"A gripping, novelistic intellectual history from the man behind 'nudge' economics."   —RICHARD REEVES, *Guardian* (UK)

"The biggest economics book of the summer, if not the year."
—BARRY RITHOLTZ, *Bloomberg View*

"The creative genius who invented the field of behavioral economics is also a master storyteller and a very funny man. All these talents are on display in this wonderful book."   —DANIEL KAHNEMAN,
winner of the Nobel Prize in Economics
and author of *Thinking, Fast and Slow*

"Richard Thaler has been at the center of the most important revolution to happen in economics in the last thirty years. In this captivating book, he lays out the evidence for behavioral economics and explains why there was so much resistance to it. Read *Misbehaving*. There is no better guide to this new and exciting economics."
—ROBERT J. SHILLER,
winner of the Nobel Prize in Economics
and author of *Finance and the Good Society*

"I would like everyone in business to buy this book and claim half the cost on expenses. The book is so enjoyable, it would be improper to claim more."   —RORY SUTHERLAND,
vice-chairman, Ogilvy & Mather UK

"Richard Thaler not only founded behavioral economics, he's also a great storyteller and observational comic. Have a seat, pour some good wine, and listen as the founder of a field narrates the fight to force economists to acknowledge the human brain."
—CHIP HEATH,
Stanford University,
coauthor of *Made to Stick*, *Switch*, and *Decisive*

Misbehaving

THE MAKING OF

BEHAVIORAL ECONOMICS

RICHARD H. THALER

W. W. NORTON & COMPANY

INDEPENDENT PUBLISHERS SINCE 1923

NEW YORK | LONDON

For information about permission to reproduce selections from this book,
write to Permissions, W. W. Norton & Company, Inc.,
500 Fifth Avenue, New York, NY 10110

For information about special discounts for bulk purchases, please contact
W. W. Norton Special Sales at specialsales@wwnorton.com or 800-233-4830

Manufacturing by RR Donnelley, Harrisonburg
Book design by Chris Welch
Production manager: Louise Mattarelliano

Library of Congress Cataloging-in-Publication Data

Thaler, Richard H., 1945–
Misbehaving : the making of behavioral economics / Richard H. Thaler. — First edition.
pages cm
Includes bibliographical references and index.
ISBN 978-0-393-08094-0 (hardcover : alk. paper)
1. Economics—Psychological aspects. I. Title.
HB74.P8T527 2015
330.01'9—dc23

2015004600

ISBN 978-0-393-35279-5 pbk.

W. W. Norton & Company, Inc.
500 Fifth Avenue, New York, N.Y. 10110
www.wwnorton.com

W. W. Norton & Company Ltd.
Castle House, 75/76 Wells Street, London W1T 3QT

1 2 3 4 5 6 7 8 9 0

To:

Victor Fuchs who gave me a year to think,
and Eric Wanner and the Russell Sage Foundation
who backed a crazy idea

And to:

Colin Camerer and George Loewenstein,
early students of misbehaving

CONTENTS

The foundation of political economy and, in general, of every social science, is evidently psychology. A day may come when we shall be able to deduce the laws of social science from the principles of psychology.

—VILFREDO PARETO, 1906

PREFACE

Before we get started, here are two stories about my friends and mentors, Amos Tversky and Daniel Kahneman. The stories provide some hints about what to expect in this book.

Striving to please Amos

Even for those of us who can't remember where we last put our keys, life offers indelible moments. Some are public events. If you are as old as I am, one may be the day John F. Kennedy was assassinated (freshman in college, playing pickup basketball in the college gym). For anyone old enough to be reading this book, September 11, 2001, is another (just getting up, listening to NPR, trying to make sense of it).

Other events are personal: from weddings to a hole in one. For me one such event was a phone call from Danny Kahneman. Although we speak often, and there are hundreds of calls that have left no trace, for this one I know precisely where I was standing. It was early 1996 and Danny had called to share the news that his friend and collaborator Amos Tversky was ill with terminal cancer and had about six months to live. I was so discombobulated that I had to hand the phone to my wife while I recovered my composure. The news that any good friend is dying is shocking, but Amos Tversky was just not the sort of person who dies at age fifty-nine. Amos, whose papers and talks were precise and perfect, and on whose desk sat only a pad and pencil, lined up in parallel, did not just die.

Amos kept the news quiet until he was no longer able to go into the office. Prior to that, only a small group knew, including two of my close friends. We were not allowed to share our knowledge with anyone except our spouses, so we took turns consoling one another for the five months that we kept this awful news to ourselves.

Amos did not want his health status to be public because he did not want to devote his last months to playing the part of a dying man. There was work to do. He and Danny decided to edit a book: a collection of papers by themselves and others in the field of psychology that they had pioneered, the study of judgment and decision-making. They called it *Choices, Values, and Frames*. Mostly Amos wanted to do the things he loved: working, spending time with his family, and watching basketball. During this period Amos did not encourage visitors wishing to express their condolences, but "working" visits were allowed, so I went to see him about six weeks before he died, under the thin disguise of finishing a paper we had been working on. We spent some time on that paper and then watched a National Basketball Association (NBA) playoff game.

Amos was wise in nearly every aspect of his life, and that included dealing with illness.* After consulting with specialists at Stanford about his prognosis, he decided that ruining his final months with pointless treatments that would make him very sick and at best extend his life by a few weeks was not a tempting option. His sharp wit remained. He explained to his oncologist that cancer is not a zero-sum game. "What is bad for the tumor is not necessarily good for me." One day on a phone call I asked him how he was feeling. He said, "You know, it's funny. When you have the flu you feel like you are going to die, but when you are dying, most of the time you feel just fine."

Amos died in June and the funeral was in Palo Alto, California, where he and his family lived. Amos's son Oren gave a short speech at the service and quoted from a note that Amos had written to him days before he died:

> I feel that in the last few days we have been exchanging anecdotes and stories with the intention that they will be remembered, at least for a while. I think there is a long Jewish tradition that history and wisdom are being transmitted from one generation to another not through

---

* While Amos was alive, a well-known joke among psychologists was that he made possible a one-item IQ test: the sooner you realized he was smarter than you, the smarter you were.

lectures and history books, but through anecdotes, funny stories, and
appropriate jokes.

After the funeral, the Tverskys hosted a traditional shiv'a gathering at their home. It was a Sunday afternoon. At some point a few of us drifted into the TV room to catch the end of an NBA playoff game. We felt a bit sheepish, but then Amos's son Tal volunteered: "If Amos were here, he would have voted for taping the funeral and watching the game."

From the time I first met Amos in 1977, I applied an unofficial test to every paper I wrote. "Would Amos approve?" My friend Eric Johnson, whom you will meet later on, can attest that one paper we wrote together took three years to get published *after* it had been accepted by a journal. The editor, the referees, and Eric were all happy with the paper, but Amos was hung up on one point and I wanted to meet his objection. I kept plugging away at that paper, while poor Eric was coming up for promotion without that paper on his vita. Fortunately Eric had written plenty of other strong papers, so my stalling did not cost him tenure. In time, Amos was satisfied.

In writing this book I took Amos's note to Oren seriously. The book is not the sort you might expect an economics professor to write. It is neither a treatise nor a polemic. Of course there will be discussions of research, but there will also be anecdotes, (possibly) funny stories, and even the odd joke.

Danny on my best qualities

One day in early 2001, I was visiting Danny Kahneman at his home in Berkeley. We were in his living room schmoozing, as we often do. Then Danny suddenly remembered he had an appointment for a telephone call with Roger Lowenstein, a journalist who was writing an article about my work for the *New York Times Magazine*. Roger, the author of the well-known book *When Genius Failed*, among others, naturally wanted to talk to my old friend Danny. Here was a quandary. Should I leave the room, or listen in? "Stay," Danny said, "this could be fun."

The interview started. Hearing a friend tell an old story about you is not an exciting activity, and hearing someone praise you is always awkward. I picked up something to read and my attention drifted— until I heard Danny say: "Oh, the best thing about Thaler, what really makes him special, is that he is lazy."

What? Really? I would never deny being lazy, but did Danny think that my laziness was my single best quality? I started waving my hands and shaking my head madly but Danny continued, extolling the virtues of my sloth. To this day, Danny insists it was a high compliment. My laziness, he claims, means I only work on questions that are intriguing enough to overcome this default tendency of avoiding work. Only Danny could turn my laziness into an asset.

But there you have it. Before reading further you should bear in mind that this book has been written by a certifiably lazy man. The upside is that, according to Danny, I will only include things that are interesting, at least to me.

---

* If you want learn more about the field of behavioral economics, keep track of recent developments and controversies, or make a comment of your own, check out the *Misbehaving* blog at misbehavingbook.org. Contributions and suggestions are welcome.

I.

BEGINNINGS:

1970–78

1

Supposedly Irrelevant Factors

Early in my teaching career I managed to inadvertently get most of the students in my microeconomics class mad at me, and for once, it had nothing to do with anything I said in class. The problem was caused by a midterm exam.

I had composed an exam that was designed to distinguish among three broad groups of students: the stars who really mastered the material, the middle group who grasped the basic concepts, and the bottom group who just didn't get it. To successfully accomplish this task, the exam had to have some questions that only the top students would get right, which meant that the exam was hard. The exam succeeded in my goal—there was a wide dispersion of scores—but when the students got their results they were in an uproar. Their principal complaint was that the average score was only 72 points out of a possible 100.

What was odd about this reaction was that the average numerical score on the exam had absolutely no effect on the distribution of grades. The norm at the school was to use a grading curve in which the average grade was a B or B+, and only a tiny number of students received grades below a C. I had anticipated the possibility that a low average numerical score might cause some confusion on this front, so I had reported how the numerical scores would be translated into actual grades in the class. Anything over 80 would get an A or A−, scores above 65 would get some kind of B, and only scores below 50 were in danger of getting a grade below C. The resulting distribution of grades was not different from normal, but this announcement had no apparent effect on the students' mood. They still hated my exam, and they were none too happy with me either. As a young professor worried about keeping my job, I was determined to do something about this, but I did not want to make my exams any easier. What to do?

Finally, an idea occurred to me. On the next exam, I made the total number of points available 137 instead of 100. This exam turned out to be slightly harder than the first, with students getting only 70% of the answers right, but the average numerical score was a cheery 96 points. The students were delighted! No one's actual grade was affected by this change, but everyone was happy. From that point on, whenever I was teaching this course, I always gave exams a point total of 137, a number I chose for two reasons. First, it produced an average score well into the 90s, with some students even getting scores above 100, generating a reaction approaching ecstasy. Second, because dividing one's score by 137 was not easy to do in one's head, most students did not seem to bother to convert their scores into percentages. Lest you think I was somehow deceiving the students, in subsequent years I included this statement, printed in bold type, in my course syllabus: "Exams will have a total of 137 points rather than the usual 100. This scoring system has no effect on the grade you get in the course, but it seems to make you happier." And indeed, after I made that change, I never got a complaint that my exams were too hard.

In the eyes of an economist, my students were "misbehaving." By that I mean that their behavior was inconsistent with the idealized model of behavior that is at the heart of what we call economic theory. To an economist, no one should be happier about a score of 96 out of 137 (70%) than 72 out of 100, but my students were. And by realizing this, I was able to set the kind of exam I wanted but still keep the students from grumbling.

For four decades, since my time as a graduate student, I have been preoccupied by these kinds of stories about the myriad ways in which people depart from the fictional creatures that populate economic models. It has never been my point to say that there is something wrong with people; we are all just human beings—homo sapiens. Rather, the problem is with the model being used by economists, a model that replaces homo sapiens with a fictional creature called homo economicus, which I like to call an Econ for short. Compared to this fictional world of Econs, Humans do a lot of misbehaving, and that means that economic models make a lot of bad predictions, predictions that can have much more serious consequences than upsetting a group of students. Virtually no economists saw the financial crisis of 2007–08 coming,* and worse, many thought that both the crash and its aftermath were things that simply could not happen.

Ironically, the existence of formal models based on this misconception of human behavior is what gives economics its reputation as the most powerful of the social sciences—powerful in two distinct ways. The first way is indisputable: of all the social scientists, economists carry the most sway when it comes to influencing public policy. In fact, they hold a virtual monopoly on giving policy advice. Until very recently, other social scientists were rarely invited to the table, and when they were invited, they were relegated to the equivalent of the kids' table at a family gathering.

The other way is that economics is also considered the most powerful of the social sciences in an intellectual sense. That power derives from the fact that economics has a unified, core theory from which nearly everything else follows. If you say the phrase "economic theory," people know what you mean. No other social science has a similar foundation. Rather, theories in other social sciences tend to be for special purposes—to explain what happens in a particular set of circumstances. In fact, economists often compare their field to physics; like physics, economics builds from a few core premises.

The core premise of economic theory is that people choose by optimizing. Of all the goods and services a family could buy, the family chooses the best one that it can afford. Furthermore, the beliefs upon which Econs make choices are assumed to be unbiased. That is, we choose on the basis of what economists call "rational expectations." If people starting new businesses on average believe that their chance of succeeding is 75%, then that should be a good estimate of the actual number that do succeed. Econs are not overconfident.

This premise of *constrained optimization*, that is, choosing the best from a limited budget, is combined with the other major workhorse of economic theory, that of *equilibrium*. In competitive markets where prices are free to move up and down, those prices fluctuate in such a way that supply equals demand. To simplify somewhat, we can say

---

* One economist who did warn us about the alarming rate of increase in housing prices was my fellow behavioral economist Robert Shiller.

that Optimization + Equilibrium = Economics. This is a powerful combination, nothing that other social sciences can match.

There is, however, a problem: the premises on which economic theory rests are flawed. First, the optimization problems that ordinary people confront are often too hard for them to solve, or even come close to solving. Even a trip to a decent-sized grocery store offers a shopper millions of combinations of items that are within the family's budget. Does the family really choose the best one? And, of course, we face many much harder problems than a trip to the store, such as choosing a career, mortgage, or spouse. Given the failure rates we observe in all of these domains, it would be hard to defend the view that all such choices are optimal.

Second, the beliefs upon which people make their choices are not unbiased. Overconfidence may not be in the economists' dictionary, but it is a well-established feature of human nature, and there are countless other biases that have been documented by psychologists.

Third, there are many factors that the optimization model leaves out, as my story about the 137-point exam illustrates. In a world of Econs, there is a long list of things that are supposedly irrelevant. No Econ would buy a particularly large portion of whatever will be served for dinner on Tuesday because he happens to be hungry when shopping on Sunday. Your hunger on Sunday should be irrelevant in choosing the size of your meal for Tuesday. An Econ would not finish that huge meal on Tuesday, even though he is no longer hungry, just because he had paid for it and hates waste. To an Econ, the price paid for some food item in the past is not relevant in making the decision about how much of it to eat now. An Econ would also not expect a gift on the day of the year in which she happened to get married, or be born. What possible difference can a date make? In fact, Econs would be perplexed by the entire idea of gifts. An Econ would know that cash is the best possible gift; it allows the recipient to buy whatever is optimal. But unless you are married to an economist, I don't advise giving cash on your next anniversary. Come to think of it, even if your spouse is an economist, this is probably not a great idea.

You know, and I know, that we do not live in a world of Econs. We live in a world of Humans. And since most economists are also human, they also know that they do not live in a world of Econs.

Adam Smith, the father of modern economic thinking, explicitly acknowledged this fact. Before writing his magnum opus, *The Wealth of Nations*, he wrote another book devoted to the topic of human "passions," a word that does not appear in any economics textbook. Econs do not have passions; they are cold-blooded optimizers. Think of Mr. Spock in *Star Trek*.

Nevertheless, this model of economic behavior based on a population consisting only of Econs has flourished, raising economics to that pinnacle of influence on which it now rests. Critiques over the years have been brushed aside with a gauntlet of poor excuses and implausible alternative explanations of embarrassing empirical evidence. But one by one these critiques have been answered by a series of studies that have progressively raised the stakes. It is easy to dismiss a story about the grading of an exam. It is harder to dismiss studies that document poor choices in large-stakes domains such as saving for retirement, choosing a mortgage, or investing in the stock market. And it is impossible to dismiss the series of booms, bubbles, and crashes we have observed in financial markets beginning on October 19, 1987, a day when stock prices fell more than 20% all around the world in the absence of any substantive bad news. This was followed by a bubble and crash in technology stocks that quickly turned into a bubble in housing prices, which in turn, when popped, caused a global financial crisis.

It is time to stop making excuses. We need an enriched approach to doing economic research, one that acknowledges the existence and relevance of Humans. The good news is that we do not need to throw away everything we know about how economies and markets work. Theories based on the assumption that everyone is an Econ should not be discarded. They remain useful as starting points for more realistic models. And in some special circumstances, such as when the problems people have to solve are easy or when the actors in the economy have the relevant highly specialized skills, then models of Econs may provide a good approximation of what happens in the real world. But as we will see, those situations are the exception rather than the rule.

Moreover, much of what economists do is to collect and analyze data about how markets work, work that is largely done with great care and statistical expertise, and importantly, most of this research does not depend on the assumption that people optimize. Two research tools that have emerged over the past twenty-five years have greatly expanded economists' repertoire for learning about the world. The first is the use of randomized control trial experiments, long used in other scientific fields such as medicine. The typical study investigates what happens when some people receive some "treatment" of interest. The second approach is to use either naturally occurring experiments (such as when some people are enrolled in a program and others are not) or clever econometrics techniques that manage to detect the impact of treatments even though no one deliberately designed the situation for that purpose. These new tools have spawned studies on a wide variety of important questions for society. The treatments studied have included getting more education, being taught in a smaller class or by a better teacher, being given management consulting services, being given help to find a job, being sentenced to jail, moving to a lower-poverty neighborhood, receiving health insurance from Medicaid, and so forth. These studies show that one can learn a lot about the world without imposing optimizing models, and in some cases provide credible evidence against which to test such models and see if they match actual human responses.

For much of economic theory, the assumption that all the agents are optimizing is not a critical one, even if the people under study are not experts. For example, the prediction that farmers use more fertilizer if the price falls is safe enough, even if many farmers are slow to change their practices in response to market conditions. The prediction is safe because it is imprecise: all that is predicted is the direction of the effect. This is equivalent to a prediction that when apples fall off the tree, they fall down rather than up. The prediction is right as far as it goes, but it is not exactly the law of gravity.

Economists get in trouble when they make a highly specific prediction that depends explicitly on everyone being economically sophisticated. Let's go back to the farming example. Say scientists learn that farmers would be better off using more or less fertilizer than has been the tradition. If everyone can be assumed to get things right as long as they have the proper information, then there is no appropriate policy prescription other than making this information freely available. Publish the findings, make them readily available to farmers, and let the magic of markets take care of the rest.

Unless all farmers are Econs, this is bad advice. Perhaps multinational food companies will be quick to adopt the latest research findings, but what about the behavior of peasant farmers in India or Africa?

Similarly, if you believe that everyone will save just the right amount for retirement, as any Econ would do, and you conclude from this analysis that there is no reason to try to help people save (say, by creating pension plans), then you are passing up the chance to make a lot of people better off. And, if you believe that financial bubbles are theoretically impossible, and you are a central banker, then you can make serious mistakes—as Alan Greenspan, to his credit, has admitted happened to him.

We don't have to stop inventing abstract models that describe the behavior of imaginary Econs. We do, however, have to stop assuming that those models are accurate descriptions of behavior, and stop basing policy decisions on such flawed analyses. And we have to start paying attention to those *supposedly irrelevant factors*, what I will call SIFs for short.

It is difficult to change people's minds about what they eat for breakfast, let alone problems that they have worked on all their lives. For years, many economists strongly resisted the call to base their models on more accurate characterizations of human behavior. But thanks to an influx of creative young economists who have been willing to take some risks and break with the traditional ways of doing economics, the dream of an enriched version of economic theory is being realized. The field has become known as "behavioral economics." It is not a different discipline: it is still economics, but it is economics done with strong injections of good psychology and other social sciences.

The primary reason for adding Humans to economic theories is to improve the accuracy of the predictions made with those theories. But there is another benefit that comes with including real people in the mix. Behavioral economics is more interesting and more fun than regular economics. It is the un-dismal science.

Behavioral economics is now a growing branch of economics, and its practitioners can be found in most of the best universities around the world. And recently, behavioral economists and behavioral scientists more generally are becoming a small part of the policy-making establishment. In 2010 the government of the United Kingdom formed a Behavioural Insights Team, and now other countries around the world are joining the movement to create special teams with the mandate to incorporate the findings of other social sciences into the formulation of public policy. Businesses are catching on as well, realizing that a deeper understanding of human behavior is every bit as important to running a successful business as is an understanding of financial statements and operations management. After all, Humans run companies, and their employees and customers are also Humans.

This book is the story of how this happened, at least as I have seen it. Although I did not do all the research—as you know, I am too lazy for that—I was around at the beginning and have been part of the movement that created this field. Following Amos's dictum, there will be many stories to come, but my main goals are tell the tale of how it all happened, and to explain some of the things we learned along the way. Not surprisingly, there have been numerous squabbles with traditionalists who defended the usual way of doing economics. Those squabbles were not always fun at the time, but like a bad travel experience, they make for good stories after the fact, and the necessity of fighting those battles has made the field stronger.

Like any story, this one does not follow a straight-line progression with one idea leading naturally to another. Many ideas were percolating at different times and at different speeds. As a result, the organizational structure of the book is both chronological and topical. Here is a brief preview. We start at the beginning, back when I was a graduate student and was collecting a list of examples of odd behaviors that did not seem to fit the models I was learning in class. The first section of the book is devoted to those early years in the wilderness, and describes some of the challenges that were thrown down by the many who questioned the value of this enterprise. We then turn to a series of topics that occupied most of my attention for the first fifteen years of my research career: mental accounting, self-control, fairness, and finance. My objective is to explain what my colleagues and I learned along the way, so that you can use those insights yourself to improve your understanding of your fellow Humans. But there may also be useful lessons about how to try to change the way people think about things, especially when they have a lot invested in maintaining the status quo. Later, we turn to more recent research endeavors, from the behavior of New York City taxi drivers, to the drafting of players into the National Football League, to the behavior of participants on high-stakes game shows. At the end we arrive in London, at Number 10 Downing Street, where a new set of exciting challenges and opportunities is emerging.

My only advice for reading the book is stop reading when it is no longer fun. To do otherwise, well, that would be just misbehaving.

2

The Endowment Effect

I began to have deviant thoughts about economic theory while I was a graduate student in the economics department at the University of Rochester, located in upstate New York. Although I had misgivings about some of the material presented in my classes, I was never quite sure whether the problem was in the theory or in my flawed understanding of the subject matter. I was hardly a star student. In that *New York Times Magazine* article by Roger Lowenstein that I mentioned in the preface, my thesis advisor, Sherwin Rosen, gave the following as an assessment of my career as a graduate student: "We did not expect much of him."

My thesis was on a provocative-sounding topic, "The Value of a Life," but the approach was completely standard. Conceptually, the proper way to think about this question was captured by economist Thomas Schelling in his wonderful essay "The Life You Save May Be Your Own." Many times over the years my interests would intersect with Schelling's, an early supporter and contributor to what we now call behavioral economics. Here is a famous passage from his essay:

> Let a six-year-old girl with brown hair need thousands of dollars for an operation that will prolong her life until Christmas, and the post office will be swamped with nickels and dimes to save her. But let it be reported that without sales tax the hospital facilities of Massachusetts will deteriorate and cause a barely perceptible increase in preventable deaths—not many will drop a tear or reach for their checkbooks.

Schelling writes the way he speaks: with a wry smile and an impish twinkle in his eye. He wants to make you a bit uncomfortable.* Here, the story of the sick girl is a vivid way of capturing the major contribution of the article. The hospitals stand in for the concept Schelling calls a "statistical life," as opposed to the girl, who represents an "identified life." We occasionally run into examples of identified lives at risk in the real world, such as the thrilling rescue of trapped miners. As Schelling notes, we rarely allow any identified life to be extinguished solely for the lack of money. But of course thousands of "unidentified" people die every day for lack of simple things like mosquito nets, vaccines, or clean water.

Unlike the sick girl, the typical domestic public policy decision is abstract. It lacks emotional impact. Suppose we are building a new highway, and safety engineers tell us that making the median divider three feet wider will cost $42 million and prevent 1.4 fatal accidents per year for thirty years. Should we do it? Of course, we do not know the identity of those victims. They are "merely" statistical lives. But to decide how wide to make that median strip we need a value to assign to those lives prolonged, or, more vividly, "saved" by the expenditure. And in a world of Econs, society would not pay more to save one identified life than twenty statistical lives.

As Schelling noted, the right question asks how much the users of that highway (and perhaps their friends and family members) would be willing to pay to make each trip they take a tiny bit safer. Schelling had specified the correct question, but no one had yet come up with a way to answer it. To crack the problem you needed some situation in which people make choices that involve a trade-off between money and risk of death. From there you can infer their willingness to pay for safety. But where to observe such choices?

Economist Richard Zeckhauser, a student of Schelling's, noted that Russian roulette offers a way to think about the problem. Here is an adaptation of his example. Suppose Aidan is required to play one

---

* Typical Schelling thought experiment: suppose there was some medical procedure that will provide some modest health benefit but is extremely painful. However, the procedure is administered with a drug that does not prevent the pain but instead erases all memory of the event. Would you be willing to undertake this procedure?

game of machine-gun Russian roulette using a gun with many chambers, say 1,000, of which four have been picked at random to have bullets. Aidan has to pull the trigger once. (Mercifully, the gun is set on single shot.) How much would Aidan be willing to pay to remove one bullet?* Although Zeckhauser's Russian roulette formulation poses the problem in an elegant way, it does not help us come up with any numbers. Running experiments in which subjects point loaded guns at their heads is not a practical method for obtaining data.

While pondering these issues I had an idea. Suppose I could get data on the death rates of various occupations, including dangerous ones like mining, logging, and skyscraper window-washing, and safer ones like farming, shopkeeping, and low-rise window-washing. In a world of Econs, the riskier jobs would have to pay more, otherwise no one would do them. In fact, the extra wages paid for a risky job would have to compensate the workers for taking on the risks involved (as well as any other attributes of the job). So if I could also get data on the wages for each occupation, I could estimate the number implied by Schelling's analysis, without asking anyone to play Russian roulette. I searched but could not find any source of occupational mortality rates.

My father, Alan, came to the rescue. Alan was an actuary, one of those mathematical types who figure how to manage risks for insurance companies. I asked him if he might be able to lay his hands on data on occupational mortality. I soon received a thin, red, hardbound copy of a book published by the Society of Actuaries that listed the very data I needed. By matching occupational mortality rates to readily available data on wages by occupation, I could estimate how much people had to be paid to be willing to accept a higher risk of dying on the job.

Getting the idea and the data were a good start, but doing the statistical exercise correctly was key. I needed to find an advisor in the

---

* The question that Zeckhauser was interested in is: how does Aidan's willingness to pay depend on the number of bullets in the gun? If all the chambers are full, Aidan should pay all he has (and can borrow) to remove even one bullet. But what if there are only two bullets loaded? What will he pay to remove one of them? And would it be more or less than what he would pay to remove the last bullet?

economics department whom I could interest in supervising my thesis. The obvious choice was the up-and-coming labor economist mentioned earlier, Sherwin Rosen. We had not worked together before, but my thesis topic was related to some theoretical work he was doing, so he agreed to become my advisor.

We went on to coauthor a paper based on my thesis entitled, naturally, "The Value of Saving a Life." Updated versions of the number we estimated back then are still used in government cost-benefit analyses. The current estimate is roughly $7 million per life saved.

While at work on my thesis, I thought it might be interesting to ask people some hypothetical questions as another way to elicit their preferences regarding trade-offs between money and the risk of dying. To write these questions, I first had to decide which of two ways to ask the question: either in terms of "willingness to pay" or "willingness to accept." The first asks how much you would pay to reduce your probability of dying next year by some amount, say by one chance in a thousand. The second asks how much cash you would demand to increase the risk of dying by the same amount. To put these numbers in some context, a fifty-year-old resident of the United States faces a roughly 4-in-1,000 risk of dying each year.

Here is a typical question I posed in a classroom setting. Students answered both versions of the question.

A. Suppose by attending this lecture you have exposed yourself to a rare fatal disease. If you contract the disease you will die a quick and painless death sometime next week. The chance you will get the disease is 1 in 1,000. We have a single dose of an antidote for this disease that we will sell to the highest bidder. If you take this antidote the risk of dying from the disease goes to zero. What is the most you would be willing to pay for this antidote? (If you are short on cash we will lend you the money to pay for the antidote at a zero rate of interest with thirty years to pay it back.)

B. Researchers at the university hospital are doing some research on that same rare disease. They need volunteers who would be willing to simply walk into a room for five minutes and expose

themselves to the same 1 in 1,000 risk of getting the disease and
dying a quick and painless death in the next week. No antidote
will be available. What is the least amount of money you would
demand to participate in this research study?

Economic theory has a strong prediction about how people should
answer the two different versions of these questions. The answers
should be nearly equal. For a fifty-year-old answering the questions,
the trade-off between money and risk of death should not be very different when moving from a risk of 5 in 1,000 (.005) to .004 (as in the
first version of the question) than in moving from a risk of .004 to .005
(as in the second version). Answers varied widely among respondents,
but one clear pattern emerged: the answers to the two questions were
not even close to being the same. Typical answers ran along these lines:
I would not pay more than $2,000 in version A but would not accept
less than $500,000 in version B. In fact, in version B many respon-
dents claimed that they would not participate in the study at any price.

Economic theory is not alone in saying the answers should be identical. Logical consistency demands it. Again consider a fifty-year-old who,
before he ran into me, was facing a .004 chance of dying in the next
year. Suppose he gives the answers from the previous paragraph: $2,000
for scenario A and $500,000 for scenario B. The first answer implies
that the increase from .004 to .005 only makes him worse off by at most
$2,000, since he would be unwilling to pay more to avoid the extra risk.
But, his second answer said that he would not accept the same increase
in risk for less than $500,000. Clearly, the difference between a risk of
.004 and .005 cannot be *at most* $2,000 and *at least* $500,000!

This truth is not apparent to everyone. In fact, even when explained,
many people resist, as you may be doing right now. But the logic is ines-
capable.* To an economist, these findings were somewhere between

---

* Technically, the answers can differ by what economists call an income or wealth
effect. You are worse off in version A than version B because if you do nothing in
version B you do not get exposed to the disease. But this effect cannot explain
differences of the magnitudes that I observed, and other surveys in which I would
hypothetically tell people in version A that they had been given (say) $50,000 did
not eliminate the disparity.

puzzling and preposterous. I showed them to Sherwin and he told me to stop wasting my time and get back to work on my thesis. But I was hooked. What was going on here? Sure, the putting-your-life-at-risk scenario is unusual, but once I began to look for examples, I found them everywhere.

One case came from Richard Rosett, the chairman of the economics department and a longtime wine collector. He told me that he had bottles in his cellar that he had purchased long ago for $10 that were now worth over $100. In fact, a local wine merchant named Woody was willing to buy some of Rosett's older bottles at current prices. Rosett said he occasionally drank one of those bottles on a special occasion, but would never dream of paying $100 to acquire one. He also did not sell any of his bottles to Woody. This is illogical. If he is willing to drink a bottle that he could sell for $100, then drinking it has to be worth more than $100. But then, why wouldn't he also be willing to buy such a bottle? In fact, why did he refuse to buy any bottle that cost anything close to $100? As an economist, Rosett knew such behavior was not rational, but he couldn't help himself.*

These examples all involve what economists call "opportunity costs." The opportunity cost of some activity is what you give up by doing it. If I go for a hike today instead of staying home to watch football, then the opportunity cost of going on the hike is the forgone pleasure of watching the game. For the $100 bottle of wine, the opportunity cost of drinking the bottle is what Woody was willing to pay Rosett for it. Whether Rosett drank his own bottle or bought one, the opportunity cost of drinking it remains the same. But as Rosett's behavior illustrated, even economists have trouble equating opportunity costs with out-of-pocket costs. Giving up the opportunity to sell something does not hurt as much as taking the money out of your wallet to pay for it. Opportunity costs are vague and abstract when compared to handing over actual cash.

---

* Rosett did not seem much troubled by this behavior. I subsequently published an article that included this anecdote, with Rosett described as Mr. R. I sent Rosett a copy of the article when it came out and received a two-word reply: "Ah fame!"

My friend Tom Russell suggested another interesting case. At the time, credit cards were beginning to come into widespread use, and credit card issuers were in a legal battle with retailers over whether merchants could charge different prices to cash and credit card customers. Since credit cards charge the retailer for collecting the money, some merchants, particularly gas stations, wanted to charge credit card users a higher price. Of course, the credit card industry hated this practice; they wanted consumers to view the use of the card as free. As the case wound its way through the regulatory process, the credit card lobby hedged its bets and shifted focus to form over substance. They insisted that if a store *did* charge different prices to cash and credit card customers, the "regular price" would be the higher credit card price, with cash customers offered a "discount." The alternative would have set the cash price as the regular price with credit card customers required to pay a "surcharge."

To an Econ these two policies are identical. If the credit card price is $1.03 and the cash price is $1, it should not matter whether you call the three-cent difference a discount or a surcharge. Nevertheless, the credit card industry rightly had a strong preference for the discount. Many years later Kahneman and Tversky would call this distinction "framing," but marketers already had a gut instinct that framing mattered. Paying a surcharge is out-of-pocket, whereas not receiving a discount is a "mere" opportunity cost.

I called this phenomenon the "endowment effect" because, in economists' lingo, the stuff you own is part of your endowment, and I had stumbled upon a finding that suggested people valued things that were already part of their endowment more highly than things that could be part of their endowment, that were available but not yet owned.

The endowment effect has a pronounced influence on behavior for those considering attending special concerts and sporting events. Often the retail price for a given ticket is well below the market price. Someone lucky enough to have grabbed a ticket, either by waiting in line or by being quickest to click on a website, now has a decision to make: go to the event or sell the ticket? In many parts of the world there is now a simple, legal market for tickets on websites such as Stubhub.com, such that ticket-holders no longer have to stand outside a venue and hawk the tickets in order to realize the windfall gain they received when they bought a highly valued item.

Few people other than economists think about this decision correctly. A nice illustration of this involves economist Dean Karlan, now of Yale University. Dean's time in Chicago—he was an MBA student then—coincided with Michael Jordan's reign as the king of professional basketball. Jordan's Chicago Bulls won six championships while he was on the team. The year in question, the Bulls were playing the Washington Bullets in the first round of the playoffs. Although the Bulls were heavily favored to win, tickets were in high demand in part because fans knew seats would be even more expensive later in the playoffs.

Dean had a college buddy who worked for the Bullets and gave Dean two tickets. Dean also had a friend, a graduate student in divinity school, who shared the same Bullets connection and had also received a pair of free tickets. Both of them faced the usual financial struggles associated with being a graduate student, although Dean had better long-term financial prospects: MBAs tend to make more money than graduates of divinity school.*

Both Dean and his friend found the decision of whether to sell or attend the game to be an easy one. The divinity school student invited someone to go to the game with him and enjoyed himself. Dean, meanwhile, got busy scoping out which basketball-loving professors also had lucrative consulting practices. He sold his tickets for several hundred dollars each. Both Dean and his friend thought the other's behavior was nuts. Dean did not understand how his friend could possibly think he could afford to go to the game. His friend could not understand why Dean didn't realize the tickets were free.

That is the endowment effect. I knew it was real, but I had no idea what to do with it.

---

* Of course, the divinity school students might make up for this disparity in the very, very long run.

3

The List

The discrepancy between buying and selling prices got my mind wandering. What else do people do that is inconsistent with the economists' model of rational choice? Once I started paying attention, so many examples cropped up that I started a list on the blackboard in my office. Here are a few that describe the behavior of some of my friends:

- *Jeffrey and I somehow get two free tickets to a professional basketball game in Buffalo, normally an hour and a half drive from where we live in Rochester. The day of the game there is a big snowstorm. We decide not to go, but Jeffrey remarks that, had we bought the (expensive) tickets, we would have braved the blizzard and attempted to drive to the game.*
- *Stanley mows his lawn every weekend and it gives him terrible hay fever. I ask Stan why he doesn't hire a kid to mow his lawn. Stan says he doesn't want to pay the $10. I ask Stan whether he would mow his neighbor's lawn for $20 and Stan says no, of course not.*
- *Linnea is shopping for a clock radio. She finds a model she likes at what her research has suggested is a good price, $45. As she is about to buy it, the clerk at the store mentions that the same radio is on sale for $35 at new branch of the store, ten minutes away, that is holding a grand opening sale. Does she drive to the other store to make the purchase?*

    On a separate shopping trip, Linnea is shopping for a television set and finds one at the good price of $495. Again the clerk informs her that the same model is on sale at another store ten minutes away for $485. Same question ... but likely different answer.
- *Lee's wife gives him an expensive cashmere sweater for Christmas. He had seen the sweater in the store and decided that it was too big of an indulgence to feel good about buying it. He is nevertheless delighted with the*

gift. Lee and his wife pool all their financial assets; neither has any sepa-
rate source of money.

- *Some friends come over for dinner. We are having drinks and waiting for*
  something roasting in the oven to be finished so we can sit down to eat. I
  bring out a large bowl of cashew nuts for us to nibble on. We eat half the
  bowl in five minutes, and our appetite is in danger. I remove the bowl and
  hide it in the kitchen. Everyone is happy.

Each example illustrates a behavior that is inconsistent with economic theory. Jeffrey is ignoring the economists' dictum to "ignore
sunk costs," meaning money that has already been spent. The price
we paid for the tickets should not affect our choice about whether to
go to the game. Stanley is violating the precept that buying and selling prices should be about the same. If Linnea spends ten minutes to
save $10 on a small purchase but not a large one, she is not valuing
time consistently. Lee feels better about spending family resources
on an expensive sweater if his wife made the decision, though the
sweater was no cheaper. And removing the cashews takes away the
option to eat some more; to Econs, more choices are always preferred
to fewer.

I spent a fair amount of time staring at the List and adding new
items, but I did not know what to do with it. "Dumb stuff people
do" is not a satisfactory title for an academic paper. Then I caught
a break. In the summer of 1976 Sherwin and I went to a conference
near Monterey, California. We were there to talk about the value of a
life. What made the conference special for me were two psychologists
who attended: Baruch Fischhoff and Paul Slovic. They both studied
how people make decisions. It was like discovering a new species. I
had never met anyone in academia with their backgrounds.

I ended up giving Fischhoff a ride to the airport. As we drove, Fischhoff told me he had completed a PhD in psychology at the Hebrew
University in Israel. There he had worked with two guys whose names
I had never heard: Daniel Kahneman and Amos Tversky. Baruch told
me about his now-famous thesis on "hindsight bias." The finding is
that, after the fact, we think that we always knew the outcome was
likely, if not a foregone conclusion. After the virtually unknown Afri-

can American senator Barack Obama defeated the heavily favored Hillary Clinton for the Democratic Party presidential nomination, many people thought they had seen it coming. They hadn't. They were just misremembering.

I found the concept of hindsight bias fascinating, and incredibly important to management. One of the toughest problems a CEO faces is convincing managers that they should take on risky projects if the expected gains are high enough. Their managers worry, for good reason, that if the project works out badly, the manager who championed the project will be blamed whether or not the decision was a good one at the time. Hindsight bias greatly exacerbates this problem, because the CEO will wrongly think that whatever was the cause of the failure, it should have been anticipated in advance. And, with the benefit of hindsight, he always knew this project was a poor risk. What makes the bias particularly pernicious is that we all recognize this bias in others but not in ourselves.

Baruch suggested that I might enjoy reading some of the work of his advisors. The next day, when I was back in my office in Rochester, I headed over to the library. Having spent all my time in the economics section, I found myself in a new part of the library. I started with the duo's summary paper published in *Science*: "Judgment Under Uncertainty: Heuristics and Biases." At the time I was not sure what a heuristic was, but it turns out to be a fancy word for a rule of thumb. As I read, my heart started pounding the way it might during the final minutes of a close game. The paper took me thirty minutes to read from start to finish, but my life had changed forever.

The thesis of the paper was simple and elegant. Humans have limited time and brainpower. As a result, they use simple rules of thumb—heuristics—to help them make judgments. An example would be "availability." Suppose I ask you if Dhruv is a common name. If you are from most countries in the world you would likely say no, but it happens to be a very common name in India, a country with a lot of people, so on a global scale it is in fact a rather common name. In guessing how frequent something is, we tend to ask ourselves how often we can think of instances of that type. It's a fine rule of thumb, and in the community in which you live, the ease with which you can recall meeting people with a given name will offer a good clue as to its actual frequency. But the rule will fail in cases in which the number of instances of some event is not highly correlated with the ease with which you can summon up examples (such as the name Dhruv). This is an illustration of the big idea of this article, one that made my hands shake as I read: using these heuristics causes people to make *predictable errors*. Thus the title of the paper: heuristics and *biases*. The concept of predictable biases offered a framework for my heretofore helter-skelter set of ideas.

A forerunner of Kahneman and Tversky was Herbert Simon, a polymath academic who spent most of his career at Carnegie Mellon University. Simon was well known in nearly every field of social science, including economics, political science, artificial intelligence, and organizational theory, but most germane to this book, he wrote about what he called "bounded rationality" well before Kahneman and Tversky came along. In saying that people have bounded rationality, Simon meant that they lack the cognitive ability to solve complex problems, which is obviously true. Yet, although he received a Nobel Prize in economics, unfortunately I think it is fair to say that he had little impact on the economics profession.* I believe many economists ignored Simon because it was too easy to brush aside bounded rationality as a "true but unimportant" concept. Economists were fine with the idea that their models were imprecise and that the predictions of those models would contain error. In the statistical models used by economists, this is handled simply by adding what is called an "error" term to the equation. Suppose you try to predict the height that a child will reach at adulthood using the height of both parents as predictors. This model will do a decent job since tall parents tend to have tall children, but the model will not be perfectly accurate, which is what the error term is meant to capture. And as long as the errors are random—that is, the model's predictions are too high or too low with equal frequency—then all is well. The errors cancel each other out. This was economists' reasoning to justify why the errors

---

* The economics prize is not one of the original Nobel Prizes laid out in Alfred Nobel's will, though it is awarded alongside them. Its full name is Sveriges Riksbank Prize in Economic Sciences in Memory of Alfred Nobel, but here I'll just call it the Nobel Prize for short. A list of laureates can be found at http://www.nobelprize.org/nobel_prizes/economic-sciences/laureates/.

produced by bounded rationality could safely be ignored. Back to the fully rational model!

Kahneman and Tversky were waving a big red flag that said these errors were not random. Ask people whether there are more gun deaths caused by homicide or suicide in the U.S., and most will guess homicide, but in fact there are almost twice as many gun deaths by suicide than homicides.* This is a *predictable* error. Even across many people, the errors will not average out to zero. Although I did not appreciate it fully at the time, Kahneman and Tversky's insights had inched me forward so that I was just one step away from doing something serious with my list. Each of the items on the List was an example of a systematic bias.

The items on the List had another noteworthy feature. In every case, economic theory had a highly specific prediction about some key factor—such as the presence of the cashews or the amount paid for the basketball game tickets—that the theory said should not influence decisions. They were all supposedly irrelevant factors, or SIFs. Much subsequent work in behavioral economics has been to show which SIFs are in fact highly relevant in predicting behavior, often by taking advantage of the systematic biases suggested in Tversky and Kahneman's 1974 paper.† By now it's a long list, far surpassing what was written on my blackboard all those years ago.

I spent an exciting few hours reading everything Kahneman and Tversky had written together, and left the library with my head spinning.

---

* In fact, just having a gun in the house increases the risk that a member of the household will commit suicide.

† In case you are wondering about the order of the names in their papers, early on Amos and Danny adopted the highly unusual strategy of alternating whose name would go first as a subtle way of signaling that they were equal partners. In economics, alphabetical order is the default option, but in psychology the order of names usually is meant to indicate relative contributions. Their solution avoided having to make a decision, paper by paper, about who had contributed more. Such evaluations can be fraught (see chapter 28).

4

Value Theory

After my day in the library, I called Fischhoff to thank him. He told me that Kahneman and Tversky were working on a new project about decision-making that should be right up my alley. Fischhoff thought that Howard Kunreuther, a professor at Wharton, might have a copy. I called Howard and struck gold. He had the draft and would send me a copy.

The paper, called "Value Theory" at the time, arrived replete with Howard's comments scrawled in the margins. It was an early version of the paper that would win Danny a Nobel Prize in 2002. (Amos would have shared the prize had he been alive.) In time the authors changed the title to "Prospect Theory."* This paper was even more germane to the List than the work on heuristics and biases. Two things grabbed me immediately: an organizing principle and a simple graph.

Two kinds of theories

The organizing principle was the existence of two different kinds of theories: normative and descriptive. Normative theories tell you the right way to think about some problem. By "right" I do not mean right in some moral sense; instead, I mean logically consistent, as prescribed by the optimizing model at the heart of economic reasoning, sometimes called rational choice theory. That is the only way I will use the word "normative" in this book. For instance, the Pythagorean theorem is a normative theory of how to calculate the length of one

---

* I asked Danny why they changed the name. His reply: "'Value theory' was misleading, and we decided to have a completely meaningless term, which would become meaningful if by some lucky break the theory became important. 'Prospect' fitted the bill."

side of a right triangle if you know the length of the other two sides. If you use any other formula you will be wrong.

Here is a test to see if you are a good intuitive Pythagorean thinker. Consider two pieces of railroad track, each one mile long, laid end to end (see figure 1). The tracks are nailed down at their end points but simply meet in the middle. Now, suppose it gets hot and the railroad tracks expand, each by one inch. Since they are attached to the ground at the end points, the tracks can only expand by rising like a draw-bridge. Furthermore, these pieces of track are so sturdy that they retain their straight, linear shape as they go up. (This is to make the problem easier, so stop complaining about unrealistic assumptions.) Here is your problem:

> Consider just one side of the track. We have a right triangle with a base of one mile, a hypotenuse of one mile plus one inch. What is the altitude? In other words, by how much does the track rise above the ground?

FIGURE 1

Guess the height of x

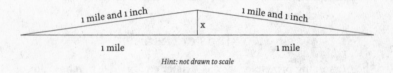

1 mile and 1 inch   1 mile and 1 inch
                    x
1 mile   1 mile

Hint: not drawn to scale

If you remember your high school geometry, have a calculator with a square root function handy, and know that there are 5,280 feet in a mile and 12 inches in a foot, you can solve this problem. But suppose instead you have to use your intuition. What is your guess?

Most people figure that since the tracks expanded by an inch they should go up by roughly the same amount, or maybe as much as two or three inches.

The actual answer is 29.7 feet! How did you do?

Now suppose we want to develop a theory of how people answer this question. If we are rational choice theorists, we assume that people will give the right answer, so we will use the Pythagorean theorem as both our normative and descriptive model and predict that people will come up with something near 30 feet. For this problem, that is a terrible prediction. The average answer that people give is about 2 inches.

This gets to the heart of the problem with traditional economics and the conceptual breakthrough offered by prospect theory. Economic theory at that time, and for most economists today, uses one theory to serve both normative and descriptive purposes. Consider the economic theory of the firm. This theory, a simple example of the use of optimization-based models, stipulates that firms will act to maximize profits (or the value of the firm), and further elaborations on the theory simply spell out how that should be done. For example, a firm should set prices so that marginal cost equals marginal revenue. When economists use the term "marginal" it just means incremental, so this rule implies that the firm will keep producing until the point where the cost of the last item made is exactly equal to the incremental revenue brought in. Similarly, the theory of human capital formation, pioneered by the economist Gary Becker, assumes that people choose which kind of education to obtain, and how much time and money to invest in acquiring these skills, by correctly forecasting how much money they will make (and how much fun they will have) in their subsequent careers. There are very few high school and college students whose choices reflect careful analysis of these factors. Instead, many people study the subject they enjoy most without thinking through to what kind of life that will create.

Prospect theory sought to break from the traditional idea that a single theory of human behavior can be both normative and descriptive. Specifically, the paper took on the theory of decision-making under uncertainty. The initial ideas behind this theory go back to Daniel Bernoulli in 1738. Bernoulli was a student of almost everything, including mathematics and physics, and his work in this domain was to solve a puzzle known as the St. Petersburg paradox, a puzzle posed by his cousin Nicolas.* (They came from a precocious

---

* The puzzle is this: Suppose you are offered a gamble where you keep flipping a coin until it lands heads up. If you get tails on your first flip you win $2, on your second flip $4, and so forth, with the pot doubling each time. Your expected winnings are ½ x $2 + ¼ x $4 + ⅛ x $8 . . . The value of this sequence is infinite, so why won't people pay a huge amount to play the bet? Bernoulli's answer was to suppose that people get diminishing value from increases in their wealth, which yields risk

family.) Essentially, Bernoulli invented the idea of risk aversion. He did so by positing that people's happiness—or utility, as economists like to call it—increases as they get wealthier, but at a decreasing rate. This principle is called diminishing sensitivity. As wealth grows, the impact of a given increment of wealth, say $100,000, falls. To a peasant, a $100,000 windfall would be life-changing. To Bill Gates, it would go undetected. A graph of what this looks like appears in figure 2.

FIGURE 2

Diminishing marginal utility of wealth

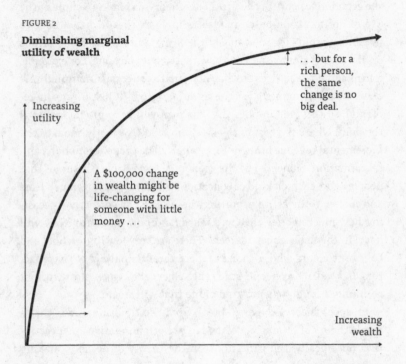

Increasing utility

... but for a rich person, the same change is no big deal.

A $100,000 change in wealth might be life-changing for someone with little money . . .

Increasing wealth

A utility function of this shape implies risk aversion because the utility of the first thousand dollars is greater than the utility of the second thousand dollars, and so forth. This implies that if your wealth is $100,000 and I offer you a choice between an additional $1,000

aversion. A simpler solution is to note that there is only a finite amount of wealth in the world, so you should be worried about whether the other side can pay up if you win. Just forty tails in a row puts your prize money at over one trillion dollars. If you think that would break the bank, the bet is worth no more than $40.

for sure or a 50% chance to win $2,000, you will take the sure thing because you value the second thousand you would win less than the first thousand, so you are not willing to risk losing that first $1,000 prize in an attempt to get $2,000.

The full treatment of the formal theory of how to make decisions in risky situations—called *expected utility theory*—was published in 1944 by the mathematician John von Neumann and the economist Oskar Morgenstern. John von Neumann, one of the greatest mathematicians of the twentieth century, was a contemporary of Albert Einstein at the Institute of Advanced Study at Princeton University, and during World War II he decided to devote himself to practical problems. The result was the 600-plus-page opus *The Theory of Games and Economic Behavior*, in which the development of expected utility theory was just a sideline.

The way that von Neumann and Morgenstern created the theory was to begin by writing down a series of axioms of rational choice. They then derived how someone who wanted to follow these axioms would behave. The axioms are mostly uncontroversial notions such as transitivity, a technical term that says if you prefer A over B and B over C then you must prefer A over C. Remarkably, von Neumann and Morgenstern proved that if you want to satisfy these axioms (and you do), then you must make decisions according to their theory. The argument is completely convincing. If I had an important decision to make—whether to refinance my mortgage or invest in a new business—I would aim to make the decision in accordance with expected utility theory, just as I would use the Pythagorean theorem to estimate the altitude of our railroad triangle. Expected utility is the right way to make decisions.

With prospect theory, Kahneman and Tversky set out to offer an alternative to expected utility theory that had no pretense of being a useful guide to rational choice; instead, it would be a good prediction of the actual choices real people make. It is a theory about the behavior of Humans.

Although this seems like a logical step to take, it is not one that economists had ever really embraced. Simon had coined the term "bounded rationality," but had not done much fleshing out of how boundedly rational people differ from fully rational ones. There were a few other precedents, but they too had never taken hold. For example, the prominent (and for the most part, quite traditional) Princeton economist William Baumol had proposed an alternative to the traditional (normative) theory of the firm (which assumes profit maximization). He postulated that firms maximize their size, measured for instance by sales revenue, subject to a constraint that profits have to meet some minimum level. I think sales maximization may be a good descriptive model of many firms. In fact, it might be smart for a CEO to follow this strategy, since CEO pay oddly seems to depend as much on a firm's size as it does on its profits, but if so that would also constitute a violation of the theory that firms maximize value.

The first thing I took from my early glimpse of prospect theory was a mission statement: *Build descriptive economic models that accurately portray human behavior.*

A stunning graph

The other major takeaway for me was a figure depicting the "value function." This too was a major conceptual change in economic thinking, and the real engine of the new theory. Ever since Bernoulli, economic models were based on a simple assumption that people have "diminishing marginal utility of wealth," as illustrated in figure 2.

This model of the utility of wealth gets the basic psychology of wealth right. But to create a better descriptive model, Kahneman and Tversky recognized that we had to change our focus from *levels* of wealth to *changes* in wealth. This may sound like a subtle tweak, but switching the focus to changes as opposed to levels is a radical move. A picture of their value function is shown further below, in figure 3.

Kahneman and Tversky focus on changes because changes are the way Humans experience life. Suppose you are in an office building with a well-functioning air circulation system that keeps the environment at what we typically think of as room temperature. Now you leave your office to attend a meeting in a conference room. As you enter the room, how will you react to the temperature? If it is the same as that of your office and the corridor, you won't give it a second thought. You will only notice if the room is unusually hot or cold rela-

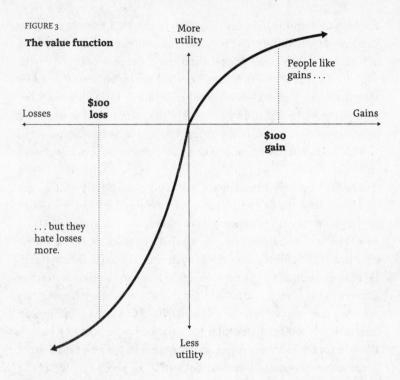

FIGURE 3

The value function

More
utility

People like
gains ...

Losses   Gains

**$100
loss**

**$100
gain**

... but they
hate losses
more.

Less
utility

tive to the rest of the building. When we have adapted to our environment, we tend to ignore it.

The same is true in financial matters. Consider Jane, who makes
$80,000 per year. She gets a $5,000 year-end bonus that she had
not expected. How does Jane process this event? Does she calculate
the change in her lifetime wealth, which is barely noticeable? No,
she is more likely to think, "Wow, an extra $5,000!" People think
about life in terms of changes, not levels. They can be changes from
the status quo or changes from what was expected, but whatever
form they take, it is changes that make us happy or miserable. That
was a big idea.

The figure in the paper so captured my imagination that I drew a
version of it on the blackboard right next to the List. Have another
look at it now. There is an enormous amount of wisdom about human
nature captured in that S-shaped curve. The upper portion, for gains,
has the same shape as the usual utility of wealth function, capturing

the idea of diminishing sensitivity. But notice that the loss function captures diminishing sensitivity also. The difference between losing $10 and $20 feels much bigger than the difference between losing $1,300 and $1,310. This is different from the standard model, because starting from a given wealth level in figure 1, losses are captured by moving down the utility of wealth line, meaning that each loss gets increasingly painful. (If you care less and less about increases in wealth, then it follows that you care more and more about decreases in wealth.)

The fact that we experience diminishing sensitivity to changes away from the status quo captures another basic human trait—one of the earliest findings in psychology—known as the Weber–Fechner Law. The Weber–Fechner Law holds that the just-noticeable difference in any variable is proportional to the magnitude of that variable. If I gain one ounce, I don't notice it, but if I am buying fresh herbs, the difference between 2 ounces and 3 ounces is obvious. Psychologists refer to a just noticeable difference as a JND. If you want to impress an academic psychologist, add that term to your cocktail party banter. ("I went for the more expensive sound system in the new car I bought because the increase in price was not a JND.")

You can test your understanding of the concept behind the Weber–Fechner Law with this example from National Public Radio's long-running show called *Car Talk*. The show consisted of brothers Tom and Ray Magliozzi—both MIT graduates—taking calls from people with questions about their cars. Improbably enough, it was hysterically funny, especially to them. They would laugh endlessly at their own jokes.[*]

In one show a caller asked: "Both my headlights went out at the same time. I took the car to the shop but the mechanic said that all I needed was two new bulbs. How can that be right? Isn't it too big of a coincidence that both bulbs blew out at the same time?"

Tom answered the question in a flash. "Ah, the famous Weber–Fechner Law!" It turns out that Tom also did a PhD in psychology and marketing supervised by Max Bazerman, a leading scholar in

---

[*] Tom Magliozzi passed away in 2014 but the show lives on in reruns, where the two brothers are still laughing.

judgment and decision-making research. So, what does the caller's question have to do with the Weber–Fechner Law, and how did this insight help Tom solve the problem?

The answer is that the two bulbs did not in fact burn out at the same time. It is easy to drive around with one bulb burned out and not notice, especially if you live in a well-lit city. Going from two bulbs to one is not always a noticeable difference. But going from one to zero is definitely noticeable. This phenomenon also explains the behavior in one of the examples on the List: being more willing to drive ten minutes to save $10 on a $45 clock radio than on a $495 television set. For the latter purchase, the savings would not be a JND.

The fact that people have diminishing sensitivity to both gains and losses has another implication. People will be risk-averse for gains, but risk-seeking for losses, as illustrated by the experiment reported below which was administered to two different groups of subjects. (Notice that the initial sentence in the two questions differs in a way that makes the two problems identical if subjects are making decisions based on levels of wealth, as was traditionally assumed.) The percentage of subjects choosing each option is shown in brackets.

PROBLEM 1. Assume yourself richer by $300 than you are today. You are offered a choice between

    A. A sure gain of $100, or   [72%]

    B. A 50% chance to gain $200 and
        a 50% chance to lose $0.   [28%]

PROBLEM 2. Assume yourself richer by $500 than you are today. You are offered a choice between

    A. A sure loss of $100, or   [36%]

    B. A 50% chance to lose $200 and
        a 50% chance to lose $0.   [64%]

The reason why people are risk-seeking for losses is the same logic that applies to why they are risk-averse for gains. In the case of problem 2, the pain of losing the second hundred dollars is less than the pain of losing the first hundred, so subjects are ready to take the risk of losing more in order to have the chance of getting back to no loss at all. They are especially keen to eliminate a loss altogether because of the third feature captured in figure 3: loss aversion.

Examine the value function in this figure at the origin, where both curves begin. Notice that the loss function is steeper than the gain function: it decreases more quickly than the gain function goes up. Roughly speaking, losses hurt about twice as much as gains make you feel good. This feature of the value function left me flabbergasted. There, in that picture, was the endowment effect. If I take away Professor Rosett's bottle of wine, he will feel it as a loss equivalent to twice the gain he would feel if he acquired a bottle; that is why he would never buy a bottle worth the same market price as one in his cellar. The fact that a loss hurts more than an equivalent gain gives pleasure is called loss aversion. It has become the single most powerful tool in the behavioral economist's arsenal.

So, we experience life in terms of changes, we feel diminishing sensitivity to both gains and losses, and losses sting more than equivalently-sized gains feel good. That is a lot of wisdom in one image. Little did I know that I would be playing around with that graph for the rest of my career.

5

California Dreamin'

Sherwin Rosen was planning to spend the summer of 1977 at Stanford and invited me to join him out west to do some more work on the value of a life. At some point that spring I learned that Kahneman and Tversky were planning to spend the academic year at Stanford. After all the inspiration their work had provided me, I could not bear the thought of leaving town just before they arrived in September.

Over spring break I flew to California to investigate housing for the summer, and at the same time try to finagle a way to stay around Stanford during the fall semester. I hoped I might get to spend some time with the complete strangers who had become my new idols. I had sent Tversky an early draft of my first behavioral paper, which at the time carried the title "Consumer Choice: A Theory of Economists' Behavior," with the implicit suggestion that only economists behave like Econs. He had sent a short but friendly reply saying we were clearly thinking along similar lines, but that was it. In the days before email, it was much more difficult to initiate a long-distance conversation.

I spent a few days begging and pleading around campus for some kind of visiting position, but after two days I had nothing. I was about to give up when I had a conversation with the storied health economist Victor Fuchs, who was the director of the National Bureau of Economic Research (NBER) office, where Sherwin and I would be working. I gave Victor my best song and dance about the List, heuristics and biases, prospect theory, and the Israeli gods who were about to descend on Stanford. Victor either got intrigued or just took pity on me and offered to put me on his grant for the fall semester. After I arrived at Stanford in July, Victor and I had frequent discussions about my deviant thoughts, and in time he would extend his offer to pay my salary until the following summer.

The Thaler family took a leisurely trip across the country in June, hitting national parks along the way, and the drive offered time to let my mind wander about ways to combine psychology and economics. Any topic was fair game for pondering. For instance: Suppose I will drive 300 miles today. How fast should I drive? If I drive at 70 miles per hour instead of 60, we will get to our destination 43 minutes sooner, which seems like enough time saved to risk a speeding ticket. But when I have only 30 miles left to go, I will only save 4.3 minutes by driving faster. That doesn't seem worth it. So, should I be gradually slowing down as I get closer to my destination? That can't be right, especially since we are going to get back in the car and drive again tomorrow. Shouldn't I have a uniform policy for the entire trip? Hmmm, put it on the List.*

Our trip's final detour was to Eugene, Oregon, to see Baruch Fischhoff and Paul Slovic, the psychologists who had originally sparked my interest in these ideas. While the family explored the town, I chatted with Baruch, Paul, and their collaborator Sarah Lichtenstein. There was also another psychologist visiting their center who, like Fischhoff, had studied with Kahneman and Tversky in graduate school, Maya Bar-Hillel. All of them would join my informal team of psychology tutors in the coming years.

At the end of the summer, the Kahneman and Tversky psychology clan arrived in force. Amos and his wife, Barbara, were visiting the Stanford psychology department. Danny and his future wife, the eminent psychologist Anne Treisman, were to be visiting the Center for Advanced Study in the Behavioral Sciences, located just up the hill from NBER.

Victor Fuchs arranged the lunch where Amos, Danny, and I first met. I don't remember much about it, except that I was uncharacteristically nervous. I can only trust that the voluble Vic kept the conversation moving. More important, the lunch introduction gave me license to walk up the hill and drop in on Danny. (Tversky's office was on campus, too far away to just drop in.) He and Tversky were finishing the paper that by now they called "Prospect Theory," and

---

* Answer: Drive the same speed the whole way. The chance of getting a ticket is proportional to the time you are driving, holding everything else constant.

I would sometimes wander in while they were working. The Center's primitive phone system made it easier to walk up the hill than to call Danny to see if he was around.

Sometimes when I stopped by to see Danny I would find the two of them at work, putting together the final version of prospect theory. When they were writing, with Danny at the keyboard, they would talk through each sentence, arguing about virtually every word. Their conversations were an odd mixture of Hebrew and English. An exchange in one language might suddenly switch to the other, with no acknowledgment of the flip. Sometimes the switch to English seemed related to the use of technical terms like "loss aversion," for which they had not bothered to invent Hebrew equivalents. But I failed to generate a viable theory for why they would switch in the other direction. It might have helped to know some Hebrew.

They spent months polishing the paper. Most academics find getting the initial ideas the most enjoyable part of research, and conducting the actual research is almost as much fun. But few enjoy the writing, and it shows. To call academic writing dull is giving it too much credit. Yet to many, dull writing is a badge of honor. To write with flair signals that you don't take your work seriously and readers shouldn't either.* "Prospect Theory" is hardly an easy read, but the writing was crystal clear because of their endless editing and Amos's perennial goal of "getting it right."

Danny and I soon began the habit of taking walks in the hills near the Center just to talk. We were equally ignorant and curious about each other's fields, so our conversations offered many learning opportunities. One aspect of these mutual training sessions involved understanding how members of the other profession think, and what it takes to convince them of some finding.

The use of hypothetical questions offers a good example. All of Kahneman and Tversky's research up to this point relied on simple scenarios, such as: "Imagine that in addition to everything you now own, you gain $400. Now consider the choice between a sure loss of $200 or a gamble in which you have a 50% chance to lose $400

---

* There are, of course, exceptions to this generalization. In that era, George Stigler and Tom Schelling come to mind as great writers.

and a 50% chance to lose nothing." (Most choose to gamble in this situation.) As Kahneman delightfully explains in his book *Thinking, Fast and Slow,* they would try these thought experiments out on themselves and if they agreed on an answer they would provisionally assume that others would answer the same way. Then they would check by asking subjects, typically students.

Economists do not put much stock in the answers to hypothetical questions, or survey questions in general for that matter. Economists say they care more about what people *do* as opposed to what they *say they would do.* Kahneman and Tversky were aware of the objections, undoubtedly raised by skeptical economists they had met, but they had little choice. A key prediction of prospect theory is that people react differently to losses than they do to gains. But it is nearly impossible to get permission to run experiments in which subjects might actually lose substantial amounts of money. Even if people were willing to participate, the university committees that review experiments using human subjects might not approve the experiments.

In the published version of prospect theory, Amos and Danny included the following defense of their methods: "By default, the method of hypothetical choices emerges as the simplest procedure by which a large number of theoretical questions can be investigated. The use of the method relies on the assumption that people often know how they would behave in actual situations of choice, and on the further assumption that the subjects have no special reason to disguise their true preferences." Essentially, they were saying that if their subjects were reasonably accurate in predicting the choices they would actually make in such cases, and their indicated choices were inconsistent with expected utility theory, then that should at least create a presumption of doubt about whether the theory is a good description of behavior.

This defense apparently satisfied the journal editor but remained a bugaboo among economists for years. Prospect theory gradually gained acceptance because it proved useful in explaining behavior in a variety of high-stakes settings where it was possible to observe actual choices, from individual investors to game show contestants. But I don't think any economist would have come up with this theory, even granting them Kahneman and Tversky's psychological insights.

An unwillingness to rely on hypothetical questions would have kept them from learning the nuances of behavior that Kahneman and Tversky were able to discern.

I found the idea that you could just ask people questions and take their answers seriously to be quite liberating. Up to then, the items on the List were merely thought experiments. It seemed obvious to me that if readers were confronted with one of my hypothetical examples, they would check their intuition and then agree that the behavior existed. (This was, of course, naïve.) And, although the survey method was not considered authoritative, it was surely better than a survey of my own intuitions.

A few years later I got a nice lesson on how to do this from the masters themselves. They took my clock radio and television shopping example from the List and turned it into shopping for a jacket and a calculator, and then asked people what they would do. Here it is, with two different versions indicated by the numbers in parentheses or brackets:

> Imagine that you are about to purchase a jacket for ($125)[$15] and a calculator for ($15)[$125]. The calculator salesman informs you that the calculator you wish to buy is on sale for ($10)[$120] at the other branch of the store, located a twenty-minute drive away. Would you make the trip to the other store?

Sure enough, real subjects said they would be more willing to take the drive to save $5 on the cheaper item, as I had conjectured, and now there was data to support it. I soon started using this method as well, though sparingly. But Danny and I would rely almost exclusively on the answers to hypothetical questions seven years later in a project about perceptions of fairness, discussed in chapter 14.

When I was not wandering the hills with Danny, I was hunkered down at NBER with nothing to do but think. Victor Fuchs played the role of guilt-inducing Jewish mother, periodically asking me about my progress. A paradox confronted me. I had what I thought was a big idea, but research proceeds through a series of small steps. And I did not know which small steps would advance the big idea. Big ideas are fine, but I needed to publish papers to stay employed. Looking back, I had what science writer Steven Johnson calls a "slow hunch." A slow hunch is not one of those "aha" insights when everything becomes clear. Instead, it is more of a vague impression that there is something interesting going on, and an intuition that there could be something important lurking not far away. The problem with a slow hunch is you have no way to know whether it will lead to a dead end. I felt like I had arrived on the shores of a new world with no map, no idea where I should be looking, and no idea whether I would find anything of value.

Kahneman and Tversky ran experiments, so it was natural to think that I should be running experiments, too. I reached out to the two founders of the then nascent field called experimental economics, Charlie Plott at Caltech and Vernon Smith, then at the University of Arizona. Economists traditionally have used historical data to test hypotheses. Smith and Plott were practitioners of and proselytizers for the idea that one could test economic ideas in the laboratory. I first took a trip down to Tucson to visit Smith.

Smith's research agenda was, at least at that time, different from the one I was imagining for myself. When he and Danny shared the Nobel Prize in economics many years later, I told a reporter that the difference between their respective research agendas that won them the prize was that Smith was trying to show how well economic theory worked and Kahneman was doing the opposite.[*]

At the time I visited him, Smith advocated using something he called the *induced value* methodology. Instead of trading actual goods or gambles, markets were created for tokens, in which each subject was given their own private value for a token. My token might be worth $8 while yours would be worth $4, meaning that these were the amounts we would receive from the experimenter if we ended up holding a token at the end of the study. Using this method, Smith was able to test economic principles such as supply and demand analysis. But I had some worries about this methodology. When you go to the store and decide whether to buy a jacket for $49, no one is telling

---

[*] I was referring to Smith's early work, cited by the Nobel committee. Later he delved into other more radical areas, including a series of experiments in which he could reliably produce an asset pricing bubble (Smith, Suchanek, and Gerry, 1998).

you how much you are willing to pay for it. You have to decide that for yourself, and that value might depend on all sorts of issues such as what the retail price of the product is, how much you have already spent on clothing this month, and whether you happened to have just gotten your tax refund. Many years later I finally got around to testing my concern about this method by replacing tokens with coffee mugs, as we will see in chapter 16.

I then combined a family trip to Disneyland with a pilgrimage to Caltech to meet Charlie Plott, who was also pioneering this field (and could easily have shared the Nobel Prize with Smith). Perhaps because of the Caltech setting, Plott liked to use a wind tunnel analogy to describe what he was doing. Rather than showing that the basic principles of economics worked in the lab, he was more interested in testing what happened when the rules of the market were changed. Charlie, for whom the word garrulous seems to have been invented, was also warm and friendly.

As kind and impressive as Smith and Plott were, I was not ready to declare myself to be exclusively, or even primarily, an experimental economist. I wanted to study "behavior" and remain open-minded about the techniques I would use. I planned to run experiments when that method seemed to be the best way of observing behavior, or sometimes to just ask people questions, but I also wanted to study the behavior of people in their natural habitats . . . if I could just figure out how to do it.

————

At some point during my year in Stanford I decided I was going "all in" on this new venture. The University of Rochester was not an ideal venue given the intellectual proclivities of the senior faculty, who were deeply wedded to traditional economic methodology, so I looked elsewhere.[*]

—

[*] Academic insiders might wonder how I landed a job in the Rochester business school after being a student in the economics department. Universities usually do not hire their own graduates. The answer is a long story, the short version of which is that I had been teaching at the business school while a graduate student, and when my first job fell through at the last minute, Bill Meckling, the school's dean, offered me a one-year position as a stopgap measure, and I ended up sticking

When you interview for a job in academia you present a paper in a faculty workshop, and that presentation, along with the papers you have written, determines whether you will get the job. My "Value of a Life" paper with Rosen was already pretty widely known, and I could have played it safe by presenting some additional work on that topic, but I wanted an environment that would tolerate a little heresy, so I presented a paper about the economics of self-control, cashews and all. Any place that would hire me after hearing that paper was likely to be at least moderately open to what came next. Fortunately, offers arrived from Cornell and Duke, and I settled on Cornell. My next move would be 90 miles down the road from Rochester.

---

around for a few more years.

6

The Gauntlet

I accepted the job at Cornell about halfway through my time at Stanford, and would start there in August 1978. I had work to do on two fronts. First, I had to produce research that showed what we could learn from the new approach I was suggesting. Second, and just as important, I had to be able to offer convincing replies to a series of one-line putdowns I would hear almost any time I presented my research. Economists had their way of doing things and would resist change, if for no other reason than that they had invested years building their own particular corner of this edifice.

This fact was brought home to me at one early conference where I gave a talk on my recent work. During the question and answer period that followed, a well-known economist asked me a question: "If I take what you are saying seriously, what am I supposed to do? My skill is knowing how to solve optimization problems." His point was that if I were right, and optimization models were poor descriptions of actual behavior, his toolkit would be obsolete.

His reaction was unusually candid. The more common response, for those who engaged at all, was to explain what I was doing wrong, and what obvious factors I had ignored. I soon had another list: reasons why economists could safely ignore behaviors such as those on the List. Among friends I would call this series of questions the Gauntlet, since any time I gave a talk about my work it felt like running a medieval gauntlet. Here are a few of the most important ones, along with the preliminary responses I had worked up at the time. To some extent people are still arguing about these points; you will see them reappear throughout the book.

As if

One of the most prominent of the putdowns had only two words: "as if." Briefly stated, the argument is that even if people are not capable of actually solving the complex problems that economists assume they can handle, they behave "as if" they can.

To understand the "as if" critique, it is helpful to look back a bit into the history of economics. The discipline underwent something of a revolution after World War II. Economists led by Kenneth Arrow, John Hicks, and Paul Samuelson accelerated an ongoing trend of making economic theory more mathematically formal. The two central concepts of economics remained the same—namely, that agents optimize and markets reach a stable equilibrium—but economists became more sophisticated in their ability to characterize the optimal solutions to problems as well as to determine the conditions under which a market will reach an equilibrium.

One example is the so-called theory of the firm, which comes down to saying that firms maximize profits (or share price). As modern theorists started to spell out precisely what this meant, some economists objected on the grounds that real managers were not able to solve such problems.

One simple example was called "marginal analysis." Recall from chapter 4 that a firm striving to maximize profits will set price and output at the point where marginal cost equals marginal revenue. The same analysis applies to hiring workers. Keep hiring workers until the cost of the last worker equals the increase in revenue that the worker produces. These results may seem innocuous enough, but in the late 1940s a debate raged in the *American Economic Review* about whether *real* managers actually behaved this way.

The debate was kicked off by Richard Lester, a plucky associate professor of economics at Princeton. He had the temerity to write to the owners of manufacturing companies and ask them to explain their processes for deciding how many workers to hire and how much output to produce. None of the executives reported doing anything that appeared to resemble "equating at the margin." First, they did not seem to think about the effect of changes in the prices of their products or the possibility of changing what they paid to workers. Counter to the theory, they did not appear to think that changes in wages would affect either their hiring or output decisions much. Instead, they reported trying to sell as much of their product as they could, and increasing or decreasing the workforce to meet that level of demand. Lester ends his paper boldly: "This paper raises grave doubts as to the validity of conventional marginal theory and the assumptions on which it rests."

The defense team for the marginal theory was headed up by Fritz Machlup, who was then at the University of Buffalo but later joined Lester at Princeton, perhaps to continue the debate in person. Machlup brushed Lester's survey data aside on the grounds that economists are not really interested in what people *say* they are doing. The theory does not require that firms explicitly calculate marginal costs and marginal revenues, he argued, but their actions nevertheless will approximate those predicted by the theory. He offered the analogy of a driver deciding when to pass a truck on a two-lane highway. The driver will not make any calculations, yet will manage to overtake the truck. An executive, he argued, would make decisions much the same way. "He would simply rely on his sense or his 'feel' of the situation . . . [and] would 'just know' in a vague and rough way, whether or not it would pay him to hire more men." Machlup was highly critical of Lester's data, but presented none of his own.

It is in the context of this debate that Milton Friedman, a young economist headed for fame, weighed in. In an influential essay called "The Methodology of Positive Economics," Friedman argued that it was silly to evaluate a theory based on the realism of its assumptions. What mattered was the accuracy of the theory's predictions. (He is using the word "positive" in his title here the way I use "descriptive" in this book, that is, as a contrast to normative.)

To illustrate his point, he traded Machlup's driver for an expert billiard player. He notes that:

> excellent predictions would be yielded by the hypothesis that the billiard player made his shots *as if* he knew the complicated mathematical formulas that would give the optimum direction of travel, could estimate by eye the angles etc., describing the location of the balls, could make lightning calculations from the

formulas, and could then make the balls travel in the direction indicated by the formulas. Our confidence in this hypothesis is not based on the belief that billiard players, even expert ones, can or do go through the process described; it derives rather from the belief that, unless in some way or other they were capable of reaching essentially the same result, they would not in fact be expert billiard players.

Friedman was a brilliant debater and his argument certainly seemed compelling. For many economists at the time this settled the issue. The *AER* stopped publishing any more rounds of the debate it had been running, and economists returned to their models free from worry about whether their assumptions were "realistic." A good theory, it seemed, could not be defeated using just survey data, even if the defenders of the theory presented no data of their own. This remained the state of play some thirty years later, when I began to have my deviant thoughts. Even today, grunts of "as if" crop up in economics workshops to dismiss results that do not support standard theoretical predictions.

Fortunately, Kahneman and Tversky had provided an answer to the "as if" question. Both their work on heuristics and biases as well as that on prospect theory clearly showed that people did not act "as if" they were choosing in accordance with the rational economic model. When the subjects in one of Kahneman and Tversky's experiments choose an alternative that is dominated by another one—that is, chosen in lieu of an alternative that is better in every way—there is no way they can be said to be acting *as if* they were making a correct judgment. There was also no way Professor Rosett's wine-buying habits could be declared rational.

In homage to Friedman, whom I genuinely admired, I titled my first behavioral economics paper "Toward a Positive Theory of Consumer Choice." The last section contained a detailed answer to the inevitable "as if" question. I too began with billiards. My main point was that economics is supposed to be a theory of everyone, not only experts. An expert billiard player might play as if he knows all the relevant geometry and physics, but the typical bar player usually aims at the ball closest to a pocket and shoots, often missing. If we are going to have useful theories about how typical people shop, save for retirement, search for a job, or cook dinner, those theories had better not assume that people behave as if they were experts. We don't play chess like a grandmaster, invest like Warren Buffett, or cook like an Iron Chef. Not even "as if." It's more likely that we cook like Warren Buffett (who loves to eat at Dairy Queen). But a snappy retort to the "as if" critique was far from sufficient; to win the argument I would need hard empirical evidence that would convince economists.

To this day, the phrase "survey evidence" is rarely heard in economics circles without the necessary adjective "mere," which rhymes with "sneer." This disdain is simply unscientific. Polling data, which just comes from asking people whether they are planning to vote and for whom, when carefully used by skilled statisticians such as Nate Silver, yield remarkably accurate predictions of elections. The most amusing aspect of this anti-survey attitude is that many important macroeconomic variables are produced by surveys!

For instance, in America the press often obsesses over the monthly announcement of the latest "jobs" data, with serious-looking economists asked to weigh in about how to interpret the figures. Where do these jobs numbers come from? They come from surveys conducted by the Census Bureau. The unemployment rate, one of the key variables in macroeconomic modeling, is also determined from a survey that asks people whether they are looking for work. Yet using published unemployment rate data is not considered a faux pas in macroeconomics. Apparently economists don't mind survey data as long as someone other than the researcher collected it.

But in 1980, survey questions were not going to overcome the "as if" grunt. There would need to be some proper data brought to bear that demonstrated that people misbehaved in their real-life choices.

Incentives

Economists put great stock in incentives. If the stakes are raised, the argument goes, people will have greater incentive to think harder, ask for help, or do what is necessary to get the problem right. Kahneman and Tversky's experiments were typically done with nothing at stake, so for economists that meant they could be safely ignored.

And if actual incentives were introduced in a laboratory setting, the stakes were typically low, just a few dollars. Surely, it was often said, if the stakes were raised, people would get stuff right. This assertion, unsupported by any evidence, was firmly believed, even in spite of the fact that nothing in the theory or practice of economics suggested that economics only applies to large-stakes problems. Economic theory should work just as well for purchases of popcorn as for automobiles.

Two Caltech economists provided some early evidence against this line of attack: David Grether and Charlie Plott, one of my experimental economics tutors. Grether and Plott had come across research conducted by two of my psychology mentors, Sarah Lichtenstein and Paul Slovic. Lichtenstein and Slovic had discovered "preference reversals," a phenomenon that proved disconcerting to economists. In brief, subjects were induced to say that they preferred choice A to choice B . . . and also that they preferred B to A.

This finding upset a theoretical foundation essential to any formal economic theory, namely that people have what are called "well-defined preferences," which simply means that we consistently know what we like. Economists don't care whether you like a firm mattress better than a soft one or vice versa, but they cannot tolerate you saying that you like a firm mattress better than a soft one *and* a soft one better than a firm one. That will not do. Economic theory textbooks would stop on the first page if the assumption of well-ordered preferences had to be abandoned, because without stable preferences there is nothing to be optimized.

Lichtenstein and Slovic elicited preference reversals when they presented subjects with a pair of gambles: one a relatively sure thing, such as a 97% chance to win $10, and the other more risky, such as a 37% chance to win $30. They called the near sure thing the "p" bet, for high probability, and the more risky gamble the "$" bet, since it offered a chance to win more money. First they asked people which gamble they preferred. Most took the p bet since they liked an almost sure win. For these subjects this means p is preferred to $. Then they asked these p bet–loving subjects: "Suppose you owned the p bet. What is the lowest price at which you would be willing to sell it?" They also asked them the same question for the $ bet. Strangely, a majority of these subjects demanded more to give up the $ bet than the p bet, indicating they liked the $ bet more. But this means they prefer the p bet to the $ bet, and the $ bet to the p bet. Blasphemy!

Grether and Plott wanted to know what was driving these weird results, and their leading hypothesis was incentives.* If the bets were real, they conjectured, this nonsense would stop. So they ran the experiments for real money, and much to their surprise, the frequency and severity of the preference reversals actually increased. Raising the stakes made things worse.

This did not put an end to the incentive objection. But at least there was one paper to cite disputing the claim that money would solve all of the problems economists had with behavioral research. And, as we will see, this has been very much a recurring theme in the debate about the validity of experimental evidence.

Learning

The style of experiment Kahneman and Tversky ran was often faulted as a "one-shot" game. In the "real world," economists argued, people have opportunities to learn. The idea is reasonable enough. We don't start out life as good drivers, but most of us do learn to drive without frequent mishaps. The fact that a clever psychologist can devise a question that will lure people in the lab into making a mistake does not necessarily imply that the same mistake would be made in the "real world." (Laboratories are thought to be unreal worlds.) Out there, people have had lots of time to practice their decision-making tasks, so they won't make the mistakes we see in the lab.

The problem with the learning story is that it assumes that we all live in a world like the Bill Murray movie *Groundhog Day*. Bill Murray's character keeps waking up and reliving the same day, over and over.

---

* They favored this hypothesis even though Lichtenstein and Slovic (1973) had replicated their studies for real money on the floor of a casino in Las Vegas. Their dismissal of this evidence might be explained by another of their hypotheses. They also explicitly entertained the possibility that the perverse results were obtained simply because the experimenters were psychologists, who were known to deceive people in experiments. Needless to say, this hypothesis did not sit well with any psychologists who stumbled onto their paper.

Once he figures out what is going on, he is able to learn because he can vary things one at a time and see what happens. Real life is not as controlled as that, and thankfully so. But as a result, learning can be difficult.

Psychologists tell us that in order to learn from experience, two ingredients are necessary: frequent practice and immediate feedback. When these conditions are present, such as when we learn to ride a bike or drive a car, we learn, possibly with some mishaps along the way. But many of life's problems do not offer these opportunities, which raises an interesting point. The learning and incentives arguments are, to some extent, contradictory. This first occurred to me in a public debate of sorts that I had with the British game theorist Ken Binmore.

At a conference organized for graduate students, Binmore and I were each giving one lecture a day. I was presenting new findings of behavioral economics and although Binmore was presenting unrelated work, he took the opportunity at the beginning of each of his lectures to reply to the one I had given the day before. After my first lecture, Binmore offered a version of the "low stakes" critique. He said that if he were running a supermarket, he would want to consult my research because, for inexpensive purchases, the things I studied might possibly matter. But if he were running an automobile dealership, my research would be of little relevance. At high stakes people would get stuff right.

The next day I presented what I now call the "Binmore continuum" in his honor. I wrote a list of products on the blackboard that varied from left to right based on frequency of purchase. On the left I started with cafeteria lunch (daily), then milk and bread (twice a week), and so forth up to sweaters, cars, and homes, career choices, and spouses (not more than two or three per lifetime for most of us). Notice the trend. We do small stuff often enough to learn to get it right, but when it comes to choosing a home, a mortgage, or a job, we don't get much practice or opportunities to learn. And when it comes to saving for retirement, barring reincarnation we do that exactly once. So Binmore had it backward. Because learning takes practice, we are more likely to get things right at small stakes than at large stakes. This means critics have to decide which argument they want to apply. If learning is crucial, then as the stakes go up, decision-making quality is likely to go down.

Markets: the invisible handwave

The most important counter-argument in the Gauntlet involves markets. I remember well the first time Amos was introduced to this argument. It came during dinner at a conference organized by the leading intellectual figure at the Rochester business school where I had been teaching, Michael Jensen. At that time Jensen was a firm believer in both rational choice models and the efficiency of financial markets. (He has changed his views in various ways since then.) I think he saw the conference as a chance to find out what all the fuss around Kahneman and Tversky was about, as well as an opportunity to straighten out two confused psychologists.

In the course of conversation, Amos asked Jensen to assess the decision-making capabilities of his wife. Mike was soon regaling us with stories of the ridiculous economic decisions she made, like buying an expensive car and then refusing to drive it because she was afraid it would be dented. Amos then asked Jensen about his students, and Mike rattled off silly mistakes they made, complaining about how slow they were to understand the most basic economics concepts. As more wine was consumed, Mike's stories got better.

Then Amos went in for the kill. "Mike," he said, "you seem to think that virtually everyone you know is incapable of correctly making even the simplest of economic decisions, but then you assume that all the agents in your models are geniuses. What gives?"

Jensen was unfazed. "Amos," he said, "you just don't understand." He then launched into a speech that I attribute to Milton Friedman. I have not been able to find such an argument in Friedman's writings, but at Rochester at that time, people attributed it to Uncle Miltie, as he was lovingly called. The speech goes something like this. "Suppose there were people doing silly things like the subjects in your experiments, and those people had to interact in competitive markets, then . . ."

I call this argument the *invisible handwave* because, in my experience, no one has ever finished that sentence with both hands remaining still, and it is thought to be somehow related to Adam Smith's

invisible hand, the workings of which are both overstated and mysterious. The vague argument is that markets somehow discipline people who are misbehaving. Handwaving is a must because there is no
logical way to arrive at a conclusion that markets transform people
into rational agents. Suppose you pay attention to sunk costs, and
finish a rich dessert after a big dinner just because you paid for the
dessert. What will happen to you? If you make this mistake often you
might be a bit chubbier, but otherwise you are fine. What if you suffer from loss aversion? Is that fatal? No. Suppose you decide to start a
new business because you are overconfident and put your chances of
success at 90%, when in fact a majority of new businesses fail. Well,
either you will be lucky and succeed in spite of your dumb decision,
or you will muddle along barely making a living. Or perhaps you will
give up, shut the business down, and go do something else. As cruel
as the market may be, it cannot make you rational. And except in rare
circumstances, failing to act in accordance with the rational agent
model is not fatal.

Sometimes the invisible handwave is combined with the incentives argument to suggest that when the stakes are high and the
choices are difficult, people will go out and hire experts to help
them. The problem with this argument is that it can be hard to find
a true expert who does not have a conflict of interest. It is illogical
to think that someone who is not sophisticated enough to choose a
good portfolio for her retirement saving will somehow be sophisticated about searching for a financial advisor, mortgage broker, or real
estate agent. Many people have made money selling magic potions
and Ponzi schemes, but few have gotten rich selling the advice, "Don't
buy that stuff."

A different version of the argument is that the forces of competition inexorably drive business firms to be maximizers, even if they are
managed by Humans, including some who did not distinguish themselves as students. Of course there is some merit to this argument,
but I think it is vastly overrated. In my lifetime, I cannot remember
any time when experts thought General Motors was a well-run company. But GM stumbled along as a badly-run company for decades.
For most of this period they were also the largest car company in the
world. Perhaps they would have disappeared from the global economy

in 2009 after the financial crisis, but with the aid of a government bailout, they are now the second largest automobile company in the world, a bit behind Toyota and just ahead of Volkswagen. Competitive forces apparently are slow-acting.

To be fair to Jensen, there is a more coherent version of his argument. Instead of arguing that markets force people to be rational, one can argue that market prices will still be rational, even if many individuals are decidedly Human. This argument is certainly plausible, perhaps even compelling. It just happens to be wrong. But how and why it is wrong is a long story that we will take up in Section VI.

For the field of behavioral economics to succeed, we needed answers to these questions. And in some quarters, we still do. But now, instead of snappy one-liners, it is possible to point to studies of real people interacting at high stakes in markets—even financial markets, where the invisible handwave would be expected to be most likely to be valid.

———

It was with the Gauntlet in my mind that I arrived at Cornell, in rural Ithaca, New York, in the fall of 1978. Ithaca is a small town with long, snowy winters, and not much to do. It was a good place to work.

While in California I had managed to finish two papers. One expounded on the List, and the other was called "An Economic Theory of Self-Control." Writing the papers was the easy part; getting them published was another story. The first paper, mentioned earlier, "Toward a Positive Theory of Consumer Choice," was rejected by six or seven major journals; I have repressed the exact count. In hindsight, I am not surprised. The paper had plenty of ideas, but little hard evidence to support them. Each rejection came with a set of referee reports, with often scathing comments that I would try to incorporate in the next revision. Still, I did not seem to be making any progress.

At some point I had to get this paper published, if for no other reason than that I needed to move on. Luckily, two open-minded economists were starting a new journal called the *Journal of Economic Behavior and Organization*. I guessed that they were anxious to get submissions, so I sent the paper to them and they published it in the inaugural issue. I had my first behavioral economics publication, albeit in a journal no one had ever heard of.

If I were going to stay in academia and get tenure at a research-focused university like Cornell, I would have to start publishing regularly in top journals. I had returned from California with two ideas at the top of my list of topics to explore. The first was to understand the psychology of spending, saving, and other household financial behavior, what has now become known as mental accounting. The second was self-control and, more generally, choosing between now and later. The next two sections of the book take up those topics.

II.

MENTAL ACCOUNTING:
1979–85

After our year together in California, Amos and Danny continued their collaboration and I would only see them occasionally at conferences. They were working on follow-up papers to "Prospect Theory" and I continued to think about consumer choice. There was one topic, however, that they and I were both thinking about, mostly independently. In a nutshell it is: "How do people think about money?" Early on I called this process "psychological accounting," but in a later paper on the topic Amos and Danny changed the name to "mental accounting," and I followed suit.

I have continued to think, write, and talk about mental accounting for the rest of my career. I still find it fascinating, exciting, and incisive; it is a lens that helps me understand the world. The next few chapters are devoted to mental accounting basics, but the topic permeates the rest of the book. Thinking about mental accounting can be contagious. You may soon find yourself blurting, "Well, that is really a mental accounting problem."

Bargains and Rip-Offs

My friend Maya Bar-Hillel was shopping for a quilt to use as a comforter on her double bed. She went to the store and found one she liked that was on sale. The regular prices were $300 for a king size, $250 for a queen size, and $200 for a double. This week only, all sizes were priced at $150. Maya could not resist: she bought the king size.

To begin any discussion of mental accounting, it helps to understand the basic economic theory of the consumer. Recall from the discussion of the endowment effect that all economic decisions are made through the lens of opportunity costs. The cost of dinner and a movie tonight is not fully captured by the financial outlay—it also depends on the alternative uses of that time and money.

If you understand opportunity costs and you have a ticket to a game that you could sell for $1,000, it does not matter how much you paid for the ticket. The cost of going to the game is what you could do with that $1,000. You should only go to the game if that is the best possible way you could use that money. Is it better than one hundred movies at $10 each? Better than an upgrade to your shabby wardrobe? Better than saving the money for a rainy day or a sunny weekend? This analysis is not limited to decisions that involve money. If you spend an afternoon reading a novel, then the opportunity cost is whatever else you might have done with that time.

Thinking like that is a right and proper normative theory of consumer choice. It's what Econs do, and in principle we should all strive to think this way most of the time. Still, anyone who tried to make every decision in this manner would be paralyzed. How can I possibly know which of the nearly infinite ways to use $1,000 will make me happiest? The problem is too complex for anyone to solve, and it is unrealistic to think that the typical consumer engages in this type of thinking. Few people think in a way that even approximates this type of analysis. For the $1,000 ticket problem, many people will consider only a few alternatives. I could watch the game on television and use the money to go visit my daughter in Providence. Would that be better? But figuring out the best alternative use of the money is not something I or anyone is capable of thinking about—not even close.*

What do people do instead? I was unsure about how to study this and other aspects of consumer decision-making, so I hired a student to interview local families to see what we could learn about what real people do. I concentrated on lower-middle-class households because spending decisions are much more important when your budget is tight.

The interviews were designed to give the participants plenty of time to talk about whatever they wanted. (We paid them a fixed amount to participate but some talked for hours.) The target respondent was the person in the household who handled the money. In married couples, more often than not this responsibility fell to the wife. The purpose of the interviews was not to collect data for an academic paper. I simply hoped to get an overall impression of how people thought about managing their household's finances. Adam Smith famously visited a pin factory to see how manufacturing worked. This was my pin factory. The interviews grounded me in reality and greatly influenced everything I later wrote about mental accounting.

The first question to deal with was one I had been pondering since the days of the List. "When is a cost a loss?" Although it had long been on my mind, my "discovery" of prospect theory heightened that interest. Recall that the value function displays loss aversion: when

---

*   Perhaps surprisingly, the one group of people that come closest to thinking this way about opportunity costs is the poor. In their recent book *Scarcity*, Sendhil Mullainathan and Eldar Shafir (2013) report that, on this dimension, the poor come closer to behaving like Econs than those who are better off, simply because opportunity costs are highly salient for them. If a $100 windfall could pay the overdue utility bill or replace the kids' shoes that are now too small, opportunity costs are front and center. However, this incessant fretting about opportunity costs takes a toll. Having to constantly worry about where the money is going to come from to pay the rent makes it hard to keep up with everything, and may contribute to some of the bad decisions made by the poor, such as taking out and rolling over payday loans.

starting from zero, it is steeper going down than going up. Losses hurt about twice as much as gains make us feel good. This raises the question: if you pay $5 for a sandwich, do you feel like you just lost $5? For routine transactions, the answer is clearly no. For one thing, thinking that way would make you miserable. Because losses are weighed about twice as heavily as gains, even trading a ten-dollar bill for two fives would be viewed as a loss with this sort of accounting. "Losing" each of the five-dollar bills would be more painful than the pleasure associated with receiving the $10. So what *does* happen when you make a purchase? And what in the world was Maya thinking when she bought that gigantic quilt?

Eventually I settled on a formulation that involves two kinds of utility: *acquisition utility* and *transaction utility*. Acquisition utility is based on standard economic theory and is equivalent to what economists call "consumer surplus." As the name suggests, it is the surplus remaining after we measure the utility of the object gained and then subtract the opportunity cost of what has to be given up. For an Econ, acquisition utility is the end of the story. A purchase will produce an abundance of acquisition utility only if a consumer values something much more than the marketplace does. If you are very thirsty, then a one-dollar bottle of water is a utility windfall. And for an Econ who owns a double bed, the acquisition utility of a quilt that fits the bed would be greater than one that hangs two feet over the side in every direction.

Humans, on the other hand, also weigh another aspect of the purchase: the perceived quality of the deal. That is what transaction utility captures. It is defined as the difference between the price actually paid for the object and the price one would normally expect to pay, the *reference price*. Suppose you are at a sporting event and you buy a sandwich identical to the one you usually have at lunch, but it costs triple the price. The sandwich is fine but the deal stinks. It produces negative transaction utility, a "rip-off." In contrast, if the price is below the reference price, then transaction utility is positive, a "bargain," like Maya's extra-large quilt selling for the same price as a smaller one.

Here is a survey question that illustrates the concept. Two groups of students in an executive MBA program who reported being regular beer drinkers were asked one of the two versions of the scenario shown below. The variations appear in parentheses and brackets.

You are lying on the beach on a hot day. All you have to drink is
ice water. For the last hour you have been thinking about how
much you would enjoy a nice cold bottle of your favorite brand of
beer. A companion gets up to go make a phone call and offers to
bring back a beer from the only nearby place where beer is sold (a
fancy resort hotel) [a small, rundown grocery store]. He says that
the beer might be expensive so asks how much you are willing to
pay for the beer. He says he will buy the beer if it costs as much
or less than what you state. But if it costs more than the price
you state, he will not buy it. You trust your friend, and there is
no possibility of bargaining with the (bartender) [store owner].
What price will you tell him?

There are several things to notice about this example, which was
fine-tuned to deal with the objections I anticipated hearing from economists. Crucially, the consumption act is identical in the two situations. The respondent gets to drink one bottle of his favorite brand
of beer on the beach. He never enters or even sees the establishment
from which the beer has been purchased, and thus does not consume
any ambience, positive or negative. Also, by ruling out any negotiation
with the seller, the respondents have no reason to disguise their true
preferences. In economists' lingo, the situation is *incentive compatible*.

With those provisos out of the way, we can proceed to the punch
line. People are willing to pay more for the beer if it was purchased
from the resort than from the convenience store. The median[*]
answers, adjusted for inflation, were \$7.25 and \$4.10.

These results show that people are willing to pay different prices
for the same beer, consumed at the same spot on the beach, depending on where it was bought. Why do the respondents care where the
beer was bought? One reason is expectations. People expect prices to
be higher at a fancy hotel, in part because the costs are quite obviously higher. Paying seven dollars for a beer at a resort is annoying but expected; paying that at a bodega is an outrage! This is the
essence of transaction utility.

---

[*]   The median is the statistical term for middle. If all the prices are ranked from
high to low, the median answer is the one with as many answers higher as lower.

Econs do not experience transaction utility. For them, the purchase location is another supposedly irrelevant factor, or SIF. It is not that Econs are immune to bargains. If someone was selling beers on the beach for ten cents, then even an Econ would be happy, but that happiness would be fully captured by the acquisition utility. Those who enjoy transaction utility are getting pleasure (or pain) from the terms of the deal per se.

Since transaction utility can be either positive or negative—that is, there can be both great deals and awful gouges—it can both prevent purchases that are welfare-enhancing and induce purchases that are a waste of money. The beer on the beach example illustrates a case where someone can be dissuaded from making a worthwhile purchase. Suppose Dennis says he would only pay $4 for the beer from the bodega, but $7 from the hotel. His friend Tom could make Dennis happier if he bought the beer at the store for $5 but told Dennis he had bought it from the hotel. Dennis would get to drink his beer thinking the deal was fine. It is only his distaste for overpaying that stops him from agreeing to this transaction without Tom's subterfuge.

For those who are at least living comfortably, negative transaction utility can prevent our consuming special experiences that will provide a lifetime of happy memories, and the amount by which the item was overpriced will long be forgotten. Good deals, on the other hand, can lure all of us into making purchases of objects of little value. Everyone has items in their closets that are rarely worn but were "must buys" simply because the deal was too good, and of course somewhere in the garage or attic is our version of Maya's quilt.

Because consumers think this way, sellers have an incentive to manipulate the perceived reference price and create the illusion of a "deal." One example that has been used for decades is announcing a largely fictional "suggested retail price," which actually just serves as a misleading suggested *reference* price. In America, some products always seem to be on sale, such as rugs and mattresses, and at some retailers, men's suits. Goods that are marketed this way share two characteristics: they are bought infrequently and quality is difficult to assess. The infrequent purchases help because consumers often do not notice that there is always a sale going on. Most of us are pleasantly surprised that when we wander in to buy a new mattress, there happens to be a sale this week. And when the quality of a product, like a mattress, is hard to assess, the suggested retail price can do double duty. It can simultaneously suggest that quality is high (thus increasing perceived acquisition utility) and imply that there is transaction utility to be had because the product is "on sale."

Shoppers can get hooked on the thrill derived from transaction utility. If a retailer known for frequent discounting tries to wean their customers away from expecting great deals, it can struggle. Several retailers have tried over the years to entice customers with something called "everyday low pricing," but these experiments usually fail.* Getting a great deal is more fun than saving a small and largely invisible amount on each item.

Macy's and JC Penney are just two U.S. retailers to have notably tried—and failed—to wean their customers off their addiction to frequent sales. In an image makeover undertaken in 2006–07, Macy's leadership specifically targeted coupons as a price reduction device, and wanted to reduce their usage. Macy's saw coupons as a threat, linking the brand too closely to less prestigious retailers such as JC Penney or Kohl's. After taking over several other department store chains across the country and rebranding them all as Macy's, they cut the use of coupons by 30% in the spring of 2007, compared to the prior spring. This did not go over well with customers. Sales plummeted, and Macy's quickly promised to return to its previous glut of coupons by the holiday season of that same year.

JC Penney similarly eschewed coupons for a brief period in 2012 in pursuit of an everyday low price strategy. Noting that less than 1% of revenues came from full-price transactions, CEO Ron Johnson in a surprisingly candid press release announced an end to what he dubbed "fake prices"—the mythical suggested retail price—and the start of a simpler pricing scheme. In addition to abolishing traditional sales via coupons, the new scheme did away with prices ending in .99, rounding

---

* A recent study finds that when U.S. supermarkets were confronted with the challenge of a Walmart entering their home market, all suffered, but those who used a promotional pricing strategy (e.g., frequent sales) experienced significantly greater revenues and long-term viability than an everyday low price strategy (Ellickson, Misra, and Nair, 2012).

them up to the nearest dollar. JC Penney claimed the end price consumers paid was effectively the same, after all these changes.

It might well be true that consumers were not paying any more under the new regime, but they were missing out on lots of transaction utility. They even lost that tiny pleasure of paying just "under" a given dollar amount, e.g., $9.99 rather than $10. The experiment was a flop. JC Penney's sales and stock price plummeted as the changes took effect in 2012. A year later, Johnson was ousted and coupons returned to JC Penney customers. But as of 2014, sales had not yet recovered. Maybe consumers did not like being told that the suggested retail prices, the source of so much transaction utility pleasure, were fake.

Sharp readers (and shoppers) might wonder about large-format discount retailers such as Walmart and Costco. These retailers successfully operate under an everyday low pricing strategy, sometimes without explicit reference to an original higher price. But they have not eliminated transaction utility; just the opposite. They have convinced their customers that the entire shopping experience is an orgy of bargain hunting, and go out of their way to reinforce that image. Along with providing genuinely low prices, Walmart also offers a variation on the old ploy of guaranteeing that they have the lowest prices available by allowing shoppers to scan their receipts into a "savings catcher" app that promises to give a refund to anyone if there is a lower price available. Unless Macy's and JC Penney wanted to give up all pretensions of offering an upscale shopping experience, they could not compete with these true low-cost providers in providing transaction utility to their customers.

For consumers, there is nothing wrong with being on the lookout for a bargain. Saving money on one purchase makes another purchase possible. But we don't want to get caught buying something we won't use just because the deal is too good to pass up. For businesses, it is important to realize that everyone is interested in a good deal. Whether it is via sales or genuine low prices, the lure of a deal will attract customers. The parking lot at Costco, a warehouse-style retailer with a reputation for low prices, always has a large number of luxury automobiles. Even affluent consumers get a kick from transaction utility.

8

Sunk Costs

Vince paid $1,000 to an indoor tennis club that entitled him to play once a week for the indoor season. After two months he developed tennis elbow, which made playing painful. He continued to play in pain for three more months because he did not want to waste the membership fee. He only stopped playing when the pain became unbearable.

When an amount of money has been spent and the money cannot be retrieved, the money is said to be sunk, meaning gone. Expressions such as "don't cry over spilt milk" and "let bygones be bygones" are another way of putting economists' advice to ignore sunk costs. But this is hard advice to follow, as the example from the List about driving to a basketball game in a blizzard, and the story of Vince and his tennis elbow, illustrate.

To make things clear, let's stipulate that if a friend invited Vince to play tennis (for free) at another club, Vince would say no because of his painful elbow. In economics lingo that means the utility of playing tennis is negative. But having paid $1,000 he continues to play, seemingly making himself worse off every time he does so. Why would he do such a thing? That is the question I wanted to answer.

Over the years I collected dozens of examples of people paying attention to sunk costs. One involved a friend, Joyce, who was fighting with her six-year-old daughter Cindy about what she should wear to school. Cindy had decided that she no longer wanted to wear dresses, only pants or shorts. Joyce insisted that Cindy had to wear three dresses that had been purchased in preparation for the beginning of first grade. Shouts of "I bought those dresses, and you are going to wear them!" began many days, with Cindy replying that she would not go to school if she had to wear a dress. I am guessing that Joyce probably asked, unhelpfully, whether Cindy thought that money grows on trees.

I was brought in as a mediator, and explained the economic logic to Joyce. The money paid for the dresses was gone, and wearing the dresses would not get it back. As long as sticking to pants and shorts would not require any new clothing purchases, then insisting that Cindy wear the dresses would not help their financial situation. Joyce was thrilled to hear this news. She hated fighting with her daughter, but genuinely felt guilty about "wasting" the purchase of those three dresses. Having an economist tell her that ignoring sunk costs is perfectly rational, even required, was all she needed. Maya Bar-Hillel started calling me the world's only clinical economist. (After her quilt purchase she became my first client.)

I may or may not have deserved that title, but I was hardly the only economist to recognize that Humans have trouble with this concept. In fact, the mistake is so common it has an official name—the *sunk cost fallacy*—and the fallacy is often mentioned in basic economics textbooks. But many people, even if they understand the concept in principle, can find it difficult to follow the advice to ignore sunk costs in practice.

Driving to the game in the blizzard, or playing tennis in pain, are mistakes no Econ would make. They rightly treat sunk costs as irrelevant. But for Humans, sunk costs linger and become another SIF, and not only for things like dinners and concerts. Many people believe that the United States continued its futile war in Vietnam because we had invested too much to quit. Barry Staw, a professor of organizational behavior, wrote a paper on what he called "escalation of commitment" and called the paper "Knee-Deep in the Big Muddy," after an antiwar song by the folk singer Pete Seeger.* Every thousand lives lost and every billion dollars spent made it more difficult to declare defeat and move on, in Staw's view. Some supposedly irrelevant factors can matter quite a lot.

Why do sunk costs matter? And why might people think that con-

---

* The song is actually titled "Waist Deep in the Big Muddy," and the lyrics illustrate the concept of escalation quite vividly as the verses go from knee-deep to waist-deep to neck-deep.

tinuing a course of action—going to the game or concert, or continuing a futile war—is worth it? As we saw in the previous chapter, when
you make a purchase at a price that does not produce any transaction
utility (or disutility), you do not feel the purchase price as a loss. You
have paid some money, and when you consume the product you will
get the pleasure of the acquisition utility and the account will clear;
your earlier cost is canceled out by your later gain. But what happens
when you buy the ticket and then skip the event?

Paying $100 for a ticket to a concert that you do not attend feels
a lot like losing $100. To continue the financial accounting analogy,
when you buy the ticket and then fail to use it you have to "recognize
the loss" in the mental books you are keeping. Going to the event
allows you to settle this account without taking a loss.

Similarly, the more you use something that you have paid for, the
better you can feel about the transaction. Here is a thought experiment. You buy a pair of shoes, perhaps because they were on sale and,
while still expensive, you could not pass up all that transaction utility. You proudly wear them to work one day and by noon your feet
hurt. After letting your feet heal, you try the shoes again, just for an
evening this time, but they still hurt. Two questions: Assuming that
the shoes never get comfortable, how many more times will you try
to wear these shoes before you give up? And, after you have stopped
wearing them, how long will they sit in the back of your closet before
you toss them or donate them to charity? If you are like most people,
the answers depend on how much you paid for the shoes. The more
you paid, the more pain you will bear before you stop wearing them,
and the longer they will take up room in your closet.

The same behavior occurs with health clubs. If you buy a membership to a gym and fail to go, you will have to declare that purchase as
a loss. In fact, some people buy a membership to help with self-control
problems regarding exercise. If I want to go to the gym and will feel bad
about wasting my membership fee, then the membership fee can help
me overcome my inertia in two ways: the membership fee is haunting
me, and there is no immediate monetary outlay when I do go. Marketing professors John Gourville and Dilip Soman conducted a clever study
at a health club to demonstrate this point. This club bills its members
twice a year. Gourville and Soman found that attendance at the club

jumps the month after the bill arrives, then tails off over time until the next bill arrives. They called this phenomenon "payment depreciation," meaning that the effects of sunk costs wear off over time.

A similar result was found by psychologist Hal Arkes, now at Ohio State University, who conducted a nice experiment with his graduate student Catherine Blumer. Students who were in line to buy season tickets to a campus theater company were randomly chosen to receive either a small or large discount on the purchase price. An important feature of the design of this experiment is that customers were already committed to make the purchase at full price before they got their discount, so experimenters could presume that the subjects who paid a discounted price valued the product as much as those who paid full price. Arkes and Blumer found that sunk costs did matter, but only for one semester. Those who paid full price went to more events in the fall semester, but by the spring attendance was the same across the three groups; apparently the students had gone to enough plays to feel they had gotten their money's worth, or had just forgotten the original purchase altogether. So sunk costs matter, at least for a while, but may be forgotten eventually.

———

In some situations, sunk costs and opportunity costs can be intertwined. I had a chance to investigate a case like this with Princeton psychologist Eldar Shafir. We got to know one another when he was a postdoctoral fellow with Amos at Stanford in 1988–89. Eldar is among the small group of psychologists who can tolerate economists long enough to have collaborated with several, and has made important contributions to behavioral economics.

Our project began with a conversation at an airport when we discovered we were booked on the same flight. I had two coupons that allowed you to upgrade to first class if space was available. At that time, frequent fliers received some of these coupons for free, and could purchase additional ones for $35. I had already used one coupon to upgrade myself when I ran into Eldar and suggested that we try to get him an upgrade as well, so that we could sit together. They did have a seat, so I gave Eldar my remaining coupon as a gift. Eldar objected, insisted on reimbursing me, and asked how much the coupon had cost me. I told

him that depended—some were free and some cost $35. So he asked me
which kind of coupon I had used. "What difference does that make?" I
asked. "I am now out of coupons and will have to buy more, so it makes
no difference which kind of coupon I gave you." "Nonsense!" he said.
"If the coupon was free then I am paying you nothing, but if it cost you
$35 then I insist on paying you that money." We continued the discus-
sion on the flight home and it led to an interesting paper.

Our question was: how long does the memory of a past purchase
linger? Our paper was motivated by our upgrade coupon incident
and by the List denizen Professor Rosett, who would drink old
bottles of wine that he already owned but would neither buy more
bottles nor sell some of the ones he owned. We ran a study using
the subscribers to an annual newsletter on wine auction pricing
called, naturally enough, *Liquid Assets*. The publication was written
by Princeton economist Orley Ashenfelter,[*] a wine aficionado, and
its subscribers were avid wine drinkers and buyers. As such, they
were all well aware that there was (and still is) an active auction
market for old bottles of wine. Orley agreed to include a survey from
us with one of his newsletters. In return, we promised to share the
results with his subscribers.

We asked:

Suppose you bought a case of good Bordeaux in the futures market for $20 a bottle. The wine now sells at auction for about $75.
You have decided to drink a bottle. Which of the following best
captures your feeling of the cost to you of drinking the bottle?
(The percentage of people choosing each option is shown in brackets.)

(a) $0. I already paid for it.   [30%]
(b) $20, what I paid for it.   [18%]
(c) $20 plus interest.   [7%]
(d) $75, what I could get if I sold the bottle.   [20%]

---

[*] From early on Orley has been a supporter of me and my misbehaving fellow
travelers, including during his tenure as the editor of the *American Economic Review*.
Nevertheless, to this day, Orley insists on calling what I do "wackonomics," a term
he finds hysterically funny.

(e) −$55. I get to drink a bottle that is worth $75 that I only paid
$20 for so I save money by drinking this bottle.   [25%]

When we included option (e), which we found greatly amusing, we
were not sure anyone would select it. We wondered whether there were
really people who are so sophisticated in their use of mental accounting that they can consider the drinking of an expensive bottle of wine
as an act that saves them money. But many people took that option
seriously, and over half of the respondents said that drinking the bottle was either free or saved them money. Of course, the correct answer
according to economic theory is $75, since the opportunity cost of
drinking the wine is selling it at that price. All Econs would pick that
answer, and in this case, so did the many economists who completed
the survey. Indeed, most of the people who gave this answer were
economists. I know this because the answers were not anonymous. We
held a lottery among those who replied, with a bottle of Bordeaux as
the prize, and to be eligible to win the prize respondents had to supply
their name and address.*

There is a small modification to this question that gets most people to respond like economists. Instead of asking people about drinking a bottle, we asked subjects how it would feel if they had dropped
and broken the bottle. A majority said they felt that dropping the
bottle costs them $75, what they could get for selling it.

The return address for the surveys was nondescript, so respondents did not know that either Eldar or I was involved. Many volunteered explanations for their answers. One, a retired engineer, wrote:
"I understand that, emotion aside, replacement cost is relevant for
economic decisions. However, my ideal feeling will be if my '89 and
'90 futures increase enough in value to sell half for my total cost and
drink the balance with only pleasure in mind, not money."

You see what he is saying? If the wine doubles in value and he sells
half, then he can drink the rest as "free." Brilliant! This ploy will make

* There is an interesting side note to this experiment. The lottery offering up
the $75 bottle of wine generated 178 respondents from a relatively affluent group
of readers. That is 42 cents per reply, and they had to pay their own postage! If you
want to get people to do stuff, lotteries can be very effective motivation.

each bottle he drinks render considerable transaction utility. Another letter came from well-known University of Chicago accounting professor Roman Weil. Roman, who became a friend when I became his colleague at Chicago, comes as close to being an Econ as anyone I have encountered.

"You left out the right answer. I feel the loss is $75 less the transaction costs of selling it (which are about $15). So, I think of the bottle as costing about $60. Since I do have plenty of wine in lifetime inventory, net realizable value is correct. If I did not have sufficient lifetime inventory, I'd use replacement cost, $75 plus commission, plus shipping—about $90. Also, you don't have the tax treatment of gain correctly. I get to enjoy tax free the capital gain. At a tax rate of 40% . . ."

But back to the survey, in which more than half the respondents are saying that drinking a $75 bottle of wine either costs them nothing or saves them money. The response raises another question: if when they *drink* the bottle they think it is free, what are they thinking when they *buy* a bottle? The next year we went back to Orley's readers with a new questionnaire. This time we asked:

Suppose you buy a case of Bordeaux futures at $400 a case. The wine will retail at about $500 a case when it is shipped. You do not intend to start drinking this wine for a decade. At the time that you acquire this wine which statement more accurately captures your feelings? Indicate your response by circling a number on each of the scales provided.

(a) I feel like I just **spent $400**, much as I would feel if I spent $400 on a weekend getaway.

1 ---- 2 ---- 3 ---- 4 ---- 5

Strongly	Strongly	
Agree	Disagree	Mean: 3.31

(b) I feel like I made a **$400 investment** which I will gradually consume after a period of years.

1 ---- 2 ---- 3 ---- 4 ---- 5

Strongly	Strongly	
Agree	Disagree	Mean: 1.94

(c) I feel like I just **saved $100**, the difference between what the futures cost and what the wine will sell for when delivered.

1 ---- 2 ---- 3 ---- 4 ---- 5

Strongly   Strongly   Mean: 2.88
Agree   Disagree

The most popular answer reveals that when buying wine to lay away for ten years before drinking, people think of the expenditure as an investment. The second choice was that they were saving money. Calling it spending came in dead last.

Although economic theory does not stipulate which of these answers is appropriate, when the answers are combined with the results of the earlier survey we clearly see some inconsistent thinking going on. It can't be right that acquiring the wine is just an "investment" and the later consumption of the wine either costs nothing or saves money. Surely the support of an expensive wine drinking habit must involve spending money at some point! Eldar and I published a paper on this, with a title that fully summarizes the findings: "Invest Now, Drink Later, Spend Never."

Notice that this way of thinking is very good for the fine wine industry, since it eliminates the spending part of consumption, a good trick if you can pull it off. Vacation time-share properties make similar use of this way of thinking. Typically, the prospective vacationer "invests" a sum of money, say $10,000, which entitles her to spend a week at the property in perpetuity, or at least until the property falls down or the company goes bankrupt. The mental accounting works this way. The original payment is an investment (not a purchase), the annual "maintenance fee" is a nuisance, but future vacations at the property are "free." Whether such an investment makes sense for a family will depend, in part, on how painful it is for them to spend money on vacations. But such investments should be seen for what they are: a way to disguise the cost of taking a vacation.

Costco, the discount retailer mentioned in the previous chapter, also uses a version of this strategy. In order to shop at Costco a customer must become a "member," which currently costs a household $55 a year. It seems likely that members view the annual fee as an "investment" and make no attempt to allocate that cost over the various purchases they make during the year. Rather, it serves as a sunk cost, offering up yet another reason to shop at Costco. Similarly, Amazon charges customers $99 a year to become a "prime member" which entitles them to "free" shipping. Again, the cost of the membership may well be viewed as an investment that does not "count" toward the cost of a particular purchase.

––––––

It is time for two confessions. Although I mostly advocate for thinking like an Econ, when it comes to mental accounting I have some notably Human tendencies. I am usually pretty good about ignoring sunk costs, especially if the sunk costs are purely monetary in nature. But like most people, if I have put a lot of work into some project I can find it difficult to give it up, even if it is clearly the right thing to do. In writing this book, for instance, my strategy for getting a first draft done was to keep writing and not worry about whether a particular passage or section would make the final cut. This process did produce a first draft, but one that was obviously too long. Some bits were going to have to be cut, and I fielded suggestions for which parts to drop from my friends and editors who read the initial draft. Many mentioned the advice, often attributed to William Faulkner, but apparently said by many, that writers have to learn to "kill their darlings." The advice has been given so often, I suspect, because it is hard for any writer to do.

When it came time to revise the manuscript, I decided to create an "outtakes" file of material that was in the first draft but was cruelly murdered. My plan is to post some of these precious masterpieces of glorious verbiage on the book's website. I don't know how many of these passages will actually get posted, but the beauty of this plan is that it doesn't matter. Merely having a place where these pieces are stored in a folder on my computer labeled "outtakes" has been enough to reduce the pain of cutting some of my favorite passages, a pain that can hurt as much as wearing those expensive, ill-fitting shoes. The bigger lesson is that once you understand a behavioral problem, you can sometimes invent a behavioral solution to it. Mental accounting is not always a fool's game.

My second confession regards wine, which, as you have guessed by now, is one of my vices. Although I fully understand the concept of opportunity cost, I admit to falling victim to a version of the same thinking articulated by the respondents to our questionnaire. If I take out an old bottle that I have stoically refrained from drinking for many years, the last thing on my mind is the price I could get for the wine if I were to sell it at an auction. In fact, I do not want to know that price! I end up like Professor Rosett. I would not dream of buying a thirty-year-old bottle of wine, but I am happy to drink one on special occasions. Just call me Human.

Buckets and Budgets

In those interviews with families that I used to inform my thinking about how households manage their finances, we learned that many households, especially those on a tight budget, used explicit budgeting rules. For families that dealt mostly in cash (credit cards were just coming into use at this time in the late 1970s), many would often use some version of an envelope system. One envelope (or mason jar) for rent, another for food, another for utilities, and so forth. In many cases the particular method used was one they had learned from their parents.

Organizations do something similar. Departments have budgets, and there are limits for specific categories within those budgets. The existence of budgets can violate another first principle of economics: money is *fungible*, meaning that it has no labels restricting what it can be spent on. Like most economic principles, this has strong logic behind it. If there is money left over in the utilities budget because of a mild winter, it will spend perfectly well at the children's shoe store.

Budgets exist for sensible, understandable reasons. In an organization, the boss does not want to have to approve every expenditure made in the organization, and budgets serve as a crude way to keep costs under control while giving employees discretion to spend as they see fit. Still, budget rules can lead to silly outcomes. Anyone who has worked in a large organization has run into the problem where there is not enough money in the assigned budget to take care of some urgent need, and there is no way to dip into money sitting idle in another budget. Money should be spent in whatever way best serves the interests of the organization or household; if those interests change, we should ignore the labels that were once assigned to various pots of money. But we don't. Labels are SIFs.

Individuals and families set their own rules, of course, but they use budgets in much the same ways. Just how explicit the budgeting rules are will often depend on how much slack is in the budget. A study by psychologists Chip Heath and Jack Soll found that most MBA students had weekly food and entertainment budgets and monthly clothing budgets. Once they had graduated and started earning more money, these budgets probably became more relaxed.

But while in graduate school, the budgets and the resulting violations of fungibility influenced their behavior. For example, Heath and Soll asked two groups of subjects whether they would be willing to buy a ticket to a play on the weekend. One group was told they had spent $50 earlier in the week going to a basketball game (same budget) while another group was told they had received a $50 parking ticket (different budget) earlier in the week. Those who had already gone to the game were significantly less likely to go to the theater, presumably because their entertainment budget for the week was already spent.

A study by economists Justine Hastings and Jesse Shapiro offers the most rigorous demonstration of the effects of mental budgeting to date. The question Hastings and Shapiro investigated is what happens to the choice of regular versus premium gasoline when the price of gasoline changes. In the United States, gasoline is typically sold in three grades based on octane: regular, midgrade, and premium. Although a question remains whether any car really requires something other than regular, a higher grade is recommended for some models, and some consumers buy a higher grade for other reasons, such as the probably erroneous belief that it is better for the engine. The authors studied what happened to the sales of premium grades of gasoline when the price of gasoline fell in 2008 by roughly 50%, from a high of about $4 a gallon to a low just below $2. Hastings and Shapiro were able to study this because they had customer purchase data from a grocery store chain that also sold gasoline.

Let's first think about what an Econ would do in this situation. Suppose a household is spending $80 a week on gasoline when the price is $4 and is buying the regular grade. Six months later the price has dropped to $2 and the household's cost has dropped to $40 a week. An Econ would think this way: First, gasoline is cheaper, so we should take more road trips. Second, we have gained the equivalent of $40 a week in take-home pay, and we can spend that on anything we want, from more date nights to higher quality beer. The $40 in extra income would be spent in the way that maximizes utility. Some of that money might be spent on improving the grade of gasoline, but only a minuscule amount. On average, if a family's income goes up by $1,000 a year, their propensity to buy something other than regular grade gasoline increases by only 0.1%. So a family of Econs might decide to treat their car to one tank a year of mid-grade gas, and spend the rest of their windfall on things more valuable.

Suppose instead a family of Humans has a gas budget, possibly kept in a mason jar in the kitchen. Like the Econ family, they will spend some of that money on taking more road trips, but they might also think, hey, gasoline is so cheap now I might as well buy the good stuff. That is exactly what Hastings and Shapiro found. The shift toward higher grades of gasoline was fourteen times greater than would be expected in a world in which money is treated as fungible. Further supporting the mental accounting interpretation of the results, the authors found that there was no tendency for families to upgrade the quality of two other items sold at the grocery stores, milk and orange juice. This is not surprising, since the period in question was right at the beginning of the financial crisis of 2007, the event that had triggered the drop in gas prices. In those scary times, most families were trying to cut back on spending when they could. The one exception to that tendency was more splurging on upscale gasoline.

Wealth, too, is often separated into various mental accounts. At the bottom of this hierarchy sits the money that is easiest to spend: cash. There is an old expression that money burns a hole in your pocket, and cash on hand seems to exist only to be spent.

Money in a checking account is slightly more out of reach than cash, but if there is money in an account labeled "savings," people are more reluctant to draw that money down. This can lead to the odd behavior of simultaneously borrowing at a high rate of interest and saving at a low rate, for example by keeping money in a savings account earning virtually no interest while maintaining an outstanding balance on a credit card that charges interest at more than

20% per year. There is what seems to be an obvious financially attractive opportunity, which is to pay off the loans with the savings. However, people may be anticipating that the strategy will backfire if they never repay the money "borrowed" from the savings account.

The most sacred accounts are long-term savings accounts, generally those dedicated for future spending, such as retirement accounts or children's education accounts. While it is true that some people do borrow from retirement savings accounts such as 401(k) plans, typically these loans are relatively small and are repaid within a few years. More dangerous to the accumulation of wealth than loans are job changes. When employees switch jobs they are often offered the chance to take their account balance in cash. Even though such cash-outs are taxable income and are subject to a 10% surcharge, many employees take the money, especially if their balance is small. This leakage can and should be addressed by making the option of rolling the account over into another retirement account as easy as possible, preferably the default.

Home equity offers an interesting intermediate case. For decades people treated the money in their homes much like retirement savings; it was sacrosanct. In fact, in my parents' generation, families strived to pay off their mortgages as quickly as possible, and as late as the early 1980s, people over sixty had little or no mortgage debt. In time this attitude began to shift in the United States, partly as an unintended side effect of a Reagan-era tax reform. Before this change, all interest paid, including the interest on automobile loans and credit cards, was tax deductible; after 1986 only home mortgage interest qualified for a deduction. This created an economic incentive for banks to create home equity lines of credit that households could use to borrow money in a tax-deductible way. And certainly it made sense to use a home equity loan to finance the purchase of a car rather than a car loan, because the interest was often lower as well as being tax deductible. But the change eroded the social norm that home equity was sacrosanct.

That norm was eventually destroyed by two other factors: the long-term decline in interest rates and the emergence of mortgage brokers. In the past three decades, interest rates in the United States have declined from double digits to essentially zero (or less, if you adjust for inflation). Adding mortgage brokers to the mix then proved fatal to the old, unwritten eleventh commandment: "Though shalt pay off thy mortgage." The role these brokers played in eroding the norm of paying off mortgages as soon as possible was to make the process of refinancing much easier. They had the relevant information in their computers, and with interest rates dropping, they had numerous opportunities to call and say, "Hey, do you want to lower your mortgage payment?" When the housing bubble arrived and drove up prices, homeowners were told they could lower their mortgage payment *and* take out a bit of extra cash too, to refinish the basement and buy a big-screen television.

At this point, home equity ceased to be a "safe" mental account. This fact is illustrated by a change in the borrowing behavior of households with a head that is aged seventy-five or older. In 1989 only 5.8% of such families had any mortgage debt. By 2010, the fraction with debt rose to 21.2%. For those with mortgage debt, the median amount owed also rose over this period, from $35,000 to $82,000 (in 2010 dollars). During the housing boom in the early 2000s, homeowners spent the gains they had accrued on paper in home equity as readily as they would a lottery windfall.

As documented in *House of Debt*, a book by economists Atif Mian and Amir Sufi, by 2000 increases in home equity had become a strong driver of consumption, especially of consumer durables. For example, in cities where house prices were booming, automobile sales also jumped, as homeowners borrowed against the increased equity in their home and used the proceeds to finance a new car. Then on the way down, the reverse happened; automobile sales crashed along with home prices, as there was no way to finance the new car purchase if a homeowner had zero home equity or was "underwater," meaning that the outstanding mortgage exceeded the value of the home. This phenomenon helps explain why the burst of the tech bubble in 2000–01 did not cause the same deep recession as the pricking of the housing bubble. Most non-wealthy households only hold stocks in their retirement accounts, which are still relatively sticky places to keep their money, especially for those with non-trivial account balances. This means that the fall in stock prices did not impact spending as much as the fall in home prices.

It remains to be seen whether the norm of paying off the mortgage before retirement will ever reemerge. If the long-expected trend of rising interest rates ever gets started, we may see people resume the habit of paying off their mortgage because refinancing will be less enticing at higher rates. Otherwise, home equity might remain a leaky bucket.

Like most aspects of mental accounting, setting up non-fungible budgets is not entirely silly. Be it with mason jars, envelopes, or sophisticated financial apps, a household that makes a serious effort to create a financial plan will have an easier time living within its means. The same goes for businesses, large or small. But sometimes those budgets can lead to bad decision-making, such as deciding that the Great Recession is a good time to upgrade the kind of gasoline you put in your car.

At the Poker Table

During my time at Cornell, a group of economics faculty members met periodically for a low-stakes poker game. It was rare that anyone won or lost more than $50 in an evening,* but I noticed that some players, in particular ones who reported the game's outcome to their spouse, behaved differently when they were winning versus when they were losing. How you are doing in the game that night, especially for stakes so small relative to net worth, should be irrelevant to how a particular hand is played. Compare someone who is down $50 in that night's poker game to another who owns 100 shares of a stock that was down 50 cents at market close. Both have lost a trivial portion of their wealth, but one of the losses influences behavior and the other does not. Losing money in the poker account only changes behavior while you are still playing poker.

This situation, in which a person is "behind" in a particular mental account, is tricky to handle in prospect theory, something Kahneman and Tversky knew well. In their original paper, they discussed a similar case at the racetrack. Because the track takes about 17% of each dollar wagered, bettors at the racetrack are collectively losing money at a rate of 17% per race. When the last race of the day comes along, most of the bettors are in the red in their racetrack mental account. How does this affect their betting? The normative prediction is "hardly at all." Just as with the poker game example, a bettor should be no more concerned with a loss of $100 in bets at the racetrack than he would be by a similar loss in his retirement savings account, which would go unnoticed. Yet Danny and Amos cite a study showing that the odds on long shots (horses with little chance

***

* This was before the beginning of the trend toward winner-take-all poker evenings inspired by the popularity of that form of wagering at poker tournaments.

of winning) get worse on the last race of the day, meaning that more people are betting on the horses least likely to win.

Kahneman and Tversky explained this finding by relying on the feature of prospect theory that people are risk-seeking when it concerns losses. As was discussed in chapter 4, if you ask people whether they would rather lose $100 for sure or choose a gamble in which they have a 50% chance of losing $200 and a 50% chance of breaking even, a majority will choose the gamble. These results are the opposite of those found when the choice is between a guaranteed gain of $100 and a 50-50 gamble for $0 or $200, where people prefer the sure thing.

As I watched how my poker buddies played when they were behind, I realized that the Kahneman and Tversky explanation was incomplete. Suppose I am down $100 at the racetrack and I would like to get back to zero to avoid closing this account in the red. Yes, I could bet $2 on a 50-to-1 long shot and have a small chance of breaking even, but I could instead bet another $100 on an even-money favorite and have a 50% chance of breaking even. If I am risk-seeking (meaning that I prefer a gamble to a sure thing that is equal to the expected outcome of the bet) why don't I make the $100 bet on the favorite and improve my chances of breaking even? Prospect theory is silent on this question, but my poker experiences suggested that Amos and Danny had the right intuition. My impression was that players who were behind were attracted to small bets that offered a slim chance for a big win (such as drawing to an inside straight) but disliked big bets that risked a substantial increase to the size of their loss, even though they offered a higher probability of breaking even.

My poker observations yielded another wrinkle on mental accounts. Players who were ahead in the game did not seem to treat their winnings as "real money." This behavior is so pervasive that casino gamblers have a term for it: "gambling with the house's money." (The casino is referred to as "the house.") Using this reasoning, when you are ahead you are betting with the casino's money, not your own. You can observe this behavior at any casino. Watch a (nonprofessional) gambler who wins some money early in the evening and you may see what I call "two-pocket" mental accounting. Take a player who has brought $300 to the casino to bet, and finds himself up $200 early in the evening. He will put $300 into one pocket and think of that money as his own money, and put the $200 worth of chips he has won in a different pocket (or more likely, on the table, ready to bet). When it comes to "house money," the expression "easy come, easy go" applies. This is about as blatant a violation of the rule that money is fungible as one can find. The money in either pocket will spend equally well.

Taking money off your colleagues is fun,* but far from scientific. So Eric Johnson, a marketing professor now at Columbia, and I started work on a real paper. This is the one I mentioned in the preface that took a while to satisfy Amos. Essentially, we wanted to replicate in the lab what I had seen at the poker table. But first we had to address the problem that had originally pushed Kahneman and Tversky to run experiments using hypothetical questions. How can you run ethical experiments in which subjects can lose money, and how can you get approval from the university review board that oversees such experiments? We solved this problem by having subjects answer a series of choices between sure things and gambles, some of which involved gains and others losses, and truthfully told them that one of the choices would be selected at random to "count" for the study. But not every gamble was equally likely to be chosen, and by making the favorable gambles the ones that were more likely to be played, we were able to assure the subjects that the chance of losing money was tiny, although we made it clear that we fully intended to collect from anyone who did lose money. If they wished, they could pay off their debt by doing some research assistance. In the end no one lost money, so we did not have to try to collect.

Here are three of the questions that were included in our study. The numbers in brackets are the percentages of subjects who chose the selected answer. In this example, an Econ who was risk averse would choose the sure thing in each of these problems, since in every case the expected outcome of the gamble is equal to the sure thing.

---

* In some cases it was also easy. Bill Green, an econometrician who was a regular in our group, and I noticed that when a certain colleague of ours got a good hand he would start bouncing up and down in his chair. This was the ultimate "tell." At some point we felt sorry for him and let him know about it, but he could not restrain himself when he got a really good hand. I kept waiting for him to take away a big prize with a fake bounce, but he never did.

PROBLEM 1. You have just won $30. Now choose between:

   (a) A 50% chance to gain $9 and a 50% chance to lose $9.   [70%]

   (b) No further gain or loss.   [30%]

PROBLEM 2. You have just lost $30. Now choose between:

   (a) A 50% chance to gain $9 and a 50% chance to lose $9.   [40%]

   (b) No further gain or loss.   [60%]

PROBLEM 3. You have just lost $30. Now choose between:

   (a) A 33% chance to gain $30 and a 67% chance to

      gain nothing.   [60%]

   (b) A sure $10.   [40%]

Problem 1 illustrates the "house money effect." Although subjects tend to be risk averse for gains, meaning that most of them would normally turn down a coin flip gamble to win or lose $9. When we told them they had just won $30, they were eager to take that gamble. Problems 2 and 3 illustrate the complex preferences in play when people consider themselves behind in some mental account. Instead of the simple prediction from prospect theory that people will be risk-seeking for losses, in problem 2 a loss of $30 does not generate risk-taking preferences *when there is no chance to break even.** But when given that chance, in problem 3, a majority of the subjects opt to gamble.

Once you recognize the break-even effect and the house money effect, it is easy to spot them in everyday life. It occurs whenever there are two salient reference points, for instance where you started and where you are right now. The house money effect—along with a tendency to extrapolate recent returns into the future—facilitates financial bubbles. During the 1990s, individual investors were steadily increasing the proportion of their retirement fund contributions to stocks over bonds, meaning that the portion of their new investments that was allocated to stocks was rising. Part of the reasoning seemed to be that they had made so much money in recent years that even if

---

* This means that the prediction from prospect theory that people will be risk-seeking in the domain of losses may not hold if the risk-taking opportunity does not offer a chance to break even.

the market fell, they would only lose those newer gains. Of course, the fact that some of your money has been made recently should not diminish the sense of loss if that money goes up in smoke. The same thinking pervaded the views of speculative investors in the boom housing market years later. People who had been flipping properties in Scottsdale, Las Vegas, and Miami had a psychological cushion of house money (no pun intended) that lured them into thinking that at worst they would be back where they started. Of course, when the market turned down suddenly, those investors who were highly leveraged lost much more than house money. Many also lost their homes.

Gambling when behind in an effort to break even can also be seen in the behavior of professional investors. Mutual fund portfolio managers take more risks in the last quarter of the year when the fund they are managing is trailing the benchmark index (such as the S&P 500) to which their returns are compared. And, much worse, many of the rogue traders that lost billions for their employers were taking on ever increasing amounts of risk at the end, in a desperate effort to break even. This behavior may have been rational from the point of view of the rogue trader, who stood to lose his job or worse if he did not recover his loss. But if true, that means management needs to pay close attention to the behavior of employees who are losing money. (Well, come to think of it, management should have been paying more attention before the rogue traders built up their big losses.) A good rule to remember is that people who are threatened with big losses and have a chance to break even will be unusually willing to take risks, even if they are normally quite risk averse. Watch out!

III.

SELF-CONTROL:

1975–88

Prospect theory and the insights provided by its value function greatly facilitated my attempt to understand mental accounting, which in turn helped me make sense of many of the items on the List. But one of those examples seemed be in a different category: the incident of removing the cashews while waiting for dinner. To an economist, removing an option can never make you better off. So why were we so happy that the bowl of cashews was safely hidden in the kitchen?

I started collecting other examples of "cashews" phenomena. Smokers paid more for their cigarettes by purchasing them one pack at a time instead of by the carton. Dieters did not stock any ice cream in the freezer. Academics (including me) would commit themselves to present a paper that was still a work in progress at a conference several months off, to give themselves an incentive to finish it. People who had trouble getting up in the morning put their alarm clocks on the other side of the room so they could not just reach over and switch off the alarm without getting out of bed.

What these examples have in common is the presence of self-control problems. We *want* to eat just a few more nuts, but are worried that if the bowl is left on the table, we will submit to temptation.

This distinction between what we want and what we choose has no meaning in modern economics, in which preferences are literally defined by what we choose. Choices are said to "reveal preferences." Imagine the following conversation between a Human who just removed a bowl of cashews with an Econ looking on.

> ECON: Why did you remove the cashews?
> HUMAN: Because I did not want to eat any more of them.
> ECON: If you did not want to eat any more nuts, then why go to the trouble of removing them? You could have simply acted on your preferences and stopped eating.
> HUMAN: I removed the bowl because if the nuts were still available, I would have eaten more.
> ECON: In that case, you prefer to eat more cashews, so removing them was stupid.

This conversation, which is obviously going nowhere, mimics many I had with economists at the time. Although it is never stated explicitly as an assumption in an economics textbook, in practice economic theory presumes that self-control problems do not exist. So my next big project was to study a supposedly nonexistent problem.

11

Willpower? No Problem

Economists have not always been so dense about self-control problems. For roughly two centuries, the economists who wrote on this topic knew their Humans. In fact, an early pioneer of what we would now call a behavioral treatment of self-control was none other than the high priest of free market economics: Adam Smith. When most people think about Adam Smith, they think of his most famous work, *The Wealth of Nations*. This remarkable book—the first edition was published in 1776—created the foundation for modern economic thinking. Oddly, the most well-known phrase in the book, the vaunted "invisible hand," mentioned earlier, appears only once, treated with a mere flick by Smith. He notes that by pursuing personal profits, the typical businessman is "led by an invisible hand to promote an end which was no part of his intention. Nor is it always the worse for the society that it was no part of it." Note the guarded language of the second sentence, which is rarely included (or remembered) by those who make use of the famous phrase, or invoke some version of the invisible handwave. "Nor it is always the worse for society" is hardly the same thing as an assertion that things will turn out for the best.

The rest of the massive book takes on almost any economics topic one can think of. For example, Smith provided the underlying theory for my PhD thesis, on the value of a life. He explained how workers had to be paid more to compensate them for taking dirty, risky, or unpleasant jobs. The famous Chicago economist George Stigler was fond of saying that there was nothing new in economics; Adam Smith had said it all. The same can be said of much of behavioral economics.

The bulk of Smith's writings on what we would now consider behavioral economics appeared in his earlier book *The Theory of Moral Sentiments*, published in 1759. It is here that Smith expounded on self-control. Insightfully, he portrayed the topic as a struggle or conflict

between our "passions" and what he called our "impartial spectator." Like most economists who find out that Smith had said it first,
I only learned about this formulation after proposing my own version, which we will get to later in this section. The crucial feature
of Smith's conception of our passions is that they are myopic, that
is, shortsighted. As he framed it, the problem is that "The pleasure
which we are to enjoy ten years hence, interests us so little in comparison with that which we may enjoy to-day."

Adam Smith was not the only early economist to have sensible intuitions about self-control problems. As behavioral economist George
Loewenstein has documented, other early treatments of "intertemporal
choice"—that is, choices made about the timing of consumption—also
stressed the importance of concepts such as "willpower," a word that
had no meaning in the economics being practiced in 1980.* Smith recognized that willpower is necessary to deal with myopia.

In 1871, William Stanley Jevons, another economics luminary,
refined Smith's observation about myopia, noting that the preference
for present consumption over future consumption diminishes over
time. We may care a lot about getting that bowl of ice cream right
now rather than tomorrow, but we would scarcely care about a choice
between this date next year versus the day before or after.

Some early economists viewed *any* discounting of future consumption as a mistake—a *failure* of some type. It could be a failure
of willpower, or, as Arthur Pigou famously wrote in 1920, it could be
a failure of imagination: "Our telescopic faculty is defective and . . .
we, therefore, see future pleasures, as it were, on a diminished scale."

Irving Fisher provided the first economic treatment of intertemporal choice that might be considered "modern." In his 1930 classic,
The Theory of Interest, he used what have become the basic teaching
tools of microeconomics—indifference curves—to show how an individual will choose between consumption at two different points of
time, given a market rate of interest. His theory qualifies as modern

---

* I once gave a talk about self-control to a group of economists at the Hebrew
University in Jerusalem. At one point I used the word "temptation," and one of the
audience members asked me to define it. Someone else in the audience jumped in
to say, "It's in the Bible." But it was not in the economists' dictionary.

both in its tools and in the sense that it is normative. He explains what a rational person *should* do. But Fisher also made clear that he did not think his theory was a satisfactory descriptive model, because it omitted important behavioral factors.

For one thing, Fisher believed that time preference depends on an individual's level of income, with the poor being more impatient than those who are better off. Furthermore, Fisher emphasized that he viewed the impatient behavior exhibited by low-income workers as partly irrational, which he described with vivid examples: "This is illustrated by the story of the farmer who would never mend his leaky roof. When it rained, he could not stop the leak, and when it did not rain, there was no leak to be stopped!" And he frowned upon "those working men who, before prohibition, could not resist the lure of the saloon on the way home Saturday night," which was then payday.

Quite evidently, from Adam Smith in 1776 to Irving Fisher in 1930, economists were thinking about intertemporal choice with Humans in plain sight. Econs began to creep in around the time of Fisher, as he started on the theory of how Econs *should* behave, but it fell to a twenty-two-year-old Paul Samuelson, then in graduate school, to finish the job. Samuelson, whom many consider to be the greatest economist of the twentieth century, was a prodigy who set out to give economics a proper mathematical foundation. He enrolled at the University of Chicago at age sixteen and soon went off to Harvard for graduate school. His PhD thesis had the audacious but accurate title "Foundations of Economic Analysis." His thesis redid all of economics, with what he considered to be proper mathematical rigor.

While in graduate school in 1937, Samuelson knocked off a seven-page paper with the modest title "A Note on the Measurement of Utility." As the title suggests, he hoped to offer a way to measure that elusive thing Econs always maximize: utility (i.e., happiness or satisfaction). While he was at it, Samuelson formulated what has become the standard economic model of intertemporal choice, the discounted utility model. I will not strain you (or myself) with any attempt to summarize the heart of this paper, but merely extract the essence our story requires.

The basic idea is that consumption is worth more to you now than later. If given the choice between a great dinner this week or one a year from now, most of us would prefer the dinner sooner rather than

later. Using the Samuelson formulation, we are said to "discount"
future consumption at some rate. If a dinner a year from now is only
considered to be 90% as good as one right now, we are said to be discounting the future dinner at an annual rate of about 10%.

Samuelson's theory did not have any passions or faulty telescopes,
just steady, methodical discounting. The model was so easy to use that
even economists of that generation could easily handle the math, and
it remains the standard formulation today. This is not to say that Samuelson thought his theory was necessarily a good description of behavior. The last two pages of his short paper are devoted to discussing what
Samuelson called the "serious limitations" of the model. Some of them
are technical, but one deserves our scrutiny. Samuelson correctly notes
that if people discount the future at rates that vary over time, then
people may not behave consistently, that is, they may change their
minds as time moves forward. The specific case he worries about is the
same one that worried earlier economists such as Jevons and Pigou,
namely, the case where we are most impatient for immediate rewards.

To understand how discounting works, suppose there is some good,
perhaps the chance to watch a tennis match at Wimbledon. If the
match is watched tonight, it would be worth 100 "utils," the arbitrary
units economists use to describe levels of utility or happiness. Consider Ted, who discounts at a constant rate of 10% per year. For him
that match would be worth 100 utils this year, 90 next year, then 81,
72, and so forth. Someone who discounts this way is said to be discounting with an *exponential* function. (If you don't know what that
term means, don't worry about it.)

Now consider Matthew, who also values that match at 100 today, but
at only 70 the following year, then 63 in year three or any time after
that. In other words, Matthew discounts anything that he has to wait
a year to consume by 30%, the next year at 10%, and then he stops discounting at all (0%). Matthew is viewing the future by looking through
Pigou's faulty telescope, and he sees year 1 and year 2 looking just one-
third of a year apart, with no real delay between any dates beyond that.
His impression of the future is a lot like the famous *New Yorker* magazine cover "View of the World from 9th Avenue." On the cover, looking
west from 9th Avenue, the distance to 11th Avenue (two long blocks) is
about as far as from 11th Avenue to Chicago, which appears to be about

FIGURE 4. *View of the World from 9th Avenue.* Saul Steinberg, cover of *The New Yorker,* March 29, 1976 © *The Saul Steinberg Foundation /Artists Rights Society (ARS), New York. Cover reprinted with permission of* The New Yorker *magazine. All rights reserved.*

one-third of the way to Japan. The upshot is that Matthew finds waiting most painful at the beginning, since it feels longer.

The technical term for discounting of this general form that starts out high and then declines is *quasi-hyperbolic discounting.* If you don't know what "hyperbolic" means, that shows good judgment on your part in what words to incorporate in your vocabulary. Just keep the faulty telescope in mind as an image when the term comes up. For the most part I will avoid this term and use the modern phrase *present-biased* to describe preferences of this type.

To see why exponential discounters stick to their plans while hyperbolic (present-biased) discounters do not, let's consider a simple numerical example. Suppose Ted and Matthew both live in London and are avid tennis fans. Each has won a lottery offering a ticket to a match at Wimbledon, with an intertemporal twist. They can choose among three options. Option A is a ticket to a first-round match this year; in fact, the match is tomorrow. Option B is a quarterfinal match at next year's tournament. Option C is the final, at the tournament to be held two years from now. All the tickets are guaranteed, so we can leave risk considerations out of our analysis, and Ted and Matthew have identical tastes in tennis. If the matches were all for this year's tournament, the utilities they would assign to them are as follows: A: 100, B: 150, C: 180. But in order to go to their favorite option C, the final, they have to wait two years. What will they do?

If Ted had this choice, he would choose to wait two years and go the final. He would do so because the value he puts right now on going to the final in two years (its "present value") is 146 (81% of 180), which is greater than the present value of A (100) or B (135, or 90% of 150). Furthermore, after a year has passed, if Ted is asked whether he wants to change his mind and go to option B, the quarterfinal, he will say no, since 90% of the value of C (162) is still greater than the value of B. This is what it means to have time-consistent preferences. Ted will always stick to whatever plan he makes at the beginning, no matter what options he faces.

What about Matthew? When first presented with the choice, he would also choose option C, the final. Right now he values A at 100, B at 105 (70% of 150) and C at 113 (63% of 180). But unlike Ted, when a year passes, Matthew will change his mind and switch to B, the quarterfinal, because waiting one year discounts the value of C by 70% to 126, which is less than 150, the current value of B. He is *time-inconsistent*. In telescope terms, referring back to the *New Yorker* cover, from New York he couldn't tell that China was any farther than Japan, but if he carried that telescope to Tokyo, he would start to notice that the trip from there to Shanghai is even farther than it was from New York to Chicago.

It bothered Samuelson that people might display time inconsistency. Econs should not be making plans that they will later change without any new information arriving, but Samuelson makes it clear that he is aware that such behavior exists. He talks about people taking steps equivalent to removing the bowl of cashews to ensure that

FIGURE 5

Initially, both Ted and Matthew would choose
to wait to see the Wimbledon final.

| ——— Ted's valuations ——— | | | | ——— Matthew's valuations ——— | | | |
MATCH	RIGHT NOW	AFTER 1 YEAR	AFTER 2 YEARS	MATCH	RIGHT NOW	AFTER 1 YEAR	AFTER 2 YEARS
First round	100	90	81	First round	100	70	63
Quarterfinal	150	135	122	Quarterfinal	150	105	95
Final	180	162	(146)	Final	180	126	(113)

A year later, Ted would still choose the final,
but Matthew would change his mind and watch the quarterfinals.

| ——— Ted's valuations ——— | | | ——— Matthew's valuations ——— | | |
MATCH	RIGHT NOW	AFTER 1 YEAR	MATCH	RIGHT NOW	AFTER 1 YEAR
First round	100	90	First round	100	70
Quarterfinal	150	135	Quarterfinal	(150)	105
Final	180	(162)	Final	180	126

their current plans will be followed. For example, he mentions purchasing whole life insurance as a compulsory savings measure. But
with this caveat duly noted, he moved on and the rest of the profession followed suit. His discounted utility model with exponential
discounting became the workhorse model of intertemporal choice.

It may not be fair to pick this particular paper as the tipping point.
For some time, economists had been moving away from the sort of folk
psychology that had been common earlier, led by the Italian economist
Vilfredo Pareto, who was an early participant in adding mathematical
rigor to economics. But once Samuelson wrote down this model and
it became widely adopted, most economists developed a malady that
Kahneman calls *theory-induced blindness*. In their enthusiasm about
incorporating their newfound mathematic rigor, they forgot all about
the highly behavioral writings on intertemporal choice that had come
before, even those of Irving Fisher that had appeared a mere seven
years earlier. They also forgot about Samuelson's warnings that his
model might not be descriptively accurate. Exponential discounting

just had to be the right model of intertemporal choice because Econs would not keep changing their minds, and the world they now studied no longer contained any Humans. This theory-induced blindness now strikes nearly everyone who receives a PhD in economics. The economics training the students receive provides enormous insights into the behavior of Econs, but at the expense of losing common-sense intuition about human nature and social interactions. Graduates no longer realize that they live in a world populated by Humans.

––––––––––

Intertemporal choice is not just an abstract concept used in theoretical economics. It plays a vital role in macroeconomics, where it underlies what is called the *consumption function*, which tells us how the spending of a household varies with its income. Suppose a government has seen its economy plunge into a deep recession and decides to give everyone a one-time tax cut of $1,000 per person. The consumption function tells us how much of the money will be spent and how much will be saved. Economic thinking about the consumption function changed quite dramatically between the mid-1930s and the mid-1950s. The way in which models of the consumption function evolved illustrates an interesting feature about how economic theory has developed since the Samuelson revolution began. As economists became more mathematically sophisticated, and their models incorporated those new levels of sophistication, the people they were describing evolved as well. First, Econs became smarter. Second, they cured all their self-control problems. Calculate the present value of Social Security benefits that will start twenty years from now? No problem! Stop by the tavern on the way home on payday and spend the money intended for food? Never! *Econs stopped misbehaving.*

This pattern in the evolution in economic theory can be seen by examining the models of the consumption function proposed by three economist heavyweights: John Maynard Keynes, Milton Friedman, and Franco Modigliani. We can begin with Keynes, who famously advocated just the sort of tax cut used in this example. In his masterwork, *The General Theory of Employment, Interest and Money,* he proposed a very simple model for the consumption function. He assumed that if a household received some incremental income, it would consume a fixed proportion of that extra income. The term he used to describe the proportion of extra income that would be consumed is the *marginal propensity to consume* (MPC). Although Keynes thought that the marginal propensity to consume for a given household was relatively constant if its income did not change dramatically, he agreed with his contemporary Irving Fisher that the MPC would vary considerably across socioeconomic classes. Specifically, he thought the propensity to spend would be highest (nearly 100%) for poor families, and decline as income rises. For the rich, a windfall of $1,000 would barely affect consumption at all, so the MPC would be close to zero. If we take the case of a middle-class family that saves 5% of any additional income earned, then Keynes predicts that the MPC from a $1,000 windfall would be 95%, or $950.

A couple of decades later, in a book published in 1957, Milton Friedman made the plausible observation that households might have the foresight to smooth their consumption over time, so he proposed the *permanent income hypothesis*. In his model, a family that is saving 5% of its income would not spend $950 extra in the year of the windfall, but instead would spread it out. Specifically, he proposed that households would use a three-year horizon to determine what their permanent income is, so would divide the extra spending evenly over the next three years. (This implies a discount rate of 33% per year.) That means that in the first year, the family would spend about $950/3, or $317.*

The next move up in sophistication came from Franco Modigliani, writing with his student Richard Brumberg. Although his work was roughly contemporaneous with Friedman's, his model was one step up the economic ladder toward the modern conception of an Econ. Rather than focus on short-term periods such as a year or even three years, Modigliani based his model on an individual's total lifetime income, and his theory was accordingly called the *life-cycle hypothesis*. The idea is that people would determine a plan when young about how to smooth their consumption over their lifetime, including retirement and possibly even bequests.

In keeping with this lifetime orientation, Modigliani shifted his focus from income to lifetime wealth. To make things simple and con-

---

* Here, and in what follows, I will also assume for simplicity that interest and inflation rates are zero, or, if you like, that they equal each other and all numbers are adjusted for inflation.

crete, let's suppose that we are dealing with someone who knows that he will live exactly forty more years and plans to leave no bequests. With these simplifying assumptions, the life-cycle hypothesis predicts that the windfall will be consumed evenly over the next forty years, meaning that the marginal propensity to consume from the windfall will be just $25 per year ($1000/40) for the rest of his life.

Notice that as we go from Keynes to Friedman to Modigliani, the economic agents are thinking further ahead and are implicitly assumed to be able to exert enough willpower to delay consumption, in Modigliani's case, for decades. We also get wildly different predictions of the share of the windfall that will be immediately spent, from nearly all to hardly any. If we judge a model by the accuracy of its predictions, as advocated by Friedman, then in my judgment the winner among the three models' ability to explain what people do with temporary changes to their income would be Keynes, modified somewhat in Friedman's direction to incorporate the natural tendency to smooth out short-run fluctuations.* But if instead we choose models by how clever the modeler is, then Modigliani is the winner, and perhaps because economists adopted the "cleverer is better" heuristic, Modigliani's model was declared best and became the industry standard.

But it is hard to be the smartest kid in the class forever, and it is possible to take the model up one more level in sophistication, as shown by Robert Barro, an economist at Harvard. First, he assumes that parents care about the utility of their children and grandchildren, and since those descendants will care about their own grandchildren, their time horizon is effectively forever. So Barro's agents plan to give bequests to their heirs, and realize that their heirs will do likewise. In this world, the predictions about how much money will be spent depend on from where the money comes. If the $1,000 windfall had come from a lucky night at the casino, Barro would make the same prediction as Modigliani about consumption. But if the windfall is a temporary tax cut that is financed by issuing government bonds, then Barro's prediction changes. The bonds will have to be repaid eventually. The beneficiary of the tax cut understands all this,

---

* If we take a longer-run problem, such as saving for retirement, then the story gets more complicated, and I would move a bit further toward Modigliani. See the discussion of the behavioral life-cycle hypothesis just below.

and realizes that his heir's taxes will eventually have to go up to pay for the tax cut he is receiving, so he won't spend any of it. Instead he will increase his bequests by exactly the amount of the tax cut.

Barro's insight is ingenious, but for it to be descriptively accurate we need Econs that are as smart as Barro.* Where should one stop this analysis? If someone even more brilliant than Barro comes along and thinks of an even smarter way for people to behave, should that too become our latest model of how real people behave? For example, suppose one of Barro's agents is a closet Keynesian, an idea that Barro would abhor, and he thinks that the tax cut will stimulate the economy enough to pay off the bonds from increased tax revenues; in that case, he will not need to alter his planned bequests. In fact, if the tax cut stimulates the economy enough, he might even be able to reduce his bequests because his heirs will be the beneficiaries of the higher economic growth rate. But notice now we need Econs who are fully conversant with both economic theory and the relevant empirical tests of effects of fiscal policy in order to know which model of the economy to incorporate in their thinking. Clearly, there must be limits to the knowledge and willpower we assume describe the agents in the economy, few of whom are as clever as Robert Barro.

The idea of modeling the world as if it consisted of a nation of Econs who all have PhDs in economics is not the way psychologists would think about the problem. This was brought home to me when I gave a talk in the Cornell psychology department. I began my talk by sketching Modigliani's life-cycle hypothesis. My description was straightforward, but to judge from the audience reaction, you would have thought this theory of savings was hilarious. Fortunately, the economist Bob Frank was there. When the bedlam subsided, he assured everyone that I had not made anything up. The psychologists remained stunned in disbelief, wondering how their economics department colleagues could have such wacky views of human behavior.†

---

* When Robert Barro and I were at a conference together years ago, I said that the difference between our models was that he assumed that the agents in his model were as smart as he was, and I assumed they were as dumb as I am. Barro agreed.

† Or, as my Cornell colleague and good friend Tom Gilovich said to me: "I never cease to be amazed by the number of convenient null hypotheses economic theory has given you."

_____

Modigliani's life-cycle hypothesis, in which people decide how much of their lifetime wealth to consume each period, does not just assume that people are smart enough to make all the necessary calculations (with rational expectations) about how much they will make, how long they will live, and so forth, but also that they have enough self-control to implement the resulting optimal plan. There is an additional unstated assumption: namely, that wealth is fungible. In the model, it does not matter whether the wealth is held in cash, home equity, a retirement plan, or an heirloom painting passed on from a prior generation. Wealth is wealth. We know from the previous chapters on mental accounting that this assumption is no more innocuous or accurate than the assumptions about cognitive abilities and willpower.

To relax the assumption that wealth is fungible and incorporate mental accounting into a theory of consumption and savings behavior, Hersh Shefrin and I proposed what we called the *behavioral life-cycle hypothesis*. We assume that a household's consumption in a given year will not depend just on its lifetime wealth, but also on the mental accounts in which that wealth is held. The marginal propensity to consume from winning $1,000 in a lottery is likely to be much higher than a similar increase in the value of a household's retirement holdings. In fact, one study has found that the MPC from an increase in the value of retirement saving can even be negative! Specifically, a team of behavioral economists showed that when investors in retirement plans earn high returns, making them richer, they *increase* their saving rates, most likely because they extrapolate this investment success into the future.

To understand the consumption behavior of households, we clearly need to get back to studying Humans rather than Econs. Humans do not have the brains of Einstein (or Barro), nor do they have the self-control of an ascetic Buddhist monk. Rather, they have passions, faulty telescopes, treat various pots of wealth quite differently, and can be influenced by short-run returns in the stock market. We need a model of these kinds of Humans. My favorite version of such a model is the subject of the next chapter.

12

The Planner and the Doer

When I starting thinking seriously about self-control problems, there was little in the economics literature upon which to draw. Like most graduate students, I knew nothing about the early scholars whose work was discussed in the previous chapter. Graduate students rarely read anything written more than thirty years ago. And there was not much new going on either. However, I did find myself motivated by the work of three scholars: one economist and two psychologists.

Robert Strotz, an economist at Northwestern University, wrote the only economics paper on self-control I found. Although many economists had been using the discounted utility model Samuelson had formulated, few aside from Strotz had paid any attention to his warnings about time inconsistency.

In this paper, published in 1955, Strotz took a deep dive into the problem, investigating the mathematical properties a person's preferences had to satisfy to ensure that once he makes a plan, he will not want to change it. We need not dwell on the technical details of the paper. Suffice to say that there was only one highly specific case (exponential discounting) in which one could be sure that people would be time-consistent, and, like Samuelson, Strotz worried that these conditions would not be met.

These worries led Strotz to engage in what has become an obligatory discussion of Homer's tale of Odysseus and the Sirens. Almost all researchers on self-control—from philosophers to psychologists to economists—eventually get around to talking about this ancient story, and for once, I will follow the traditional path.

Recall the setup. The Sirens were an ancient version of an all-female rock band. No sailor could resist the call of their songs. But any sailor who submitted to the temptation of trying to steer his ship close to the rocks would find himself shipwrecked. Odysseus wanted to both hear the music and live to tell about it. He devised a two-part plan to succeed.* The first part was to make sure that his crew did not hear the Sirens' call, so he instructed them to fill their ears with wax. The second part of the plan was to have his crew bind him to the mast, allowing Odysseus to enjoy the show without risking the inevitable temptation to steer the ship toward the rocks.

This story illustrates two important tools that people use to confront self-control problems. For the crew, the strategy was to remove the cues that would tempt them to do something stupid. Out of sight, out of mind. For himself, Odysseus chose a *commitment strategy*: he limited his own choices to prevent self-destruction. It was his version of removing the bowl of cashews. Strotz confessed to employing a commitment strategy himself, to accommodate his academic calendar year pay schedule: "I select the option of having my annual salary dispersed to me on a twelve- rather than nine-month basis, although I could use the interest!"

By the time I was thinking about self-control problems in 1978, Strotz's paper was already more than twenty years old, and there was no one else in economics who seemed interested (though Tom Schelling would soon chime in). I turned to psychology for inspiration. Surely, I thought, there would be a vast literature in psychology on delay of gratification. Dead wrong. Although many psychologists are now interested in self-control problems, in the late 1970s that was not the case. But I did unearth two treasures.

The first was the work of Walter Mischel, which is now quite well known. Mischel, then at Stanford, was running experiments at a day care center on the school's campus. A kid (age four or five) was asked into a room by the experimenter and given a choice between a small reward now and a larger reward a bit later. The rewards were treats such as marshmallows or Oreo cookies. The child was told that he could have one Oreo right now, or any time he wanted it, but if he could wait until the experimenter came back, he could have three Oreos. At any time the kid could ring a bell and the experimenter would return and give him the small reward.

* In truth, Odysseus was not clever enough to think up this plan himself. He got some good advice from Circe, a goddess who specialized in herbs and drugs. Go figure.

Most of the children found this task excruciatingly difficult, but the circumstances in which the child was waiting mattered. In some versions of the experiment the treats were on a plate right in front of the kid. The sight of those Oreos had the same effect on most children that the Sirens' tunes had on Odysseus. Waiting time averaged barely over a minute. But if the rewards were out of sight (and thus more out of mind), the average kid could hold out for eleven minutes. Children also could wait longer if they were told to think about something "fun" instead of the reward itself.

The earliest of these experiments were run in the late 1960s and early 1970s. About ten years later, as an afterthought, Mischel and his colleagues thought it would be interesting to see what had happened to the children who had been the subjects in these experiments, so they tracked down as many of the 500 or so original participants as they could find, and eventually found about a third of them who agreed to be interviewed once a decade. Somewhat surprisingly, the amount of time a kid waited in one of those experiments turned out to be a valid predictor of many important life outcomes, from SAT scores to career success to drug use. This was a particularly surprising result, because Mischel himself had done considerable research showing that so-called personality traits were not very useful in predicting behavior, even in the present, much less the future.

Mischel has priceless videos from some of the early experiments that demonstrate the difficulty kids had in exerting self-control. There is one kid I am particularly curious about. He was in the toughest setup, in which the bigger prize, three delicious Oreo cookies, was sitting right in front of him. After a brief wait, he could not stand it anymore. But rather than ring the bell, he carefully opened each cookie, licked out the yummy white filling, and then put the cookie back together, arranging the three cookies as best he could to avoid detection. In my imagination, this kid grows up to be Bernie Madoff.

The other behavioral scientist whose work captured my attention was a practicing psychiatrist named George Ainslie who was doing research in his spare time, while holding a job treating patients in a veterans' hospital. In a paper published in 1975, which I had studied carefully during my year at Stanford, Ainslie summarized everything academics knew about self-control at the time.

I learned from Ainslie that there existed a large literature studying delay of gratification in nonhuman animals such as rats and pigeons. In a paradigm similar to Mischel's, experimenters would give an animal a choice between a small, immediate reward and a delayed, larger reward. The animals had to press (or peck) a lever to get a reward, and, after extensive training, they would learn the length of the delays and amounts of food they could expect from pressing one lever or the other. By varying the delays and sizes of the rewards, the experimenter could estimate the animals' time preferences, and most studies found that animals display the same discounting pattern that leads to preference reversals in humans. Animals discount hyperbolically, and have self-control problems too!*

Ainslie's paper also provides a long discussion of various strategies for dealing with self-control problems. One course of action is commitment: removing the cashews or tying yourself to the mast. Another is to raise the cost of submitting to temptation. For example, if you want to quit smoking, you could write a large check to someone you see often with permission to cash the check if you are seen smoking. Or you can make that bet with yourself, what Ainslie calls a "private side bet." You could say to yourself, "I won't watch the game on television tonight until I finish [some task you are tempted to postpone]."

———————

Armed with the insights of Strotz, Mischel, and Ainslie, I set out to create a conceptual framework to discuss these problems that economists would still recognize as being economics. The crucial theoretical question I wanted to answer was this: if I know I am going to change my mind about my preferences (I will not limit myself to a few more cashew nuts, as I intend, rather I will eat the entire bowl), when and why would I take some action to restrict my future choices?

We all have occasions on which we change our minds, but usually

———————

* Some researchers have tried a version of the marshmallow/Oreo experiment on animals. Most go for the immediate reward, but one particularly clever African gray parrot named Griffen was shown to display better self-control than most preschoolers (Zielinski, 2014).

we do not go to extraordinary steps to prevent ourselves from deviating from the original plan. The only circumstances in which you would want to commit yourself to your planned course of action is when you have good reason to believe that *if you change your preferences later, this change of preferences will be a mistake.*

Removing the cashews is smart because eating the entire bowl will ruin your appetite, and you would rather not have your dinner consist entirely of cashew nuts. Likewise, a smart kid who participated in one of Mischel's experiments would be wise to say to the experimenter, "Next time you have Oreos to give away, please do not offer me the 'one cookie now' option, or even mention the word Oreo. Just wait fifteen minutes and bring me my three cookies."

At some point in pondering these questions, I came across a quote from social scientist Donald McIntosh that profoundly influenced my thinking: "The idea of self-control is paradoxical unless it is assumed that the psyche contains more than one energy system, and that these energy systems have some degree of independence from each other." The passage is from an obscure book, *The Foundations of Human Society.* I do not know how I came by the quote, but it seemed to me to be obviously true. Self-control is, centrally, about conflict. And, like tango, it takes (at least) two to have a conflict. Maybe I needed a model with two selves.

As intuitively appealing as this idea was to me, any sort of two-self model had the disadvantage of being considered radical in economics but passé in psychology: not a great combination. Few economists, including me when I was getting started on this work, were aware of Adam Smith's discussion of the battle between our passions and our impartial spectator. To most the idea just seemed wacky. Academic psychologists at that time were no longer much enamored of Freud with his id, ego, and superego, and the two-system view that is now very much in vogue had yet to emerge.* With much trepidation, I quietly trotted out the idea among friends. A sketch of the con-

---

* The two-system model articulated by Kahneman in *Thinking, Fast and Slow* was not the way he and Tversky originally thought about their research. One of Danny's main reasons for writing the book was because he thought recasting their original work using the framework of a fast, automatic system and a slow, reflexive system offered an insightful new perspective on their earlier findings.

cept appeared in my "Toward a Positive Theory of Consumer Choice" paper, but I knew I needed something more formal, which in economics means a credible amount of math. I recruited Hersh Shefrin, a mathematical economist who was at the University of Rochester at the same time I was there, to join the effort.

Hersh was the first of many coauthors I have worked with over the years. When we began talking about these questions, his chief qualifications were that he was good at math and he did not think my ideas were completely crazy. The latter was more important, since economists who are better at math than me are easy to find. In many ways Shefrin and I were polar opposites. Hersh was serious, meticulous, studious, and religious, including being a student of the Talmud, the encyclopedic compendium of ancient Jewish scholarly writing. I had none of those qualities, but we still managed to get along well. Most importantly, Hersh laughed at my jokes. We worked together in the way I had seen Amos and Danny work, through endless talking. And when it came to writing our first paper, we would talk through each sentence, just as I had watched them do. Although we began our conversations while we were colleagues at Rochester, I soon moved to Cornell and Hersh departed for sunny California at Santa Clara University, not far from Stanford. We wrote just two papers together, but Hersh got hooked on doing behavioral economics and soon formed a highly successful collaboration with Meir Statman, a colleague at Santa Clara, doing research on behavioral finance.

Our model is really based on a metaphor. We propose that at any point in time an individual consists of two selves. There is a forward-looking "planner" who has good intentions and cares about the future, and a devil-may-care "doer" who lives for the present.* The key question for any model of this behavior was deciding how to characterize interactions between the two. One possibility would be to make the planner and doer players who interact as competitors in a game, using the branch of mathematics and economics called game theory as the

---

* Tom Schelling started writing on this topic soon after I did. Our views were very much in the same spirit, but he was less convinced than I was that the longsighted set of preferences is more likely to be "right." See, for example, Schelling (1984).

core model. We rejected this idea because we did not think that the doer engages in strategic behavior; he is more of a passive creature who simply lives for the moment. He reacts to what is in front of him and consumes until sated. Instead, we chose a formulation based on the theory of organizations, namely a principal–agent model. In this choice we were undoubtedly influenced by the fact that agency theory, as it was called, was a focus of discussion at the University of Rochester Graduate School of Business while I was teaching there. Michael Jensen and the then dean of the school, William Meckling, had written a famous paper on the topic in 1976. I was not sure that they would approve of this application of their ideas, but that was part of the fun.

In a principal–agent model the principal is the boss, often the owner of a firm, and the agent is someone to whom authority is delegated. In the context of an organization, tensions arise because the agent knows some things that the principal does not, and it is too costly for the principal to monitor every action that the agent takes. The agent in these models tries to make as much money as possible while minimizing effort. In response, the firm adopts a set of rules and procedures (incentive schemes and accounting systems, for example) that are designed to minimize the costs of the conflicts of interest between the principal and the agents employed at the firm. For example, a salesperson might get paid mostly on commission, have to turn in receipts to document travel expenses, and be forbidden to fly first class.

In our intrapersonal framework, the agents are a series of short-lived doers; specifically, we assume there is a new doer each time period, say each day. The doer wants to enjoy himself and is completely selfish in that that he does not care at all about any future doers. The planner, in contrast, is completely altruistic. All she* cares about is the utility of the series of doers. (Think of her as a benevolent dictator.) She would like them to be collectively as happy as possible, but she has limited control over the actions of the doers, especially if

---

* Amos always referred to the planner as a female. I will do likewise in his honor. And since men are generally more like doers than women are, I will use the male pronoun for doers. Just call me a sexist.

a doer is aroused in any way, such as by food, sex, alcohol, or an urgent desire to go outside and goof off on a nice day.

The planner has two sets of tools she can use to influence the actions of the doers. She can either try to influence the decisions that the doers make through rewards or penalties (financial or otherwise) that still allow them *discretion*, or she can impose *rules*, such as commitment strategies, which limit the doers' options.

Consider a simple, albeit contrived, example just to illustrate the ideas. Suppose Harry is out camping alone in a remote cabin with no means of communicating with the outside world. He was dropped off by a small plane and will be picked up again in ten days. Originally, he had plenty of food to eat (water is plentiful), but a hungry bear wandered by and walked off with every food item he had except for ten energy bars that either escaped the bear's attention or did not suit his epicurean tastes. Since there is no way to communicate with the plane, and Harry is not good at scavenging for food, he will have to make the ten energy bars last until the plane comes back to pick him up. Of course, Harry is equipped with a planner and a doer. How will his planner deal with this problem?

Let's assume that the planner values each doer's consumption equally (so does not discount the consumption of distant doers relative to current ones). The doers have diminishing marginal utility for food, meaning that the first energy bar is more enjoyable than the second, and so forth, but they eat until the last bite yields no additional pleasure, and then stop. In this setup, the planner would consider the best outcome to be to eat one energy bar per day, thus giving each of the ten doers the same amount of utility.* In other words, the planner would like to impose the same kind of consumption smoothing the Econs are supposed to do if they follow the life-cycle hypothesis. To some extent, the planner is trying to get the doers to act more like Econs. If it were technologically feasible, the planner would adopt a commitment strategy that left no discretion to the doers, thus eliminating any risk of misbehaving. A cabin that came

---

* For the sake of simplicity, I will ignore the possibility that the one-energy-bar-per-day diet makes the doers increasingly hungry as time passes.

equipped with ten programmable safes, each of which can be set to open at a specific time, would be ideal.* This is the best possible outcome from the planner's perspective.

But the cabin is unlikely to have those safes, so what can the planner do? All ten energy bars are sitting in the cupboard available to be eaten. What happens then? If the planner does not intervene, the first doer, who does not care at all about the welfare of future doers, will eat until he is full; that is, up until the point that eating one more bite of an energy bar will make him less happy. Let's say that point comes after eating three energy bars. The second day, the doer also eats three more energy bars, as does the doer of day three. Then when the fourth day comes along, the current doer eats one energy bar for breakfast—the last of the ten left—and soon starts getting hungry. The rest of the week is no fun.

Somehow, the planner has to keep the early doers from bingeing on the energy bars in the first few days. If there are no commitment strategies available, the only other tool the planner has in our model is guilt. Through some process of indoctrination, either by the planner herself or by parents and society, doers can be made to feel bad about leaving future doers with nothing to eat. But imposing guilt is costly. In the energy bar example, the planner is unable to make the doer start feeling bad only after consuming the first energy bar. Instead, she has to make each bite of the energy bar less pleasurable.

This is illustrated in figure 6. The highest line represents the doer's utility for eating energy bars without guilt, and the doer consumes up until the point where the utility is maximized, at three energy bars. The next highest line illustrates the case where enough guilt has been applied to get the doer to stop eating after two energy bars, and the lowest line shows the case where the doer stops after eating one. The thing to notice about this figure is that when guilt is employed, life is less pleasurable. The only way to

---

* Such technology does exist. The Kitchen Safe (kitchensafe.com) is a plastic container than the user can lock for any period of time. The manufacturers recommend it for anything tempting, from candy to smartphones to car keys. I received one from a thoughtful student. Naturally it was filled with cashews. In a world of Econs, there would be no demand for such a product.

make the doer eat fewer energy bars is to make eating them less enjoyable. Another way to think about this is that employing will-power requires effort.

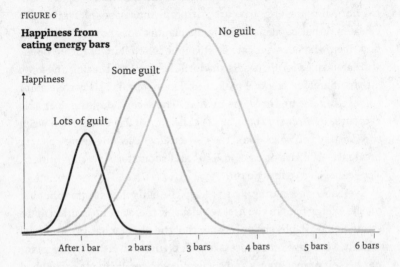

FIGURE 6

Happiness from eating energy bars

This analysis suggests that if one can implement perfect rules, life will be better. The strategy of using programmable safes, each containing one energy bar, achieves much more satisfaction than the guilt-induced diet. Strotz accomplished this goal by asking his employer to pay him in twelve monthly increments, from September through August, rather than in nine, from September to May. The latter plan would yield more interest since the money comes in more quickly, but he has to save up enough over the course of the academic year to ensure he has money to live on during the summer, not to mention to go on a family vacation.

Why not always use rules? One reason is that externally enforced rules may not be easily available. Even if you arrange to get a healthy dinner delivered to your home each night, ready to eat, there will be nothing stopping you from also ordering a pizza. Also, even if such rules are available, they are inflexible by design. If Professor Strotz opts for the September-to-May pay schedule, the money comes in earlier, so he might be able to take advantage of an opportunity to buy something on sale during the winter—say, a new lawnmower—that will be more expensive in the summer. But if his salary is spread out over twelve months he may not have enough slack in the budget to buy a lawnmower in winter. Of course, the flip side is that if he takes the money early he has to have the discipline to make it last through the summer.

This same principle applies in organizations. If the principal knows exactly what the agent should do in every situation, then she can create a rulebook that is never to be violated. But we have all had the frustration of dealing with a low-level agent who is working under such rules and does not have the discretion to do something that is obviously sensible but had not been anticipated, and is therefore "not allowed."

Of course, there are other techniques of control, used by both organizations and individuals, which involve keeping track of expenditures. In organizations, these techniques are called accounting. Similarly, as we saw earlier, Humans use mental accounting, with the help of envelopes, mason jars, and retirement savings plans, to accomplish the same purpose. Notice that the failure to treat various pots of money as fungible, as Econs would do, is what makes such accounting strategies feasible.

I should stress that Shefrin and I did not think that there were actually two different people inside your head. Ours is an "as if" model that is meant to provide a useful way of thinking about self-control problems. We did include a footnote in our second paper noting that one could think of the planner as residing in the prefrontal cortex region of the brain, which is associated with conscious, rational thinking, whereas the doer can be associated with the limbic system. For those who are familiar with the two-system model such as the one Kahneman describes in *Thinking, Fast and Slow*, it is reasonable to think of the planner as the slow, reflective, contemplative System 2 while the doers are the fast, impulsive, intuitive System 1. Recent research in neuro-economics offers some support for this interpretation. But for practical purposes, it does not matter whether the model has a physiological basis. It is a metaphor that helps us think about how to incorporate self-control into economics.

I still find the planner–doer model the most useful way to think about self-control problems, but it has not proven to be the favorite formal model of the next generation of behavioral economists. David Laibson, a behavioral economist at Harvard, pioneered what has turned out to be the model of choice in his PhD dissertation, published in 1997. Two other behavioral economic theorists, Matthew Rabin and Ted O'Donoghue, elaborated on this approach, which most economists now just refer to using the two Greek letters that represent the important variables: beta (β) and delta (δ). The subtleties of the model are difficult to explain without going into some detail, but references to the key papers are provided in the endnotes. The crucial advantage that the beta–delta model has over the planner and the doer is mathematical simplicity. It is the smallest possible modification of Samuelson's basic model that can capture the essential aspects of self-control.

Here is a simple way of thinking about how the beta–delta model works. Suppose that for any time period far enough away to be considered "later," a person does not discount time at all, meaning that the discount rate is zero. But anything considered "now" is privileged and tempting, and anything considered "later" is worth only half as much. In the Wimbledon example discussed earlier, the first-round match that would be valued at 100 this year would only be worth 50 next year or any year thereafter. Such preferences are "present-biased" since they put so much weight on now versus later, and they lead to time-inconsistent choices.

Even in this highly simplified version of the model, it is possible to illustrate many interesting subtleties about intertemporal choice; these subtleties depend in part on whether people are aware of their self-control problems. When David Laibson wrote his first paper on this subject he assumed that agents were "sophisticated," meaning that they knew they had this pattern of time preferences. As a graduate student trying to get a job with a paper on behavioral economic theory (a category that was then essentially unknown), it was clever of David to characterize the model this way. David's agents were pure Econs except for one detail; they had problematic time preferences. When O'Donoghue and Rabin decided to join the party they considered a more radical approach, in which agents have present-biased preferences but are unaware of their affliction. Such agents are considered "naïve."

Not surprisingly, neither of these simple formulations portrays a fully accurate description of behavior. I share a view held by all three authors that the "truth" is somewhere in between the two extremes: partial naiveté. Most of us realize that we have self-control problems, but we underestimate their severity. We are naïve about our level of sophistication. In particular, we suffer from what George Loewenstein has called "hot-cold empathy gaps." When we are in a cool, reflective mood—say, contemplating what to eat at dinner on Wednesday after just having finished a satisfying brunch on Sunday—we think we will have no trouble sticking to our plan to eat healthy, low-calorie dinners during the week. But when Wednesday night comes along and friends suggest going out to a new pizza place featuring craft beers, we end up eating and drinking more than we would have predicted on Sunday, or even on Wednesday before arriving at the restaurant with its tempting aromas wafting from the wood-burning oven, not to mention an intriguing list of special brews to sample. For such cases we may need a planner to have established a rule—no midweek beer and pizza outings—and then to think of a way of enforcing that rule.

In the time since I first removed that bowl of cashews, behavioral scientists have learned a lot about self-control problems. This knowledge is proving important in dealing with many of society's biggest problems, as we will see later on.

INTERLUDE

Misbehaving in the Real World

I f behavioral economics is supposed to offer a more realistic description of how people behave, then it should be helpful in practical settings. Although most of my time early in my career was devoted to academic research about mental accounting and self-control, I did have the occasional opportunity to venture out into the real world, or as close as one can get to that in Ithaca. I soon found that these ideas had practical business applications, especially relating to pricing. Here are two examples.

Greek Peak

At Cornell I got to know a student, David Cobb, who encouraged me to meet his brother, Michael. A local to the area and an avid skier, Michael was determined to make a career in the ski business and had landed a job as marketing director at Greek Peak, a family-owned operation near Ithaca. At the time, the resort was in serious financial difficulties. A few winters with less than the usual amount of snow and a tough economy had created a situation where the company had to borrow heavily to get through the off-season, and this was at a time when interest rates were high, even for good credit risks, which Greek Peak was not. The resort simply had to increase revenues and decrease debt, or it would go bankrupt. Michael needed help and suggested a barter exchange. He would give me and my kids lift tickets and set the kids up with ski equipment. In return, I would try to help him get the business back in the black.

It quickly became apparent that Greek Peak would have to increase prices if they were going to turn a profit. But any increase large enough to generate a profit would put their ticket prices nearly on par with well-known ski resorts in Vermont or New Hampshire. Opera-

tional costs per skier were not much different than they were at those
bigger resorts, but Greek Peak had only five chair lifts and less skiable
terrain. How could we justify charging a similar price to the larger
resorts, and do so without significantly reducing the number of skier
visits? And how could we retain the price-sensitive local market,
including students at Cornell and other nearby colleges?

In mental accounting terms, the lift ticket prices of the famous
Vermont ski resorts would be a salient reference point for Greek Peak
customers, and they would expect to pay significantly less since the
product was distinctly inferior. What Greek Peak had going for it was
proximity. It was the nicest place to ski in central New York, and getting to Vermont was a five-hour drive. Greek Peak was also the closest
option for people living due south, including in Scranton, Philadel-
phia, and even Washington DC. Busloads of skiers would arrive from
these cities every weekend.

I urged Michael to rethink Greek Peak's revenue model, making use
of principles from behavioral economics. The first problem to solve was
how to raise the ticket price without losing too many customers. We
adopted a plan of gradually raising the price over a period of years, thus
avoiding a sudden jump that might create backlash. To partially justify the higher prices we tried to improve the skier experience, to make
the purchase seem less of a rip-off.* I remember one early idea I had
along these lines. There was a short racecourse on the side of one of
the trails, where a skier could run through a series of slalom gates and
receive an official time that was broadcast over loudspeakers. Younger
skiers enjoyed the competitive aspect of this, and the gates were close
enough together that speeds were safe. The price charged to use the
racecourse was one dollar. A dollar was not a lot to pay, but the fee was
a damn nuisance. Getting access to your money while on a ski hill is
a pain. You have to take off your thick, clumsy gloves and dig down to

---

* In mental accounting terms, going to Greek Peak and paying the retail price did
provide positive acquisition utility for most customers, especially the locals who
were able to drive just thirty minutes, ski for a day, and be home for dinner, without
paying for a hotel room. That is a luxury available to residents of Salt Lake City and
other places in close proximity to ski resorts, but not to most people. The problem
was in the perceived transaction utility, since the price did not seem reasonable
compared to bigger resorts that were not charging much more.

whichever layer you are keeping your money in. Then, in this case, you had to feed a one-dollar bill into a vending machine–style slot. Given how well those machines work in the best of circumstances, you can imagine the failure rate once exposed to the elements.

I asked Michael and the owner, Al, how much money they were making from the racecourse. It was a small amount of money, perhaps a few thousand dollars a year. Why not make this free, I asked? We can improve the skier experience at a trivial cost. This was a no-brainer. And it got Michael and Al thinking about other things they could do to improve the quality and, importantly, the perceived value of their product.

Another example involved ski instructors. The instructors' main business was teaching new skiers, especially groups of schoolkids— obviously an important way to grow the customer base. But instructors had a lot of downtime. Someone got the clever idea to set up a free ski clinic on the mountain. A skier would wait at a designated spot on the trail, and then ski though a few gates with the action captured on video. An instructor stationed at the bottom would show the skier a replay of the video and offer a few pointers. "Free lessons!"

Even if these enhancements were making higher lift ticket prices more palatable, we still had to worry about the price-sensitive local market. Here we had a nice existing model to work from. The resort offered university students a package of six weekday lift tickets at a heavily discounted price if purchased by October 15. These were popular and provided a good source of early revenue. I suspect the students also liked the fact that the deal was called a six-pack. Even subtle beer references appeal to the college crowd.

We wondered whether we could offer something like the six-pack to the local non-student market as well. The goal was to offer the locals a deal that would not be available to the out-of-town skiers who drove in once or twice a year. To these skiers, the price of the lift ticket was only a small portion of the trip's expense, which included transportation, food, and lodging. A few dollars more for the lift ticket was unlikely to sway the decision about whether to make the trip, especially given the lack of nearby competition. We ended up with a solution called the ten-pack. It included five weekend tickets and five weekday tickets and was sold at 40% off the retail price when purchased by October 15.

Ten-packs turned out to be wildly popular with the locals. There are a few behavioral factors that explain their popularity. The first is obvious: 40% off sounds like a great deal. Lots of transaction utility. Second, the advance purchase decoupled the purchase decision from the decision to go skiing. As with wine mental accounting, the initial purchase could be viewed as an "investment" that saves money, making a spur-of-the-moment decision to go skiing on a sunny Friday after a recent snowfall costless to implement. That the customer may have gone out for a nice dinner the previous weekend would not put the recreation mental account in the red; the skiing was "free." And from the resort's point of view, it was better than free—it was a sunk cost.* As the season progressed, skiers would be eager to use some of their tickets to avoid wasting the money invested in the ten-pack, and they might bring along a friend who would pay full price. (The tickets were not transferrable.)

Ten-packs also were popular because skiing is one of those activities that people resolve to do more of next year. "Last year I only got out three times, which is ridiculous given that Greek Peak is so nearby. This year, I am going to take off a few days from work and go when it isn't crowded." As with paying for a gym membership to encourage more exercise, the skiers' planners liked the idea of committing to ski more often this winter. Buying the ten-pack was a good way to do that and save money at the same time.

After a few years, six-packs, ten-packs, and season passes accounted for a substantial portion of the resort's revenue, and this early money eliminated the need to borrow to stay afloat until the start of the season in December. Selling all these tickets in advance also hedged against a warm winter without much snow. While ski resorts can make snow, it has to be cold enough for the machines to work. Also—

---

* Of course, not everyone falls for this trap. Before Michael started giving us free lift tickets, I had purchased an after-school skiing program for my daughter Maggie, who was in seventh grade. One week Maggie announced that she was going to skip skiing to go to a dance at the school. The next week, she said she was also going to skip because a friend was having a birthday party. "Hey Maggie," I said, "are you sure about this? We paid a lot for that after-school ski program!" Maggie just said: "Ha! Sunk costs!" Only the daughter of an economist would come up with that line.

and this drives ski resort owners crazy—even if it has been cold, if there is no snow on the ground in town, people are less likely to think about going skiing, regardless of conditions at the resort.

After three years of selling the ten-packs, Michael did some analysis and called me with the results. Recall that ten-packs were sold at just 60% of the regular season retail price. "Guess what percentage of the tickets is being redeemed?" Michael asked. "Sixty percent!" The resort was selling the tickets at 60% of the retail price but only 60% of them were being redeemed. In essence they were selling the tickets at full price and getting the money several months earlier: a huge win.

This outcome did not seem to upset the clientele, most of whom repurchased ten-packs the following year. Even those who did not use many of their tickets would blame themselves, not the resort. Of course, there were customers that would end up with nearly all their tickets unused at the end of the season. Some would ask, hopefully, whether they could use the tickets the following season. They were politely told no, the tickets were explicitly sold as being good only this year. But Al designed a special offer for these customers. They were told that if they bought a ten-pack again this year, their unused tickets from the previous year would remain valid. Of course a customer who only went skiing two or three times last year is unlikely to go more than ten times this year, but the offer sounded good. Although I don't think many people were foolish enough to buy another ten-pack simply for this reason, they did seem to appreciate that the resort was making an effort to be "fair," something we will soon see can be important to keeping customers happy.

A final pricing challenge for Greek Peak was to figure out what to do early in the season, when, shortly after the first snowfall, the resort would open but often with only one lift running. Avid skiers who had been waiting since the previous March would show up for the first runs of a new season. What price should they be charged? Al's policy had been to look out his window at the mountain and the weather, and then tell the ticket sellers the price, often half off the regular price. Of course, most of the skiers who arrived had no idea what the price would be; they only knew the retail price. Only true diehards might have been able to unravel Al's pricing strategy for the early season. I call this a "secret sale." A customer comes up to the cash register prepared to pay retail and the seller says, "Oh, that item is on sale for 50% off." It might generate goodwill, but it is not a brilliant pricing strategy, because the customer was ready to pay the full price. Reducing the price only makes sense if it increases current sales or perhaps future sales by building customer loyalty.

Michael and I came up with a new strategy. Early in the season, or for that matter, any time only part of the mountain was open for skiing, pricing followed a set formula. Skiers would pay full price to ski that day, but would get a coupon good for up to 50% off their next visit, depending on how many chair lifts were operating. Since customers were expecting to pay full price, this offer seemed generous, and the coupon might induce them to come back, and perhaps buy lunch and a beer as well.

Michael once told me a story that captures how popular these coupons were. A guy shows up for his first ski outing of the year and has picked up a brand new ten-pack. He is standing in line to exchange one of these coupons for a lift ticket and overhears the ticket seller explain to the customer in front of him that she will get a 50%-off coupon that she can use toward her next purchase. This sounds so good to him that he puts the ten-pack back in his pocket and shells out for a full-priced ticket. I have always wanted to know whether he used that half-off coupon before he finished his ten-pack. We will never know.

We do know that building a solid revenue base before the season started accomplished the goal of getting the resort out of debt and reducing its dependence on the amount of snowfall during the season. Both Michael* and I moved on, but I can report that Greek Peak is still in business.

My day at GM

For years, American automobile manufacturers had a seasonal sales problem. New car models would be introduced in the fall of each year,

---

* Alas, Michael passed away just as this book was being finished. We both enjoyed comparing our distant memories of this episode as I was writing this passage. I already miss him.

and in anticipation of the new models, consumers became reluctant to buy "last year's" model. Manufacturers did not seem to anticipate this pattern and would reliably have a substantial inventory of unsold cars on dealers' lots in August, taking up the space needed to show off new models. Inevitably, car companies offered sales promotions to move the excess inventory.

One innovation was the rebate, introduced by Chrysler in 1975, and quickly followed by Ford and GM. The car companies would announce a temporary sale whereby each buyer of a car would receive some cash back, usually a few hundred dollars. A rebate seems to be just another name for a temporary sale, but they seemed to be more popular than an equivalent reduction in price, as one might expect based on mental accounting. Suppose the list price of the car was $14,800. Reducing the price to $14,500 did not seem like a big deal, not a just-noticeable difference. But by calling the price reduction a rebate, the consumer was encouraged to think about the $300 separately, which would intensify its importance. This bit of mental accounting was costly, at least in New York State where I was living, because the consumer had to pay sales tax on the rebate. Using the numbers in the example above, the consumer would pay sales tax on the full purchase price of $14,800 and would then get a check back from the manufacturer for $300, not $300 plus the 8% sales tax. But more to the point, rebates were starting to lose some of their luster, and cars were again piling up in dealers' lots.

Then someone at GM headquarters got an idea. Ford and Chrysler had been trying discounted auto loans as an alternative or supplement to rebates. What if GM tried offering a highly discounted rate as a sales inducement? At a time when the going interest rate for a car loan was 10% or more, General Motors offered a loan at just 2.9%. Consumers could choose either a rebate or the discounted loan. The loan offer had an unprecedented effect on sales. There were news reports of consumers sprawled on the hoods of cars at a dealership claiming a particular car before anyone else could buy it.

Around this time, I noticed a small story in the *Wall Street Journal*. A reporter had crunched the numbers and discovered that the economic value of the low-interest-rate loan was less than the value of the rebate. In other words, if consumers used the rebate to increase the down payment they made on the car, thus reducing the amount they had to borrow (though at a higher rate), they would save money. Taking the loan deal was dumb! But it was selling a lot of cars. Interesting.

At this time, one of my Cornell colleagues, Jay Russo, was consulting for GM, so I went to talk to him. I told Jay about this puzzle and said that I might have a simple psychological explanation. The rebate was a small percentage of the price of the car, but the car loan being offered was less than a third of the usual rate. That sounds like a much better deal. And few people besides accountants and *Wall Street Journal* reporters would bother to do the math, especially since this was in an era that predated spreadsheets and home computers.

Jay asked me to write up a brief note about my observation that he could share with people at GM. I did, and to my surprise about a week later I got a call from General Motors headquarters. My note had found its way to someone in the marketing department, and he wanted to talk to me about it in person. I said sure, come on by.

This gentleman flew from Detroit to Syracuse and drove the hour and a quarter down to Ithaca. We chatted about my idea for about an hour, at most. He left, spent a few hours strolling the campus, and went back to Detroit. I went to Jay to find out what this was about and he put it bluntly. "He was here to count your heads." What? "Yeah, he wanted to see if you had two heads, didn't bathe, or were in some other way unsafe to bring to see his bosses. He will report back to HQ."

Apparently I passed the test. A few days later I got a call asking whether I would be willing to come to Detroit. This had the potential to be my first paid consulting gig, I could use the money, so I quickly agreed. Besides, I was damn curious.

If you have seen Michael Moore's documentary film *Roger and Me*, you have seen my destination: the GM headquarters building. I found it very strange. It was huge, and new cars were on display everywhere inside, in the hallways and lobbies. In my first meeting, a vice president of marketing gave me my schedule for the day. I had a series of half-hour meetings with different people in the marketing department. Many of them also seemed to be vice presidents. In that first meeting I asked who was in charge of evaluating the low-interest-rate promotion, which reduced the price of the cars sold by hundreds of millions of dollars. My host was not certain, but assured me it had to be one of the people I would be meeting. By the end of the day I would know.

During the day several people described how the interest rate of 2.9% had been determined. Apparently Roger Smith, the CEO, had called a meeting to determine how they were going to deal with surplus inventory that year and someone had suggested a promotion based on lower interest rates. Everyone agreed this was a great idea. But what rate should they use? One manager suggested 4.9%. Another said 3.9%. After each suggestion, someone would be sent to make some calculations. Finally, someone suggested 2.9%, and Roger decided he liked the sound of that number. The whole process took less than an hour.

But when I asked people who would evaluate the promotion and decide what to do next year, I got blank stares followed by, "Not me." The day ended in the office of my host. I reported that, as far as I could tell, no one would be thinking about these questions, and this struck me as a mistake. He suggested that I write him a proposal for what might be done.

After what I had learned during my visit, I was pretty sure I did not want this consulting job, but I did send him a short proposal making two suggestions for what I thought they should do. First, figure out why the promotion had worked so well. Second, make a plan for the future, especially since they should expect that Ford and Chrysler were likely to copy GM's successful promotion.

After a month I received a curt reply. My recommendation had been discussed by top management and was rejected. The company had instead resolved to better plan its production and avoid excess summer inventory. This would eliminate the need to evaluate the promotion and plan for the future, since there would be no more end-of-model-year sales. I was astounded. A huge company had spent hundreds of millions of dollars on a promotion and did not bother to figure out how and why it worked. Michael Cobb at tiny Greek Peak was thinking more analytically than the industrial behemoth General Motors.

As I have learned over the years, and will discuss further in subsequent chapters, the reluctance to experiment, test, evaluate, and learn that I experienced at General Motors is all too common. I have continued to see this tendency, in business and government, ever since, though recently I have had the chance to try to change that ethos in government settings.

Oh, and about that claim that they had a plan to eliminate excess inventory in future summers? It was violated the next summer, the summer after that, and, as far as I know, every summer since. Over-confidence is a powerful force.

IV.

WORKING WITH DANNY:

1984-85

After our year in Stanford, Amos and Danny decided to immigrate to North America. Amos stayed on at the Stanford psychology department and Danny moved to the psychology department at the University of British Columbia in Vancouver. Part of the allure of UBC was that Amos and Danny would be a two-hour flight away from each other and in the same time zone. They continued to work together, talking daily and visiting each other often.

Because we all started new jobs the same year, we were on the same sabbatical schedule. In 1984–85 I would get my first one, and Amos and Danny would be on leave too. Our year at Stanford had been so transformative for me that when it came time to think about my research leave, I naturally hoped to hook up with one or both of them. After various machinations, I ended up in Vancouver with Danny. Amos, meanwhile, headed off to Israel.

I got an office at the UBC business school, which was a good place for me to hang out since it had an excellent finance department and I was in the midst of trying to learn more about that field. But the main thing I did that year was work with Danny and his collaborator, the environmental economist Jack Knetsch, who taught at nearby Simon Fraser University. Like the year at Stanford, this year in Vancouver offered me the rare opportunity for full immersion in research. Apart from the year in Stanford, it would be the most productive year of my life.

14

What Seems Fair?

Danny and Jack invited me to join them in a project they had recently started that was closely related to my "beer on the beach" question, which investigated what makes an economic transaction seem like a "good deal" (i.e., what makes people willing to pay more for a beer purchased at a fancy resort than at a rundown shack). The topic Danny and Jack had begun to study was: what makes an economic transaction seem "fair"? Someone might resist paying as much for a beer sold at a shack as for one sold at a fancy resort because, in his or her mind, it's not fair for the shack owner to be charging such a high price.

This project was made possible by an arrangement Jack Knetsch had made with the Canadian government, which gave us access to free telephone polling. Apparently there was a program that was training the unemployed to be telephone interviewers, whatever that entails, and they needed questions for the trainees to ask. If we faxed a bunch of questions each Monday morning, they would fax us back the responses Thursday night. That gave us Friday and the weekend to figure out what we had learned from the week's questions and to write some new ones for the following week. Today this sort of research can be done online using services like Amazon's "Mechanical Turk," but back then weekly access to a random sample of a few hundred residents of Ontario (and later British Columbia) was an incredible luxury. We were able to try out lots of ideas, get quick feedback, and learn in the best possible way: theory-driven intuition tested by trial and error.

Here is an example of the kind of question we were asking:

A hardware store has been selling snow shovels for $15. The morning after a large snowstorm, the store raises the price to $20.

Rate this action as: Completely fair, acceptable, somewhat unfair, or very unfair.

We decided to simplify the presentation of the data by combining the first two answers and calling them "acceptable," and the last two, which we labeled "unfair." Here were the responses for this question (each question had about 100 respondents):

Acceptable 18%   Unfair 82%

Now, you might be saying, "Duh! What kind of jerk would raise the price of snow shovels the morning after a snowstorm?" But raising the price is exactly what economic theory says will and *should* happen! This easily could be a question from a basic economics course in business school. "There is a fixed supply of snow shovels, and a sudden increase in demand. What will happen to the price?" In that class, the correct answer is to say that the price will go up enough so that everyone who is willing to pay that price will get one. Raising the price is the only way to assure that the snow shovels will end up being owned by those who value them most (as measured by their willingness to pay).

One of the things MBAs learn in business school is to think like an Econ, but they also forget what it is like to think like a Human. This is another example of Kahneman's notion of theory-induced blindness. Indeed, when I posed the snow shovel fairness question to my MBA students, their responses were in accord with standard economic theory:

Acceptable 76%   Unfair 24%

Ours was a purely descriptive exercise. We did not intend to be moral philosophers or to render judgment about what "is" or "should be" fair. Instead, we were trying to do what you might call experimental philosophy. We were trying to learn what ordinary citizens, albeit Canadians, think is fair. More specifically, we were trying to learn what actions by firms make people angry. It turns out that raising the price of snow shovels after a blizzard really pisses people off. There is even a name for this practice: gouging. The usual definition of "gouge" is "to make a hole or groove with a sharp instrument." When a store raises the price of snow shovels the day after a blizzard, people feel very much like someone has poked them with a sharp object. And indeed, in many places there are laws against gouging, suggesting that people find the practice offensive. We wanted to figure out what other business practices Humans hate.

Any polling question that produced something interesting would be run again using different variations to make sure there was nothing special about, say, snow shovels. Here is another example, inspired by my three-year-old daughter Jessie and her ever-present doll Joey. Joey was no ordinary doll; he was a Cabbage Patch doll, which for reasons mysterious to me but obvious to many young girls had become a fad among the preschool set. By Christmastime, there were no Cabbage Patch dolls to be found anywhere, and many parents were desperate. Thus, this item:

> A store has been sold out of the popular Cabbage Patch dolls for a month. A week before Christmas a single doll is discovered in a storeroom. The managers know that many customers would like to buy the doll. They announce over the store's public address system that the doll will be sold by auction to the customer who offers to pay the most.

Acceptable 26%   Unfair 74%

This answer raises an interesting follow-up question: what is it that makes the auction unpopular? Is it that the doll will go to someone affluent enough to win the auction, or is it that the store owner has opted to extract every possible penny from a desperate parent with a toddler waiting anxiously for Christmas Eve?

To find out, we asked the same question to another group of respondents but added one extra sentence stating that the proceeds will be donated to UNICEF. That yielded an acceptable rating of 79%. Auctioning a doll is fine if the proceeds go to charity, unless the "charity" is the owner's wallet.

Even this conclusion has to be tempered. In another scenario, we

said that a small town was suffering from a flu epidemic, and there
was only one package of medicine remaining. Would it be fair for the
pharmacist to auction off the medicine? Of course people hated the
auction, but in this case they hated it even if the money went to charity. People understand that many luxuries are only available to the
affluent. But, at least for most people, health care occupies a different category. Most European countries (as well as Canada) provide
health care to their citizens as a basic right, and even in America,
where this view is resisted in certain quarters, we do not turn unin-
sured accident victims away at the emergency room. Similarly, no
country permits a free market in organs, although Iran does have a
market for kidneys. For most of the world, the idea that a rich person
who needs a kidney should be allowed to pay a poor person to donate
one is considered "repugnant," to use the word favored by economist
Alvin Roth to describe such market transactions.

In many situations, the perceived fairness of an action depends
not only on who it helps or harms, but also on how it is framed. To
test these kinds of effects, we would ask two versions of a question
to different groups of respondents. For example, consider this pair of
questions, with the differences highlighted in italics:

A shortage has developed for a popular model of automobile,
and customers must now wait two months for delivery. *A dealer
has been selling these cars at list price. Now the dealer prices this model
at $200 above list price.*

Acceptable 29%   Unfair 71%

A shortage has developed for a popular model of automobile,
and customers must now wait two months for delivery. *A dealer
has been selling these cars at a discount of $200 below list price. Now
the dealer sells this model only at list price.*

Acceptable 58%   Unfair 42%

This pair of questions illustrates a useful point that came up in our
discussion in chapter 2 of merchants imposing surcharges for using

a credit card. Any firm should establish the highest price it intends to charge as the "regular" price, with any deviations from that price called "sales" or "discounts." Removing a discount is not nearly as objectionable as adding a surcharge.

One principle that emerged from our research is that perceptions of fairness are related to the endowment effect. Both buyers and sellers feel entitled to the terms of trade to which they have become accustomed, and treat any deterioration of those terms as a loss. This feeling of ownership of the usual conditions of sale is particularly true when a seller starts to charge for something that has traditionally been given away for free or included in the price. In this way, the status quo becomes a reference point. If restaurants started charging extra to be able to sit down while you eat, that would be violating the existing norm that dinner meals include a chair, although it does not have to be comfortable. Nevertheless, citizens think that firms and employers are entitled to make a (reasonable) profit. Firms are not expected to give away their products. One implication is that raising prices because costs have increased is almost always judged to be fair.

Perceptions of fairness also help explain a long-standing puzzle in economics: in recessions, why don't wages fall enough to keep everyone employed? In a land of Econs, when the economy goes into a recession and firms face a drop in the demand for their goods and services, their first reaction would not be to simply lay off employees. The theory of equilibrium says that when the demand for something falls, in this case labor, prices should also fall enough for supply to equal demand. So we would expect to see that firms would reduce wages when the economy tanks, allowing them to also cut the price of their products and still make a profit. But this is not what we see: wages and salaries appear to be sticky. When a recession hits, either wages do not fall at all or they fall too little to keep everyone employed. Why?

One partial explanation for this fact is that cutting wages makes workers so angry that firms find it better to keep pay levels fixed and just lay off surplus employees (who are then not around to complain). It turns out, however, that with the help of some inflation, it is possible to reduce "real" wages (that is, adjusted for inflation) with much

less pushback from workers. The next pair of questions illustrates
this point.

> A company is making a small profit. It is located in a commu-
> nity experiencing a recession with substantial unemployment
> but no inflation. There are many workers anxious to work at the
> company. The company decides to decrease wages and salaries
> by 7% this year.

Acceptable 38%   Unfair 62%

> A small company is making a small profit. It is located in a com-
> munity experiencing a recession with substantial unemploy-
> ment *and inflation of 12%.* The company decides to *increase salaries
> only 5% this year.*

Acceptable 78%   Unfair 22%

Notice that the spending power of the employees is the same for
the two versions of the problem, but the reactions are quite different.
An actual cut in the nominal wage is viewed as a loss and is therefore
unfair, whereas failing to keep up with inflation is judged acceptable
since the nominal wage is still going up. This is one of many reasons
why some economists (including me) felt that central banks should
have been willing to tolerate a bit more inflation after the financial
crisis. Even 3% inflation might have allowed firms to effectively cut
real wages enough to speed the jobs recovery that has been so slow in
most of the world.

––––––––

Of course, it is one thing to discover what actions by firms make
people angry, and it is quite another to ask whether firms obey these
fairness norms. I do not know of any systematic study of this question, but I suspect that most successful firms intuitively understand
the norms we uncovered and at least try to avoid giving the appear-
ance of behaving unfairly.

The value of seeming fair should be especially high for firms that plan to be in business selling to the same customers for a long time, since those firms have more to lose from seeming to act unfairly. In fact, after a hurricane, the cheapest place in the country to buy ply-wood is often the area that has been hardest hit. For example, after Hurricane Katrina devastated New Orleans, Home Depot and other chains loaded up trucks with emergency supplies of food and bottled water to give away. At the same time, such a natural disaster will induce some entrepreneurial folks to load a truck with plywood in a nearby city and sell it in the devastated areas for whatever price it will fetch. In this case, both sellers are profit-maximizing. The chain store is establishing a reputation for fair dealing that will have long-term payoffs, whereas the "temporary entrepreneurs" will be back home in a couple days with a tidy profit and either a slightly guilty conscience or pride in their efforts to help improve the allocation of scarce resources, depending on their point of view.

But firms don't always get these things right. The fact that my MBA students think it is perfectly fine to raise the price of snow shovels after a blizzard should be a warning to all business executives that their intuitions about what seems fair to their customers and employees might need some fine-tuning.

Consider the case of an initiative taken by First Chicago in the mid-1990s, when it was the largest bank in the Chicago metropolitan area. Top management was concerned that the retail banking division was not making enough profits. To trim costs, they decided to encourage customers to make greater use of recently introduced automatic teller machines (ATMs). Although most people had become comfortable taking money out of such a machine, some customers were reluctant to use an ATM to deposit checks. Instead, they would go to a teller for that service, and full-fledged technophobes continued to go to the teller to get cash (and perhaps chat with a favorite teller). The bank decided to give customers an incentive to switch to ATMs by charg-ing three dollars to use a teller for a transaction that could be done at an ATM.

The bank was proud of this innovation and announced it with great fanfare, along with a new lineup of checking account options. The public reaction was immediate and fierce. A local paper's front-page headline read: "FIRST CHICAGO LOSES TOUCH WITH HUMANS."

The story went on to say: "The First National Bank of Chicago today introduced an innovative lineup of checking accounts designed to bring its products up to date with the way customers prefer to bank in the 1990s. And what is it the bank thinks customers prefer in the 1990s? Paying a $3 fee for the privilege of doing business with a bank teller."

The competition was quick to pounce. One bank put a "Free Teller" sign on its branch right off one of the local expressways. Another ran this radio ad:

> **MAN:** I was looking over my bank statement, and I am wondering . . .
> **TELLER:** Is that a question?
> **MAN:** What? Well, yes.
> **TELLER:** Questions are extra—six dollars.
> **MAN:** What?!
> **TELLER:** Nine dollars.

You get the idea. Even the late night comedian Jay Leno picked up on it: "So, if you want to talk to a human, it's three dollars. But the good news is, for $3.95 you can talk dirty to her, so that's okay."

The bank attracted all this bad publicity for a three-dollar fee that very few people would actually pay. Yet it took until December 2002, after First Chicago had been purchased by a national bank, for the new management team to announce that they were abandoning the policy. "We've been presumptuous about our market share here. We haven't done a great job in Chicago."

The CEO of Coca-Cola also discovered the hard way that violating the norms of fairness can backfire. Douglas Ivester, aged fifty-two, appeared to be on his way to the job of chairman when he abruptly resigned after a push from several board members including legendary investor Warren Buffett. Although several actions contributed to his downfall, one speech in Brazil attracted the most attention. At a press conference, Mr. Ivester was asked about tests Coke was running with vending machines that could change price dynamically. He replied: "Coca-Cola is a product whose utility varies from moment to moment. In a final summer championship, when people meet in a stadium to have fun, the utility of a cold Coca-Cola is very high. So it is fair that it should be more expensive. The machine will simply make this process automatic." As the *Wall Street Journal* stated in a story about his downfall, Mr. Ivester seemed to have a "tin ear." An editorial cartoon captured the feelings of the general public perfectly with an image of a customer walking away from a Coke vending machine with a can in his hand, looking back to see an arm reaching out of the machine and picking his pocket.

Firms continue to fail at the basics of business fairness. Consider the case of Whitney Houston, the pop singer who died suddenly on February 11, 2012. It was to be expected that there would be a spike in the demand for her recordings, now largely sold online at sites such as iTunes. How did Apple and Sony (the owner of the recording rights) react to the death? Was this a propitious time to jack up the price?

Someone (or possibly, some pricing algorithm) seemed to think so. About twelve hours after her death, the price of Houston's 1997 album *The Ultimate Collection* increased on the U.K. iTunes site from £4.99 ($7.86) to £7.99 ($12.58), a 60% increase in price. The price of *Whitney— The Greatest Hits* later increased from £7.99 to £9.99, a 25% increase.

The *Guardian* was the first news organization to break the story. Customer ire was originally directed toward Apple, but later Sony was blamed for the hike. Regardless of who was to blame, fans were outraged. The *Daily Mail* quoted one customer as saying: "To say I am angry is an understatement and I feel it is just a case of iTunes cashing in on the singer's death, which in my opinion is totally parasitic." The anger in this case might have been particularly acute because in the case of online downloads there is no sense in which the albums have become scarce. Unlike snow shovels after a blizzard, iTunes cannot run out of copies of an album to be downloaded.

This story was not widely known in the United States, where prices did not spike, and certainly it did not appear to affect sales in the U.S. According to Nielsen SoundScan, there were 101,000 Whitney Houston albums sold in the U.S. the week after her death (up from 1,700 the week before) and 887,000 individual song downloads (compared to 15,000 the week before). I do not know whether sales in the U.K. were as strong, but even if they were, a price increase may not have been wise. As usual in these cases when demand has suddenly risen, a seller has to trade off short-term gain against possible long-term loss of good will, which can be hard to measure.

A reasonable question to ask at this point is whether firms are always punished for acting "unfairly." Sure, First Chicago got hammered in the media for its three-dollar charge to see a teller, but airlines have been adding fees one after another without appearing to cause irreparable harm to the individual airlines that lead the way, or the industry as a whole. Why not? Airline travelers can't be happy about the new fees for checked baggage, nor the crammed overhead bins that have become the norm since baggage fees were added. In this case, as in many others, the key is what happens after the first mover adds a new fee that might be perceived as unfair. If the competition follows the first mover's lead, then customers may be peeved but have little choice if they must consume the product in question. Had the other major banks in the area followed First Chicago's example and added a teller fee, customers might well have gotten used to the idea and reluctantly accepted it. But any large first mover who takes an action that violates the norms of fairness runs considerable risks if competitors do not follow suit.

My takeaway from these examples is that temporary spikes in demand, from blizzards to rock star deaths, are an especially bad time for any business to appear greedy. (There are no good times to appear greedy.) One prominent new firm that appears to be ignoring this advice is Uber, the innovative smartphone-driven car service that has entered many markets around the world. One feature of Uber's business model is that prices can fluctuate depending on demand. Uber refers to this practice as "surge pricing." When demand is high, for whatever reason, prices go up, and customers requesting a car are notified of the current price multiple. Customers can then choose to accept the higher price, turn it down and seek alternative transportation, or hope that the surge will be short-lived and wait for Uber to notify them that the surge is over. Uber does not make their pricing formulas public, but there have been media reports of surge multiples more than ten times the regular price. Unsurprisingly, multiples this large have led to complaints.

Uber has defended surge pricing on the basis that a higher price will act as an incentive for more drivers to work during peak periods.

It is hard to evaluate this argument without seeing internal data on the supply response by drivers, but on the face of it the argument does not seem to be compelling. First of all, you can't just decide on the spur of the moment to become an Uber driver, and even existing drivers who are either at home relaxing or at work on another job have limited ability to jump in their cars and drive when a temporary surge is announced. One indication of the limits on the extent to which the supply of drivers can respond quickly is the very fact that we have seen multiples as high as ten. If thousands of drivers were ready to leap into their cars when a surge is announced, large surges in price would be fleeting.

Regardless of whether Uber can instantly increase its supply of drivers, the high multiples charged during a blizzard in New York City attracted the attention of the New York State attorney general. (Raising the price of snow shovels is not the only thing that makes people mad during a snowstorm.) It turns out that New York has one of those anti-gouging laws I referred to earlier. Specifically, firms are prohibited from charging "unconscionable excessive prices" during any "abnormal disruption of the market," which can be anything from a storm to a power outage to civil disorder. Note that the language of the law captures some of the emotions people have about this issue. Excessive would seem to be enough, but this law bans *unconscionably* excessive prices.

The State of New York and Uber reached an agreement that in such abnormal disruptions of the market, Uber would limit its surge pricing using a formula. It would first search for the highest multiples charged on four different days during the sixty days that precede the "abnormal disruption." The fourth highest price would then serve as a cap on the surge that could be charged in the emergency period. In addition, Uber voluntarily offered to donate 20% of its additional revenues during these periods to the American Red Cross.

I think it showed bad judgment on the part of Uber management to wait until the attorney general forced them into this concession. If they wanted to establish good long-term relationships with their customers, they should have thought of something like it themselves. Just imagine that Uber existed on September 11, 2001, when the planes struck the World Trade Center. Would it have been a smart move for Uber to have a special "9/11 surge special" of twenty times the usual fare, sending many of the cars in the area off to Greenwich?* This insensitivity to the norms of fairness could be particularly costly to Uber since the company has had to fight political battles in many of the cities it enters. Why create enemies in order to increase profits a few days a year?†

Don't get me wrong. I love Uber as a service. But if I were their consultant, or a shareholder, I would suggest that they simply cap surges to something like a multiple of three times the usual fare. You might wonder where the number three came from. That is my vague impression of the range of prices that one normally sees for products such as hotel rooms and plane tickets that have prices dependent on supply and demand. Furthermore, these services sell out at the most popular times, meaning that the owners are intentionally setting the prices too low during the peak season.

I once asked the owner of a ski lodge why he didn't charge more during the Christmas week holiday, when demand is at a peak and rooms have to be booked nearly a year in advance. At first he didn't understand my question. No one had ever asked why the prices are so *low* during this period when prices are at their highest. But once I explained that I was an economist, he caught on and answered quickly. "If you gouge them at Christmas they won't come back in March." That remains good advice for any business that is interested in building a loyal clientele.

One businessman who understands this lesson better than most is Nick Kokonas, the co-owner, with celebrity chef Grant Achatz, of two of the best restaurants in Chicago: Alinea and Next. The concept at Next is highly original. The menu changes completely three times a year. The themes can vary as widely as a dinner in Paris from 1906, to Thai street food, to an homage to El Bulli, a restaurant in Catalonia,

* I asked one Uber driver in California how he would feel about surge pricing being applied if there was a wildfire in some town and people had to get out. He said: "In that situation, I would want to offer rides for free!"

† A similar episode occurred in Sydney, Australia, during a hostage crisis in the center of the city. Prices surged, probably based on some algorithm that was not fine-tuned to special circumstances. After online criticism, some Humans at Uber decided to offer free rides and to refund people who had paid (Sullivan, 2014).

Spain, that was a foodie mecca until it closed in 2011. When Next was scheduled to open in April 2011, they announced that all their meals (as well as those at Alinea) would be sold by tickets, with the ticket prices varying according to the day of the week and the time of day. Following the usual fairness norms, the prices do not vary all that much. The most expensive price, for Saturday night at eight, is only about 25% more than the cheapest time, 9:45 on Wednesday. As a result, the prime-time tables sell out almost immediately (some to customers who buy season tickets to all three meals that year), and typically the only tables available are at the cheaper off-peak times.

When Next first opened and the excitement was at its peak, two economists from Northwestern University tried to explain to Mr. Kokonas that he was doing this all wrong, and that he should instead have auctioned off each reservation so as to maximize his profits. Kokonas strongly disagreed with this advice, and has a long blog entry explaining why. Here is the key sentence in his blog: "It is incredibly important for any business, no matter how great the demand, not to charge a customer more than the good or service is worth—even if the customer is willing to pay more." He felt that even if someone was willing to pay $2,000 to eat at Next, that customer would leave feeling, "Yeah, that was great but it wasn't worth $2,000." And crucially, Kokonas believes that such a customer will not come back, and may share his disgruntled experience with other potential diners.*

Kokonas is now offering his online ticket-selling software to other high-end restaurants. It will be interesting to see whether the restaurants that adopt the ticket model also adopt his pricing strategy of "underpricing" the (expensive) tables at peak times. The ones that want to stay in business for the long haul would be well advised to do so.

---

* Notably, an even larger organization—the NFL—recognizes and ascribes to this same piece of advice. In an interview with economist Alan B. Krueger, the NFL's VP for public relations, Greg Aiello, explained that his organization takes a "long-term strategic view" toward ticket pricing, at least for the Super Bowl. Even though the high demand for Super Bowl tickets might justify significantly higher prices (and short-term profits—he calculates the profit increase as on the same scale as all advertising revenues), the organization intentionally keeps these prices reasonable in order to foster its "ongoing relationship with fans and business associates" (Krueger, 2001).

15

Fairness Games

One question was very much on the minds of Danny, Jack, and me while we were doing our fairness project. Would people be willing to punish a firm that behaves unfairly? Would a customer who was charged $500 for a taxi ride that is normally priced at $50 try to avoid using that service again, even if they liked the service? We designed an experiment in the form of a game to investigate.

One player, the Proposer, is given a sum of money known as the "pie." He is told to offer the other player, called the Responder, the portion of the pie he is willing to share. The Responder can either accept the offer, leaving the remaining amount to the Proposer, or can reject it, in which case both players get nothing.

It was important that this game be played for real money, so we abandoned our telephone polling bureau and did our research with students at the University of British Columbia and Cornell. We devised a very simple way to play the game and get as much data as possible for a given research budget. Players were chosen at random to play the role of Proposer or Responder. Then they filled out a simple form like this one for Responders. In our game the pie was $10.

If you are offered $10 will you accept?	Yes _____	No _____
If you are offered $9.50 will you accept?	Yes _____	No _____
...		
...		
If you are offered $0.50 will you accept?	Yes _____	No _____
If you are offered nothing will you accept?	Yes _____	No _____

We asked the questions in this way because we were worried that many Proposers would offer half, which would not give us much insight into the preferences of the Responders, who were our primary focus.

Using the standard economics assumptions that people are selfish and rational, game theory has a clear prediction for this game. The Proposer will offer the smallest positive amount possible (50 cents in our version) and the Responder will accept, since 50 cents is more than nothing. In contrast, we conjectured that small offers would be rejected as "unfair." That conjecture turned out to be right. Typically, offers that did not exceed 20% of the pie, $2 in our game, were rejected.

We were delighted with this outcome of our cute little game, but we soon discovered that three German economists led by Werner Güth had published a paper on precisely this game three years earlier. They used exactly the same methods and had a snappy name for it: the Ultimatum Game. Danny was crestfallen when he heard this news, worried as always that his current idea would be his last. (This is the same man who would publish a global best-seller at age seventy-seven.)

Jack and I reassured Danny that he probably still had some good ideas left, and we all pressed on to think of another game to go along with the first one. Our research on this game was conducted in two stages. In the first stage we gave students in a classroom setting the following choice: "You have the opportunity to divide $20 between you and another anonymous student in this class. You have two choices: you can take $18 and give the other student $2, or you can split the money evenly, so that you each get $10." (While everyone made the choice, the subjects were told that only some of them would be selected at random to be paid.) Because the second player is forced to take whatever she is offered, this game has become known as the Dictator Game.

We did not have a strong opinion about how the Dictator Game would come out. Our primary interest was in the second game, let's call it the Punishment Game, in which we went to a different class and told the students there about the Dictator Game experiment. Then we gave students a choice. "You have been paired with two students who played [the Dictator Game] but were not selected to be paid. One, E, divided the money evenly, while the other, U, divided the money unevenly. He took $18 and gave his counterpart $2. You have the following choice. Would you like to evenly split $12 with U or $10 with E?"

Another way to phrase the choice in the Punishment Game is: "Are you willing to give up a dollar to share some money with a student who behaved nicely *to someone else*, rather than share with a student who was greedy in the same situation?" We thought that the Punishment Game, like the Ultimatum Game, would tell us whether people are willing to give something up to punish someone who behaves in a manner they consider "unfair."

Somewhat surprisingly to us (or at least to me), the students in the Dictator stage of our game were remarkably nice. Nearly three quarters (74%) chose to divide the money equally. Of more interest to us, the results of the Punishment stage were even stronger. Fully 81% of the subjects chose to share $10 with a "fair" allocator rather than $12 with an "unfair" allocator.

It is important to stress what should and should not be inferred from the results of both of these experiments. There is clear evidence that people dislike unfair offers and are willing to take a financial hit to punish those who make them. It is less clear that people feel morally obliged to make fair offers. Although it is true that in the Ultimatum Game the most common offer is often 50%, one cannot conclude that Proposers are trying to be fair. Instead, they may be quite rationally worried about being rejected. Given the empirical evidence on respondents' behavior, the profit-maximizing strategy in the Ultimatum Game is for the Proposer to offer about 40% of the pie. Lower offers start to run the risk of being rejected, so a 50% offer is not far from the rational selfish strategy.

Whether the offers made by Proposers are driven by fairness or selfish concerns, the outcomes of the Ultimatum Game appear to be quite robust. Proposers make offers of close to half the pie, and Responders tend to reject offers of less than 20%. The game has been run in locations all around the world, and with the exception of some remote tribes the results are pretty similar. Nevertheless, one question that people have long wondered about is whether the tendency to reject small offers in the Ultimatum Game persists as stakes increase. A natural intuition shared by many is that as the stakes go up, the minimum offer that will be accepted goes down as a fraction of the total pie. That is, if when playing for $10 the average minimally acceptable offer is $2, then when the stakes are raised to $1,000, would people accept less than $200?

Investigating this hypothesis has been plagued by two problems: running a high-stakes version of the Ultimatum Game is expensive, and most Proposers make "fair" offers. Experimenters in the United States ran a version of the Ultimatum Game for $100, and the results did not differ much from lower-stakes games. Even more telling is evidence from running the game in poor countries, where the cost of living allows experimenters to raise the stakes even higher. For example, Lisa Cameron ran Ultimatum Game experiments in Java using both low stakes and truly high stakes (approximately three months' income for the subjects). She found virtually no difference in the behavior of Proposers when she raised the stakes.

There is another class of games that takes up the question of whether people are purely selfish (at least when dealing with strangers), as Econs are presumed to be. These are games about cooperation. The classic game of this variety is the well-known Prisoner's Dilemma. In the original setup, there are two prisoners who have been arrested for committing some crime and are being held and interrogated separately. They each have a choice: they can confess their crime or remain silent. If they both remain silent, the police can only convict them of a minor offense with a sentence of one year. If they both confess, they each get five years in jail. But if one confesses and the other stays silent, the confessor gets out of jail free while the other serves ten years in jail.

In the more general version of this game without the prisoner cover story, there are two strategies, cooperate (stay silent) or defect (confess). The game theoretic prediction is that both players will defect because, no matter what the other player does, it is in the selfish best interest of each player to do so. Yet when this game is played in the laboratory, 40–50% of the players cooperate, which means that about half the players either do not understand the logic of the game or feel that cooperating is the just the right thing to do, or possibly both.

The Prisoner's Dilemma comes with a great story, but most of us don't get arrested very often. What are the implications of this game for normal life? Consider a related game called the Public Goods Game. To understand the economic significance of this game, we turn back to the great Paul Samuelson, who formalized the concept of a public good in a three-page paper published in 1954. The guy did not belabor things.

A public good is one that everyone can consume without diminishing the consumption of anyone else, and it is impossible to exclude anyone from consuming it. A fireworks display is a classic example. Samuelson proved that a market economy will undersupply public goods because no one will have an incentive to pay much of anything for them, since they can be consumed for free. For years after Samuelson's paper, economists assumed that the public goods problem could not be solved unless the government stepped in and provided the good, using taxes to make everybody pay a share.

Of course, if we look around, we see counterexamples to this result all the time. Some people donate to charities and clean up campgrounds, and quite miraculously, at least in America, most urban dog owners now carry a plastic bag when they take their dog for a "walk" in order to dispose of the waste. (Although there are laws in place supposedly enforcing this norm, they are rarely enforced.) In other words, some people cooperate, even when it is not in their self-interest to do so.

Economists, psychologists, and sociologists have all studied this problem using variations on the following simple game. Suppose we invite ten strangers to the lab and give each of them five one-dollar bills. Each subject can decide how many (if any) dollar bills he wishes to contribute to the "public good" by privately putting that money into a blank envelope. The rules of the game are that the total contributions to the public good envelope are doubled, and then the money is divided equally among all the players.

The rational, selfish strategy in the Public Goods Game is to contribute nothing. Suppose that Brendan decides to contribute one dollar. That dollar is doubled by the experimenter to two dollars and then is divided among all the players, making Brendan's share of that contribution 20 cents. So for each dollar he contributes, Brendan will lose 80 cents. Of course other subjects are happy about Brendan's anonymous contribution, since they each get 20 cents as well, but they will not be grateful to him personally because his contribution was anonymous. Following Samuelson's logic, the prediction from economic theory is that no one will contribute anything. Notice that by being selfishly rational in this way, the group ends up with half as much money as they would have had if everyone contributed their entire stake, because if everyone contributed $5, that amount would be doubled, and everyone would go home with $10. The distinguished economist and philosopher Amartya Sen famously called people who always give nothing in this game rational fools for blindly following only material self-interest: "The *purely* economic man is indeed close to being a social moron. Economic theory has been much preoccupied with this rational fool."

As with the Prisoner's Dilemma, the standard economics prediction that no one will cooperate in the Public Goods Game turns out to be false. On average, people contribute about half their stake to the public good. There is still a public goods problem, meaning that public goods are not supplied in as great a quantity as people would want if they could all somehow agree to be cooperative, but the undersupply is about half as severe as the rational selfish model predicts—well, with one important proviso. When the game was played by economics graduate students, the contribution rate was only 20%, leading the sociologists Gerald Marwell and Ruth Ames to write a paper titled "Economists Free Ride: Does Anyone Else?"

A wisecracking economist might answer the question posed by Marwell and Ames's title with "experienced players." A robust finding in public goods experiments is that if a group of subjects play the game repeatedly, cooperation rates steadily fall, from the usual 50% down to nearly zero. When this result was first discovered, some economists argued that the initial high cooperation rates were due to some confusion on the part of the subjects, and when they played the game repeatedly, they learned that the rational selfish strategy was the right one. In 1999, the experimental economist James Andreoni tested this interpretation with a brilliant twist. After groups of five subjects played the game for the announced ten rounds and watched cooperation rates fall, the subjects were told that they would play another ten rounds of the game with the same players. What do you think happens?

If people have learned that being selfish is the smart thing to do, then cooperation rates should remain low after the restart, but that is not what happened. Instead, in the first round of the new game, cooperation rates jumped back to the same level as the first round of the initial experiment. So repeated play of the Public Goods Game does not teach people to be jerks; rather it teaches them that they are playing with (some) jerks, and no one likes to play the role of the sucker.

Further research by Ernst Fehr and his colleagues has shown that, consistent with Andreoni's finding, a large proportion of people can be categorized as *conditional cooperators*, meaning that they are willing to cooperate if enough others do. People start out these games willing to give their fellow players the benefit of the doubt, but if cooperation rates are low, these conditional cooperators turn into free riders. However, cooperation can be maintained even in repeated games if players are given the opportunity to punish those who do not cooperate. As illustrated by the Punishment Game, described earlier, people are willing to spend some of their own money to teach a lesson to those who behave unfairly, and this willingness to punish disciplines potential free riders and keeps robust cooperation rates stable.

———

A few years after my time with Danny in Vancouver, I wrote an article about cooperation with the psychologist Robyn Dawes. In the conclusion, we drew an analogy with the roadside stands one would often see in the rural areas around Ithaca. A farmer would put some produce for sale out on a table in front of his farm. There was a box with a small slot to insert the payment, so money could be put in but not taken out. The box was also nailed to the table. I thought then, and think now, that farmers who use this system have a pretty good model of human nature in mind. There are enough honest people out there (especially in a small town) to make it worthwhile for the farmer to put out some fresh corn or rhubarb to sell. But they also know that if the money were left in an open box where anyone could take all of it, someone eventually would.

Economists need to adopt as nuanced a view of human nature as the farmers. Not everyone will free ride all the time, but some people are ready to pick your pocket if you are not careful. I keep a photograph of one of those farm stands in my office for inspiration.

16

Mugs

At some point during the Vancouver year, the economist Alvin Roth, who was then deeply involved with experimental methods, organized a conference at the University of Pittsburgh. The goal was to present the first drafts of papers that would later be published in a small book called *Laboratory Experimentation in Economics: Six Points of View*. The contributors were major figures in the experimental economics community including Al, Vernon Smith, and Charlie Plott. Danny and I represented the new behavioral wing of the experimental economics community.

For Danny and me, the most interesting discussion was about my beloved endowment effect. Both Vernon and Charlie claimed we didn't have convincing empirical evidence for this phenomenon. The evidence I had presented was based on a paper written by Jack Knetsch along with an Australian collaborator, John Sinden. Their experiment was delightfully simple. Half the subjects were chosen at random to receive three dollars; the other half got lottery tickets. The winner of the lottery would receive her choice between $50 in cash and $70 in vouchers for use at the local bookstore. After some time passed during which the subjects completed some other task, each group was given a choice. Those who did not have a lottery ticket were told they could buy one for $3, while the others were told that they could sell their lottery tickets for $3.

Notice that both groups are being asked the same question: "Would you rather have the lottery ticket or three dollars?" According to economic theory, it should not make any difference whether subjects had originally received the money or the lottery ticket. If they value the ticket at more than $3 they should end up with one; if they value the ticket at less than $3 they should end up with the money. The results clearly rejected this prediction. Of those who began with a lottery ticket, 82% decided to keep it, whereas of those who started out with the money, only 38% wanted to buy the ticket. This means that people are more likely to keep what they start with than to trade it, even when the initial allocations were done at random. The result could not be any stronger or clearer.

Charlie and Vernon's critique came right from the list of complaints discussed in chapter 6, "The Gauntlet." First, they thought that subjects might have been confused; they would have preferred an experiment in which the subjects had an opportunity to learn. Second, they invoked a version of the invisible handwave to argue that the misbehaving observed in the Knetsch and Sinden experiment would disappear if the subjects were making choices in a market context, meaning buyers and sellers trading and prices fluctuating. Danny and I returned to Vancouver with a mission: design an experiment that would convince Plott and Smith that the endowment effect was real.

Naturally, since Jack had conducted the original experiment and was part of our fairness team, we joined forces with him on the new design. The discussion with Charlie and Vernon also led us to recognize that the endowment effect, if true, will reduce the volume of trade in a market. Those who start out with some object will tend to keep it, while those who don't have such an object won't be that keen to buy one. We wanted to come up with a design that could exploit this prediction.

The basic idea was to build on Jack's original study and add a market. To make the case airtight, we wanted to show that the results were not an unintended consequence of the particular methods we employed. We decided to use one of Smith's favorite experimental devices—induced value—to our advantage. As was mentioned in chapter 5, Vernon had used this methodology in many of his pioneering early experiments demonstrating how well markets can work. Recall that when using this method, subjects buy and sell tokens that are worthless outside the laboratory. They are each told their own personal value for a token, a value that is redeemable at the end of the experiment if the subject has a token. Seth is told that if he ends up with a token at the end of the experiment, he can sell it back to the experimenter for (say) $2.25, while Kevin is told that he can get $3.75 for a token. We used this method because we did not expect anyone to have an endowment effect for a token any more than they would have an endowment effect for a particular twenty-dollar bill.

Figure 7 illustrates how this market is supposed to work. Suppose we have twelve subjects and we have assigned induced vales to them at random, varying from 25 cents to $5.75. We then line up these subjects, with the subject given the highest induced value on the left and the one with the lowest value on the right, as shown in panel A. We then hand out six tokens at random to these subjects, as is illustrated in panel B. We now conduct a market by asking subjects to answer a series of simple questions. Those who own a token would get a form such as this one:

| At a price of 6.00 | I will sell _____ | I will not sell _____ |
| At a price of 5.50 | I will sell _____ | I will not sell _____ |

The lowest price at which a seller is willing to part with their token is called their *reservation price*. Someone with a valuation of $4.25 would be willing to sell at a price of $4.50 but not at $4, so her reservation price would be $4.50. Potential buyers would receive a similar form asking about their willingness to buy a token over the same range of prices. What does economic theory predict will happen? If the market works well, the six subjects who value the tokens the most, the ones on the left, will end up owning the tokens. In this example, that means that subjects 7, 8, and 11 will buy tokens from subjects 2, 5, and 6, as illustrated in panel C.

We can figure out the price that will make this market "clear," meaning equate supply and demand, by working from the two ends of the distribution toward the middle. Subject 11 will have no trouble finding a price at which Subject 2 will give up his token, so they are bound to make a deal. The same applies to Subjects 8 and 5. But to get Subject 7 to buy a token from Subject 6, the price will have to be between their two reservation prices. Since we only allowed prices in increments of 50 cents, the market-clearing price will be $3.

FIGURE 7

A: Students are arranged in order of how much they value a token.
These values were assigned before the experiment.

Values tokens most   Values tokens least

$5.75 $5.25 $4.75 $4.25 $3.75 $3.25 $2.75 $2.25 $1.75 $1.25 $0.75 $0.25

B: Then we randomly distribute six tokens among the students.

$5.75 $5.25 $4.75 $4.25 $3.75 $3.25 $2.75 $2.25 $1.75 $1.25 $0.75 $0.25

C: Then we open the market for trading.
Here, it takes three trades to reach equilibrium.

Value tokens **most**   Value tokens **least**

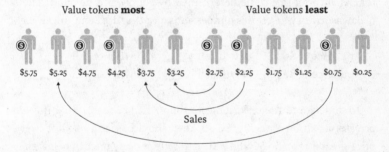

$5.75 $5.25 $4.75 $4.25 $3.75 $3.25 $2.75 $2.25 $1.75 $1.25 $0.75 $0.25

Sales

Since both the values and the tokens are being handed out at random, the particular outcome will differ each time, but on average the six people with the highest valuations will have been allocated half of the tokens, and as in this example, they will have to buy three tokens to make the market clear. In other words, the predicted volume of trading is half the number of tokens distributed.

Now suppose we repeat the experiment, but this time we do it with some good such as a chocolate bar. Again we could rank the subjects from high to low based on how much they like the chocolate bar, but in this case we are not telling the subjects how much they like the good; they are determining that themselves. Now we distribute the chocolate bars at random, just as in the token experiment, and ask the same series of questions. What should happen? The theory yields exactly the same prediction. On average, half of the chocolate bars will change hands, moving from those who don't care so much for chocolate (or are on a diet) to the chocoholics who can't wait to start munching on one of those bars. But if there is an endowment effect, the people who are randomly assigned chocolate bars will value them more than those who don't, and the volume of trade will be lower as a result. This is the prediction we wanted to test.

The first experiment with this design was run when I returned to Cornell in the fall of 1985. I commandeered an advanced undergraduate class in law and economics to run the experiment. In this case there were forty-four students, so there were twenty-two tokens handed out at random, and every subject was given his or her private value. Then, token owners were told that there would be a market for tokens with a price to be determined by supply and demand. Their task was to answer a series of questions, quoting different prices, e.g.:

At a price of $6.25   I will sell _____   I will not sell _____
At a price of $5.75   I will sell _____   I will not sell _____

To understand the task, subjects simply had to realize that if their private valuation was, say, $6.50, they should agree to sell at every price greater than $6.50 and refuse to sell for every price of below that amount. The lowest price at which they would be willing to sell is called the seller's "reservation price." Buyers also received private values and a similar form to fill out that yielded their reservation prices, i.e., the highest price at which they would be willing to buy. To be sure that everyone understood what was going on, we did this three times.

We then ran the markets right in front of the class while they watched. To do this, one simply uses the tools of supply and demand taught in any introductory economics class. Specifically, we took all the reservation prices of the sellers and ranked them from lowest to highest, and ranked the buyers' reservation prices from highest to lowest. If the highest bid by a buyer is greater than the lowest offer by a seller, then we have at least one sale. If the second highest bid by a buyer is greater than the second lowest offer by a seller, then we have two sales, and so forth until the highest bid is less than the lowest ask. All trades happen at the same price, namely the price at which the number of tokens demanded is equal to the number supplied.

Recall that we predict about eleven trades—matching half of the twenty-two buyers with half of the twenty-two sellers—will occur. In the three trials the actual number of trades was twelve, eleven, and ten, so the market was working fine and the subjects demonstrably understood what they were being asked to do.

We were now ready for the experiment that mattered, where we would use real goods instead of the tokens. In preparation for the experiment, I went over to the campus bookstore to see what products I could buy to use in the study. I wanted something that the students might want and was not too expensive, since we had to buy twenty-two of each item. Eventually I settled on two objects: a coffee mug with the Cornell insignia and a nice ballpoint pen that came in a box. The mugs cost $6 each, and the pens were $3.98 each. In the case of the pens, the price tag was left on the box.

We began by putting a coffee mug in front of every other student. The students who got a mug were owners and potential sellers; the others were potential buyers. Everyone was told to inspect the mug, either their own or their neighbor's, to ensure they all had equal information about the products. Then we conducted exactly the same market that we had used for the tokens. To allow for learning, one of Plott and Smith's requirements, we said that we would do this four times and pick one of the trials at random to "count." As with the tokens, economic theory predicts that the number of trades will be about eleven, but we were predicting significantly fewer trades because of the endowment effect.

Our prediction was right. On the four successive markets, the number of trades were four, one, two, and two respectively: not even close to eleven. The reason was apparent. Those who got the mugs were reluctant to sell them; the median reservation price for sellers was $5.25 in each of the four rounds. But those who did not have a mug were not eager to buy one; the median reservation price for buyers was $2.75 in one round and $2.25 in the others.

We repeated the experiment with the pens. The students who did not get a mug got a pen, so everyone had a chance to be a buyer and a seller. The students were not wild about these pens, but the results were about the same. The number of trades varied between four and five, and the ratio of selling to buying prices was again in the neighborhood of 2:1.

We ran numerous versions of these experiments to answer the complaints of various critics and journal referees, but the results always came out the same. Buyers were willing to pay about half of what sellers would demand, even with markets and learning. Again we see that losses are roughly twice as painful as gains are pleasurable, a finding that has been replicated numerous times over the years.

––––––––––––

The endowment effect experiments show that people have a tendency to stick with what they have, at least in part because of loss aversion. Once I have that mug, I think of it as mine. Giving it up would be a loss. And the endowment effect can kick in very fast. In our experiments, the subjects had "owned" that mug for a few minutes before the trading started. Danny liked to call this the "instant endowment effect." And while loss aversion is certainly part of the explanation for our findings, there is a related phenomenon: inertia. In physics, an object in a state of rest stays that way, unless something happens. People act the same way: they stick with what they have unless there is some good reason to switch, or perhaps despite there being a good reason to switch. Economists William Samuelson and Richard Zeckhauser have dubbed this behavior "status quo bias."

Loss aversion and status quo bias will often work together as forces that inhibit change. Think of people who lose their jobs because a plant or a mine closes down, and in order to find work, they would have to both take up another line of work and give up the friends, family, and home to which they have become attached. Helping people get back to work can often be met with inertia. We will return to this concept later in the context of public policy. For now, let me just offer an amusing example of status quo bias.

In the years since our mugs paper was published in 1990, there have been dozens, perhaps hundreds of follow-up studies, some critical of our findings, others exploring what psychologists call the boundary conditions of the phenomenon, meaning the limits on when it will be observed and when it will not. There is one thing that nearly all these studies have in common: coffee mugs. Thousands of university insignia coffee mugs have been purchased and given away by economists and psychologists, all because at the Cornell bookstore one day, a coffee mug caught my eye. Someone that makes mugs with university insignias owes me dinner.

————

Near the end of my year in Vancouver, Danny made an offhand comment that was, as usual, wise. We were gossiping about some academic we both knew and Danny said: "You know, at some point people reach an age at which they can no longer be considered 'promising.' I think it is about the time they turn forty." I am sure that Danny did not know my exact age, but I was thirty-nine. By the time classes resumed and I returned to Cornell, I would be forty. Damn. I had kind of enjoyed being "promising."

V.

ENGAGING WITH THE
ECONOMICS PROFESSION:
1986–94

By the time I returned to Cornell from my year in Vancouver, I had been working full time on my risky behavioral economics endeavor for eight years. And either despite or because of this endeavor, depending on whom you ask, I had managed to get tenure at Cornell and had several papers in the pipeline to be published in top journals. I was finding the project that had once looked very much like a fool's errand as much fun as ever, and it kept a roof over my family's head. The biggest problem was that, aside from our engagement with the experimental economics community, Amos, Danny, and I were mostly talking to one another. That state of affairs was about to change.

17

The Debate Begins

Behavioral economics got its first major public hearing shortly after I returned to Cornell from Vancouver. In October 1985, two University of Chicago Graduate School of Business professors—Robin Hogarth, a psychologist, and Mel Reder, an economist—organized a conference at the University of Chicago, home of many ardent defenders of the traditional way of doing economics. Rationalists and behavioralists were to come together and try to sort out whether there was really any reason to take psychology and behavioral economics seriously. If anyone had been laying odds on who would win this debate, the home team would have been considered the strong favorite.

The behavioral team was led by Herb Simon, Amos, and Danny, and was buttressed by Kenneth Arrow, an economic theorist who, like Paul Samuelson, deserved to win several Nobel Prizes in economics, though he had to settle for just one. The younger behavioral crowd, which included Bob Shiller, Richard Zeckhauser, and me, were given speaking roles as discussants.

The rationalists' team was formidable, with Chicago locals serving as team captains: Robert Lucas and Merton Miller. Eugene Fama and my thesis advisor, Sherwin Rosen, were given the roles of panel moderators, but were clearly part of the Chicago-based rationalists' side. The two-day meeting was held in a large auditorium, and every seat was taken. Thinking back on it, this conference was a highly unusual event. I don't think I have ever been to another one quite like it.

Amos presented a new paper that he and Danny had written for the occasion. It offered some violations of economic principles that economists found especially disconcerting. One was their now famous Asian disease problem, which goes as follows:

Two groups of subjects are told that 600 people are sick from some Asian disease, and a choice has to be made between two policies. The choices offered to the first group are:

Policy A will save 200 people for sure.

Policy B offers a one-third chance to save everyone but a two-thirds chance that all 600 patients will die.

When presented with this choice, most people take the safe option A.

In the alternative version, the subjects are again given two choices:

If they go with option C, 400 will die for sure.

If they choose option D, there is a one-third chance of killing no one and a two-thirds chance of killing everyone.

In this case, a majority preferred the risky option D.

Offhand, there does not appear to be anything remarkable about these choices, but a little arithmetic reveals that policy A is the same as C, and policy B is the same as D, so it is not logical for respondents to prefer A over B but D over C. And yet they did, and the same results were obtained with a similar problem posed to a group of physicians. Results like this clearly made the rational camp uncomfortable. Econs would certainly not misbehave so blatantly.

Danny then presented some of our work on fairness, including our Ultimatum and Dictator Game experiments. These findings were not any more popular. The economists thought that fairness was a silly concept mostly used by children who don't get their way, and the skeptics just brushed aside our survey data. The Ultimatum Game experiments were a bit more troubling, since actual money was at stake, but of course it wasn't all that much money, and all the usual excuses could be raised.

The talk that gave me the most to think about, and the one I have gone back to read again most often, was by Kenneth Arrow. Arrow's mind goes at light speed, and his talks tend to be highly layered fugues, with digressions inserted into digressions, sometimes accompanied by verbal footnotes to obscure scholars from previous centuries, followed by a sudden jump up two or three levels in the outline that he has in his head. While you work to digest a profound nugget disguised as a throwaway line, he has leapt back to the main argument and you are left scrambling to catch up. On this occasion, however, his talk can be summarized easily: rationality (meaning optimization) is neither necessary nor sufficient to do good economic theory.

Arrow began by dumping on the idea that rationality is necessary. "Let me dismiss a point of view that is perhaps not always articulated but seems implicit in many writings. It seems to be asserted that a theory of the economy must be based on rationality, as a matter of principle. Otherwise there can be no theory." Arrow noted that there could be many rigorous, formal theories based on behavior that economists would not be willing to call rational. As an example, he noted that the standard theory of the consumer states that when prices change, the consumer will solve the new optimization problem and choose a new "best" set of goods and services that still satisfies the budget constraint. Yet, he noted, one could easily build a theory based on habits. When prices change, the consumer chooses the affordable bundle that is closest to what she was consuming before. Arrow could have gone even further. For example, we could have rigorous theories as bizarre as "choose the bundle with brand names in order to maximize the occurrences of the letter K." In other words, formal models need not be rational; they don't even have to be sensible. So we should not defend the rationality assumption on the basis that there are no alternatives.

As for whether rationality alone is "sufficient"—meaning that by itself, it alone can deliver important predictions—Arrow argued convincingly that rationality alone does not get you very much. To derive useful results, theorists have to add auxiliary assumptions, such as assuming that everyone has the same utility function, meaning the same tastes. This assumption is not only demonstrably false, but it immediately leads to all kinds of predictions that are inconsistent with the facts. We are not Econs and we are certainly not *identical* Econs.

Arrow also noted an inconsistency inherent in the behavior of an economic theorist who toils for months to derive the optimal solution to some complex economic problem, and then blithely assumes that the agents in his model behave as if they are capable of solving the same problem. "We have the curious situation that scientific analysis imputes scientific behavior to its subjects." At the end of the talk, Arrow declared his allegiance: "Obviously I am accepting the insight of Herbert Simon on the importance of recognizing that rationality is bounded."

But my role in this conference was not just listening to academics I admired; I was given the intimidating task of acting as the discussant for a set of three papers authored respectively by Herbert Simon, Danny Kahneman with Amos Tversky, and Hillel Einhorn with Robin Hogarth (the conference organizer). In this situation, I largely agreed with what the authors had said, so I was not sure what to do. Discussants are expected to critique and elaborate. For me to just say, "Yeah, what he said," would not serve me well. The papers that I thought had real conceptual problems were slated for sessions yet to come. I also had to keep in mind that I was at the "kids' table"; there were two Nobel laureates on the program (Arrow and Simon), several others in the audience, and half a dozen more that were to win prizes later. How could I make my points to such a big-league crowd without seeming presumptuous?

I ended up deciding that my best strategy was to employ some humor. This can be risky, but I have found that if people are laughing, they tend to be more forgiving. I based my discussion on an obscure essay by George Stigler, one of the wittiest economists of his generation, and as a Chicago faculty member, he was sitting in the rationalists' cheering section of the audience. Stigler's essay was called the "The Conference Handbook," and it, in turn, was based on an ancient joke:

> A new prisoner arrives at a jail where everyone else has been locked up for a long time. He notices that occasionally someone shouts out a number, and everyone else laughs. He asks his cellmate what is going on and is told that they have been in jail so long together that they have all heard all the jokes that anyone knows, so to save time they have numbered the jokes. After hearing a few more numbers followed by howls of laughter, he decides to try it himself and shouts out "Thirty-nine!" No one laughs. He asks his cellmate why no one laughed and was told, "Well, some people just can't tell a joke."

Stigler's essay proposed to apply the joke numbering system at conferences and departmental seminars where the same tiresome comments are repeated again and again. Stigler offered several introductory remarks, indicated by letters, followed by thirty-two specific comments that he suggested could be referenced by number. I quoted his introductory comment F, figuring we might hear a version of it soon: "It is good to have a non-specialist looking at our problem. There is always a chance of a fresh viewpoint, although usually, as in this case, the advantages of the division of labor are reaffirmed."

In this spirit, I offered what I called the "Psychology and Economics Conference Handbook." My idea was to list the tiresome comments I had been hearing anytime I gave a talk, those described in chapter 6 on the Gauntlet, along with suggested retorts. I figured that announcing them in advance might preempt some of the participants from hauling them out later. You can guess by now some of the comments: 1. If the stakes are high enough, people will get it right. 2. In the real world, people will learn and avoid these mistakes. 3. In aggregate, the errors will cancel . . . And so forth. For each one, I explained why the comment was not as devastating as the person delivering it might have thought.

I then concluded:

> I will end my remarks with the following two false statements.
>
>   *1. Rational models are useless.*
>
>   *2. All behavior is rational.*
>
> I have offered these false statements because both sides in the debate that will be taking place at this conference and at similar conferences in the future have a tendency to misstate the other side's views. If everyone would agree that these statements are false, then no one would have to waste any time repudiating them.

People seemed to like the discussion. I even got a thumbs-up from Stigler as I was leaving the podium. The rest of the first day of the conference was reasonably calm.

The morning of the second day began with the announcement that Franco Modigliani had won the Nobel Prize in economics, in part for work that he had done jointly with Merton Miller, one of the primary speakers scheduled for the second day. Modigliani was then at MIT, but he had earlier been a colleague of Herb Simon's at Carnegie Mellon, and at Simon's urging the conference sent Modigliani a congratulatory telegram. That morning, Miller could not be blamed if he was thinking that this good news for his mentor and collaborator was bad news for him. Modigliani won the prize alone, and Miller might have felt that he had missed his chance. It turned out that he would win a Nobel Prize five years later, but he had no way of knowing that at the time. Nor did he know that morning, in this pre-Internet era, that the prize had been awarded primarily for Modigliani's work on saving and consumption—the life-cycle hypothesis— rather than for his work with Miller on corporate finance.

In the morning festivities surrounding the news, Miller spoke briefly about Modigliani's research. The press had asked him to summarize the work he had done with Modigliani, and, with his usual sharp wit, he said they had shown that if you take a ten-dollar bill from one pocket and put it into a different pocket, your wealth does not change. This line got a big laugh, to which Miller replied: "Don't laugh. We proved it rigorously!"

The joke was meant to refer to their so-called "irrelevance theorem," which proved that, under certain assumptions, it would not matter whether a firm chose to pay a dividend or instead use that money to repurchase their own shares or reduce their debts. The idea is that investors should care neither where money is stashed nor how it is paid out. But the joke actually applied equally well to the life-cycle hypothesis, since in that theory the only determinant of a household's consumption is its wealth, not the manner in which that wealth is held, say in cash, retirement savings, or home equity. Both theories take as a working hypothesis that money is fungible. We have already seen that in the case of the life-cycle hypothesis, this assumption is wrong. It turns out, all jokes aside, the assumption was equally questionable in corporate finance, which was the topic of Miller's talk that afternoon.

Miller's paper had been provoked by a behavioral finance paper by Hersh Shefrin, my self-control collaborator, and Meir Statman, a colleague of Shefrin's at Santa Clara University. In particular, they were offering a behavioral explanation for an embarrassing fact. One of the key assumptions in the Miller–Modigliani irrelevance theorem was the absence of taxes. Paying dividends would no longer be irrelevant if dividends were taxed differently than the other ways firms return money to their shareholders. And given the tax code in the United States at that time, firms should not have been paying dividends. The embarrassing fact was that most large firms *did* pay dividends.

The way taxes come into play is that income, including dividend income, was then taxed at rates as high as 50% or more, whereas capital gains were taxed at a rate of 25%. Furthermore, this latter tax was only paid when the capital gain was realized, that is, when the stock was sold. The effect of these tax rules was that shareholders would much rather get capital gains than dividends, at least if the shareholders were Econs. Importantly, a firm could easily transform a dividend into a capital gain by using the funds that would go to paying dividends to repurchase shares in the firm. Instead of receiving a dividend, shareholders would see the price of their shares go up, and would save money on their tax bill. So the puzzle was: why did firms punish their tax-paying shareholders by paying dividends? (Those who pay no taxes, such as endowments or those saving in a tax-free account, would be indifferent between the two policies.)

Shefrin and Statman's answer relied on a combination of self-control and mental accounting. The notion was that some shareholders—retirees, for instance—like the idea of getting inflows that are mentally categorized as "income" so that they don't feel bad spending that money to live on. In a rational world, this makes no sense. A retired Econ could buy shares in companies that do not pay dividends, sell off a portion of his stock holdings periodically, and live off of those proceeds while paying less in taxes. But there is a long-standing notion that it is prudent to spend the income and leave the principal alone, and this idea was particularly prevalent in the generation of retirees around in 1985, all of whom had lived through the Great Depression.[*]

---

[*] For a long time foundations and endowments operated in the same way, which was to leave the principal alone and spend the "income," tending to push them to hold bonds and stocks that paid large dividends. Gradually this practice was recognized as silly, and these organizations adopted a more sensible rule, such as to spend a given percentage (say 5%) of a three-year moving average of the value of the endowment, allowing them to choose investments based on their long-term

It is fair to say that Merton Miller was not a fan of the Shefrin and Statman paper. In his talk, he did not disguise this disdain, saying that the behavioral approach might have applied to his own Aunt Minnie and a few others like her, but that that was as far as it went.

The written version of Miller's paper was less strident than his presentation, but was nevertheless quite odd. Most of the paper was devoted to a lucid tutorial on the very puzzle that Shefrin and Statman were trying to explain, rather than a critique of their hypothesis. In fact, I know of no clearer explanation for why, in a land of Econs, firms would not pay dividends under the tax regime then in place. Miller agreed that firms should not pay dividends, but most did so. He also agreed that the model that best described how firms decided how much to pay out in dividends was the one proposed by the financial economist John Lintner, a model Miller labeled "behavioral." In Lintner's model, firms only increase dividends when they are confident that earnings have gone up enough such that dividends will not have to be cut in the future. (Had the model been written later, Lintner might have used loss aversion to help explain why firms are so reluctant to cut dividends.) Lintner had arrived at this model after using the unfashionable strategy of interviewing the chief financial officers of many large companies. About this model Miller said: "I assume it to be a behavioral model, not only from its form, but because no one has yet been able to derive it as the solution to a maximization problem, despite thirty years of trying!"

So let's summarize Miller's paper. *Theory tells us that firms should not pay dividends and yet they do. And a behavioral model admittedly best describes the pattern by which they pay them.* This sounds like a paper written by someone who has come to praise behavioral finance, not bury it. But Miller was neither ready to praise nor to concede. He wrote: "The purpose of this paper has been to show that the rationality-based market equilibrium models in finance in general and of dividends

---

potential rather than their cash payouts. This change in policy allowed endowments to invest in new asset classes such as venture capital funds, which often do not pay any returns for many years.

in particular are alive and well—or at least in no worse shape than other comparable models in economics at their level of aggregation." So, the strongest statement Miller could muster was to say that the standard rational model of financial markets—the efficient market hypothesis, to which we will turn in the next section, on finance—was not quite dead.

Not only did Miller concede that the best model of how firms pay dividends is behavioral, but he was also happy to grant the same about how individual investors behave. He said: "Behind each holding may be a story of family business, family quarrels, legacies received, divorce settlements, and a host of other considerations almost totally irrelevant to our theories of portfolio selection. That we abstract from all these stories in building our models is not because the stories are uninteresting, but because they may be too interesting and thereby distract us from the pervasive market forces that should be our principal concern." Take a moment to absorb that: we should ignore the reasons why people do things, not because they are uninteresting, but because they are *too* interesting. I, for one, had trouble keeping track of which side of the case Miller was arguing.

Miller's talk came in the afternoon session of the last day, chaired by Eugene Fama, another Chicago faculty member and a strong defender of the rational point of view. The other speaker during that session was Allan Kleidon, who like Miller was not so much presenting new research of his own, but rather attacking a paper by Robert Shiller that we will discuss in detail in chapter 24. Shiller was given the role of discussant, along with two efficient market defenders, Richard Roll and Steve Ross. Shefrin and Statman could only heckle from the audience. Clearly, during this part of the program the deck was stacked. Chalk it up to home field advantage.

Shiller was thrust into the unusual role of discussing a paper that critiqued his own work without having the chance to present his original research in any detail. Yet his remarks were, as usual for him, calm and well reasoned. He noted that both Miller and Kleidon had referred to Thomas Kuhn's model of scientific revolutions, in which paradigms change only once a significant number of empirical anomalies are accepted as valid violations of the received wisdom. The papers by Kleidon and Miller amounted to a declaration that the revolution was, thankfully, not yet upon us. Here is the beginning of Shiller's reply: "Maybe something as dramatic as a scientific revolution is in store for us. That does not mean, however, that the revolution would lead to 'the abandonment of assumptions of rational expectations in favor of mass psychology.'" Instead, he explained: "I tend to view the study of behavioral extensions of these efficient market models as leading in a sense to the enhancement of the efficient market models. I could teach the efficient market models to my students with much more relish if I could describe them as extreme special cases before moving to the more realistic models." Well said and still true.

As usual after such meetings, or after debates between political candidates, both sides were confident that they had won. The debate between behavioral finance researchers and defenders of the efficient market hypothesis was just beginning, and has been continuing for the last thirty years, but in some ways it all began that afternoon in Chicago. We will see where that debate has taken us in the next section of the book.

18

Anomalies

An important aspect of Thomas Kuhn's model of scientific revolutions, which came up at the end of the Chicago conference, is that paradigms change only once experts believe there are a large number of anomalies that are not explained by the current paradigm. A few scattered unexplained facts are not enough to upend the conventional wisdom. That conference was not the first time that the links between Kuhn's ideas and what I was trying to do had crossed my mind. It was a topic I had thought about, but only on the sly. As someone who had until recently still been in the "promising" stage of his career, it would be viewed as brash, unseemly, and self-destructive to talk about my own work as something that could be part of a "revolution." My goal was much more modest: just get a few more papers published and begin to establish the case that adding some psychology to economics was an activity worth pursuing. But I had certainly read Kuhn's path-breaking book *The Structure of Scientific Revolutions*, and had secretly spent idle moments wondering whether anything like a paradigm shift could ever be possible in economics.

A paradigm shift is one of the rare cataclysmic events in science when people make a substantial break with the way the field has been progressing and pursue a new direction. The Copernican revolution, which placed the sun at the center of the solar system, is perhaps the most famous example. It replaced Ptolemaic thinking, in which all the objects in our solar system revolved around the Earth. Given that the planets do not revolve around the Earth, it now seems odd to think that anyone could have made a geocentric model work at all. But for centuries astronomers using the geocentric system had in fact managed to do a pretty good job of explaining the movements of the planets, albeit with numerous somewhat ad hoc modifications of the basic model that were called epicycles: mini-circles around a main circular path along which the planets were thought to be rotating around the Earth.

At the Chicago conference, the speakers who were defending the status quo usually mentioned the idea of a paradigm shift with evident horror, with the gist of their remarks being that there was no reason to think we were standing on the precipice of a revolution. Of course, that they kept invoking it suggested there was at least some reason for concern among traditionalists. Their defense was usually to pick apart any given result and explain why it was not as critical as it seemed. If necessary, defenders of the traditional paradigm could always find some economics version of an epicycle with which to rationalize an otherwise embarrassing fact. And each single anomaly could be dismissed as a one-off puzzle, for which a satisfactory explanation was sure to exist if one looked hard enough. To create a real paradigm shift, I felt that we would require a whole series of anomalies, each calling for its own ad hoc explanation. At exactly the right time and place in my life, an opportunity to compile and document such a list of anomalies fell into my lap, and I had the good sense to seize the chance.

———

Sometime after returning to Ithaca from my year in Vancouver, I was at a conference sitting next to the economist Hal Varian, then a well-known theorist who later went on to become the chief economist at Google. Hal was telling me about a new journal that the American Economic Association was starting called the *Journal of Economic Perspectives*. Hal was an advisory editor. The editorial board was thinking about commissioning regular features for the journal. The clever Barry Nalebuff would write one on economics-based brainteasers and puzzles. Hal and I came up with an idea for a feature that I might write on anomalies. The editor of the journal, Joseph Stiglitz, who enjoys stirring the pot, was easily convinced, and the concept was approved. Four times a year I had a platform to write about anomalies. These could be documentation that supposedly irrelevant factors actually matter, or any other set of facts that were inconsistent with the standard way of doing economic theory.

I quoted Thomas Kuhn in the opening passage of the first install-
ment of the series, which appeared in the first issue of the journal,
published in 1987.

> *"Discovery commences with the awareness of anomaly, i.e., with
> the recognition that nature has somehow violated the paradigm-
> induced expectations that govern normal science."*
> —Thomas Kuhn

WHY A FEATURE ON ANOMALIES?

*Consider the following problem. You are presented with four cards
lying on the table before you. The cards appear as shown:*

FIGURE 8

*Your task is to turn over as few cards as possible to verify whether
the following statement is true:* Every card with a vowel on one side
has an even number on the other side. *You must decide in advance
which cards you will examine. Try it yourself before reading further.*

*When I give this problem to my class, the typical ranking of the cards
in terms of most to least often turned over is A, 2, 3, B. It is not surprising
that nearly everyone correctly decides to turn over the A. Obviously, if
that card does not have an even number on the other side the statement
is false. However, the second most popular choice (the 2) is futile. While
the existence of a vowel on the other side will yield an observation consistent with the hypothesis, turning the card over will neither prove the
statement correct nor refute it.*

*Rather, to refute the statement, one must choose to turn over the 3,
a far less common choice. As for the least popular choice, the B, that one
must be flipped over as well, since a vowel might be lurking on the other
side. (The problem, as stated here, did not specify that numbers are always*

on one side and letters on the other— although that implicit assumption is commonly made by solvers.) Two lessons emerge from this problem (based on Wason, 1968). First, people have a natural tendency to search for confirming rather than disconfirming evidence, as shown by the relative popularity of the 2 over the 3. This tendency is called the confirmation bias. Second, the confirmation bias can be accentuated when unwarranted assumptions make some kinds of disconfirming evidence seem unlikely, as illustrated by the unpopularity of turning over the B.

This feature will report successful searches for disconfirming evidence— economic anomalies. As suggested by Thomas Kuhn, an economic anomaly is a result inconsistent with the present economics paradigm. Economics is distinguished from other social sciences by the belief that most (all?) behavior can be explained by assuming that agents have stable, well-defined preferences and make rational choices consistent with those preferences in markets that (eventually) clear. An empirical result is anomalous if it is difficult to "rationalize," or if implausible assumptions are necessary to explain it within the paradigm. Of course, "difficult" and "implausible" are judgments, and others might disagree with my assessment. Therefore, I invite readers to submit brief explanations (within the paradigm or otherwise) for any of the anomalies I report. To be considered for publication, however, proposed explanations must be falsifiable, at least in principle. A reader who claims that an alleged anomaly is actually the rational response to taxes should be willing to make some prediction based on that hypothesis; for example, the anomaly will not be observed in a country with no taxes, or for non-taxed agents, or in time periods before the relevant tax existed. Someone offering an explanation based on transaction costs might suggest an experimental test in which the transaction costs could be eliminated, and should be willing to predict that the effect will disappear in that environment.

I wrote a column in every issue, that is, quarterly, for nearly four years. The articles were about ten to twelve published pages, short enough to make them a quick read, but long enough to give a fair amount of detail. Each article ended with a "Commentary" section in which I tried to explain the significance of the findings.

I can't say that I had a grand plan when I started writing these columns. I made a list of topics, and off the top of my head I knew I could write at least ten, so the question was what to write about first and how to get the right tone. Having recently written two papers about what makes people angry, I was fully aware that this enterprise could backfire. It was also incredibly time-consuming. Many of the topics were well outside my field of expertise, so in those cases I recruited a coauthor who was a specialist in the field. But I still had to do a lot of boning up on new topics, since I ended up writing the final versions of all of them. That meant that these columns were taking time away from what most academics would consider to be "real research," meaning discovering new facts, developing new theories, and publishing papers in refereed journals.[*]

The potential payoff, however, was huge. The AEA at one point conducted a survey of its members to see what they thought of the new journal. They asked members whether they read it and specifically whether they read the features. Half the members of the AEA who responded to the survey reported that they read the "Anomalies" feature "regularly," whatever that means. To put this in perspective, the average article written in a specialized academic journal is probably lucky to find 100 readers. These anomalies articles were reaching over 5,000 economists. When recruiting coauthors, I could truthfully tell them that more people were likely to read this article than anything else they would ever write. The same was true for me, of course. I had eyeballs. What should I put in front of them?

My goal was to cover a broad spectrum of anomalies and to find examples that relied on a wide variety of empirical methods, includ-

---

[*] One of the joys of writing the Anomalies columns was that the editors themselves handled the refereeing process, and every paper also received true "editing" to make it intelligible for non-specialists. Tim Taylor, an economist who can also write, has ably performed that task from the beginning, and he is still at it. At most academic journals the editors make sure the economics is right and a copyeditor checks for typos and style, but no one is making suggestions on how to make the article more readable. Early on Tim caught on to the power of defaults. He would rewrite every article, send his new draft along, and then tell authors they were free to opt out of any of his suggestions. By the way, the *Journal of Economic Perspectives* is available free online to anyone at www.aeaweb.org/jep, including all the back issues. It is a great place to learn about economics.

ing many that used market data, to help dispense with the myth that anomalies only occur in the laboratory. Of the fourteen columns I wrote in those first four years, only five were primarily based on experimental data. The others were far-ranging, though many were related to finance, for the simple reason that those were both the most surprising and most disturbing to the defenders of the standard paradigm.

I should note that I did not have satisfactory behavioral explanations for every anomaly. Some were just empirical facts that did not line up with theoretical predictions. For example, the first two columns were about "calendar" effects in the stock market. These results are just weird. Consider just a sample of them: Stocks tend to go up on Fridays and down on Mondays. January is a good month in which to hold stocks, particularly the early part of the month, and especially for the shares of small companies. Finally, the days before holidays, often Fridays, are particularly good. A burst of papers had documented these results. All logical, and some illogical, explanations for these effects could be rejected. I had no explanation either, but they were certainly anomalies.

Another anomaly came from bettors at the racetrack. Racetracks in the United States and in many other parts of the world (excluding Britain) use what are called pari-mutuel betting systems, where the odds are determined by the amount of money bet on each horse, rather than a fixed amount set in advance. In the simplest case of bets to win, the track first removes its predetermined share of the betting pool, typically around 17%, and then those who bet on the winning horse divide the rest of the money. The horse that the crowd thinks has the best chance to win is called the favorite, while the horses with small chances to win, say with odds greater than 10 to 1, are called longshots.

If the track takes 17% of the bets and the betting market is efficient, then all bets should have the same expected return, namely minus 17%. If you bet $100, you expect to get back $83 on average, from the odds-on favorite to the longest of longshots. But that is not what the data show. The return in betting on favorites is much better than betting on longshots. For example, a bet made on an even-money favorite will return 90 cents for each dollar bet, but a bet on a 100-to-1 longshot only returns about 14 cents on the dollar. And, remember from our earlier discussion of gambling and the breakeven effect (chapter 10), the return in betting on longshots is even worse on the last race of the day.

After writing fourteen columns in consecutive issues, I took a break. These columns were lightly edited and published in book form with the title *The Winner's Curse* (the title of one of the columns). I then wrote a few more on an occasional basis, though without the quarterly deadline, their appearances becoming increasingly irregular. The last appeared in 2006. Shortly thereafter, the column was officially retired. The editor of the journal at that time, Andrei Shleifer, declared that their purpose had been served. That was a polite way of saying that my job chronicling anomalies had ended. I was fired.

Forming a Team

The "Anomalies" columns served the purpose of showing the economics profession that there were lots of facts that did not line up with the traditional models. They helped establish the case for adopting a new way of doing economics based on Humans rather than Econs. But economics is a big discipline, and I was one lazy man. To create a new field would require a team. How could I do anything to encourage others to join the fun? There was no field manual available to consult on how to make that happen.

Of course, new fields emerge all the time, and they usually do so without any coordination. Someone writes a paper on a new topic that opens up new lines of inquiry, such as game theory in the 1940s. Soon others read about it, think that the topic seems interesting, and decide to try to make a contribution of their own. If things go well, enough people are soon doing research in the area to start having conferences on the topic, and eventually a journal dedicated to the subject matter emerges. But this is a slow process, and I was yearning for people to talk to besides Amos and Danny. In the late 1980s, there were really just three people besides me who thought of themselves as behavioral economists. One was George Loewenstein, whose work was mentioned in the section on self-control. Another was Robert Shiller, who appeared above and plays a starring role in the next section, and the third was Colin Camerer.

I first met Colin when he was on the academic job market. At that point he had picked up an MBA and was nearly done with a PhD from the University of Chicago, and he had not yet turned twenty-one. Colin has made many important contributions to behavioral economics. Two stand out. First, he more or less invented the field of behavioral game theory, the study of how people actually play games, as opposed to standard game theory, which studies how Econs would play games if they knew that everyone else playing was also an Econ. More recently, he has been at the forefront of neuro-economics, which uses techniques such as brain imaging to learn more about how people make decisions.

Colin has many talents. While still a teenager in grad school, he formed a record company and signed the famously satirical punk band called the Dead Milkmen. One of their "hits" was "Watching Scotty Die." Colin is also a skilled mimic. His Gene Fama and Charlie Plott are particularly good. Personally, I think his Thaler is only so-so.

Although the additions of Camerer, Loewenstein, and Shiller to the field were all important milestones, I knew that behavioral economics as an academic enterprise would flounder unless it could acquire a critical mass of researchers with a variety of research skills. Fortunately, there was someone else who had the same goal, and could also contribute some resources. That man was Eric Wanner.

———————

Eric Wanner was a program officer at the Alfred P. Sloan Foundation when he took an interest in combining psychology and economics. Eric is a psychologist by training, but I think he is an economist by predilection, and he relished the chance to see if these two fields could somehow find common ground. He sought out the advice of Amos and Danny about how he could help make this happen. Danny, who prides himself on being a pessimist, remembers telling Eric that he "could not see any way to honestly spend much money on this endeavor," but they both suggested to Eric that he talk to me. After Eric and I met at the Sloan Foundation in New York, Eric convinced the foundation to provide the funding to support my year in Vancouver visiting Danny.

Soon after I returned to Cornell, Eric left Sloan to become the president of the Russell Sage Foundation, also located in New York. Although behavioral economics was not at the core of the stated mission of the foundation—which is to address important social policy issues such as poverty and immigration—the board was sufficiently anxious to hire Eric that they agreed to let him bring his behavioral economics agenda along with him. Naturally, he had no more idea of how to go about nurturing a new field than I did, but we put our heads together and tried to figure it out on the fly.

Our first idea seemed like a good one at the time. Since the goal was to combine economics and psychology, we decided to organize occasional meetings of psychologists and economists and hope that sparks would fly. We invited three groups of people: distinguished psychologists who were willing to endure a day spent talking to economists, some senior economists who were known to have an open mind about new approaches to doing economics, and the few hardcore folks who were engaged in doing research.

Eric is a persuasive guy, and as a result of his charm and armtwisting, the collection of psychologists who showed up at our initial meeting was truly astonishing. We had not just Amos and Danny, but also Walter Mischel, of the Oreo and marshmallow experiment fame, Leon Festinger, who formulated the idea of cognitive dissonance, and Stanley Schachter, one of the pioneers of the study of emotions. Together they were the psychology version of the dream team. Some of the friendly economists who agreed to participate were also an all-star cast: George Akerlof, William Baumol, Tom Schelling, and Richard Zeckhauser. The hard-core group was Colin, George, Bob, and me. Eric also invited Larry Summers to come to the inaugural meeting, but Larry couldn't come and suggested inviting one of his recent students, Andrei Shleifer. It was at that meeting that I first met the rambunctious Andrei, who would later become my collaborator. Jon Elster, the eclectic Norwegian philosopher who seems to be knowledgeable in nearly every intellectual domain, rounded out the group.

Given the amazing lineup, the couple meetings we had did not turn out to be very productive. I have two vivid memories. One is of Leon Festinger making wry wisecracks, interrupted only by his frequent trips to the foundation's patio for a smoking break. The other was a plea from William Baumol for us to move beyond the discovery of anomalies. He thought that our anomaly-mining, as he called the activity, had served its purpose, but that we now had to move on to a more constructive agenda. But he had no suggestion about what that constructive agenda should be.

I think the real problem we faced was a general one that I have learned with experience. Interdisciplinary meetings, especially those with high-level agendas (reduce poverty, solve climate change) tend to be disappointing, even when the attendees are luminaries, because academics don't like to talk about research in the abstract—they want to see actual scientific results. But if scientists from one field start presenting their research findings in the manner that the colleagues in their field expect, the scientists from other disciplines are soon overwhelmed by technical details they do not understand, or bored by theoretical exercises they find pointless.*

Whether or not my gloomy assessment of interdisciplinary conferences is correct, the presence and enthusiastic participation of the collection of all-star psychologists at these meetings, held at the Russell Sage Foundation's office in New York, were both encouraging and misleading regarding the future of the field—encouraging because such luminaries were taking the time to come and seemed to think that the mission was both worthy and sensible, but misleading because they reinforced the belief we all held at the time, which was that if there were to be a successful field called behavioral economics, it would have to be a truly interdisciplinary effort with psychologists and economists working together. It was natural for Amos, Danny, and me to think that, because we had learned so much from one another and had begun to produce actual joint research.

That turned out to be a poor forecast. Although there are a handful of psychologists who have formed successful collaborations with economists over the years, Drazen Prelec and Eldar Shafir being notable examples, behavioral economics has turned out to be primarily a field in which economists read the work of psychologists and then go about their business of doing research independently.† One of our

---

* There are some exceptions to this generalization, such as neuroscience, where scientists from many different fields have productively worked together, but in that case they coalesced around specific tools like brain scans. I don't want to say that all interdisciplinary meetings are a waste of time. I am just saying that in my experience, they have been disappointing.

† To be clear, the field of judgment and decision-making that was kick-started by Kahneman and Tversky in the 1970s continues to thrive. Their annual meeting,

early participants, Stanley Schachter, is a case in point. He tried his hand at doing some research on the psychology of the stock market, but grew frustrated with the reactions he got from the referees at mainstream finance and economics journals and eventually abandoned the research program.

There are several possible reasons why psychologists might have failed to engage. First, since few have any attachment to the rational choice model, studying departures from it is not considered inherently interesting. A typical reaction would be: "Of course people pay attention to sunk costs! Who would have thought otherwise?" Second, the psychology that behavioral economists have ended up using is not considered cutting-edge to psychologists. If psychologists started using supply and demand curves in their research papers, economists would not find the idea very exciting. Finally, for some reason the study of "applied" problems in psychology has traditionally been considered a low-status activity. Studying the reasons why people fall into debt or drop out of school has just not been the type of research that leads academic psychologists to fame and glory, with the notable exception of Robert Cialdini.

Furthermore, we behavioral economists have not been particularly successful in generating new psychology of our own, which might breed the kind of cross-fertilization that we originally expected. Most of the advances in the field have been to figure out how best to modify the tools of economics to accommodate Humans as well as Econs, rather than discovering new insights about behavior. Of the emerging group of economists that have become the leaders of the field, only George Loewenstein has really created much new psychology. Although trained as an economist, George is really a talented psychologist as well, a fact that might be partially attributed to

---

sponsored by the Society for Judgment and Decision Making, attracts over 500 scholars whose work often intersects with behavioral economics. There are also a number of notable behavioral scholars in marketing, including my old friend Eric Johnson, several of my former students, and many others who do research on topics such as mental accounting and self-control. My point is that a typical meeting of behavioral economists does not include any psychologists, and I am one of the few economists who regularly attends the SJDM meeting.

good genes. His middle initial F stands for Freud; Sigmund was his great-grandfather.

———————

Although this effort to get economists and psychologists working together did not succeed, Eric Wanner remained committed to helping foster the field, even if it consisted almost entirely of economists. The Russell Sage Foundation's small size meant that it could not be the primary source of research funding if the field were to grow beyond a few hard-core members, so Eric convinced the board to continue to support the field in a limited and highly unusual way. And unlike the initial effort, it has been a huge success.

Here is the plan Eric devised. In 1992, the foundation formed a group of researchers called the Behavioral Economics Roundtable, gave them a modest budget, and tasked them with the goal of fostering growth in the field. The initial members of the Roundtable were George Akerlof, Alan Blinder, Colin Camerer, Jon Elster, Danny Kahneman, George Loewenstein, Tom Schelling, Bob Shiller, Amos Tversky, and I, and within reason, we could spend the money we were given any way we wanted.

The Roundtable members decided that the most useful way to spend our limited budget (which began at $100,000 per year) was to foster and encourage the entry of young scholars into the field. To do this, we organized two-week intensive training programs for graduate students to be held during the summer. No university was then teaching a graduate course in behavioral economics, so this program would be a way for students from all over the world to learn about the field. These two-week programs were officially called the Russell Sage Foundation Summer Institutes in Behavioral Economics, but from the beginning everyone referred to them as the Russell Sage summer camps.

The first summer camp was held in Berkeley in the summer of 1994. Colin, Danny, and I were the organizers, with several other Roundtable members joining for a few days as faculty members. We also had some guest stars, such as Ken Arrow, Lee Ross (a social psychologist), and Charlie Plott. In the spirit of encouraging young scholars to join the field, we also invited two economists who had received their degrees quite recently to participate: Ernst Fehr and Matthew

Rabin. Both had independently decided to take up careers in behavioral economics.

Ernst Fehr is the most aptly named economist I know. If you had to think of a single adjective to describe him it would be "earnest," and the topic that has interested him most is fairness. An Austrian by birth, Ernst has become a central figure in the behavioral economics movement in Europe, with a base at the University of Zürich in Switzerland. Like Colin, he has also become a prominent practitioner of neuro-economics.

The first paper by Fehr that captured our attention was experimental. He and his coauthors showed that in a laboratory setting, "firms" that elected to pay more than the minimum wage were rewarded with higher effort levels by their "workers." This result supported the idea, initially proposed by George Akerlof, that employment contracts could be viewed partially as a gift exchange. The theory is that if the employer treats the worker well, in terms of pay and working conditions, that gift will be reciprocated with higher effort levels and lower turnover, thus making the payment of above-market wages economically profitable.

In contrast, Matthew Rabin's first behavioral paper was theoretical, and was at that time the most important theory paper in behavioral economics since "Prospect Theory." His paper was the first serious attempt to develop a theory that could explain the apparently contradictory behavior observed in situations like the Ultimatum and Dictator Games. The contradiction is that people appear altruistic in the Dictator Game, giving away money to an anonymous stranger, but also seem to be mean to others who treat them unfairly in the Ultimatum Game. So, does increasing the happiness of someone else make us happier too, or does it make us less happy, perhaps because of envy? The answer, Rabin suggested, hinges on reciprocity. We are nice to people who treat us nicely and mean to people who treat us badly. The finding discussed earlier, that people act as "conditional cooperators," is consistent with Rabin's model.

Matthew is also a character. His normal attire is a tie-dyed T-shirt, of which he seems to have an infinite supply. He is also very funny. I was one of the referees who were asked to review his fairness paper when he submitted it for publication in the *American Economic Review*.

I wrote an enthusiastic review supporting publication, but added, without providing any details, that I was disturbed that he had left out an important footnote that had appeared in an earlier draft. The footnote referred to the game economists refer to as "chicken," in which the first person to concede to the other loses. Here was his footnote, which was restored in the published version: "While I will stick to the conventional name for this game, I note that it is extremely speciesist—there is little evidence that chickens are less brave than humans and other animals."

So we had an all-star faculty lined up for our summer camp, plus the up-and-coming young guys, Fehr and Rabin. But having never done this before, we did not know whether anyone would apply. We sent an announcement to the chairs of the leading economics departments around the world and hoped someone would want to come. Fortunately, over 100 students applied, and the group of thirty that we picked was packed with the future stars of the field.

These summer camps have continued in alternate years ever since. After Danny and I grew too busy/tired/old/lazy to organize and participate in the entire two-week program, it was taken over by younger generations. For a while Colin and George organized it, and David Laibson and Matthew Rabin have run the last several camps.

One indicator of the success of these summer camps is that David was a student at the first one, so the group is becoming self-generating. Many of the other faculty members who participate now are also camp graduates. I should be clear that we make no claims about turning these young scholars into stars. For example, David Laibson had already graduated from MIT and taken a job at Harvard before he arrived at our summer camp. Others were also clearly stars in the making. Instead, the primary accomplishment of the summer camps was to increase the likelihood that some of the best young graduate students in the world would seriously consider the idea of becoming behavioral economists, and then to provide them with a network of like-minded economists they could talk to.

The talent level of the campers that first year is evidenced by the number who have gone on to fame. One was Sendhil Mullainathan, who had just completed his first year of graduate work at Harvard. I had gotten to know Sendhil when he was an undergraduate at Cornell, completing degrees in economics, mathematics, and computer science in three years. It was not hard to see that he had the talent to do almost anything, and I tried my best to interest him in psychology and economics. Luckily for the field, my pitch worked, and it was his budding interest in behavioral economics that tipped him from computer science to economics for his graduate training. Among his other accomplishments, Sendhil founded the first behavioral economics nonprofit think tank, called ideas42. He, Matthew, and Colin have received a so-called "genius" award from the MacArthur Foundation.

Other notable first-year campers were Terry Odean, who essentially invented the field of individual investor behavior, Chip Heath, who with his brother Dan has published three successful management books, and two of my future coauthors, who will soon make their appearances in this book: Linda Babcock and Christine Jolls.

In the summer of 2014 we held our tenth summer camp, and I have yet to miss one. There are now about 300 graduates, many holding positions at top universities around the world. It is largely the research produced by those summer camp graduates that has turned behavioral economics from a quirky cult activity to a vibrant part of mainstream economics. They all can thank Eric Wanner for helping them get started. He is the behavioral economics' founding funder.

20

Narrow Framing on the Upper East Side

The contributions of the Russell Sage Foundation to behavioral economics were not limited to the creation of the Roundtable. The foundation also has a wonderful program for visiting scholars, who spend a year in New York living in a subsidized apartment near the foundation's office on the Upper East Side. A scholar's only responsibility is to show up for a tasty—and dare I say it, free—lunch. The rest of your time is available to spend thinking and writing. For the academic year 1991–92 Colin Camerer, Danny, and I had applied as a team, and Danny's wife, Anne Treisman, also a psychologist, also joined as a visiting scholar. As a bonus, Amos made periodic visits, so we were poised to have a great year. Danny and I hoped to somehow recreate the magic we had experienced earlier at Stanford and Vancouver. But the stars were not aligned.

It did not help that I was going through a divorce, and an enormous fire burned Anne and Danny's Berkeley home to the ground. But those were only two of the distractions we had to overcome. Over the six years since we had been in Vancouver, we had both become too busy to ignore everything else and work intensively on a joint project. We had PhD students who needed attention, Danny and Anne had a lab full of graduate students back in Berkeley, and we all had colleagues at our home universities who wanted us to weigh in on various departmental dramas. Our days of being able to work on one thing, seven days a week, for months at a time, had ended.

But there was an idea in the air that we were both thinking about independently, and this idea also played a role in the project I worked on with Colin. The idea is called "narrow framing," and it is related to a more general mental accounting question: when are economic events or transactions combined, and when are they treated separately? If you go on a vacation, is each component of the cost of the trip (travel, hotel, meals, outings, gifts) considered a separate trans-action, or are they pooled into the vacation category and evaluated together, as they would be in an all-inclusive cruise trip? The specific question that Danny and I were each pondering is: when do people get themselves into trouble by treating events one at a time, rather than as a portfolio?

Danny's work on this problem arose in a project with Dan Lovallo, a graduate student at Berkeley who joined us that year as our research assistant. Their idea was that managerial decision-making was driven by two countervailing, but not necessarily offsetting, biases: bold forecasts and timid choices. The bold forecasts come from Danny's distinction between the "inside view" and the "outside view."

To convey the distinction, Danny tells the story of a book project. The full story is described in detail in *Thinking, Fast and Slow*, but for those who have shamefully failed to memorize that book, here is the short version. A team of scholars with different backgrounds was tasked with the job of devising a curriculum on decision-making for middle school students. After working on the project for several months, Danny started to wonder how long it might take to complete. He took a poll of the various team members, having each write down their guess separately to get a set of independent guesses. The estimates for time to completion ranged from eighteen to thirty months. Then Danny realized that one member of the team was an expert in curriculum development, and had observed many such teams in action over the years. So Danny asked this expert to evaluate their team compared to the others he had seen, and based on his experience to say how much longer the project would take. The expert, whose own guess had been among those in the range between eighteen and thirty months, became a bit sheepish. He reluctantly told the group that in his experience, no group had fin-ished a similar task in less than seven years, and worse, 40% of the teams never finished!

The difference between the expert's two estimates illustrates Dan-ny's distinction between the inside and outside views. When the expert was thinking about the problem as a member of the project team, he was locked in the inside view—caught up in the optimism that comes with group endeavors—and did not bother thinking about what psychologists call "base rates," that is, the average time for similar projects. When he put on his expert hat, thereby taking the outside view, he naturally thought of all the other projects he'd known and made a more accurate guess. If the outside view is fleshed out carefully and informed with appropriate baseline data, it will be far more reliable than the inside view.

The problem is that the inside view is so natural and accessible that it can influence the judgments even of people who understand the concept—indeed, even of the person who coined the term. After learning of Amos's illness and short life expectancy, Amos and Danny decided to edit a book that contained a collection of papers on decision-making, but Amos passed away before the book was completed. Danny had the daunting task of writing an introduction that they had intended to write together. Amos died in June 1996, and I remember talking to Danny that fall about the book and when he thought it would be done. He said it shouldn't take more than six months. I started laughing. Danny got the joke and said sheepishly, "Oh, you are thinking of *that* book [meaning the one featured in his story about the inside view]. *This* book is completely different. It is just a collection of papers, most of them already published. I just have to get a few stragglers to finish their new papers and complete the introduction." The book came out, shortly after the last paper arrived and the introduction was finished, in 2000, almost four years later.

The "timid choices" part of the Kahneman and Lovallo story is based on loss aversion. Each manager is loss averse regarding any outcomes that will be attributed to him. In an organizational setting, the natural feeling of loss aversion can be exacerbated by the system of rewards and punishment. In many companies, creating a large gain will lead to modest rewards, while creating an equal-sized loss will get you fired. Under those terms, even a manager who starts out risk neutral, willing to take any bet that will make money on average, will become highly risk averse. Rather than solving a problem, the organizational structure is making things worse.

Here's an example to show how this works. Sometime shortly after our year in New York, I was teaching a class on decision-making to a group of executives from a company in the print media industry. The company owned a bunch of publications, primarily magazines, and each executive in the audience was the head of one of the publications, which were run pretty much independently. The CEO of the firm was also in attendance, sitting in the back of the room, watching and listening. I put to the executives this scenario: Suppose you were offered an investment opportunity for your division that will yield one of two payoffs. After the investment is made, there is a 50% chance it will make a profit of $2 million, and a 50% chance it will lose $1 million. (Notice that the expected payoff of this investment is $500,000, since half the time they gain $2 million—an expected gain of $1 million—and half the time they lose a million—an expected loss of half a million. The company was large enough that a million-dollar loss, or even several of them, would not threaten its solvency.) I then asked by a show of hands who would take on this project. Of the twenty-three executives, only three said they would do it.

Then I asked the CEO a question. If these projects were "independent"—that is, the success of one was unrelated to the success of another—how many of the projects would you want to undertake? His answer: all of them! By taking on the twenty-three projects, the firm expects to make $11.5 million (since each one is worth an expected half million), and a bit of mathematics reveals that the chance of losing any money overall is less than 5%. He considered undertaking a collection of projects like this a no-brainer.

"Well, that means *you* have a problem," I responded to the CEO. "Because you are not going to get twenty-three of these projects—you are only getting three. You must be doing something wrong, either by hiring wimpy managers who are unwilling to bear risks, or, more likely, by creating an incentive system in which taking this sort of a risk is not rewarded." The CEO smiled knowingly but stayed silent, waiting to see what the other participants would say. I turned to one of the managers who had said he would not undertake the project and asked him why not. He said that if the project was a success, he would probably get a pat on the back and possibly a bonus, say three months' income. But if the project failed, he thought there would be a decent chance he would be fired. He liked his job and didn't want to risk it on a coin flip in which he only stood to gain three months' income.

Narrow framing prevents the CEO from getting the twenty-three projects he would like, and instead getting only three. When broadly considering the twenty-three projects as a portfolio, it is clear that the firm would find the collection of investments highly attractive, but when narrowly considering them one at a time, managers will be reluctant to bear the risk. The firm ends up taking on too little risk. One solution to this problem is to aggregate investments into a pool where they can be considered as a package.

The value of this sort of aggregation was brought home to me on a brief consulting job with a large pharmaceutical company. Like all major drug companies, this one spent over a billion dollars a year on research and development, investigating thousands of new compounds in the hope of finding the next blockbuster drug. But blockbuster drugs are rare. Even for a large firm, finding one every two or three years would be considered good, and with so many drugs being investigated, any one of them has expected returns that look a lot like a lottery ticket—there is a very small chance of a very large prize. You might think a company that lays out billions on investments that offer very small chances of an occasional windfall has figured out how to think about risk, but you would be wrong, because they had only figured this out with respect to research and development.

The project I happened to be working on was related to marketing and pricing, not research and development. An employee came up with a proposal to run experiments investigating different ways that certain drugs might be priced, with one of the goals being to improve "compliance," which is medical parlance for taking the medicine that your doctor has prescribed. For some drugs, especially those that do not relieve pain or have other obvious beneficial effects for the user, many patients stop taking their medicine. In certain cases, such as taking the recommended drugs after having a heart attack, the benefits are demonstrably large. Any improvement to compliance offered the chance for a true win-win. Patients would be healthier, medical spending would fall, and the drug company would make more money since it would sell more pills. In spite of this potential upside, we were told that running the trials to attempt to communicate directly with consumers that we had devised would be too risky. This was wrong-headed thinking. Of course the idea might not pan out—that is why you run experiments.* But the cost of the experiment was tiny, compared to the size of the company. It just looked risky compared to the particular manager's budget. In this example, narrow framing prevented innovation and experimentation, two essential ingredients in the long-term success of any organization.

Both this example of the risk-averse manager and the story of the CEO who would have liked to take on twenty-three risky projects, but would only get three, illustrate an important point about principal–agent problems. In the economics literature, such failures are usually described in a way that implicitly puts the "blame" on the agent for taking decisions that fail to maximize the firm, and acting in their own self-interest instead. They are said to make poor decisions because they are maximizing their *own* welfare rather than that of the organization. Although this depiction is often apt, in many cases the real culprit is the boss, not the worker.

In order to get managers to be willing to take risks, it is necessary to create an environment in which those managers will be rewarded for decisions that were value-maximizing *ex ante*, that is, with information available at the time they were made, even if they turn out to lose money *ex post*. Implementing such a policy is made difficult by hindsight bias. Whenever there is a time lapse between the times when a decision is made and when the results come in, the boss may have trouble remembering that he originally thought it was a good idea too. The bottom line is that in many situations in which agents are making poor choices, the person who is misbehaving is often the principal, not the agent. The misbehavior is in failing to create an environment in which employees feel that they can take good risks and not be punished if the risks fail to pay off. I call these situations

---

* A recent experiment shows that behavioral interventions can work in this domain, although it uses technology that did not exist at this time. Simply texting patients to remind them to take their prescribed medications (in this study, for lowering blood pressure or cholesterol levels) reduced the number of patients who forgot or otherwise failed to take their medications from 25% to 9% (Wald et al., 2014).

"dumb principal" problems. We will discuss a specific example of such a case a bit later in the context of sports decision-making.

————————

The previous stories illustrate Danny's take on narrow framing. My own project on this topic was with a PhD student who had arrived recently at Cornell to study finance, Shlomo Benartzi. Shlomo would turn out to be an important solution to my laziness problem. Shlomo is high-energy and impossible to discourage. He also mastered the fine art of "bugging me," as we came to define it. Often I would say to Shlomi, as everyone calls him, "I am just too busy, I can't think about this right now." Shlomi: "Okay, when do you think you can get to it?" Me: "Oh, maybe two months from now, not before." Two months to the day later, Shlomi would call. Are we ready to work? Of course Shlomi had figured out that I was taking the inside view in thinking that I would have more time in just two months, but he would call nonetheless, and eventually I would get around to working on his current project. As a result of his "bugging," as well as a fountain of interesting ideas, I have written more papers with him than anyone else.

Shlomo and I were interested in an anomaly called the *equity premium puzzle*. The puzzle was first announced, and given the name, by Raj Mehra and Edward Prescott in a 1985 paper. Prescott was a surprising person to announce an anomaly. He was and remains a hard-core member of the conservative, rational expectations establishment. His work in this domain, called "real business cycles," would later win him a Nobel Prize. And unlike me, Prescott did not have declaring anomalies as part of his agenda. I suspect he found this one to be a bit embarrassing given his worldview, but he and Mehra knew they were on to something interesting.

The term "equity premium" is defined as the difference in returns between equities (stocks) and some risk-free asset such as short-term government bonds. The magnitude of the historical equity premium depends on the time period used and various other definitions, but for the period that Mehra and Prescott studied, 1889–1978, the equity premium was about 6% per year.

The fact that stocks earn higher rates of return than Treasury bills is not surprising. Any model in which investors are risk averse predicts it: because stocks are risky, investors will demand a premium over a risk-free asset in order to be induced to bear that risk. In many economics articles, the analysis would stop at that point. The theory predicts that one asset will earn higher returns than another because it is riskier, the authors find evidence confirming this prediction, and the result is scored as another win for economic theory.

What makes the analysis by Mehra and Prescott special is that they went beyond asking whether economic theory can explain the existence of an equity premium, and asked if economic theory can explain how large the premium actually is. It is one of the few tests I know of in economics where the authors make a statement about the permissible magnitude of some effect.* After crunching the numbers, Mehra and Prescott concluded that the largest value of the equity premium that they could predict from their model was 0.35%, nowhere near the historical 6%.† Investors would have to be implausibly risk averse to explain the historical returns. Their results were controversial, and it took them six years to get the paper published. However, once it was published, it attracted considerable attention and many economists rushed in to offer either excuses or explanations. But at the time Shlomo and I started thinking about the problem, none of the explanations had proven to be completely satisfactory, at least to Mehra and Prescott.

We decided to try to find a solution to the equity premium puzzle. To understand our approach, it will help to consider another classic article by Paul Samuelson, in which he describes a lunchtime conversation with a colleague at the MIT faculty club. Samuelson noted that he'd read somewhere that the definition of a coward is someone who refuses to take either side of a bet at 2-to-1 odds. Then he turned to

---

*   They were able to do this because, for technical reasons, the standard theory makes a prediction about the relation between the equity premium and the risk-free rate of return. It turns out that in the conventional economics world, when the real (inflation-adjusted) interest rate on risk-free assets is low, the equity premium cannot be very large. And in the time period they studied, the real rate of return on Treasury bills was less than 1%.

†   That might not look like a big difference, but it is huge. It takes seventy years for a portfolio to double if it's growing at 1% per year, and fifty-two years if it's growing at 1.35%, but only ten years if it's growing at 7%.

one of his colleagues, an economic historian named E. Carey Brown, and said, "Like you, Carey."

To prove his point, Samuelson offered Brown a bet. Flip a coin, heads you win $200, tails you lose $100. As Samuelson had anticipated, Brown declined this bet, saying: "I won't bet because I would feel the $100 loss more than the $200 gain." In other words, Brown was saying: "I am loss averse." But then Brown said something that surprised Samuelson. He said that he did not like one bet, but would be happy to take 100 such bets.

This set Samuelson thinking, and he soon came back with a proof that Brown's preferences were not consistent, and therefore not rational by economics standards. Specifically, he proved, with one proviso, that if someone is not willing to play one bet, then he should not agree to play multiple plays of that bet. The proviso is that his unwillingness to play a single bet is not sensitive to relatively small changes in his wealth, specifically any wealth level that could be obtained if he played out all of the bets. In this case, he could lose as much as $10,000 (if he loses all 100 bets) and win as much as $20,000 (if he wins every bet). If Brown had a substantial retirement nest egg he probably made or lost that amount of money frequently, so it was probably safe to assume that his answer to Samuelson's question would not change if he were suddenly $5,000 richer or poorer.*

Here is the logic of Samuelson's argument. Suppose Brown agrees to play the 100 bets, but after playing 99 of the bets, Samuelson offers him the chance to stop, thus making the last bet optional. What will Brown do? Well, we know that he does not like one bet, and we are in the range of wealth for which this applies, so he stops. Now, suppose that we do the same thing after 98 bets. We tell him that each of the last two bets is now optional. What will Brown do? As a trained economist, he will use backward induction, which just means starting at the end and working back. When he does, he will know that when he reaches the choice of taking the single bet number 100 he will turn it down, and realizes that this implies that bet 99 is also essentially a

---

* It is crucial to Samuelson's argument that he is using the traditional expected utility of wealth formulation. Mental accounting misbehavior such as the house money effect is not permitted in this setup because wealth is fungible.

single bet, which he again does not like, so he also says no to bet 99. But if you keep applying this logic sequentially, you get to the result that Brown will not take the first bet. Thus Samuelson's conclusion: If you don't like one bet, you shouldn't take many.

This result is quite striking. It does not seem unreasonable to turn down a wager where you have a 50% chance to lose $100, especially since $100 in the early 1960s was worth more than $750 now. Not many people are willing to risk losing that much money on a coin flip, even with a chance to win twice as much. Although the 100-bet combination seems quite attractive, Samuelson's logic is unassailable. As he restated it once in another of his short papers, this time consisting entirely of words with one syllable:* "If it does not pay to do an act once, it will not pay to do it twice, thrice, . . . or at all." What is going on here?

Samuelson did more than point out that his colleague had made a mistake. He offered a diagnosis teased at in the title of the paper: "Risk and Uncertainty: A Fallacy of Large Numbers." In Samuelson's view, the mistake Brown made was to accept the 100 plays of the gamble, and he thought Brown made this mistake because he misunderstood the statistical principle called the law of large numbers. The law of large numbers says that if you repeat some gamble enough times, the outcome will be quite close to the expected value. If you flip a coin 1,000 times, the number of heads you get will be pretty close to 500. So Brown was right to expect that if he played Samuelson's bet 100 times, he was unlikely to lose money. In fact, his chance of losing money is just 1 in 2300. The mistake Samuelson thought Brown was making was to ignore the possibility of losing a substantial amount. If you play the bet once you have a 50% chance of losing, but the most you can lose is $100. If you play it 100 times, your chance of losing is tiny, but there is some, admittedly infinitesimal, chance of losing $10,000 by flipping 100 tails in a row.

In our take on this betting scenario, Benartzi and I thought Sam-

---

* Well not quite entirely. Here is how he ends the paper. "No need to say more. I've made my point. And, save for the last word, have done so in prose of but one syllable." And truth be told, he slipped in the word "again" somewhere in the paper, no doubt by accident. I owe this reference, and the spotting of the "again," to the sharp-eyed Maya Bar-Hillel.

uelson was half right. He was right that his colleague had made a mistake. It is illogical, in Samuelson's setup, to refuse one bet but accept many. But where Samuelson criticized Brown for taking the many bets, we thought his mistake was to turn down the one. Narrow framing was responsible. Criticizing the acceptance of the 100-bet option is really misplaced. On average Brown expects to win $5,000 by accepting this parlay, and the chance of losing any money is tiny. The chance of losing a lot of money is even tinier. Specifically, the chance of losing more than $1,000 is about 1 in 62,000. As Matthew Rabin and I wrote in an "Anomalies" column on this topic: "A good lawyer could have you declared legally insane for turning down this gamble." But if it is crazy to turn down the 100 bets, the logic of Samuelson's argument is just reversed; you should *not* turn down one! Shlomo and I called this phenomenon "myopic loss aversion." The only way you can ever take 100 attractive bets is by first taking the first one, and it is only thinking about the bet in isolation that fools you into turning it down.

The same logic applies to investing in stocks and bonds. Recall that the equity premium puzzle asks why people would hold so many bonds if they expect the return on stocks to be 6% per year higher. Our answer was that they were taking too short-term a view of their investments. With a 6% edge in returns, over long periods of time such as twenty or thirty years, the chance of stocks doing worse than bonds is small, just like (though perhaps not as good odds as) the chance of losing money in Samuelson's original 100-bet game.

To test this hypothesis, Shlomo and I ran an experiment using recently hired non-faculty employees at the University of Southern California, which has a defined contribution retirement plan in which employees have to decide how to invest their retirement funds. In the United States these are often called 401(k) plans, a term that is derived from a provision in the tax code that made them legal. We told each subject to imagine that there were only two investment options in this retirement plan, a riskier one with higher expected returns and a safer one with lower expected returns. This was accompanied by charts showing the distribution of returns for both of the funds based on the returns for the past sixty-eight years. The riskier fund was based on the returns of an index of large U.S.

companies, while the safer fund was based on the returns of a portfolio of five-year government bonds. But we did not tell subjects this,
in order to avoid any preconceptions they might have about stocks
and bonds.

The focus of the experiment was on the way in which the returns
were displayed. In one version, the subjects were shown the distribution of annual rates of return; in another, they were shown the distribution of simulated average annual rates of return for a thirty-year
horizon (see figure 9). The first version captures the returns people
see if they look at their retirement statements once a year, while the
other represents the experience they might expect from a thirty-year
invest-and-forget-it strategy. Note that the data being used for the
two charts are exactly the same. This means that in a world of Econs,
the differences in the charts are SIFs and would have no effect on the
choices people make.

FIGURE 9

Distribution of one-year returns

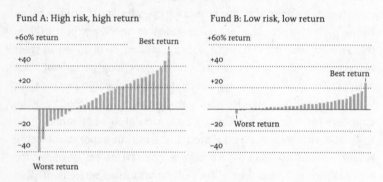

Distribution of average annual returns over 30 years

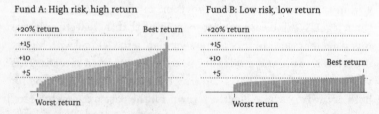

For our Human subjects, the presentation of the data had a huge effect. The employees shown the annual rates of return chose to put 40% of their hypothetical portfolio in stocks, while those who looked at the long-term averages elected to put 90% of their money into stocks. These results, and others, go against Samuelson's hypothesis about people overestimating the risk-reducing effect of repeated plays. When people see the actual data, they love the riskier portfolio.

An implication of this analysis is that the more often people look at their portfolios, the less willing they will be to take on risk, because if you look more often, you will see more losses. And in fact, that is an implication I later explored with Kahneman and Tversky. This would be the only paper that Amos, Danny, and I published together (along with Danny's then-student Alan Schwartz, now a professor of medical decision-making at the University of Illinois at Chicago). The paper was published in 1997 in a special issue of the *Quarterly Journal of Economics* dedicated to Amos's memory. We had to finish the writing of the paper without him.

The paper reports an experiment in which student subjects at Berkeley were given the job of investing the money of a portfolio manager for a university endowment. Of course, they were only pretending to be portfolio managers, but the amount of money they earned in the experiment did depend on how their investments turned out. Their earnings varied from $5 to $35 in less than an hour, so it was real enough for them. As in the previous experiment, the subjects had only two investment options, a riskier one with higher returns and a safer one with lower returns. In this case, what we varied was how often the subjects got to look at the results of their decisions. Some subjects saw their results eight times per simulated calendar year of results, while others only saw their results once a year or once every five years. As predicted by myopic loss aversion, those who saw their results more often were more cautious. Those who saw their results eight times a year only put 41% of their money into stocks, while those who saw the results just once a year invested 70% in stocks.

These experimental findings have recently been replicated in a natural experiment made possible by a regulatory change in Israel. A paper by Chicago Booth PhD student Maya Shaton investigates what happened in 2010 when the government agency that regulates retirement savings funds changed the way funds report their returns. Previously, when an investor checked on her investments, the first number that would appear for a given fund was the return for the most recent month. After the new regulation, investors were shown returns for the past year instead. As predicted by myopic loss aversion, after the change investors shifted more of their assets into stocks. They also traded less often, and were less prone to shifting money into funds with high recent returns. Altogether this was a highly sensible regulation.

These experiments demonstrate that looking at the returns on your portfolio more often can make you less willing to take risk. In our "myopic loss aversion" paper, Benartzi and I used prospect theory and mental accounting to try to explain the equity premium puzzle. We used historical data on stocks and bonds and asked how often investors would have to evaluate their portfolios to make them indifferent between stocks and bonds, or want to hold a portfolio that was a 50-50 mixture of the two assets. The answer we got was roughly one year. Of course investors will differ in the frequency with which they look at their portfolios, but once a year has a highly plausible ring. Individuals file tax returns once a year; similarly, while pensions and endowments make reports to their boards on a regular basis, the annual report is probably the most salient.

The implication of our analysis is that the equity premium—or the required rate of return on stocks—is so high because investors look at their portfolios too often. Whenever anyone asks me for investment advice, I tell them to buy a diversified portfolio heavily tilted toward stocks, especially if they are young, and then scrupulously avoid reading anything in the newspaper aside from the sports section. Crossword puzzles are acceptable, but watching cable financial news networks is strictly forbidden.[*]

---

[*] Of course, this is not to say that stocks always go up. We have seen quite recently that stocks can fall 50%. That is why I think the policy of decreasing the percentage of your portfolio in stocks as you get older makes sense. The target date funds used as default investment strategies in most retirement plans now follow this strategy.

During our year at Russell Sage, Colin and I would frequently take taxis together. Sometimes it was difficult to find an empty cab, especially on cold days or when a big convention was in town. We would occasionally talk to the drivers and ask them how they decided the number of hours to work each day.

Most drivers work for a company with a large fleet of cabs. They rent the cab for a period of twelve hours, usually from five to five, that is, 5 a.m. to 5 p.m., or 5 p.m. to 5 a.m.* The driver pays a flat amount to rent the cab and has to return it with the gas tank full. He keeps all the money he makes from the fares on the meter, plus tips. We started asking drivers, "How do you decide when to quit for the day? Twelve hours is a long time to drive in New York City traffic, especially while trying to keep an eye out for possible passengers. Some drivers told us they had adopted a target income strategy. They would set a goal for how much money they wanted to make after paying for the car and the fuel, and when they reached that goal they would call it a day.

The question of how hard to work was related to a project Colin, George Loewenstein, and I had been thinking about; we called it the "effort" project. We had discussed the idea for a while and had run a few lab experiments, but we had yet to find an angle we liked. We decided that studying the actual decision-making of cab drivers might be what we had been looking for.

All drivers kept a record of each fare on a sheet of paper called a trip sheet. The information recorded included the time of the pickup, the destination, and the fare. The sheet also included when the driver returned the car. Somehow, Colin managed to find the manager of a taxicab company who agreed to let us make copies of a pile of these trip sheets. We later supplemented this data set with two more we obtained from the New York City Taxi and Limousine commissioner. The data analysis became complicated so we recruited Linda Bab-

---

* The 5 p.m. turnover is particularly maddening since it occurs just as many people are leaving work. And with many of the fleets located in Queens, far from midtown Manhattan, drivers often start to head back to the garage at 4, turning their off-duty sign on. A recent study found that this results in 20% fewer cabs on the road between 4 and 5 p.m., when compared to an hour before. See Grynbaum (2011) for the full story.

cock, a labor economist and Russell Sage summer camp graduate
with good econometrics skills, to join us.

The central question that the paper asked is whether drivers
work longer on days when the effective wage is higher. The first
step was to show that high- and low-wage days occur, and that
earnings later in the day could be predicted by earnings during the
first part of the day. This is true. On busy days, drivers make more
per hour and can expect to make more if they work an additional
hour. Having established this, we looked at our central question
and got a result economists found shocking. The higher the wage,
the less drivers worked.

Basic economics tells us that demand curves slope down and supply curves slope up. That is, the higher the wage, the more labor that
is supplied. Here we were finding just the opposite result! It is important to clarify just what these results say and don't say. Like other
economists, we believed that if the wages of cab drivers doubled, more
people would want to drive cabs for a living. And even on a given
day, if there is a reason to think that a day will be busy, fewer drivers
will decide to take that day off and go to the beach. Even behavioral
economists believe that people buy less when the price goes up and
supply more when the wage rises. But in deciding how long to work
on a given day that they have decided to work, the drivers were falling into a trap of narrowly thinking about their earnings one day at a
time, and this led them to make the mistake of working less on good
days than bad ones.*

Well, not all drivers made this mistake. Driving a cab is a *Groundhog Day*–type learning experience, in which the same thing happens every day, and cab drivers appear to learn to overcome this bias
over time. We discovered that if we split each of our samples in half

---

* Recall the earlier discussion of Uber and surge pricing. If some of their drivers
behaved this way, it would limit the effectiveness of the surge in increasing the
supply of drivers. The key question, which is impossible to answer without access
to their data, is whether many drivers monitor the surge pricing when they are not
driving and hop in their cars when prices go up. If enough drivers respond this way,
that would offset any tendency for drivers to take off early after hitting the jackpot
on a 10x fare. Of course the surge may help divert cabs to places where demand is
higher, assuming the surge lasts long enough for the taxis to get there.

according to how long the subjects had been cab drivers, in every case the more experienced drivers behaved more sensibly. For the most part, they drove more when wages were higher, not lower. But of course, that makes the effect even stronger than average for the inexperienced drivers, who look very much like they have a target income level that they shoot for, and when they reach it, they head home.

To connect this with narrow framing, suppose that drivers keep track of their earnings at a monthly rather than a daily level. If they decided to drive the same amount each day, they would earn about 5% more than they do in our sample. And if they drove more on good days and less on bad days, they would earn 10% more over the same amount of hours. We suspected that, especially for inexperienced drivers, the daily income target acts as a self-control device. "Keep driving until you make your target or run up against the twelve-hour maximum" is an easy rule to follow, not to mention justify to yourself or a spouse waiting at home. Imagine instead having to explain that you quit early today because you didn't make very much money. That will be a long conversation, unless your spouse is an economist.

The cabs paper was also published in that special issue of the *Quarterly Journal of Economics* dedicated to the memory of Amos.

VI.

FINANCE:

1983–2003

Aside from the discussion of my work with Benartzi on the equity premium puzzle, I have left something out of the story so far: the investigation of behavioral phenomena in financial markets. This topic was, fittingly, a risky one to delve into, but one that offered the opportunity for high rewards. Nothing would help the cause of behavioral economics more than to show that behavioral biases matter in financial markets, where there are not only high stakes but also ample opportunities for professional traders to exploit the mistakes made by others. Any non-Econs (amateurs) or non-Econ behavior (even by experts) should theoretically have no chance of surviving. The consensus among economists, and especially among those who specialized in financial economics, was that evidence for misbehaving would be least likely to be found in financial markets. The very fact that financial markets were the least likely place to harbor behavioral anomalies meant that a victory there would make people take notice. Or, as my economist friend Tom Russell once told me, finance was like New York in Frank Sinatra's famous song: "If you can make it there, you can make it anywhere."

But the smart money was betting against us making it anywhere near New York, New York. We were likely to be stuck in Ithaca, New York.

21

The Beauty Contest

It is difficult to express how dubious people were about studying the behavioral economics of financial markets. It was one thing to claim that consumers did strange things, but financial markets were thought to be a place where foolish behavior would not move market prices an iota. Most economists hypothesized—and it was a good starting hypothesis—that *even if* some people made mistakes with their money, a few smart people could trade against them and "correct" prices—so there would be no effect on market prices. The efficient market hypothesis, mentioned in chapter 17 about the conference at the University of Chicago, was considered by the profession to have been proven to be true. In fact, when I first began to study the psychology of financial markets back in the early 1980s, Michael Jensen, my colleague at the Rochester business school, had recently written: "I believe there is no other proposition in economics which has more solid empirical evidence supporting it than the Efficient Market Hypothesis."

The term "efficient market hypothesis" was coined by University of Chicago economist Eugene Fama. Fama is a living legend not just among financial economists, but also at Malden Catholic High School near Boston, Massachusetts, where he was elected to their athletic hall of fame, one of his most prized accomplishments.* After graduating from nearby Tufts University with a major in French, Fama headed to the University of Chicago for graduate school, and he was such an obvious star that the school offered him a job on the faculty when he graduated (something highly unusual), and he never left. The Booth School of Business recently celebrated his fiftieth anniver-

---

* When asked which he was more proud of, the hall of fame designation or his Nobel Prize, Gene said the former, pointing out that it had fewer recipients.

sary as a faculty member. He and Merton Miller were the intellectual leaders of the finance group at Chicago until Miller died, and to this day Fama teaches the first course taken by finance PhD students, to make sure they get off to the right start.

The EMH has two components, which are somewhat related but are conceptually distinct.* One component is concerned with the rationality of prices; the other concerns whether it is possible to "beat the market." (I will get to how the two concepts are related a bit later.)

I call the first of these propositions "the price is right," a term I first heard used to describe the stock market by Cliff Smith, a colleague at the University of Rochester. Cliff could be heard bellowing from the classroom in his strong southern accent, "The price is riiiight!" Essentially, the idea is that any asset will sell for its true "intrinsic value." If the rational valuation of a company is $100 million, then its stock will trade such that the market cap of the firm is $100 million. This principle is thought to hold both for individual securities and for the overall market.

For years financial economists lived with a false sense of security that came from thinking that the price-is-right component of the EMH could not be directly tested—one reason it is called a hypothesis. Intrinsic value, they reasoned, is not observable. After all, who is to say what the rational or correct price of a share of General Electric, Apple, or the Dow Jones Industrial Average actually is? There's no better way to build confidence in a theory than to believe it is not testable. Fama tends not to emphasize this component of the theory, but in many ways it is the more important part of the EMH. If prices are "right," there can never be bubbles. If one could disprove this component of the theory, it would be big news.†

---

* One of my many finance tutors over the years has been Nicholas Barberis, who was a colleague of mine for a while at the University of Chicago and now teaches at Yale. My discussion here draws upon our survey of behavioral finance (Barberis and Thaler, 2003).

† Experimental economists have conducted numerous experiments in which bubbles are predictably created in the laboratory (Smith, Suchanek, and Williams, 1988; Camerer, 1989; Barner, Feri, and Plott, 2005), but financial economists put little credence in such demonstrations, in part because they do not offer the opportunity for professionals to intervene and correct the mispricing.

Most of the early academic research on the EMH stressed the second component of the theory, what I call the "no free lunch" principle—the idea that there is no way to beat the market. More specifically it says that, because all publicly available information is reflected in current stock prices, it is impossible to reliably predict future prices and make a profit.

The argument supporting this hypothesis is intuitively appealing. Suppose a stock is selling for $30 a share, and I know for certain that it will soon sell for $35 a share. It would then be easy for me to become fabulously wealthy by buying up shares at prices below $35 and later selling them when my prediction comes true. But, of course, if the information I am using to make this prediction is public, then I am unlikely to be the only one with this insight. As soon as the information becomes available, everyone who is in possession of this news will start buying up shares, and the price will almost instantaneously jump to $35, rendering the profit opportunity fleeting. This logic is compelling, and early tests of the theory appeared to confirm it. In some ways, Michael Jensen's PhD thesis provided the most convincing analysis. In it he showed that professional money managers perform no better than simple market averages, a fact that remains true today. If the pros can't beat the market, who can?

––––––––––

It is somewhat surprising that it was not until the 1970s that the efficient market hypothesis was formally proposed, given that it is based on the same principles of optimization and equilibrium that other fields of economics adopted much earlier. One possible explanation is that financial economics as a field was a bit slower to develop than other branches of economics.

Finance is now a highly respected branch of economics, and numerous Nobel Prizes have been awarded to economists whose primary work was in finance, including a recent prize in 2013.* But it

––––––––––

* The 2013 prize went to Gene Fama and Bob Shiller, whose debates you will read about in this chapter and in chapter 17, along with my fellow Chicago economist Lars Hansen, whose views lie somewhere in the large space between, or perhaps off to the side of, Fama and Shiller.

was not always so. Although some of the intellectual giants of the field, such as Kenneth Arrow, Paul Samuelson, and James Tobin, all made important contributions to financial economics in the 1950s and 1960s, finance was not a mainstream topic in economics departments, and before the 1970s, in business schools finance was something of an academic wasteland. Finance courses were often similar to accounting courses, where students learned the best methods to figure out which stocks were good investments. There was little in the way of theory, and even less rigorous empirical work.

Modern financial economics began with theorists such as Harry Markowitz, Merton Miller, and William Sharpe, but the field as an academic discipline took off because of two key developments: cheap computing power and great data. The data breakthrough occurred at the University of Chicago, where the business school got a grant of $300,000 to develop a database of stock prices going back to 1926. This launched the Center for Research in Security Prices, known as CRSP (pronounced "crisp").

CRSP released its first database in 1964, and research in the field immediately took off, with University of Chicago locals leading the way. Chief among these were Miller, Fama, and a group of exceptional graduate students including Michael Jensen, Richard Roll (a distinguished scholar and longtime professor at UCLA), and Myron Scholes, the co-inventor of the Black–Scholes option-pricing model. Research proceeded quickly. By 1970 the theory and evidence supporting the EMH was sufficiently well-established that Fama was able to publish a comprehensive review of the literature that stood for many years as the efficient market bible. And just eight years after Fama had established this foundation, Jensen would publish the sentence declaring the efficient market hypothesis to be proven. Ironically, the sentence appears in the preface to a special issue of the *Journal of Financial Economics* that was devoted to anomalies, that is, papers reporting purported departures from the efficient market hypothesis.

The confidence Jensen and others had in the EMH was perhaps based as much in the compelling logic of the idea as it was in the empirical data. When it came to financial markets, the invisible handwave was damn convincing, and no one was putting up much resistance. Furthermore, the 1970s was a period in which a similar revolution was taking place in macroeconomics. Models based on rational expectations were on the rise, and the popularity of Keynesian economics amongst academic economists was on the decline. Perhaps for this reason, Keynes's writings were no longer required reading by graduate students. This is unfortunate, because had he been alive, Keynes might have made the debate more even-handed. He was a true forerunner of behavioral finance.

Keynes is now remembered primarily for his contributions to macroeconomics and especially for his controversial argument that governments should use fiscal policy to stimulate demand during recessions or depressions. Regardless of your views about Keynesian macroeconomics, you would be foolish to dismiss his thoughts on financial markets. To me, the most insightful chapter of his most famous book, *The General Theory of Employment, Interest and Money*, is devoted to this subject. Keynes's observations were based in part on his considerable experience as an investor. For many years, he successfully managed the portfolio of his college at Cambridge, where he pioneered the idea of endowments investing in equities.

As we discussed earlier, many economists of his generation had pretty good intuitions about human behavior, but Keynes was particularly insightful on this front. He thought that emotions, or what he called "animal spirits," played an important role in individual decision-making, including investment decisions. Interestingly, Keynes thought markets were more "efficient," to use the modern word, in an earlier period at the beginning of the twentieth century when managers owned most of the shares in a company and knew what the company was worth. He believed that as shares became more widely dispersed, "the element of real knowledge in the valuation of investments by those who own them or contemplate purchasing them . . . seriously declined."

By the time he was writing the *General Theory* in the mid-1930s, Keynes had concluded that markets had gone a little crazy. "Day-to-day fluctuations in the profits of existing investments, which are obviously of an ephemeral and non-significant character, tend to have an altogether excessive, and even an absurd, influence on the market." To buttress his point, he noted the fact that shares of ice companies were higher in summer months when sales are higher. This fact is surprising because in an efficient market, stock prices reflect the long-run value of a company, a value that should not reflect the fact that is it warm in the summer and cold in the winter. A predictable seasonal pattern in stock prices like this is strictly verboten by the EMH.[*]

Keynes was also skeptical that professional money managers would serve the role of the "smart money" that EMH defenders rely upon to keep markets efficient. Rather, he thought that the pros were more likely to ride a wave of irrational exuberance than to fight it. One reason is that it is risky to be a contrarian. "Worldly wisdom teaches that it is better for reputation to fail conventionally than to succeed unconventionally." Instead, Keynes thought that professional money managers were playing an intricate guessing game. He likened picking the best stocks to a common competition in the male-dominated London financial scene in the 1930s: picking out the prettiest faces from a set of photographs:

> Professional investment may be likened to those newspaper competitions in which the competitors have to pick out the six prettiest faces from a hundred photographs, the prize being awarded to the competitor whose choice most nearly corresponds to the average preferences of the competitors as a whole: so that each competitor has to pick, not those faces which he himself finds prettiest, but those which he thinks likeliest to catch the fancy of the other competitors, all of whom are looking at the problem from the same point of view. It is not a case of choosing those which, to the best of one's judgment, are really the prettiest, nor even those which average opinion genuinely thinks the prettiest. We have reached the third degree where we devote our intelligences to anticipating what average opinion

---

[*]   Whether or not such a pattern in prices is verboten, a recent paper finds support for Keynes's story about the price of ice companies. Firms with seasonal businesses have higher prices when their earnings are higher (Chang et al., 2014).

expects the average opinion to be. And there are some, I believe, who practice the fourth, fifth, and higher degrees.

I believe that Keynes's beauty contest analogy remains an apt description of how financial markets work, as well as of the key role played by behavioral factors, though it may be a bit hard to get your head around. To understand the gist of his analogy, and appreciate its subtlety, try out this puzzle.

Guess a number from 0 to 100 with the goal of making your guess as close as possible to two-thirds of the average guess of all those participating in the contest.

To help you think about this puzzle, suppose there are three players who guessed 20, 30, and 40 respectively. The average guess would be 30, two-thirds of which is 20, so the person who guessed 20 would win.

Make a guess before continuing. Really, you should try it: the rest of this chapter will be more fun if you have tried the game yourself.

Is there anything you would have liked to ask before making your guess? If so, what would it be? We will return to it in a minute. Now, let's ponder how someone might think about how to play this game.

Consider what I will call a zero-level thinker. He says: "I don't know. This seems like a math problem and I don't like math problems, especially word problems. I guess I will pick a number at random." Lots of people guessing a number between 0 and 100 at random will produce an average guess of 50.

How about a first-level thinker? She says: "The rest of these players don't like to think much, they will probably pick a number at random, averaging 50, so I should guess 33, two-thirds of 50."

A second-level thinker will say something like: "Most players will be first-level thinkers and think that other players are a bit dim, so they will guess 33. Therefore I will guess 22."

A third level thinker: "Most players will discern how the game works and will figure that most people will guess 33. As a result they will guess 22, so I will guess 15."

Of course, there is no convenient place to get off this train of thinking. Do you want to change your guess?

Here is another question for you: What is the Nash equilibrium for this scenario? Named for John Nash, the subject of the popular book (and biopic) *A Beautiful Mind*, the Nash equilibrium in this game is a number that if everyone guessed it, no one would want to change their guess. And the only Nash equilibrium in this game is zero. To see why, suppose everyone guessed 3. Then the average guess would be 3 and you would want to guess two-thirds of that, or 2. But if everyone guessed 2 you would want to guess 1.33, and so forth. If and only if all participants guessed zero would no one want to change his or her guess.

Perhaps you have now formulated the question that might have been worth asking before submitting your guess: who are the other players, and how much math and game theory do they know? If you are playing at your local bar, especially late in the evening, other people are probably not thinking too deeply, so you might make a guess around 33. Only if you are at a conference of game theorists would you want to guess a number close to zero.

Now let's see how this game is related to Keynes's beauty contest. Formally, the setups are identical. In the guess-the-number game, you have to guess what other people are thinking that other people are thinking, just as in Keynes's game. In fact, in economics, the "number guessing game" is commonly referred to as the "beauty contest."

This delightful game was first studied experimentally by the German economist Rosemarie Nagel, who teaches at Pompeu Fabra University in Barcelona. Thanks to the *Financial Times* newspaper, in 1997 I had the opportunity to replicate her findings in a large-scale experiment. The *FT* had asked me to write a short article about behavioral finance, and I wanted to use the guess-the-number game to illustrate Keynes's beauty contest. Then I had an idea: could they run the game as a contest a few weeks before my article appeared? That way I could present fresh data from *FT* readers along with my article. The *FT* agreed, and British Airways offered up two business-class tickets from London to the U.S. as the prize. Based on what you know now, what would be your guess playing with this crowd?

The winning guess was 13. The distribution of guesses is shown in figure 10. As you can see, many readers of the *Financial Times* were clever enough to figure out that zero was the Nash equilibrium for this game, but they were also clueless enough to think it would be the winning guess.* There were also quite a few people who guessed 1, allowing for the possibility that a few dullards might not fully "get it" and thus raise the average above zero.†

FIGURE 10

Distribution of FT reader guesses

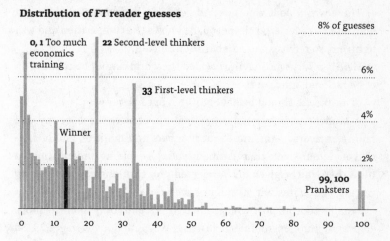

Many first and second level thinkers guessed 33 and 22. But what about the guesses of 99 or 100; what were those folks up to? It turns out that they all came from one student residence at Oxford University. Contestants were limited to one entry, but someone up to some mischief had completed postcards on behalf of all of his housemates. It fell to my research assistants and me to make the call on whether these entries were legal. We decided that since each card had a dif-

---

* This is another case where the normative economic theory, here the Nash equilibrium of zero, does a terrible job as a descriptive theory, and is equally bad as a source of advice about what number to guess. There is now a burgeoning literature of attempts to provide better descriptive models.

† Another reason why some contestants guessed 1 was that they had noticed a sloppy bit of writing in the contest rules, which asked people to guess a number *between* 0 and 100. They thought that the "trick" was that the word "between" implied that guesses of 0 and 100 were disallowed. This had little bearing on the results, but I learned from the experience and switched the word "between" to "from," as I did when posing the problem above.

ferent name attached, we would leave them in, and collectively they moved the winning guess from 12 to 13. Luckily, no one from that house had guessed 13.

We asked participants to write a short explanation of their logic, which we would use as a tie-breaker. Their explanations provided an unexpected bonus. Several were quite clever.[*]

There was a poet who guessed zero: "So behaviourists observe a bod, an FT reader, ergo clever sod, he knows the competition and will fight 'em, so reduces the number ad infinitum."

Here is a Tory who, having decided the world cannot be counted on to be rational, guessed 1:

"The answer should be naught [0] . . . but Labour won."

A student who guessed 7 justified his choice: "Because my dad knows an average amount about numbers and markets, and he bottled out at ten." Note that like many young people, he underestimated his father. Had he given his father credit for thinking one level *beyond* the average contestant, he might have won!

Finally, another poet who guessed 10: "Over 67 only interests fools; so over 45 implies innumeracy rules. 1 to 45 random averages 23. So logic indicates 15, leaving 10 to me."

As illustrated by all these *FT* guessers, at various levels of sophistication, we see that Keynes's beauty contest analogy is still an apt description of what money managers try to do. Many investors call themselves "value managers," meaning they try to buy stocks that are cheap. Others call themselves "growth managers," meaning they try to buy stocks that will grow quickly. But of course no one is seeking to buy stocks that are expensive, or stocks of companies that will shrink. So what are all these managers really trying to do? They are trying to buy stocks that will go up in value—or, in other words, stocks that they think *other* investors will *later* decide should be worth more. And

---

[*] Others were not so clever. At least three people who guessed 33 reported having used the random number generating function in Excel to determine that, if people choose at random from 0 to 100, the average will be 50! Maybe I have too high hopes for the mathematical sophistication of *Financial Times* readers, but I would have thought they could figure out that the average of a number picked at random between 0 and 100 is 50 without using Excel. This confirmed my long-held suspicion that many people use spreadsheets as an alternative to thinking.

these other investors, in turn, are making their own bets on others' *future* valuations.

Buying a stock that the market does not fully appreciate today is fine, as long as the rest of the market comes around to your point of view sooner rather than later! Remember another of Keynes's famous lines. "In the long run, we are all dead." And the typical long run for a portfolio manager is no more than a few years—maybe even just a few months!

22

Does the Stock Market Overreact?

T he opportunity for me to do some research on financial markets was made possible by the first graduate student I had convinced to join me in the study of psychology and economics, Werner De Bondt. I met Werner in the fall of 1978, my first semester at Cornell. Werner, a Belgian exchange student, was by far the best student in the class I taught on economics and public policy in the fall and was again a standout in another course I taught in the spring. I encouraged him to continue his studies and get a PhD, which he did after serving a stint in the Belgian military. We had just one problem: Werner's true love was finance, a topic about which I knew very little.

Fortunately, although I had never taken a course in finance, I had picked up the basics while on the faculty at the University of Rochester Graduate School of Business. Many of the leading faculty members at the school were in finance, and the topic permeated the place. The plan was that I would supervise Werner's thesis if we could figure out a way to inject psychology into the mix, and the finance faculty would make sure we used all the generally accepted financial economics methods so that in the unlikely event we stumbled onto something interesting, the results would be taken seriously. Some of my colleagues told me that I was committing professorial malpractice by encouraging Werner to pursue this topic, but he was unconcerned. De Bondt was, and is, a true intellectual, interested only in finding truth. So he and I learned finance together, with him doing most of the teaching.

For his thesis, Werner wanted to take a hypothesis from psychology and use it to make a prediction about some previously unobserved effect in the stock market. There were easier things to try. For instance, he might have offered a plausible behavioral explanation for some already observed effect in the stock market, as Benartzi and I had done when trying to explain why stocks earn much higher returns than bonds (the equity risk premium). But the problem with a new explanation for an old effect is that it's hard to prove your explanation is correct.

Take, for example, the fact of high trading volume in security markets. In a rational world there would not be very much trading—in fact, hardly any. Economists sometimes call this the Groucho Marx theorem. Groucho famously said that he would never want to belong to any club that would have him as a member. The economist's version of this joke—predictably, not as funny—is that no rational agent will want to buy a stock that some other rational agent is willing to sell. Imagine two financial analysts, Tom and Jerry, are playing a round of golf. Tom mentions that he is thinking of buying 100 shares of Apple. Jerry says, that's convenient, I was thinking of selling 100 shares. I could sell my shares to you and avoid the commission to my broker. Before they can agree on a deal, both think better of it. Tom realizes that Jerry is a smart guy, so asks himself, why is he selling? Jerry is thinking the same about Tom, so they call off the trade. Similarly, if everyone believed that every stock was correctly priced already—and always would be correctly priced—there would not be very much point in trading, at least not with the intent of beating the market.

No one takes the extreme version of this "no trade theorem" literally, but most financial economists agree, at least when pressed, that trading volume is surprisingly high. There is room for differences of opinion on price in a rational model, but it is hard to explain why shares would turn over at a rate of about 5% per month in a world of Econs. However, if you assume that some investors are overconfident, high trading volume emerges naturally. Jerry has no trouble doing the trade with Tom, because he thinks that he is smarter than Tom, and Tom thinks he's smarter than Jerry. They happily trade, each feeling a twinge of guilt for taking advantage of his friend's poor judgment.

I find the overconfidence explanation of why we observe such high trading volume highly plausible, but it is also impossible to prove that it is right. Werner and I wanted to do something more convincing. We wanted to use a finding from psychology to predict something not pre- viously known about financial markets and, even better, something that financial economists thought could not happen. Piece of cake.

Our plan was to use a Kahneman and Tversky finding: that people are willing to make extreme forecasts based on flimsy data. In one of the pair's classic experiments illustrating this point, subjects were asked to predict the grade point average (GPA) for a group of students based on a single fact about each one. There were two* conditions. In one condition, subjects were told the decile of the student's GPA— that is, whether it fell in the top 10% (top decile, between the 90th and 100th percentile), the next 10% (between the 80th and 90th per- centile), and so forth. The other group was not told anything about grades, but was instead given a decile score for each student on a test of "sense of humor."

Decile GPA is an excellent predictor of actual GPA, of course, so if you are told that Athena is in the top decile in GPA, you can reason- ably predict that she has appropriately high grades, say 3.9 out of 4.0. But any correlation between sense of humor and GPA is likely to be weak, if it exists at all.

If the subjects in Kahneman and Tversky's experiment behaved rationally, those given percentile GPA would offer much more extreme (very high or low) predictions of actual GPA than those given mea- sures of a test of sense of humor. Subjects who were told only about sense of humor should make forecasts that differ little from the aver- age GPA at that school. In short, they shouldn't let the sense of humor score influence their prediction much, if at all. As shown in figure 11, this did not happen. The forecasts based on sense of humor are nearly as extreme as the forecasts based on decile GPA. In fact, the predicted GPA for students who scored in the top decile in sense of humor was predicted to be the same as the GPA of those who were in the top decile based on GPA! One way to characterize this result is to say that the subjects *overreacted* to information about a student's sense of humor.

---

* There was actually a third condition I am leaving out for simplicity, in which subjects were told a student's decile score on a test of mental concentration. The results of this condition lie between the other two.

FIGURE 11

Predictions of grade point average

Subjects were willing to guess a GPA as high
for those who scored in the top decile for sense
of humor as for those with a top decile GPA.

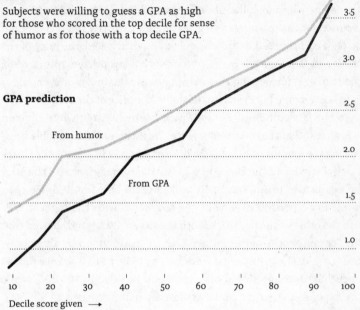

GPA prediction

From humor

From GPA

Decile score given ⟶

Would investors behave the same way, responding to "ephemeral
and non-significant" day-to-day information, as Keynes had asserted?
And, if investors did overreact, how could we show it?

Circumstantial evidence for overreaction already existed, namely
the long-standing tradition of "value investing" pioneered by investment guru Benjamin Graham, author of the classic investment bibles
Security Analysis, co-written with David Dodd and first published in
1934, and *The Intelligent Investor,* first published in 1949. Both books are
still in print. Graham, like Keynes, was both a professional investor
and a professor. He taught at Columbia University, where one of his
students was the legendary investor Warren Buffett, who considers
Graham his intellectual hero. Graham is often considered the father
of "value investing," in which the goal is to find securities that are
priced below their intrinsic, long-run value. The trick is in knowing
how to do this. When is a stock "cheap"? One of the simple measures
that Graham advocated in order to decide whether a stock was cheap

or expensive was the price/earnings ratio (P/E), the price per share divided by annual earnings per share. If the P/E ratio is high, investors are paying a lot per dollar of earnings, and implicitly, a high P/E ratio is a forecast that earnings will grow quickly to justify the current high price. If earnings fail to grow as quickly as anticipated, the price of the stock will fall. Conversely, for a stock with a low price/earnings ratio, the market is forecasting that earnings will remain low or even fall. If earnings rebound, or even remain stable, the price of the stock will rise.

In the last edition of *The Intelligent Investor* written while Graham was alive (others have revised it since), he includes a simple table illustrating the efficacy of his approach. Starting in 1937, he took the thirty stocks included in the Dow Jones Industrial Average (some of the largest companies in America) and ranked them based on P/E. He then formed two portfolios—one of the ten stocks with the highest P/Es and the other of the ten stocks with the lowest P/Es—and showed that the "cheap" stocks outperformed the expensive group by an impressive margin. Over the period from 1937 to 1969, a $10,000 investment in the cheap stocks would have increased in value to $66,900, while the expensive stock portfolio would only have increased to $25,300. (Buying the entire original thirty-stock portfolio would have produced $44,000.) Implicitly, Graham was offering a kind of behavioral explanation for this finding. Cheap stocks were unpopular or out of favor, while expensive stocks were fashionable. By being a contrarian, Graham argued, you could beat the market, although not all the time. Graham noted that his strategy of buying the cheapest members of the Dow Jones Industrials would not have worked over an earlier period, 1917–33, and he cautioned that "Undervaluations caused by neglect or prejudice may persist for an inconveniently long time, and the same applies to inflated prices caused by overenthusiasm or artificial stimulants." That advice was worth heeding during the technology bubble of the late 1990s, when value investing performed spectacularly badly, since the most expensive stocks, the Internet darlings, kept increasing in price, leaving those boring value stocks behind.

Many in the investment community revered Benjamin Graham, but by the early 1980s most academic financial economists considered his work passé. A simple strategy of buying "cheap" stocks was obviously inconsistent with the Efficient Market Hypothesis, and Graham's methods were hardly state of the art. The data for the returns on the various Dow portfolios had undoubtedly been constructed by hand. Now researchers had digitized data files such as CRSP for stock prices and COMPUSTAT, which collected financial accounting data. When these two data sources came together, much more comprehensive studies were possible, and results like Graham's that used a small number of stocks over a relatively short time period were considered little more than anecdotes.

It was not so much that anyone had refuted Graham's claim that value investing worked; it was more that the efficient market theory of the 1970s said that value investing *couldn't* work. But it did. Late that decade, accounting professor Sanjoy Basu published a thoroughly competent study of value investing that fully supported Graham's strategy. However, in order to get such papers published at the time, one had to offer abject apologies for the results. Here is how Basu ended his paper: "In conclusion, the behavior of security prices over the fourteen-year period studied is, perhaps, not completely described by the efficient market hypothesis." He stopped just short of saying "I am sorry." Similarly, one of Eugene Fama's students at the University of Chicago, Rolf Banz, discovered another anomalous finding, namely that portfolios of small firms outperformed portfolios of large firms. Here is his own apologetic conclusion in his paper published in 1981: "Given its longevity, it is not likely that it is due to a market inefficiency but it is rather evidence of a pricing model misspecification." In other words, there must be something left out of the model because market efficiency cannot be wrong.

An investor named David Dreman made bolder claims related to Graham. Dreman had founded his own investment company and had somehow stumbled onto the work of Kahneman and Tversky. He was the first person to suggest an explicitly psychological explanation for the value effect, one based on the tendency for people to extrapolate the recent past into the future. Dreman published his ideas in 1982 in a book aimed at a popular audience titled *The New Contrarian Investment Strategy*. Unlike Basu and Banz, he offered no apologies for his ideas, but because it was a book for nonspecialists it did not make much of an impression on the academic finance community. But Werner and I read the book and took notice.

Following Dreman's thinking led us to a plausible hypothesis. Suppose that the "P/E effect" is caused by overreaction: high P/E stocks (known as growth stocks because they are going to have to grow like crazy to justify their high prices) have gone up "too high" because investors have made overly optimistic forecasts of future growth rates, and low P/E stocks, or value stocks, have sunk "too low," because investors are excessively pessimistic. If true, the subsequent high returns to value stocks and low returns to growth stocks represent simple regression toward the mean.

Examples of regression toward the mean can be found in every aspect of life. If a basketball player scores 50 points in a game, a personal best, it is highly likely that he will score fewer points the next game. And similarly, if he scores three points, his worst game in two years, it is almost certain that he will do better the next game. Children of seven-foot-tall basketball players are tall—but not usually as tall as that. And so forth. Werner and I thought that the same process might be at work in the stock market, too. Companies that are doing well for several years in a row gather an aura implying that they are a "good company," and will continue to grow rapidly. On the other hand, companies that have been losers for several years become tagged as "bad companies" that can't do anything right. Think of it as a form of stereotyping at the corporate level. If this corporate stereotyping is combined with the tendency to make forecasts that are too extreme, as in the sense of humor study, you have a situation that is ripe for mean reversion. Those "bad" companies are not as bad as they look, and on average are likely to do surprisingly well in the future.

Predicting mean reversion in the stock market would not seem to be a particularly radical hypothesis, except for one thing: the EMH says it can't happen. The price-is-right component says that stock prices will not diverge from intrinsic value, so, by definition, can't be "cheap." And the no-free-lunch component says that you cannot beat the market because all information is already captured in the current price. As the past history of the stock's returns and its P/E ratio are clearly known, they cannot predict future price changes. They are SIFs. Finding evidence of mean reversion would constitute a clear violation of the EMH. So we decided to see if we could find that evidence.

Our study was simple. We would take all the stocks listed on the

New York Stock Exchange (which, at that time, had nearly all of the largest companies) and rank their performance over some time period long enough to allow investors to get overly optimistic or pessimistic about some company, say three to five years. We would call the best performing stocks "Winners" and the worst performers "Losers." Then we would take a group of the biggest Winners and Losers (say the most extreme thirty-five stocks) and compare their performance going forward. If markets were efficient, we should expect the two portfolios to do equally well. After all, according to the EMH, the past cannot predict the future. But if our overreaction hypothesis were correct, Losers would outperform Winners.

Such a finding would accomplish two things. First, we would have used psychology to predict a new anomaly. Second, we would be offering support for what we called "generalized overreaction." Unlike the Kahneman and Tversky experiment in which subjects were overreacting to measures of sense of humor when predicting GPA, we were not specifying what investors were overreacting to. We were just assuming that by driving the price of some stock up or down enough to make it one of the biggest winners or losers over a period of several years, investors were likely to be overreacting to *something*.

The results strongly supported our hypothesis. We tested for overreaction in various ways, but as long as the period we looked back at to create the portfolios was long enough, say three years, then the Loser portfolio did better than the Winner portfolio. Much better. For example, in one test we used five years of performance to form the Winner and Loser portfolios and then calculated the returns of each portfolio over the following five years, compared to the overall market. Over the five-year period after we formed our portfolios, the Losers outperformed the market by about 30% while the Winners did worse than the market by about 10%.

Not long after getting these results, we caught a lucky break. Hersh Shefrin had been asked to organize a session at the American Finance Association (AFA) annual meeting, and invited Werner and me to present our findings there. At that time the *Journal of Finance*, the official print outlet of the AFA, produced one issue per year that was devoted entirely to papers from the annual meeting. The way it worked is that the person organizing the session could nominate one paper from the session, and the current president of the AFA would choose some of those papers to publish. The selected papers were published just months later, and did not go through the formal process of peer review. Poor Hersh had a dilemma. Should he recommend his own paper that he would present at the conference, or ours? (The third paper in our session was not eligible because it had been submitted for publication already.) Hersh combined the wisdom of Solomon with a little old-fashioned chutzpah and nominated both papers. Here is where the luck comes in. The president of the American Finance Association that year was the late Fischer Black, the co-inventor of the Black–Scholes option pricing formula. Black was a bit of a renegade, and he chose to publish both papers.

My paper with Werner, published in 1985, has since become well known. But I am convinced that if Hersh hadn't offered the back door entrée to the journal, it would have taken years to get the results published, or the paper might not have been published at all. First of all, everyone "knew" that our results—which were clear violations of the EMH—had to be wrong, so referees would have been highly skeptical. And there is no way we would have agreed to write an apologetic conclusion of the sort that had been foisted on Professor Basu. Werner was too principled, and I was too stubborn.

The Reaction to Overreaction

With the facts confirmed—that "Loser" stocks did earn higher returns than the market—there was only one way to save the no-free-lunch component of the EMH, which says it is impossible to beat the market. The solution for the market efficiency folks was to fall back on an important technicality: it is not a violation of the efficient market hypothesis if you beat the market by taking on more risk. The difficulty comes in knowing how to measure risk.

This subtlety was first articulated by Eugene Fama. He correctly pointed out that all tests of the no-free-lunch component of market efficiency were actually "joint tests" of two hypotheses: market efficiency and some model of risk and return. For example, suppose someone found that new firms have higher returns than old firms. This would seemingly be a rejection of market efficiency; because the age of a firm is known, it cannot be used to "beat" the market. But it would not be a definitive rejection of market efficiency because one could plausibly argue that new firms are riskier than old ones, and that their higher returns are just the compensation rational investors require to bear the additional risk.

This joint hypothesis argument applies to any apparent violation of the EMH, including those of Graham, Basu, Dreman, and others who claimed that value stocks were good investments. If our Loser portfolio was riskier than the Winner portfolio, then the observed higher rate of return *could* be the compensation rational investors demand to invest in risky portfolios. The central question became whether to accept our interpretation of our findings as evidence of *mispricing*,* which goes against the EMH, or to say they were attributable to risk.

---

* One note about some confusing terminology: In this chapter and the next one, when I use the term "mispricing" I mean that a stock price will *predictably* move in

To answer that question, you need a way to measure risk. Assuredly the stocks in the Loser portfolio are *individually* risky, and some of those companies actually may go bankrupt. But in our study we had already accounted for this risk. If one of the stocks in either of the portfolios was delisted by the New York Stock Exchange (because of bankruptcy, for example), then our computer programs hypothetically "sold" the stock at whatever price could be obtained if it were listed on another exchange, or we recorded the investment as total loss. So the possibility of stocks going bankrupt was not the hidden source of risk that could explain our results.

Still, those Loser stocks certainly did *look* risky. And might not scary-looking stocks, such as those whose prices had plummeted, have to earn a higher rate of return (a "risk premium") in the market? You might think so, but such thinking was not kosher in modern financial economics. At that time, the right and proper way to measure the risk of a stock was to use the capital asset pricing model (CAPM) developed independently by financial economists John Lintner and William Sharpe.

According to the CAPM, the only risk that gets rewarded in a rational world is the degree to which a stock's return is correlated with the rest of the market. If you form a portfolio composed of a bunch of highly risky stocks whose prices bounce around a lot, the portfolio itself will not be especially risky if the price movements of each of the component stocks are independent of one another, because then the movements will on average cancel out. But if the returns on the stocks are positively correlated, meaning they tend to go up and down together, then a portfolio of volatile stocks remains pretty risky; the benefits of diversification conferred by holding a portfolio of the stocks are not as great. In this way, according to the CAPM, the correct measure of the riskiness of a stock is simply its correlation

---

some direction, up or down, so much so that an investor could hypothetically take advantage of it for a "free lunch." This is the first illustration of the subtle ways in which the two components of the EMH are intertwined. It is reasonable to think that stocks that are priced "too low" will eventually beat the market, but De Bondt and I had no conclusive evidence that the Losers' prices diverged from their intrinsic value, just that they earned higher returns.

with the rest of the market, a measure that is called "beta."* Roughly speaking, if a stock has a beta of 1.0, then its movements are proportional to the overall market. If a stock has a beta of 2.0, then when the market goes up or down by 10% the individual stock will (on average) go up or down by 20%. A stock that is completely uncorrelated with the market has a beta of zero.

The efficient market hypothesis could be reconciled with our results if the Loser stocks had high betas and thus were risky according to the CAPM, and the Winner stocks had low betas, meaning they were less risky. But we had already checked this out ourselves and reported the results in the paper; in fact, we had found the opposite pattern. For example, in the tests we ran using Winner and Loser portfolios based on three-year "formation periods" and followed by three-year "test periods," the average beta for the Winners was 1.37 and for the Losers was 1.03. So the Winners were actually *riskier* than the Losers. Adjusting for risk using the standard methods of the profession made our anomalous findings even more anomalous!

To rescue the no-free-lunch aspect of the EMH, someone would have to come up with another way to show that the Loser portfolio was riskier than the Winner portfolio. The same would be true for any measure of "value," such as low price/earnings ratios or low ratios of the stock price to its book value of assets, an accounting measure that represents, in principle, what shareholders would get if the company were liquidated. By whatever measure one used, "value stocks" outperformed "growth stocks," and to the consternation of EMH advocates, the value stocks were also less risky, as measured by beta.

It was one thing for renegades like us, portfolio managers like Dreman, and dead guys like Benjamin Graham to claim that value stocks beat the market, but this fact was only declared to be officially true when the high priest of efficient markets, Eugene Fama, and his younger colleague who would become his regular collaborator, Ken-

----

* Just to avoid any confusion, I should mention that this "beta" has nothing to do with the beta in the beta–delta models of present bias in chapter 12. All I can say is that economists like Greek letters and beta comes early in the alphabet.

neth French, published similar findings. In part provoked by our initial findings and those of Banz, who had documented the small firm effect, in 1992 Fama and French began publishing a series of papers documenting that both value stocks and the stocks of small companies did indeed earn higher returns than predicted by the CAPM. In 1996 they officially declared the CAPM to be dead, in a paper with the provocative title "The CAPM Is Wanted, Dead or Alive."

While Fama and French were ready to declare the CAPM dead, they were not ready to abandon market efficiency. Instead, they proposed what is now known as the Fama–French Three Factor Model, in which, in addition to the traditional beta, two extra explanatory factors were added to rationalize the anomalous high returns to small companies and value stocks. Fama and French showed that the returns on value stocks are correlated, meaning that a value stock will tend to do well when other value stocks are doing well, and that the same is true for small-cap stocks. But Fama and French were forthright in conceding that they did not have any theory to explain *why* size and value should be risk factors. Unlike the capital asset pricing model, which was intended to be a normative theory of asset prices based on rational behavior by investors, there was no theoretical reason to believe that size and value *should* predict returns. Those factors were used because empirical research had shown them to matter.

To this day, there is no evidence that a portfolio of small firms or value firms is observably riskier than a portfolio of large growth stocks. In my mind, a paper titled "Contrarian Investment, Extrapolation, and Risk" published in 1994 by financial economists Josef Lakonishok, Andrei Shleifer, and Robert Vishny settled any remaining questions about whether value stocks are riskier. They are not. It also convinced the authors of the paper, since they later started a highly successful money management firm, LSV Asset Management, which is based on value investing.

Although their paper convinced me, it did not convince Fama and French, and the debate has continued for years as to whether value stocks are mispriced, as behavioralists argue, or risky, as rationalists claim. The topic is still debated, and even Fama concedes that it is impossible to say whether the higher returns earned by value stocks are due to risk or overreaction. But in late-breaking news, Fama and

French have announced a new five-factor model. The new factors are one that measures a firm's profitability (which predicts high returns) and another that captures how aggressively a firm invests (which predicts low returns). In a nice twist of fate, profitability is another trait that Benjamin Graham looked for in judging the attractiveness of a firm as an investment. So in some ways, the venerable Ben Graham has been given a Fama–French seal of approval, since they also endorse value and profitability. And it is difficult to tell a plausible story in which highly profitable firms are riskier than firms losing money.

So, in the time since Sharpe and Lintner created the CAPM in the early 1960s, we have gone from a one-factor model to a five-factor model, and many practitioners would add a sixth factor: momentum. Firms that have done well over the last six to twelve months tend to keep doing well for the next six to twelve months. Whether there are five or six factors, I believe that in a rational world, the only factor that would matter is the first one, good old beta, and beta is dead. And the others? In a world of Econs, they would all be SIFs.

24

The Price Is Not Right

Recall that the efficient market hypothesis has two components: you can't beat the market (there is no free lunch), and prices are "right." The work Werner and I did primarily questioned the first principle. Meanwhile, another battle was brewing about the rationality of the aggregate stock market that addressed the second principle. Robert Shiller, now a professor at Yale University, published a paper in 1981 with a striking result.

To understand Shiller's findings, it helps to first think about what *should* determine a stock's price. Suppose a foundation decides to buy a share of stock today and hold it forever. In other words, they are never going to sell the stock—so the only money they will ever get back are the dividends they receive over time. The value of the stock should be equal to the "present value" of all the dividends the foundation will collect going forward for forever, meaning the amount of money that the flow would be worth, after appropriately adjusting for the fact that money tomorrow is worth less than money today.* But because we don't exactly know how much a given stock will pay in dividends over time, the stock price is really just a forecast—the market's expectation of the present value of all future dividend payments.

An important property of rational forecasts—as a stock price is supposed to be—is that the predictions cannot vary more than the thing being forecast. Imagine you are trying to forecast the daily high temperature in Singapore. The weather doesn't vary much in this Southeast Asian city-state. Typically the high temperature is around 90°F

---

* If the foundation ever sells the stock, then we would also include the price they get when they sell it, discounted back to the present. If they hold the stock long enough, this will have a negligible effect on the analysis.

(32°C). On a really hot day it might reach 95°F. A "cold" day might top out at 85°F. You get the idea. Predicting 90°F every day would never be far off. If some highly intoxicated weather forecaster in Singapore was predicting 50°F one day—colder than it ever actually gets—and 110°F the next—hotter than it ever gets—he would be blatantly violating the rule that the predictions can't vary more than the thing being forecast.

Shiller's striking result came from applying this principle to the stock market. He collected data on stock prices and dividends back to 1871. Then, starting in 1871, for each year he computed what he called the "ex post rational" forecast of the stream of future dividends that would accrue to someone who bought a portfolio of the stocks that existed at the time. He did this by observing the actual dividends that got paid out and discounting them back to the year in question. After adjusting for the well-established trend that stock prices go up over long periods of time, Shiller found that the present value of dividends was, like the temperature in Singapore, highly stable. But stock prices, which we should interpret as attempts to forecast the present value of dividends, are highly variable. You can see the results in figure 12. The nearly flat

FIGURE 12

Do stock prices move too much?

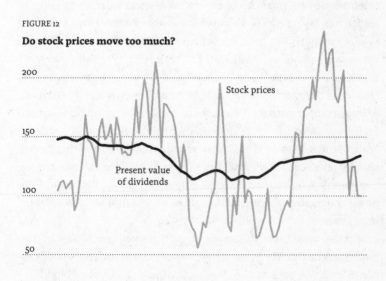
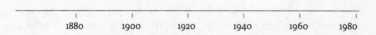

line is the present value of dividends, while the line jumping around like the forecasts of a drunk weatherman is actual stock prices, both of which have be adjusted to remove the long-term upward trend.

Shiller titled his paper "Do Stock Prices Move Too Much to Be Justified by Subsequent Changes in Dividends?" To judge by figure 12, the answer was yes. Shiller's results caused a firestorm in finance circles. Various papers were written attacking his methods and conclusions, one of which was gleefully heralded by critics as the "Shiller Killer." (You may recall that one of those papers, written by Allan Kleidon, was presented at the Chicago conference discussed in chapter 17.)

Academic economists still quibble about the right way to conduct Shiller's test. But I believe that the debate was effectively settled a few years later, on Monday, October 19, 1987, and the days that surrounded it. That Monday, stock prices fell dramatically all around the world. The carnage started in Hong Kong and moved west, as markets opened in Europe and then the United States. In New York, prices fell over 20%, after having already fallen more than 5% the previous Friday. Crucial for our purposes, Monday the 19th was a day without any important news, financial or otherwise. No war started, no political leader was assassinated, and nothing else of note occurred. (For the sake of comparison, the U.S. stock market dropped 4.4% the day after the Japanese bombed Pearl Harbor.) Yet prices were falling precipitously all around the world. No one could say why. The volatility continued for the next few days. In the United States, the S&P 500 index of large company stocks rebounded a robust 5.3% on Tuesday, jumped another 9.1% on Wednesday, only to crash by 8.3% on Monday the 26th. The headline in the *Wall Street Journal* at the end of that month should have been, "Robert Shiller proven right: financial markets are too volatile." In a rational world, prices only change in reaction to news, and during that week, the only news was that prices were moving crazily.

If prices are too variable, then they are in some sense "wrong." It is hard to argue that the price at the close of trading on Thursday, October 15, and the price at the close of trading the following Monday— which was more than 25% lower—can *both* be rational measures of intrinsic value, given the absence of news.

When Shiller wrote his original paper, he did not think of it in psychological terms. He was merely reporting facts that were hard to rationalize. Not surprisingly, I read the paper through a behavioral lens, and saw him as a potential co-conspirator. When he came to give a talk at Cornell in the spring of 1982, he, Werner De Bondt, and I took a long walk around campus, and I encouraged him to think about his paper from what we would now call a behavioral perspective. I don't know whether our conversation had anything to do with it, but two years later he wrote a paper that was a behavioral bombshell. The paper, titled "Stock Prices and Social Dynamics," embraced the heretical idea that social phenomena might influence stock prices just as much as they do fashion trends. Hemlines go up and down without any apparent reason; might not stock prices be influenced in other similar ways that seem to be beyond the standard economist's purview? Bob's agenda in this paper was in some ways more radical than my own. Imagine trying to convince economists that fashion matters, when many have only recently retired their tweed sport jackets with leather patches. Years later, in a book with George Akerlof, Shiller would use Keynes's term "animal spirits" to capture this notion of whimsical changes in consumer and investor attitudes.

———

Although I have portrayed Shiller's research as primarily relevant to the price-is-right aspect of the EMH, it is also relevant to the no-free-lunch component. To see why, it is useful to recall the findings about value investing. Value stocks, either those with very low price/earnings ratios or extreme past losers, predictably outperform the market. One can also compute a price/earnings ratio for the overall market. Does the same principle apply—that is, can you beat the market by buying stocks when they are relatively cheap and avoiding them when they are relatively expensive? My best answer to this question, which Shiller audaciously took on, is "Yes, but . . ."

For an exercise like this, Shiller's preferred method is to divide the market price of an index of stocks (such as the S&P 500) by a measure of earnings averaged over the past ten years. He prefers this long look-back at earnings because it smooths out the temporary fluctuations that come over the course of the business cycle. A plot of this ratio is shown in figure 13.

FIGURE 13

Long-term stock market price/earnings ratios

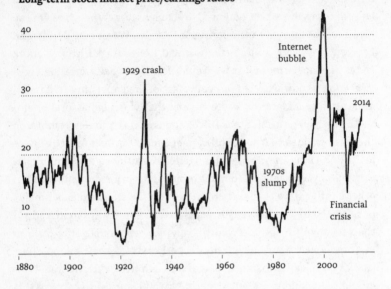

With the benefit of hindsight, it is easy to see from this chart what an investor would have liked to do. Notice that when the market diverges from its historical trends, eventually it reverts back to the mean. Stocks looked cheap in the 1970s and eventually recovered, and they looked expensive in the late 1990s and eventually crashed. So there appears to be some predictive power stemming from Shiller's long-term price/earnings ratio. Which brings us to that "but." The predictive power is not very precise.

In 1996 Shiller and his collaborator John Campbell gave a briefing to the Federal Reserve Board warning that prices seemed dangerously high. This briefing led Alan Greenspan, then the Fed's chairman, to give a speech in which he asked, in his usual oblique way, how one could know if investors had become "irrationally exuberant." Bob later borrowed that phrase for the title of his best-selling book, which was fortuitously published in 2000 just as the market began its slide down. So was Shiller's warning right or wrong?* Since his warning

---

* For the record, I also thought that technology stocks were overpriced in the late 1990s. In an article written and published in 1999, I predicted that what we were

came four years before the market peaked, he was wrong for a long time before he was right! This lack of precision means that the long-term price/earnings ratio is far from a sure-fire way to make money. Anyone who took Shiller's advice in 1996 and bet heavily on the market falling would have gone broke before he had a chance to cash in.

The same is true in the housing market. One of Bob Shiller's many admirable qualities is that he has long been an avid collector of data, from the historical data on stock prices back to 1871 that made his original paper feasible, to surveys of investor sentiment, to measures of home prices. The latter endeavor, done with his friend Chip Case, a real estate economist at Tufts University, created the now widely used Case–Shiller Home Price Index. Before Case and Shiller came along, indicators of home prices were not very reliable because the mix of homes sold in a given month could vary greatly, skewing the average. Case and Shiller had the clever idea to create an index based on repeat sales of the same home, thus controlling for the quality of the home and its location.

A plot of the long-term growth in U.S. home prices since 1960 is shown in figure 14. The chart relies on data on home price sales collected by the government up to 2000, after which the Case-Shiller data become available so both data sources are used. All the prices are adjusted for inflation. The plot shows that home prices grew modestly for most of the period up until the mid-1990s, after which prices shot up. Furthermore, after a long period during which the ratio of the purchase price of a home to the cost of renting a similar home hovered around 20:1, home prices diverged sharply from this long-term benchmark. Looking at these data, Shiller warned of the dangers of a housing bubble, a warning that turned out to be right, eventually. But at the time, one could never be sure whether we were in a bubble or whether something in the economy had changed, causing much higher price-to-rental ratios to be the new normal.

---

currently experiencing would become known as the Great Internet Stock Bubble (Thaler, 1999b). But like Shiller, I would have written the same thing two years earlier if I had gotten around to it (remember, I was and remain a lazy man). Having made one correct prediction about the stock market, I am resolving not to make any more.

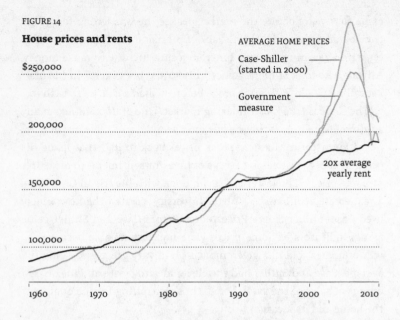

FIGURE 14

House prices and rents

AVERAGE HOME PRICES

$250,000

Case-Shiller
(started in 2000)

Government
measure

200,000

150,000

20x average
yearly rent

100,000

1960   1970   1980   1990   2000   2010

I should stress that the imprecision of these forecasts does not mean they are useless. When prices diverge strongly from historical levels, in either direction, there is some predictive value in these signals. And the further prices diverge from historic levels, the more seriously the signals should be taken. Investors should be wary of pouring money into markets that are showing signs of being overheated, but also should not expect to be able to get rich by successfully timing the market. It is much easier to detect that we may be in a bubble than it is to say when it will pop, and investors who attempt to make money by timing market turns are rarely successful.

———

Although our research paths have taken different courses, Bob Shiller and I did become friends and co-conspirators. In 1991, he and I started organizing a semiannual workshop on behavioral finance hosted by the National Bureau of Economic Research. Many of the landmark papers in behavioral finance have been presented there, and the conference has helped behavioral finance become a thriving and mainstream component of financial economics research.

25

The Battle of Closed-End Funds

Shiller's work wounded the price-is-right component of the efficient market hypothesis, but it was not considered a fatal attack. Disputes about methodology still lingered. And, although it was hard to justify what happened that week in October 1987, efficient market advocates were unwilling to rule out a rational explanation. In the spring of 1988, the University of Chicago held a conference about the crash, and one panel included Eugene Fama and me. Gene spoke first and said the market should be congratulated for how quickly it had reached its new equilibrium, meaning that something must have happened to cause people to revise down their estimates of the future returns on the stock market, and prices had adjusted immediately, just as they "should."

When it was my turn to speak, I asked the assembled experts if they thought that the present value of dividends had fallen 20% on Black Monday, as it was called. Only a few hands went up, and Gene's was not among them. I raised my eyebrow as if to say, "Well?" Gene shot his hand up in the air, smiling. He was not ready to concede, but kept his good sense of humor.

A smoking gun would be required to convince Fama and the rest of the efficient market clan. But as we saw earlier, intrinsic value cannot be determined with precision, which makes it hard to prove that stock prices deviate from intrinsic value. One possible approach to testing whether prices are "right" is to employ an important principle at the very heart of the EMH: the *law of one price*. The law asserts that in an efficient market, the same asset cannot simultaneously sell for two different prices. If that happened, there would be an immediate arbitrage opportunity, meaning a way to make a series of trades that are guaranteed to generate a profit at no risk. Imagine that gold sells for $1,000 an ounce in New York and $1,010 an ounce in London. Someone could buy gold contracts in New York and sell them in London, and if the transaction costs of making that trade are small, money can be made until the two prices converge. The existence of a multitude of smart traders who are constantly on the lookout for violations of the law of one price guarantees that it should hold, almost precisely and instantaneously. Finding a violation would strike at a core tenet of the EMH.

And yet a violation was surprisingly easy to find. In fact, it had already been written about by, among others, Benjamin Graham. The law-breaking suspect was a type of mutual fund called a closed-end fund.

With a more familiar open-end fund, investors can at any time put money into the fund or take money out, and all transactions are conducted at a price determined by the value of the fund's underlying assets, the so-called Net Asset Value (NAV) of the fund. Imagine a fund that only buys shares in Apple Corporation, and one share of the Apple fund gets you one share of Apple stock. Suppose Apple is selling for $100 a share, and an investor wants to invest $1,000. The investor sends the fund $1,000 and gets back ten shares of the fund. If the investor later wants to withdraw from the fund, the amount returned will depend on the current price of Apple. If the price has doubled to $200 a share, when the investor cashes out she will get back $2,000 (less fees charged by the fund). The term "open-end" means that the assets managed by the fund can grow or shrink depending on the preferences of its investors.

A closed-end fund works differently. Managers of the fund raise an initial amount of money, say $100 million, and that is it. No new money can be invested, and money cannot be withdrawn. (You can see the appeal of starting such a fund to the portfolio managers. Investors can't withdraw their money!) Shares of the fund trade in the market, so if an investor wants to sell her shares, she has to do so at the fund's market price. Go back to the hypothetical Apple fund example and suppose now the fund is organized as a closed-end fund, and as before, one share of the fund gets you one share of Apple stock. What is the market price for the Apple closed-end fund? One would assume net asset value, namely, the current price of Apple. If it were anything else, the law of one price would be violated, since it would be possible to buy Apple shares at two different prices, one determined by the market price of Apple shares, and the other by the price of the Apple fund.

The EMH makes a clear prediction about the prices of closed-end fund shares: they will be equal to NAV. But a look at any table of the prices of closed-end fund shares reveals otherwise (see figure 15). These tables have three columns: one for the fund's share price, one for the NAV, and another for the discount or premium measuring the percentage difference between the two prices. The very fact that there are three columns tells you that market prices are often different from NAV. While funds typically sell at discounts, often in the range of 10–20% below NAV, funds sometimes sell at a premium. This is a blatant violation of the law of one price. And an investor does not have to do any number-crunching to detect this anomaly, since it is displayed right there in the table. What is going on?

FIGURE 15

Premia and discounts on selected closed-end funds

FUND	NAV	MARKET PRICE	PREMIUM OR DISCOUNT
Gabelli Utility Trust (GUT)	$6.28	$7.42	+18.2 %
BlackRock Hlth Sciences (BME)	38.94	42.48	+9.1
First Tr Spec Fin&Finl (FGB)	7.34	7.62	+3.8
DNP Select Income Fund (DNP)	10.50	10.55	+0.4
First Tr Energy Inc & Gr (FEN)	37.91	35.83	−5.5
ASA Gold & Prec Met Ltd (ASA)	11.24	10.19	−9.3
BlackRock Res & Comm Str (BCX)	11.78	9.93	−15.7
Firsthand Technology Val (SVVC)	29.70	18.59	−37.4

As of Dec. 31, 2014

I did not know much about closed-end funds until I met Charles Lee. Charles was a doctoral student in accounting at Cornell, but his background hinted that he might have some interest in behavioral finance, so I managed to snag him as a research assistant during his first year in the program. When Charles took my doctoral class in behavioral economics, I suggested closed-end funds as a topic for a course project. He took the challenge.

Around the time that Charles finished his paper for my class, Larry Summers had just written the first of a series of papers with three of his former students about what they called "noise traders." The term "noise traders" comes from Fischer Black, who had made "noise" into a technical term in finance during his presidential address to the American Finance Association, using it as a contrast to the word "news." The only thing that makes an Econ change his mind about an investment is genuine news, but Humans might react to something that does not qualify as news, such as seeing an ad for the company behind the investment that makes them laugh. In other words, SIFs are noise, and a noise trader, as Black and Summers use the term, makes decisions based on SIFs rather than actual news.

Summers had earlier used more colorful language to capture the idea that noise might influence asset prices. He has an infamous but unpublished solo-authored paper on this theme that starts this way: "THERE ARE IDIOTS. Look around."* Three graduate students who had met when they shared a suite during their first year as undergraduates—Brad De Long, Andrei Shleifer, and Robert Waldmann—joined Summers to produce a more rigorous, thorough, and polite version of the "idiots" paper. The model they proposed used closed-end funds as an example of the type of asset that their model might help understand, but they had not done any empirical testing. Charles and I thought we might be able to build on some of the work Charles had done for his term paper to fill in that gap, and we asked Andrei Shleifer, who had recently joined the faculty at the University of Chicago, to join us on this project. Charles, Andrei, and I then wrote a paper on closed-end funds, noting that there were four puzzles associated with these funds.

When closed-end funds are started they are usually sold by brokers, who add a hefty commission of around 7% to the sale price. But within six months, the funds typically trade at a discount of more than 10%. So the first puzzle is: why does anyone buy an asset for $107 that will predictably be worth $90 in six months? This pattern had

---

* The only copy of this paper I have been able to find is one Fischer Black faxed to Summers with his handwritten comments on it. Next to the opening phrase about "IDIOTS" Black writes: "I call them 'noise traders.' They trade on noise as if it were information."

induced Benjamin Graham to refer to closed-end funds as "an expensive monument erected to the inertia and stupidity of stockholders." This was a more polite way of saying "THERE ARE IDIOTS," which remains the only satisfactory answer to this first puzzle.*

The second puzzle is the existence of the discounts and premia mentioned earlier. Why does the fund trade at a price that is different from the value of its holdings?

The third puzzle is that the discounts (and premia) vary quite a bit, across time and among funds. This is an important point because it rules out many simple explanations for the existence of discounts. One such explanation had held that the discount was necessary to compensate investors for the fact that the funds charge fees or mismanage the portfolio. But if factors like this were the explanation, why do the discounts bounce around so much? Neither the fees nor the management vary much over time.

The fourth puzzle is that when a closed-end fund selling at a discount decides to change its structure to an open-end fund, often under pressure from shareholders when it is selling at a large discount, its price converges to NAV. This fact rules out the possibility that net asset value was miscalculated. Collectively, the four puzzles created an efficient market conundrum.

The primary goal of our paper was to draw a bit more attention to these puzzles. But our main research contribution was to understand a bit more about why discounts vary over time. We exploited an important fact about the U.S.-based closed-end funds we were studying: individual investors, as opposed to institutions, are the primary owners of these funds. We postulated that individual investors acted as the noise traders in this market; they would be more flighty than professional investors, such as pension funds and endowments, and thus they would be subject to shifting moods of optimism or pessimism, which we dubbed "investor sentiment." We conjectured that when individual investors are feeling perky, discounts on closed-end funds shrink, but when they get depressed or scared, the discounts

---

* To be clear, it can be quite smart to invest in closed-end funds when they sell at a discount, but it is foolish to buy one when it is first issued and a commission is being charged.

get bigger. This approach was very much in the spirit of Shiller's take on social dynamics, and investor sentiment was clearly one example of "animal spirits."

The question was how to measure investor sentiment. To do so, we exploited the fact that individual investors are also more likely than institutional investors to own shares of small companies. Institutions shy away from the shares of small companies because these shares do not trade enough to provide the liquidity a big investor needs, and institutions such as mutual funds don't buy shares of closed-end funds or other mutual funds because their customers don't like the idea of paying two sets of fees. So, if the investor sentiment of individuals varies, we figured it would show up both in the discounts on closed-end funds and on the relative performance of small companies versus big companies. (Although shares in small companies do better on average, the difference varies, and in some periods big firms outperform small ones.)

That is exactly what we found. The average discount on closed-end funds was correlated with the difference in returns between small and large company stocks; the greater the discount, the larger the difference in returns between those two types of stocks. This finding was the equivalent of finding footprints for Bigfoot or some other creature that is thought to be a myth.

As I have said, we were by no means the first to write about closed-end funds. Economist Rex Thompson wrote his thesis on closed-end funds, and found that a strategy of buying the funds with the biggest discounts earned superior returns (a strategy also advocated by Benjamin Graham). The well-known efficient market guru Burton Malkiel, author of the perpetual best-seller *A Random Walk Down Wall Street*, has also advocated such a strategy. Nevertheless, our paper made some people upset, and it infuriated Merton Miller, the Nobel Prize–winning financial economist at the University of Chicago who was Shleifer's senior colleague.

To this day I do not know exactly what about our paper made Miller so upset, but I suspect that while others had written about these funds before, we were the first to do so since Graham without following the mannerly procedure of apologizing and making excuses for our anomalous findings. Instead, we seemed to be enjoying ourselves.

On top of that, we were using one annoying anomaly, the small firm effect, to help explain another one, persistent discounts on closed-end funds. This is, for an Econ, the equivalent of taking the Lord's name in vain while working on the Sabbath.

Miller jumped into attack mode. We submitted our paper to the *Journal of Finance*, and the editor, René Stulz, sent it out to referees. Meanwhile, we learned that Miller was lobbying Professor Stulz to reject our paper. To his credit, Stulz accepted our paper and told Miller that if he disagreed with our findings, he should follow the usual procedure of writing a comment on the paper and submitting it to the *Journal*.

Miller took Stulz up on this suggestion. He recruited Nai-fu Chen, a fellow Chicago professor, and Raymond Kan, a graduate student, to help with the research, and they submitted a comment on our paper. Miller was a sharp-witted guy, and the comment was written in his usual swashbuckling style. They started their paper this way: "Charles Lee, Andrei Shleifer, and Richard Thaler (1991) claim to solve not one, but two, long-standing puzzles—discounts on closed-end funds and the small firm effect. Both, according to Lee et al., are driven by the same waves of small investor sentiment. Killing two such elusive birds with one stone would be a neat trick indeed if Lee et al. could bring it off. But they can't."

I won't bore you with the substance of the debate, which was mostly about technical details. Following tradition, we wrote a "reply" to appear in the same issue of the journal, and introduced new data to buttress our claims, something Miller considered a violation of the usual protocol of such debates. He insisted on a reply to our reply, which meant that, following tradition, we as the original authors would get to throw the last set of stones.

Naturally, in the final two comments both sides declared victory. I don't know who won, but I do know that the unprecedented four-part pissing contest about our paper attracted a lot of attention. Thanks to Professor Miller, hundreds of financial economists were nudged to read our original paper, so by attacking us, Miller ended up doing us a big favor. Many readers of the *Journal of Finance* might otherwise not have noticed a paper about closed-end mutual funds. But nothing attracts attention more than a good fight.

26

Fruit Flies, Icebergs, and Negative Stock Prices

T he debate with Merton Miller obscured the most important point about closed-end funds: the blatant violation of the law of one price. It was as if we had discovered a unicorn and then had a long fight about what to call the color of the beast's coat. Years later, after I had joined the University of Chicago, I revisited the law of one price with a Chicago colleague, Owen Lamont.

At that time Owen was not really a behavioral economist. He was just an open-minded researcher who enjoyed stirring the pot and had a good eye for interesting problems. Owen is always a favored choice for the role of discussant at the behavioral finance seminars that Shiller and I organize at NBER. Zingers abound at these meetings, and Owen may hold the record for most points scored. Once he was asked to discuss a paper in which the authors had measured option traders' anxiety levels during the trading day. The sensor technology employed was nifty, but a lot of us wondered what we should take away from this exercise. Owen opened his discussion with a summary: "The authors have definitively rejected the hypothesis that these traders are blocks of wood."

The interesting problem Owen had spotted was a blatant violation of the law of one price involving a company called 3Com. 3Com's main business was in networking computers using Ethernet technology, but through a merger they had also acquired Palm, the maker of what at the time was considered a very spiffy handheld computer called the Palm Pilot. In the summer of 1999, when the stock of any respectable Silicon Valley technology company seemed to double every month or two, 3Com was being neglected, and its stock price was flat. 3Com management adopted a plan of action to increase its share price, and the plan involved divesting itself of its interest in Palm. On March 2,

2000, 3Com sold a fraction of its stake in Palm to the general public. In this transaction, called an equity carve-out, 3Com sold about 4% of its stake in Palm in the initial public offering, sold about 1% to a consortium of firms, and retained ownership of 95% of the shares.

This action in and of itself should worry efficient market advocates. What difference does it make whether Palm is located within 3Com or out on its own? If prices are "right," then splitting a company up into two parts should not raise its value unless the parent company, 3Com in this case, was doing something dysfunctional in its management of Palm that was keeping that division from thriving. But of course, the 3Com management did not say they were getting a divorce from Palm to allow it to get out from under their mismanagement. Instead, they implied that Palm would somehow be magically worth more as a separate company than as a part of the parent company. Undoubtedly, they were hoping that as a separate company Palm would be valued more like the sexy technology companies around at that time, such as eBay, AOL, and Amazon. An efficient market advocate would be skeptical of this move. In a market consisting only of Econs, the value of 3Com is equal to the value of Palm plus the value of the rest of 3Com, and splitting them up would have no effect on the total value of the enterprise.

But Econs were clearly not driving the stock prices of technology firms in the late 1990s. Puzzling as it might be, carving out Palm seemed to work. When the plan to separate Palm from the rest of the company was first announced on December 13, 1999, 3Com was selling for about $40 a share, and by the time the initial public offering for the Palm shares took place, on March 1, 2000, the 3Com price had risen to over $100 a share. That is quite a return for taking the costly step of turning Palm into a separate company! But the truly bizarre part was yet to come.

The way the spin-off would work is that initially only 5% of the value of Palm would be sold to outside investors. 3Com would retain the rest of the shares. Then, after a period of a few months, each 3Com shareholder would receive 1.5 shares of Palm. Here is where the law of one price comes into play. As soon as the initial shares of Palm were sold and started trading, 3Com shareholders would essentially have two separate investments. A single share of 3Com included 1.5 shares of Palm plus an interest in the remaining parts of 3Com, or what in the finance literature is called the "stub value" of 3Com. In a rational world, the price of a 3Com share would be equal to the value of the stub plus 1.5 times the price of Palm.

Investment bankers marketing the shares of Palm to be sold in the initial public offering had to determine what price to charge. As excitement about the IPO kept building, they kept raising the price, finally settling on $38 a share, but when Palm shares started trading, the price jumped and ended the day at a bit over $95. Wow! Investors did seem to be wildly enthusiastic about the prospect of an independent Palm company.

So what should happen to the price of 3Com? Let's do the math. Each 3Com share now included 1.5 shares of Palm, and if you multiply $95 by 1.5 you get about $143. Moreover, the remaining parts of 3Com were a profitable business, so you have to figure that the price of 3Com shares would jump to *at least* $143, and probably quite a bit more. But in fact, that day the price of 3Com *fell*, closing at $82. That means that the market was valuing the stub value of 3Com at minus $61 per share, which adds up to minus $23 billion! You read that correctly. The stock market was saying that the remaining 3Com business, a profitable business, was worth minus $23 billion.

FIGURE 16

In a rational world, the price of a 3Com share would be equal to 1.5 times the price of Palm plus the "stub" value of 3Com.

3COM	=	PALM	X **1.5**	+	S
Cost of one share of 3Com		1.5 times the price of one share of Palm			The "stub" value of 3Com

But when markets closed, prices were irrational. If you solve for s, you find that 3Com's stub value is a negative number.

$82	=	$95	X **1.5**	+	-$61
Cost of 1 share of 3Com		1.5 times the price of one share of Palm			The "stub" value of 3Com

There is a first principle of finance even more fundamental than the law of one price, which is that a stock price can never be negative. You can throw your shares away if you want to, and shareholders have limited liability, so the absolute lowest a stock price can fall to is zero. No company can be worth minus $100, much less minus $23 billion. But that is what the market was saying.

Think of it another way. Suppose an Econ is interested in investing in Palm. He could pay $95 and get one share of Palm, or he could pay $82 and get one share of 3Com that includes 1.5 shares of Palm *plus* an interest in 3Com. That does not seem to be a tough decision! Why buy Palm directly when you can get more shares for less money by buying 3Com, plus get a stake in another company thrown in for free?

This was a colossal violation of the law of one price. In fact it was so colossal that it was widely publicized in the popular press. Nevertheless, the value of the 3Com stub remained negative for several months.

How could this happen? Two ingredients are necessary for a violation of the law of one price to emerge and persist. The first is that you need some investors with an inexplicable desire to own a pure, unadulterated version of Palm rather than one watered down with extra money and a share of a profitable company. In other words, you need noise traders, a.k.a. Summers's IDIOTS. And note that even if some people buy Palm knowing it is overvalued but hoping to sell it to idiots later at an overvalued price—well, you still need some idiots to make it all work.

The other thing that is necessary for this to happen is that something must be preventing the "smart money" from driving the prices back to where they are supposed to be. The merely "sensible" investor would simply buy 3Com instead of Palm. But a true Econ would go one step further. The smart-money trade in this situation is to buy undervalued 3Com shares and sell short an appropriate number of shares of Palm. Then, when the deal is completed, the investor sells the shares of Palm he receives, uses those shares to repay his loan, and is left with a profit equal to whatever price 3Com is selling for as a stand-alone company. This is a trade that cannot lose. Why wasn't everyone trying to do it, given that it was so widely known? The problem was that so few shares of Palm were sold in the initial public offering that there were not enough to satisfy everyone who wanted to borrow them: the demand from people who wanted to borrow shares to sell them short exceeded the supply of shares available to lend. This meant that the smart money was unable to drive the relative prices of Palm and 3Com into a rational equilibrium where the price of 3Com was at least 1.5 times the price of Palm.[*]

The Palm/3Com story is not unique.[†] Back in 1923, a young Benjamin Graham noticed that DuPont owned a large number of shares of General Motors and strangely, the market value of DuPont was about the same as its stake in GM. In spite of the fact that DuPont was a highly profitable firm, its stub value was close to zero. Graham made the smart trade, buying DuPont and selling GM short, and made a bundle when the price of DuPont went up.

But things don't always work out so well for the smart investors. For many years, there were two kinds of shares of the merged company Royal Dutch Shell. Royal Dutch shares traded in New York and the Netherlands, and Shell shares traded in London. According to the terms of the merger agreement that created this company in 1907, 60% of the profits would go to Royal Dutch shareholders and 40% would go to Shell shareholders. The law of one price stipulates that the ratio of the prices of the two classes of shares should be 60/40 or 1.5. But did the two share prices always trade at that ratio? No! Sometimes the Royal Dutch shares traded as much as 30% too low, and other times they traded as much as 15% too high. Noise traders appear to have particular difficulty with multiplying by 1.5.

In this case, the smart trade is to buy whichever is the cheaper version of the stock and sell the expensive version short. Unlike the case

---

[*]   It was possible to find some shares to borrow if you had time on your hands. In fact, at the time, there was a finance PhD student at the University of Chicago who was determined to make money on 3Com/Palm. He opened accounts at every discount brokerage house and spent all of his time trying to borrow shares of Palm to sell short. Whenever he got Palm shares he would sell them short and use the proceeds to buy the number of shares of 3Com required to hedge his bet. When the deal was finalized a few months later, he made a tidy profit and bought a sports car that he nicknamed the Palm-mobile. The moral of this story is that it was possible to make tens of thousands of dollars from this anomaly, but not tens of millions.

[†]   A similar situation arose in mid-2014 when Yahoo's holdings of Alibaba were calculated to be worth more than the whole of Yahoo (Jackson, 2014; Carlson, 2014).

of Palm and 3Com, both versions of the stock were widely traded and easy to borrow, so what prevented the smart money from assuring that the shares traded at their appropriate ratio of 1.5? Strangely, nothing! And crucially, unlike the Palm example, which was sure to end in a few months, the Royal Dutch Shell price disparity could and did last for decades.* Therein lies the risk. Some smart traders, such as the hedge fund Long Term Capital Management (LTCM), did execute the smart trade, selling the expensive Royal Dutch shares short and buying the cheap Shell shares. But the story does not have a happy ending. In August 1998, because of a financial crisis in Asia and a default on Russian bonds, LTCM and other hedge funds started to lose money and needed to reduce some of their positions, including their Royal Dutch Shell trade. But, not surprisingly, LTCM was not the only hedge fund to have spotted the Royal Dutch Shell pricing anomaly, and the other hedge funds had also lost money in Russia and Asia. So at the same time that LTCM wanted to unwind its position in Royal Dutch Shell, so did other hedge funds, and the spread moved against them, meaning that the expensive version got *more* expensive. Within weeks, LTCM had collapsed from this and other "arbitrage" opportunities that got worse before they got better.

The LTCM example illustrates what Andrei Shleifer and his frequent coauthor Robert Vishny call the "limits of arbitrage." In fact, in a paper they published on this topic in 1997, a year before these events occurred, they quite cannily described a hypothetical situation much like what LTCM experienced. When prices start to move against a money manager and investors start to ask for some of their money back, prices will be driven further against them, which can cause a vicious spiral. The key lesson is that prices can get out of whack, and smart money cannot always set things right.

---

* When I described this anomaly to the CEO of a large pension fund sometime in the 1990s, he said I must be wrong because surely the smart money would just buy whichever shares were cheaper. I said, "Really? I believe your fund owns millions of dollars of the more expensive version," and offered to bet a fancy dinner that I was right. He wisely didn't bet. His fund was partly indexed to the S&P 500, which then included the Dutch version that was selling at a premium.

———————

Owen and I wrote an academic paper about the Palm–3Com episode boldly titled "Can the Market Add and Subtract?" and presented it at the finance workshop at the University of Chicago. At the end of the workshop Gene Fama questioned the significance of examples such as this one and closed-end funds. He pointed out that these are relatively minor financial assets. So, although the results were in conflict with the EMH, he argued that the stakes were too small to worry about.

My view was that these special cases are finance's equivalent of geneticists' fruit flies. Fruit flies are not a particularly important species in the grand scheme of things, but their ability to quickly reproduce offers scientists the chance to study otherwise difficult questions. So it is with finance's fruit flies. These are the rare situations in which we can say something about intrinsic value. No one can say what the price of 3Com or Palm should be, but we can say with great certainty that after the spin-off, the price of 3Com had to be at least 1.5 times the price of Palm. I suggested that examples like this one were the tip of the iceberg of market mispricing. Gene's view was that we had beheld the entire iceberg.

What are the implications of these examples? If the law of one price can be violated in such transparently obvious cases such as these, then it is abundantly clear that even greater disparities can occur at the level of the overall market. Recall the debate about whether there was a bubble going on in Internet stocks in the late 1990s. There was no way to prove at the time, or even now, that the pricing of technology stocks was too high. But if the market could not get something as simple as Palm and 3Com right, it certainly seemed possible that the technology-heavy NASDAQ index could be overpriced as well. It does not seem to be a coincidence that the expensive part of the Palm/3Com trade was the sexy Palm division and the inexpensive part was the sleepier 3Com parent. The same could be said when contrasting the rise in prices of sexy tech stocks versus sleepy industrials.

So where do I come down on the efficient market hypothesis? It should be stressed that as a *normative* benchmark of how the world should be, the EMH has been extraordinarily useful. In a world of Econs, I believe that the EMH would be true. And it would not have been possible to do research in behavioral finance without the rational model as a starting point. Without the rational framework, there are no anomalies from which we can detect misbehavior. Furthermore, there is not as yet a benchmark behavioral theory of asset prices that could be used as a theoretical underpinning of empirical research. We need some starting point to organize our thoughts on any topic, and the EMH remains the best one we have.

When it comes to the EMH as a *descriptive* model of asset markets, my report card is mixed. Of the two components, using the scale sometimes used to judge the claims made by political candidates, I would judge the no-free-lunch component to be "mostly true." There are definitely anomalies: sometimes the market overreacts, and sometimes it underreacts. But it remains the case that most active money managers fail to beat the market. And as the story about Royal Dutch Shell and LTCM shows, even when investors can know *for sure* that prices are wrong, these prices can still stay wrong, or even get more wrong. This should rightly scare investors who think they are smart and want to exploit apparent mispricing. It is possible to make money, but it is not easy.[*] Certainly, investors who accept the EMH gospel and invest in low-cost index funds cannot be faulted for that choice.

I have a much lower opinion about the price-is-right component of the EMH, and for many important questions, this is the more important component. How wrong do I think it is? Notably, in Fischer Black's essay on noise, he opines that "we might define an efficient market as one in which price is within a factor of 2 of value, i.e., the price is more than half of value and less than twice value. The factor of 2 is arbitrary, of course. Intuitively, though, it seems reasonable to me, in the light of sources of uncertainty about value and the strength of the forces tending to cause price to return to value. By this definition, I think almost all markets are efficient almost all of the time. 'Almost all' means at least 90%."

---

[*] Full disclosure: Since 1998 I have been a partner in a money management firm called Fuller and Thaler Asset Management that invests in U.S. equities by finding situations where investors' behavioral biases are likely to cause mispricing. The fact that we are still in business suggests that we have either been successful at using behavioral finance to beat the market, or have been lucky, or both.

I am not sure whether "90% of the time" is a satisfactory definition of "almost all" of the time, but more importantly, a factor of 2 strikes me as a very wide margin to call a market efficient. Just think about all the housing units built during the real estate bubble that are still worth only half of what their value was at the peak. The people who bought those homes would probably disagree with an assessment that the housing market was acting efficiently during the boom. Furthermore, Black died in 1996, before the technology and real estate bubbles. I think if he were still around he could be convinced to revise that assessment to "right within a factor of 3." The NASDAQ index lost more than two-thirds of its value from its peak in 2000 to its trough in 2002, and the decline is almost certainly due to initial exuberance. (It can certainly not be blamed on the Internet proving to be a disappointment.)

My conclusion: the price is often wrong, and sometimes very wrong. Furthermore, when prices diverge from fundamental value by such wide margins, the misallocation of resources can be quite big. For example, in the United States, where home prices were rising at a national level, some regions experienced especially rapid price increases and historically high price-to-rental ratios. Had both homeowners and lenders been Econs, they would have noticed these warning signals and realized that a fall in home prices was becoming increasingly likely. Instead, surveys by Shiller showed that these were the regions in which expectations about the future appreciation of home prices were the most optimistic. Instead of expecting mean reversion, people were acting as if what goes up must go up even more.

Moreover, rational lenders would have made the requirements for getting a mortgage stricter under such circumstances, but just the opposite happened. Mortgages were offered with little or no down payment required, and scant attention was paid to the creditworthiness of the borrowers. These "liar loans" fueled the booms, and policy-makers took no action to intervene.

This lesson is one of the most important to take away from the research about market efficiency. If policy-makers simply take it as a matter of faith that prices are always right, they will never see any need to take preventive action. But once we grant that bubbles are possible, and the private sector appears to be feeding the frenzy, it can make sense for policy-makers to lean against the wind in some way.

Central banks around the world have had to take extraordinary measures to help economies recover from the financial crisis. The same people who complain most about these extraordinary recovery measures are also those who would object to relatively minor steps to reduce the likelihood of another catastrophe. That is simply irrational.

VII.

WELCOME TO CHICAGO:

1995–PRESENT

During what amounted to a job interview at the University of Chicago for a position at what is now called the Booth School of Business, I had a lunch meeting with several of the finance faculty members. As we left the business school to walk over to the faculty club where we would have lunch, I spotted a twenty-dollar bill lying on the sidewalk, right outside the building. Naturally I picked it up, and then everyone started laughing. We were laughing because we all realized the irony of this situation. There is an old joke that says a Chicago economist would not bother to pick up a twenty-dollar bill on the sidewalk because if it were real, someone would already have snagged it. There is no such thing as a free lunch or a free twenty-dollar bill. But to a heretic like me, that twenty looked real enough to be worth bending over.

My appointment was not without some controversy in the school. Predictably, Merton Miller was not too happy about it, even though my primary appointment would not be in finance. Instead, I would

join the behavioral science group that was made up primarily of psychologists, which I viewed as a plus. I would have the opportunity to
build the kind of group of behavioral scientists with strong disciplin-
ary training that I had long thought should exist in a top business
school, and while so doing, I would have a chance to learn more about
psychology, a field in which my knowledge was quite narrow.

I am not privy to the internal conversations the faculty had at the
time my appointment was considered, but a magazine reporter interviewed Gene Fama and Merton Miller after I arrived, wondering why
they were letting a renegade like me join them. Gene, with whom I
have always had a good relationship, replied that they wanted me
nearby so that they could keep a close eye on me, his tongue firmly
in cheek. The reporter pressed Miller a bit harder, specifically asking him why he had not blocked my appointment. This was obviously
an impertinent question, to which Miller might well have replied,
"None of your business." Instead, he said that he had not blocked the
appointment "because each generation has got to make its own mistakes." Welcome to Chicago!

Law Schooling

I spent the academic year 1994–95 as a visiting professor at MIT's Sloan School of Management in order to spend some time with France Leclerc, who was then on their faculty in the marketing department. It was during that year that we both accepted faculty positions at the University of Chicago Graduate School of Business (as it was then called), and we later married.* While at MIT I got a call from Orley Ashenfelter—the economist who had let Eldar Shafir and me use his wine newsletter to study mental accounting—asking whether I might give a plenary talk on the applications of behavioral economics to the law at a conference he was organizing. "We need some of that wackonomics," he said. I told Orley that the topic was definitely interesting, but I knew nothing about the field of law. I said I would look for a knowledgeable collaborator and get back to him.

One of the participants in our first summer camp, Christine Jolls, was a prime prospect. She was just finishing up both her PhD in economics at MIT and her law degree at Harvard, and was a hard worker. Christine was game, and as we tossed around topics to cover we soon came up with enough material for a decent talk, so I told Orley we would accept his invitation. The basic idea was to think about how the field of law and economics, as currently practiced, should be modified to accommodate recent findings in behavioral economics.

The traditional law and economics approach was based exclusively on models of Econs. Many of the articles took many pages to reach the conclusion that things would turn out for the best if markets were left alone to sort things out. Many of the arguments depended implicitly on some form of the invisible handwave.

Our idea was to introduce some of the essential elements of behav-

---

* France has now switched from marketing to photography. In my highly biased opinion, her images are worth a look. See for yourself at franceleclerc.com.

ioral economics into such arguments and see how they would have
to be modified. By this point I had adopted the pedagogical device of
calling these essential elements "the three bounds": bounded rationality, bounded willpower, and bounded self-interest. In law and economics these properties of Humans had heretofore been assumed to
be thoroughly unbounded.

I ended up having to miss the conference, leaving Christine to give
the talk solo, but it went over well enough that we thought it was
worth expanding into an academic paper. We planned to get busy on
that once we both settled into our new jobs. She had been hired by
Harvard Law School and would join their faculty at the same time
that I was arriving at Chicago.

The stars must have been in some kind of fortuitous alignment,
because when I arrived at Chicago, the first faculty member I met
from outside the business school was Cass Sunstein, a professor at
the law school. Cass had already been collaborating with Danny and
was excited about behavioral economics. In the world of academic
law, Cass is a rock star. Although nominally his specialty is constitu-
tional law, he has written articles and books on nearly every branch of
the law, and is widely admired. We had lunch a couple times and hit it
off well. His enthusiasm is catching, and his encyclopedic knowledge
is astonishing. At some point I suggested to Christine that we should
consider asking Cass to join our behavioral law and economics project. It was not a hard sell. Adding Cass to your research team is a bit
like adding Lionel Messi to your pick-up soccer game. Soon we were
off and running. And I mean running, because Cass is fast.

It took only a few months for the three of us to produce a draft of a
paper that we titled "A Behavioral Approach to Law and Economics." It
was the longest paper I have ever written. To law professors, the longer a
paper is, the better, and there can never be too many footnotes. The published version of the paper came in at 76 pages and 220 footnotes, and it
was only this short because I kept complaining of its excessive length.

When we had a draft ready to submit for publication, I learned that
the process is very different in legal circles than in economics. In economics, you are only allowed to submit your article to one journal at a
time. If they reject it, you can try another one. But law reviews allow
authors to submit to several at once, which we did. The *Stanford Law*

Review was the first to get back to us with an acceptance, and soon after another law review was expressing interest as well. We had bargaining power, so I made a suggestion. Since the editors were so keen to get this article, and it was bound to be controversial, why not get them to solicit a commentary from a prominent representative of the law and economics inner circle to be published in the same issue, with us having the opportunity to reply? I had in mind how the debate with Merton Miller and his team had attracted a lot of attention to the closed-end funds paper, and I thought this might have a similar effect.

The obvious choice to provide the critical commentary was the legal scholar Richard Posner. Posner is considered by many to be the founder of modern law and economics, and he has written the definitive treatise on the subject, revised numerous times. The field Posner helped create introduced formal economic reasoning into legal scholarship. From the beginning, law and economics was primarily based on traditional, Chicago-style economics, so he had a considerable investment in the approach to which we were offering an alternative.

We knew that Posner would find much to criticize in our approach, and we also knew that he could knock off a comment quickly. In spite of his serving both as a part-time law professor and federal judge on the Seventh Circuit in Chicago (one step below the Supreme Court), his research productivity is legendary. As the economist Robert Solow so colorfully put it: "Posner evidently writes the way other men breathe." Writing a comment on our long article would not take him much time.

Although we had a good hunch about what Posner might think of our paper, any uncertainty about which parts of the paper he would find to be most objectionable was resolved the day before the three of us were to present our paper at the University of Chicago Law School. That morning we received a letter from him with his comments. The letter, which ran many single-spaced pages, was highly critical, and quite emotional. Posner told us he had written up his thoughts so that he could remain silent during our talk, knowing that others would be anxious to speak as well. Maybe he thought it would serve as a good commitment strategy.

Before getting to what the arguments were about, some background is required. When Richard Posner and others of his generation started the law and economics movement, there were many legal scholars who were uncomfortable with some of the conclusions of their work, but they lacked the economic training to put up a good fight. At that time, the few law professors that had any formal training in economics were using the traditional approach based on models of Econs, and legal scholars who tried to challenge the conclusions of such papers often felt bullied if they entered the ring against the law and econ crowd, who could brush aside critiques with a condescending "Well, you just don't understand." As a result, at our workshop some attendees would be defending the old-time religion, like Posner, while others might be (quietly) rooting for the underdogs to score some points against the bullies.

Cass and Christine both thought I should present the paper. They argued that I had more battle experience, or at least that was their story. They were nearby, and I kept expecting to look over at them and find them hiding under the table.

I began by reminding everyone that standard law and economics assumes that people have correct beliefs and choose rationally. But suppose they don't? How should law and economics change? Our paper offered an illustrative example based on a new policy that had been adopted by the Chicago police department. Parking tickets had traditionally been placed on a car's front windshield, held down by the wiper blade. The new policy was to issue tickets that were printed on bright orange paper and were attached by some sticky substance to the driver's side window, where they were highly visible to drivers passing by. We pointed out that such a policy was smart from a behavioral perspective, since it might increase the perceived probability of getting a ticket, thus discouraging illegal parking at almost no cost.* This example may not seem either profound or controversial, but remember that part of the received wisdom in law and economics is that people have correct beliefs, including about the probability of getting caught committing some crime, and base their decisions about whether to commit a crime, from illegal parking to robbing a bank, by calculating the expected gains and losses. If it were possible to change the perception of the chance of getting caught by just changing the color and location of parking tickets, without changing the actual probability of being caught, then it might be possible to do the same for more serious crimes. This thought was pure heresy.

---

* Later we would call this a nudge.

Judge Posner remained quiet for about five minutes, but then he could no longer contain himself. Why, he asked out of the blue, were we ignoring evolution? Didn't evolutionary biology explain many of the odd behaviors discussed in the paper, such as turning down small offers in the Ultimatum Game, or ignoring sunk costs? Couldn't evolution explain these and all our other "cognitive quirks" (a slyly deprecating term he insisted on using)? His thought was that if humans had evolved to pay attention to sunk costs, or resist unfair offers in the Ultimatum Game, then such behavior must be good for us, in some sense, and therefore rational. Problem solved.

I assured him that I was not a creationist and accepted evolution as a scientific fact. I added that there was no doubt that many of the aspects of human behavior that we were talking about had evolutionary roots. But, I argued, accepting the theory of evolution as true does not mean that it needs to feature prominently in an economic analysis. We know people are loss averse; we don't need to know whether it has an evolutionary explanation. (Amos used to joke that there once were species that did not display the endowment effect, but they are now extinct.) Furthermore, the real point of behavioral economics is to highlight behaviors that are in conflict with the standard rational model. Unless we change the model to say that people pay attention to sunk costs, the model will make poor predictions. At this point Posner was completely exasperated. "You are completely unscientific!" he cried, in utter despair. I had resolved to remain calm so I just smiled at this outburst, said, "Okay then," and moved on. There was much more contentious material still to come, and I was determined not to get into a shouting contest, especially with a federal judge!

The biggest fight was about something called the Coase theorem. The Coase theorem is named for its inventor, Ronald Coase, who had been a faculty member at University of Chicago Law School for many years. The theorem can be easily stated: in the absence of transaction costs, meaning that people can easily trade with one another, resources will flow to their highest-valued use.[*]

---

[*] Another important proviso of the Coase theorem, along with no transaction costs, is that the stakes be "small" relative to the wealth of the disputing parties. I will ignore it for the purposes of this discussion.

The logic is easy to explain. I will follow Coase's lead and explain it with a simple numerical example. Suppose that Alexa and Julia are college roommates. Julia is quiet and studious, but Alexa is boisterous and likes to play loud music while she studies, which disturbs Julia. Julia complains to the dorm resident advisor, Hallie, who is empowered to settle disputes like this. Hallie can choose one of two alternatives: she can give Alexa the right to play her music as loud as she likes, or she can give Julia the right to quiet during certain hours. The Coase theorem makes a strong and surprising prediction: Hallie's decision will have no effect on how much music Alexa will play. Rather, that will depend simply on whether Alexa likes her music more than Julia hates it.

The result is surprising but the logic is simple. Suppose Alexa is willing to pay $5 per night to blast her music, and Julia is willing to pay $3 a night for silence. If Julia is awarded the right to silence, then, according to the Coase theorem, Alexa will pay Julia some amount between $3 and $5 for the right to play her music, an amount Julia will accept. Both will be happier this way than if Alexa couldn't play her music but no money changed hands; that is, after all, why they're both agreeing to the transaction. And if Alexa wins the right to play her music, Julia will be unwilling to pay her enough to stop, since her value of silence is less than Alexa's joy of music. Either way, Julia will have to find somewhere else to study if she wants quiet.

The reason this result is important for the law is that judges often decide who owns a certain right, and the Coase theorem says that if transaction costs are low, then what the judge decides won't actually determine what economic activities will take place; the judge will just decide who has to pay. The article that includes this result, entitled "The Problem of Social Cost," is one of the most cited economics articles of all time.

The argument I have sketched up to this point crucially depends on the stated assumption that the costs involved in the two parties coming to an efficient economic agreement are small to nonexistent. Coase is upfront about this. He says: "This is, of course, a very unrealistic assumption." Although many applications of the Coase theorem ignore Coase's warning, we wanted to show that the result was wrong, even when it could be shown that transaction costs were essentially zero. To do so, we presented the results of the mug experiments that were discussed in chapter 16, the results of which are summarized in figure 17.

FIGURE 17

A: Students ranked by how much they valued a Cornell mug.

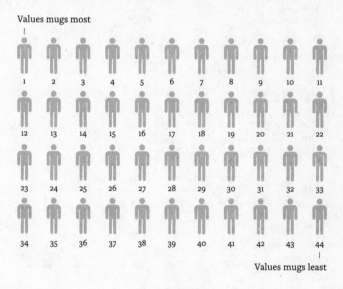

B: As with the tokens, we assigned mugs randomly to the students.

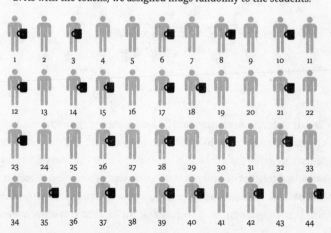

FIGURE 17

C: This is how we'd expect things to turn out if the Coase Theorem is right:

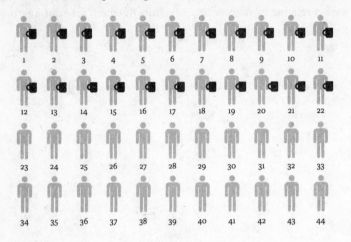

FIGURE 17

D: Instead, it looked something like this:

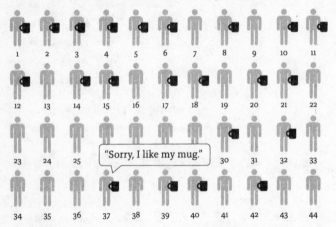

"Sorry, I like my mug."

Recall that the first stage of the experiments involved tokens that were redeemable for cash, with each subject told a different personal redemption value for a token, meaning the cash they could get for it if they owned one at the end of the experiment. The Coase theorem predicts that the students who received the highest personal valuations for their tokens would end up owning them; that is what it means to say that resources flow to their highest valued use. And that is what happened. The market worked perfectly, just as the theory predicted, which also meant that transaction costs must not be inhibiting trade in any meaningful way.

But the Coase theorem is not meant to be limited to tokens for which people are told their personal values. It says that the same thing should happen when we replace the tokens with real goods, such as coffee mugs. So when we gave every other student a coffee mug, the Coase theorem predicts that the students who liked the mugs most should end up owning them, and since the mugs were randomly assigned, about half the mugs should trade. Yet we found that trading volume was much lower than that: resources were not flowing at the rate predicted. And the reason was the endowment effect: people given mugs valued them about twice as much as people not given the mugs. How goods were allocated *did* affect who would end up owning the mugs. In other words, the Coase theorem worked in theory, when trading for tokens redeemable for cash, but it did not work in practice, when trading for real-world objects like coffee mugs. Questioning the Coase theorem at a law and economics workshop! That was high treason.

One of the unfortunate aspects of the University of Chicago at that time, one that is thankfully no longer the case, was that there was an undue tolerance for scholars who would spout the Chicago School traditional lines, loudly and frequently. One example was the economist John Lott, who had strung together a series of visiting appointments allowing him to be at the university for several years. Lott is most famous for writing a book entitled *More Guns, Less Crime*. As the title suggests, the thesis of the book is that if we just made sure every American was armed at all times, no one would dare commit a crime, a claim that other researchers have strongly disputed.* Lott was a frequent attendee and active participant at workshops. His style resembled that of a pit bull.

At this workshop, Lott was present and looking annoyed, so I hoped he was not packing a gun. His wife, Gertrude (also an economist), was in the crowd as well and asked a question about the mugs

---

* The latest findings by Stanford Law professor John Donoghue and his colleagues suggest that if anything, the passage of so-called "right to carry" laws increases crime rates (Aneja, Donohue III, and Zhang, 2014).

study. Couldn't the low trading of the mugs be explained by transaction costs? I explained that the tokens experiment had ruled out this explanation—after all, the tokens had the same transaction costs as the mugs, and the tokens did trade as much as the theory predicted. She seemed satisfied, but then Lott jumped in to "help." "Well," he asked, "couldn't we just call the endowment effect itself a transaction cost?" I was shocked by this comment; transaction costs are supposed to be the *cost* of doing a transaction—not the *desire* to do a transaction. If we are free to re-label preferences as "costs" at will so that behavior appears to be consistent with the standard theory, then the theory is both untestable and worthless. So instead of trying to reason with Lott, I turned to Posner and asked him whether he would now concede that I was not the *least* scientific person in the room. Posner smiled, nodded his agreement, and everyone in the room who could see him laughed. But Posner was not in Lott's line of sight, so I saw him angrily asking people around him what had happened. I quickly moved on to another topic.

———

The fact that the strongest resistance to behavioral economics came from those who had the greatest investment in building up the rational actor model raised an amusing possibility. Might their objections be more evidence in support of the sunk-cost fallacy? Of course, I could not say to my critics that by clinging to their beloved theories they were merely paying attention to sunk costs, but I could introduce the one bit of new experimental data we had included in the paper. The data came from a version of the Ultimatum Game.

In the usual version of the Ultimatum Game, the experimenter provides the money that the participants divide. Now we had created a version in which the experimenter makes money! We asked students to bring $5 to class for the purpose of an in-class demonstration. (Participation was voluntary.) Then each student filled out a form indicating how he would play a $10 version of the Ultimatum Game, with the money coming from the $5 each player had contributed. Players indicated their contingent decisions both as Proposer and as Responder, were told that they would be randomly assigned to one of those roles, and then were paired with another, anonymous student who had been given the other role.[*]

If sunk costs don't matter, then the outcome of this game should be identical to the one where the experimenter provides the money. The sunk cost of $5 is a SIF. But economists might think that if the students had to provide their own money, they will take the experiment more seriously and therefore act more rationally. We found exactly the opposite. Although the Proposers behaved very similarly to participants in previous versions of the game where the money came from the experimenter, with most offering to share at least 40% of the $10, the Responders, the ones we were really interested in, changed their behavior in a manner that made the results even more inconsistent with the predictions of the standard theory.

Rather than doing the rational self-interested thing of agreeing to take any positive offer (the smallest offer allowed in our version was 50 cents), when the Responders were playing with what they considered to be their own money (rather than "house money") they became even more concerned with being treated fairly. In the experiments Kahneman, Knetsch, and I had run years before, the average minimum request by Responders was $1.94. In these new experiments, that average jumped to $3.21 for a group of MIT MBA students, $3.73 for Chicago MBA students, and $3.35 for Chicago law students. And in all three groups, many of the Responders demanded their full $5 back. Making the experiment more "real" had made the Responders *less* consistent with self-interested income maximization! As we had hoped, the audience greeted this result with some consternation.

This experiment was germane to the behavioral analysis of the Coase theorem. Willingness to walk away from an "unfair" offer is another reason why the predictions of the Coase theorem often fail. I had discovered this firsthand many years earlier in Rochester. Our

* The experiment makes money because the students had provided the stakes and many offers were rejected, meaning that both players got nothing. We always figured out a way of returning this money to the students, often by playing the beauty contest game discussed earlier and giving the leftover money to the winner.

home there had a willow tree in the backyard that shed its leaves late in the fall and continued to do so even after snow arrived. This made raking the leaves especially arduous. The tree was located very close to the border of my neighbor's land, and the neighbor hated that tree. He asked me to have the tree removed.

I was ambivalent about the tree. It was nice to look at and provided some shade, factors that roughly offset the cleanup issue. Still, in the interest of neighborhood harmony I inquired about the cost of removing the tree and found out the price was $1,000, roughly one month's income for me at the time. I was not willing to pay that much money to get rid of the tree. But I knew the Coase theorem. In fact, I was teaching a course in which it played a central role. So I went to talk to my neighbor and told him that, while the tree did not bother me, if he felt strongly about it, I would let him arrange to remove it at his own expense. He thought this was the most outrageous suggestion he ever heard, slammed the door in my face, and never broached the subject again.

When people are given what they consider to be unfair offers, they can get angry enough to punish the other party, even at some cost to themselves. That is the basic lesson of the Ultimatum Game. As the willow tree story illustrates, the same can occur in situations in which the Coase theorem is often applied. After a lawsuit, both sides are typically upset with each other, and this is particularly true for the person who loses the case. For the Coase theorem to work, that losing party has to be willing to make an offer to the other side if he puts a greater value on the property right he just lost. But if people are angry, the last thing they want to do is talk to the other side. Law professor Ward Farnsworth documented this reluctance by interviewing attorneys from over twenty civil cases in which injunctive relief was sought and either granted or denied after full litigation before a judge. In not a single case did the parties even attempt to negotiate after the court had issued its order.

In addition to the Coase theorem, the other part of the paper that got people's blood boiling was something we left for the very end of it—the topic of paternalism. The core principle underlying the Chicago School's libertarian beliefs is *consumer sovereignty*: the notion that people make good choices, and certainly better choices than anyone

else could make for them. By raising the specters of bounded rationality and bounded self-control, we were undercutting this principle. If
people make mistakes, then it becomes conceivable, at least in principle, that someone could help them make a better choice.

We knew this was treacherous, inflammatory territory for the Chicago law and economics crowd, so we approached the topic in the mildest
possible manner using a term Cass had coined: "anti-antipaternalism."
The double negative implied that we were not ready to put forward a
positive argument *for* paternalism. Instead, we noted that the knee-
jerk claim that it is impossible to help anyone make a better decision is
clearly undercut by the research. The short, two-page section on this
topic was followed by a longer section on "behavioral bureaucrats." It
was, for Cass and me, the first of many times that we went out of our
way to say that if the government bureaucrat is the person trying to
help, it must be recognized that the bureaucrat is also a Human, subject to biases. Frustratingly, no matter how many times we repeat this
refrain, we continue to be accused of ignoring it.

After the workshop, we retreated to the faculty club. Christine had
a glass of wine, I had a double scotch, and Cass had three Diet Cokes—
his strongest and favorite elixir. We had not converted any of the key
participants, but we had survived. Better still, we had confirmed that
our paper was going to cause a stir.

Postscript: It is not possible to say what impact our paper had. We do
know that it has been frequently cited, but cannot determine whether
we successfully nudged anyone to take up the cause of behavioral law
and economics. What I can say is that today there is a lot of behavioral law and economics research being done, enough to fill an 800-
page *Oxford Handbook of Behavioral Economics and the Law*, edited by
Eyal Zamir and Doron Teichman. One of the prominent contributors to this field, UCLA law professor Russell Korobkin, is ready to
declare victory: "The battle to separate the economic analysis of legal
rules and institutions from the straitjacket of strict rational choice
assumptions has been won." Ever fearful of overconfidence, I am not
ready to declare "mission accomplished," but for sure we can safely
declare "mission launched."

28

The Offices

Normally the Booth School of Business at the University of Chicago is a research hotbed. You can almost feel those scientific frontiers creak as they are pushed ever outward. Except, that is, for a few months in the spring of 2002. During that period, research, at least among the tenured faculty members of the school, took a pause. Offices needed to be picked.

The task at hand was seemingly simple. After years in charming but cramped and rustic quarters on the university's main quadrangle, the business school was building a new home two blocks away. Designed by the world-famous architect Rafael Viñoly, it was to be a stunning, modern edifice with a spectacular atrium. The site was across the street from the famous Robie House, the first home built by Frank Lloyd Wright, and Viñoly had paid subtle homage to Wright in designing the corner of the building that faces Wright's iconic house. The palatial building was full of light, and virtually everyone was looking forward to the move. All that was left to do was to decide who would get which office. What could go wrong?

There are many possible ways to assign offices, but the deans settled on an unusual process. There would be an office draft. Faculty would receive a time slot to pick, and then choose any open office, with full knowledge of all the selections made up to that point. This all seems fine, but there remained the important question of how the order would be determined. Seniority seems like one obvious choice, but there is a famous saying around Chicago that you are only as good as your last paper. Strike seniority as a possibility. A lottery was also not seriously considered; office locations were too important to leave entirely to chance.

The deans decided that the selection order would be based on "merit," and the judge of that merit would be Deputy Dean for Faculty John Huizinga. He already had the duty of negotiating with new faculty members over the terms of their contracts, as well as that of dealing with any current faculty members who were unhappy with their teaching assignments, pay, colleagues, students, research budget, or anything else. In spite of several years on the job, John was greatly admired by the faculty, who considered him an honest, if at times blunt, straight shooter.[*]

The other deans had the sense to make it clear that this job was going to be handled solely by John, to whom all complaints should be taken. After considerable deliberation, he announced how the picking order (and pecking order) would be determined. First, there would be a certain number of categories (bins, they were called, a term from statistics). John would decide how many bins there would be, and which faculty members would be assigned to each bin, but the order *within each bin* would be determined by random drawing. The number of bins was not announced, and has still not been revealed. As we will see, this created some ambiguity about the process.

On the day of the draft, faculty members would have fifteen minutes each to select their office. They would do so with the aid of one of the architects working on the project. The building was a steel cage at this point, so it would not be possible to go see the offices, but architectural drawings and a scale model of the building were made available. Two other rules of interest: offices could not be traded and, after one senior faculty member inquired, the deans emphatically ruled out the possibility of buying an earlier draft pick from a colleague. This ruling, and the fact that the school decided not to simply auction off the draft picks, reveals that even at the University of Chicago Booth School of Business—where many favor an open market in babies and organs—some objects are simply too sacred to sell in the marketplace: faculty offices.

It appeared most of the faculty had expected a process vaguely like this, and nearly all the senior faculty were content in the knowledge

---

[*] John was also a big basketball fan who would regularly win the NBA fantasy basketball league. A few years after this episode, he ended up serving as agent for the 7-foot-6-inch basketball star Yao Ming.

that they would be chosen to make one of the early picks. A few weeks of calm ensued.

In time, all the faculty members received an email announcing that the draft would occur in a few weeks, and that our time to pick was, say, from 10:15 to 10:30 a.m. on a Wednesday. The email gave no hint about the pecking order. We were in the dark . . . for about thirty minutes. Anil Kashyap, a hyperenergetic senior faculty member in the finance and economics groups, took it upon himself to make the draft order known to everyone. An email went out asking people to reply with their time slot. Within hours, the basic outline of the draft order became clear.

Seniority had not been ignored altogether. All the tenured full professors would choose before the (untenured in our system) associate professors, who would pick before the assistant professors, who would pick before the adjuncts, and so forth. The order of the picks within the groups of untenured faculty members seemed clearly random, and at that point the junior faculty went back to work, trying to get tenure and have a chance to do work in one of those senior faculty offices someday. Meanwhile, all hell broke loose among the senior faculty members.

John has never revealed to me (or anyone else, as far as I know) exactly how the draft order for the senior faculty was determined. What follows is my best guess.* I believe that there were three full-professor bins. The first bin (bin A) had about a dozen people who were considered stars and/or were the obvious senior figures in their respective groups. There was at least one faculty member from each faculty group, such as accounting, economics, and so forth, but there were several people from finance, which is by far the largest department. So far, so good. No one would have complained if Gene Fama had been given the first choice. He was the most distinguished faculty member in the draft pool.

Bin B contained most of the rest of the tenured faculty, and bin C consisted of faculty members who were no longer doing active

---

* I did show John a draft of this chapter and asked for comments. He neither confirmed nor denied the details of my reconstruction of how things went, but he did concede that I had the basic facts right.

research. In a classy move, John had slotted himself as the last tenured faculty member to choose. I believe that John selected people to be in the first bin with several purposes in mind. One was to reward those who had made significant contributions to the school. Another was to scatter the star faculty members around the building; the most attractive offices were those in corners and as such they were far apart, since the five-story building takes up an entire city block with faculty offices spread over the top three floors.

The most distressed people were the ones in bin B who thought they deserved to have been in bin A, and then got unlucky in the lottery within their bin. There were several people in this category, but the angriest of them all was "Archie."* Someone else from his department, "Clyde," had been included in bin A, and he had lucked into the second pick. Meanwhile, Archie was picking near the end of the second group, after two of his much younger colleagues.

To call Archie furious at this turn of events is a serious understatement. He was hopping mad, or jumping mad if there is such a thing. He was corybantic, if that means anything to you. As far as Archie was concerned, the entire draft had been rigged and the considerable evidence to the contrary would not sway him. The first pick had gone to Doug Diamond, one of the most respected and likable members of the faculty but not a household name outside of academia. Fama was third. I remember thinking at the time that the only person who was truly happy with their spot in the draft was Doug. But no one was as unhappy as Archie.

About a day after the draft order was pieced together, Anil Kashyap got back to work and decided that it was essential to test how this draft would play out. Someone with a high pick might be interested to see the "neighborhoods" that could develop out of the later picks. We conducted a "mock" draft via email. A spreadsheet was passed around by email from Doug, to Clyde, to Gene, and so forth, on which everyone would indicate their choice of office.

Someone circulated floor plans but the faculty demanded more information, specifically the size of each office and whether the office

---

* When people in this chapter are identified by first name only, they are real characters but with fictitious names.

had a thermostat. There were thermostats in about one in three offices and, at least in theory, the occupant of the office could control the temperature with the thermostat. I suggested to John that they install "placebo" thermostats in the rest of the offices to make everyone happy, and based on my experience with the thermostat in the office I chose, the placebos would have been equally effective in controlling the temperature. The mock draft took days to complete, leading to loud complaints of "Where the hell is X, doesn't he read his email?" Everyone was captivated by the exercise, so we ran it again to see if things would change. This was important!

Finally, the day of the draft arrived, and we began making picks at 8:30 in the morning. The only early hiccup was when someone picked an office that someone below him had claimed in a mock draft, producing a "That was my office, you bastard!" It seems that the endowment effect can occur even for an office that was selected in what had been clearly labeled a practice exercise. Then, something strange happened. Picking at 1:15, the finance professor Luigi Zingales had his eye on a fifth-floor office near where his corporate finance colleagues were congregating. Luigi is suspicious by nature—he attributes it to his Italian upbringing—and he questioned the estimated square footage of the office he had selected.

The architect tried to put him off, but Luigi persisted. She hauled out the real floor plans only to discover that he was right. The office he had selected was 20 square feet smaller than indicated. (The offices are all large, mostly between 180 and 230 square feet.) Luigi quickly switched his pick to a larger one nearby, and went back to his office to share his discovery. Naturally, he had not mentioned his suspicion to anyone before making his choice, lest he lose his competitive advantage. Word travelled quickly. People who had picked earlier were descending on the office that was being used for the selection process, demanding that their office be remeasured. Other mistakes in the office size estimates were found and people wanted to switch. Mayhem! John, who was out of town at a conference, was finally reached, and sometime around 3 p.m. the draft was suspended for remeasurement.

It took a few days for the new measurements to be announced, and this time the unhappy people included some with early picks. A few of their offices had "shrunk," and they wanted to switch to offices that others, lower in the draft, had taken. John now weighed in via email. The draft would start over the following week. People were free to switch their picks; however, *they could not choose any office that someone had already taken, even if that person were drafting later.* More uproar. Around this time, John wandered into the faculty lounge during lunchtime wearing a pair of plastic Groucho Marx glasses, as if he were there incognito. It brought the house down, but the ranks of the pissed off did not laugh quite as loudly.

Postmortem

A year or so later, we moved into the new building and for the most part all was well. In hindsight, the most remarkable thing about the entire fiasco is that, except for the nine corner offices, the rest of the offices are pretty much the same. They are all nice, much nicer than what we had in the old building. Sure, some are a bit bigger than others, and some have slightly nicer views, but many of the differences that are now apparent were not fully appreciated at the time of the draft. For example, the offices on the fifth floor were grabbed early, perhaps on the basis of a flawed "higher is better" heuristic, but there is no view advantage to the fifth floor versus the fourth, and it has the disadvantage of being served by only one of the three elevator banks in the building, and the busiest one at that. The offices along the north face of the building have the nicest views, including the Chicago skyline, but were not among the first offices picked.

If the north exposure, with its neutral light and attractive views, was the value buy in this market, the overhyped commodity was square footage. The difference between an office of 190 square feet and one of 210 square feet is not a noticeable difference. Most people who visit the school don't even realize that offices differ in size. But if the only thing you are staring at on a spreadsheet is a list of offices with their measurements, this factor is bound to be overweighted. If there is a number, people will use it.

In hindsight I think that some of the furor created by explicitly ranking the faculty members could have been mitigated if the process had been a bit more transparent. For example, it might have been a good idea to make the number of bins public. This would have at least reassured Clyde that he had not been deliberately slotted into one of the later picks.

I also put a bit of the blame on the architect, Rafael Viñoly, and his team. Although they had dutifully spent hundreds of hours talking to students, faculty, and administrators about how the building would be used, and the result is a space both aesthetically pleasing and highly functional, no one told the architect how the offices would be assigned. Had he known, he might have avoided corner offices altogether. One small change he could have made, even late in the game, was to make the office that Doug Diamond took a bit smaller. Doug's office is on the fifth floor, on the northeast corner, and, to rub salt in the wounds of the unlucky, it is the biggest office of them all. At the time I suggested that, if possible, the architect should chop some of his office off and give it to one of his neighbors, so that there would be a less obvious first choice. But he was only an architect; the term "choice architect" had not yet been invented.

29

Football

Of the many unique aspects of the so-called job of being a pro-fessor at a top research university, the one that I most prize is the freedom to think about almost anything I find interest-ing and still get to call it work. You have already seen that I managed to write a paper about the mental accounting of wine drinkers. The next two chapters delve into other domains that on the surface may seem frivolous: player selection in the National Football League, and decision-making by contestants on television game shows. What the topics have in common is that they provided unique ways of studying decision-making at high stakes, and thus a reply to those critics who kept (and keep) bringing up the claim from the Gauntlet that behav-ioral biases go away when the stakes are high enough.

One version of this critique, which applies to the study of the National Football League, comes from Gary Becker, the most distin-guished of the many practitioners of Chicago price theory.* I will call this critique the Becker conjecture. Becker believed that in competi-tive labor markets, only people who are able to perform their jobs like Econs are able to land the key positions. Becker made this conjecture when he was asked his opinion of behavioral economics. "Division of labor strongly attenuates if not eliminates any effects [caused by bounded rationality.] . . . [I]t doesn't matter if 90 percent of people can't do the complex analysis required to calculate probabilities. The 10 percent of people who can will end up in the jobs where it's required." In this chapter, we test the Becker conjecture. Does it apply

---

* Sadly, Gary Becker died in 2014 while this book was being written. He was one of the most imaginative economists I have ever met. I am sorry that he is not around to tell me what he thinks of this book. I am sure I would have learned something from his comments, even if I disagreed. The cliché "he is a gentleman and a scholar" was an apt description of Gary.

to the owners, general managers, and coaches of the teams in the National Football League? Spoiler alert: it doesn't.

My research about the National Football League was done with my former student Cade Massey, who now teaches at the Wharton School of Business. Similar to my experience with Werner DeBondt, I first met Cade when he was an MBA student, during my first year at the University of Chicago. I was impressed with his intuitive understanding of what makes people tick, and what makes a research project interesting. I encouraged him to continue his studies and pursue a PhD, and luckily for both of us, as well as for the students who are fortunate enough to take a class from him, he agreed to do so.

Our football paper is nominally about a peculiar institution called the NFL draft. In the NFL, teams get to pick players in a manner similar to the way we picked offices. And, not to worry: it is not necessary to care about American football to understand this chapter and its implications. In the end, this is a chapter about a problem that every organization faces: how to choose employees.

Here is how the NFL draft works. Once a year in late spring, the teams select prospective players. Almost all the candidates have been playing football at an American college or university, giving the professional scouts and general managers an opportunity to see how they play. The teams take turns choosing players, with the order of the picks determined by the teams' records the previous year. The team with the worst record picks first and the team that wins the championship picks last. There are seven rounds of the draft, meaning each team starts out with seven "picks," though there are additional picks handed out for reasons that are not important to our story. For the initial contract period, usually four or five years, an athlete can only play for the team that drafted him. When that contract runs out or the player is dropped from the team, the player is declared a free agent, and he can sign with whatever team he wants.

A key feature of this environment, which differs from the Chicago Booth office draft, is that teams are allowed to trade their picks. For example, the team with the fourth pick might agree to give up that pick in return for two or more later picks. There are a sufficient number of trades (over 400 in our sample) to make it possible to infer how teams value the right to pick earlier. Teams can also trade picks this year for picks in future years, which provides a way of examining the teams' time preferences.

Before we started this project, Cade and I had a strong hunch that there was some serious misbehaving going on in this environment. Specifically, we thought that teams were putting too high a value on the right to pick early in the draft. Part of this feeling was based on observing a few extreme examples. One of the most famous involved a larger-than-life character named Mike Ditka, a legendary former player who became the coach of the New Orleans Saints.

In the 1999 draft, Ditka decided that the only thing stopping the Saints from winning a championship soon was the acquisition of one player, a running back named Ricky Williams. The Saints owned the number twelve pick, and Ditka was worried that Williams would be snapped up before their turn came, so he announced publicly that he would be willing to trade away all of his picks if he could get Williams (not the smartest negotiation strategy). When it was the Washington Redskins' turn at the fifth pick and Ricky Williams was still available, the Saints were able to complete the trade Ditka wanted, although at a very steep price. Specifically, to move from the twelfth pick to the fifth pick, the Saints gave up all the picks they had in the current draft plus their first- and third-round picks the following year. Those latter picks turned out to be particularly costly to give away, because the Saints ended up as the second worst team in the league in 1999, meaning they gave away the second pick in the entire draft in 2000. Clearly, snagging Williams was not enough to turn the team around, and Ditka was fired. Williams played four years for the Saints and was a very good but not transformative player, and the team could have used the help of all the players they might have acquired with the draft picks they traded away. Cade and I wondered: why would anyone make such a trade?

The Saints' trade was just an extreme example of the general behavior we thought we would find, namely overvaluing the right to pick early. Five findings from the psychology of decision-making supported our hypothesis that early picks will be too expensive:

1. *People are overconfident.* They are likely to think their ability to discriminate between the ability of two players is greater than it is.

2. *People make forecasts that are too extreme.* In this case, the people whose job it is to assess the quality of prospective players—scouts—are too willing to say that a particular player is likely to be a superstar, when by definition superstars do not come along very often.

3. *The winner's curse.* When many bidders compete for the same object, the winner of the auction is often the bidder who most overvalues the object being sold. The same will be true for players, especially the highly touted players picked early in the first round. The winner's curse says that those players will be good, but not as good as the teams picking them think. Most teams thought that Ricky Williams was an excellent prospect, but no one loved him as much as Mike Ditka.

4. *The false consensus effect.* Put basically, people tend to think that other people share their preferences. For instance, when the iPhone was new I asked the students in my class two anonymous questions: do you own an iPhone, and what percentage of the class do you think owns an iPhone? Those who owned an iPhone thought that a majority of their classmates did as well, while those who didn't thought iPhone ownership uncommon. Likewise in the draft, when a team falls in love with a certain player they are just *sure* that every other team shares their view. They try to jump to the head of the line before another team steals their guy.

5. *Present bias.* Team owners, coaches, and general managers all want to win *now*. For the players selected at the top of the draft, there is always the possibility, often illusory, as in the case of Ricky Williams, that the player will immediately turn a losing team into a winner or a winning team into a Super Bowl champion. Teams want to win now!

So our basic hypothesis was that early picks were overvalued, meaning that the market for draft picks did not satisfy the efficient market hypothesis. Fortunately, we were able to get all the data we needed to rigorously test this hypothesis.

The first step in our analysis was just to estimate the market value of picks. Since picks are often traded, we could use the historical trade data to estimate the relative value of picks. If you want to get the fifth pick and you have the twelfth pick, as Ditka did, how much do you normally have to throw in to make that trade? The outcome of that analysis is shown in figure 18 below. The dots are specific trades that we used to estimate the curve. There are two things that jump out from this figure. The first is that it is very steep: the first pick is worth about five times as much as the thirty-third pick, the first one taken in the second round. In principle, a team with the first pick could make a series of trades and end up with five early picks in the second round.

FIGURE 18

Average value by NFL draft order relative to the first pick

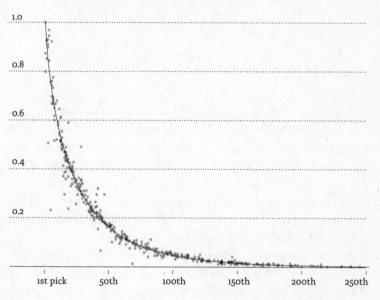

The other thing to notice about this figure is how well the curve fits the data. The individual trades, represented by the dots, lie very close to the estimated line. In empirical work you almost never get such orderly data. How could this happen? It turns out the data line up so well because everyone relies on something called the Chart, a table that lists the relative value of picks. Mike McCoy, a minority owner of the Dallas Cowboys who was an engineer by training, originally estimated the Chart. The coach at the time, Jimmy Johnson, had asked him for help in deciding how to value potential trades, and McCoy eyeballed the historical trade data and came up with the Chart. Although the Chart was originally proprietary information only known by the Cowboys, eventually it spread around the league, and now everyone uses it. Figure 19 shows how highly the chart values first-round picks.

FIGURE 19

"The Chart"

PICK	VALUE	PICK	VALUE	PICK	VALUE	PICK	VALUE
1	3,000	9	1,350	17	950	25	720
2	2,600	10	1,300	18	900	26	700
3	2,200	11	1,250	19	875	27	680
4	1,800	12	1,200	20	850	28	660
5	1,700	13	1,150	21	800	29	640
6	1,600	14	1,100	22	780	30	620
7	1,500	15	1,050	23	760	31	600
8	1,400	16	1,000	24	740	32	590

When Cade and I tracked down Mr. McCoy, we had a nice conversation with him about the history of this exercise. McCoy stressed that it was never his intention to say what value picks *should* have, only the value that teams had used based on prior trades. Our analysis had a different purpose. We wanted to ask whether the prices implied by the chart were "right," in the efficient market hypothesis sense of the term. Should a rational team be willing to give up that many picks in order to get one of the very high ones?

Two more steps were required to establish our case that teams valued early picks too highly. The first of these was easy: determine how much players cost. Fortunately, we were able to get data on player compensation. Before delving into those salaries, it is important to understand another peculiar feature of the National Football League labor market for players. The league has adopted a salary cap, meaning an upper limit on how much a team can pay its players. This is quite different from many other sports, for example Major League Baseball and European soccer, where rich owners can pay as much as they want to acquire star players.

The salary cap is what makes our study possible. Its existence means that each team has to live within the same budget. In order to win regularly, teams are forced to be economical. If a Russian oligarch wants to spend hundreds of millions of dollars to buy a soccer superstar, one can always rationalize the decision by saying that he is getting utility from watching that player, as with buying an expensive piece of art. But in the National Football League, acquiring an expensive player, or giving away lots of picks to get a star like Ricky Williams, involves explicit opportunity costs for the team, such as the other players that could have been hired with that money or drafted with those picks. This binding budget constraint means that the only way to build a winning team is to find players that provide more value than they cost.

The league also has rules related to rookie salaries. The compensation of first-year players, by draft order, is shown in figure 20. The figures we use here are the official "cap charge" that the team is charged, which includes the player's salary plus an amortization of any signing bonus paid up front. Figure 20 shares many features of figure 18. First of all, the curve is quite steep. High picks are paid much more than lower-round picks. And again, the data are highly regular because the league pretty much dictates how much players are paid in their initial contracts.

FIGURE 20

Average compensation by draft order

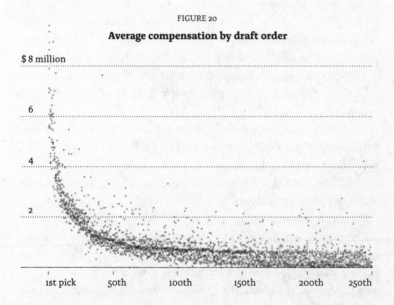

So high picks end up being expensive in two ways. First, teams have to give up a lot of picks to use one (either by paying to trade up, or in opportunity cost, by declining to trade down). And second, high-round picks get paid a lot of money. The obvious question is: are they worth it?

Another way of asking this question is: what would have to be true to make the price of early picks rational, and is it in fact true? The price says that, on average, the first player taken in the draft is five times better than the thirty-third player. That fact alone does not tell us anything, since players' values can vary by much more than a 5:1 ratio. Some players are perennial all-stars who can transform a team. Others are complete busts that cost the team a lot of money and provide little in return. In fact, high-profile busts actually hurt performance because the teams are unable to ignore sunk costs. If a team is paying a high draft pick a lot of money, it feels under a lot of pressure to put him in the game, regardless of how well he is playing.

The key appears to be how good a team's managers are at distinguishing between stars and busts. Here is a simple thought experiment. Suppose you rank all the players taken at a given position (quarterback, wide receiver, etc.) by the order in which they were picked. Now take two players drafted consecutively, such as the third running back and the fourth. What is the chance that the player taken earlier is better by some objective measure? If the teams were perfect forecasters, then the player taken first would be better 100% of the time. If the teams have no ability, then the earlier pick will be better half the time, like flipping a coin. Take a guess at how good teams are at this task.

In reality, across the entire draft, the chance that the earlier player will be better is only 52%. In the first round it is a bit higher, 56%.* Keep that thought in mind, both as you read the rest of this chapter and the next time you want to hire someone and are "sure" you have found the perfect candidate.

Although this result gives a strong hint of how our analysis would come out, it is worthwhile to provide an outline of our more thorough evaluation. We followed the performance of each player drafted during our study period for the duration of his initial contract. Then, for each player-year, we assigned an economic value to the performance of

---

* These statistics use the simple metric of "games started" to determine who is better. We use this simple metric because it can be measured for players at any position. However, these results and others I will mention are similar even if we use more fine-grained performance measures, such as yards gained for a wide receiver or running back.

that player; in other words, we estimated the value the player provided to the team that year. We did so by looking at how much it would cost to hire an equivalent player (by position and quality) who was in the sixth, seventh, or eighth year of his contract, and was thus being paid the market rate, because after his initial contract ran out he became a free agent. A player's performance value to the team that drafted him is then the sum of the yearly values for each year he stays with the team until his initial contract runs out. (After that, to retain him, they will have to pay the market price or he can jump to another team.)

In figure 21, we plotted this total "performance value" for each player, sorted by draft order, as well as the compensation curve shown in figure 20. Notice that the performance value curve is downward-sloping, meaning that teams do have some ability to rate players. Players who are taken earlier in the draft are indeed better, but by how much? If you subtract the compensation from the performance value, you obtain the "surplus value" to the team, that is, how much more (or less) performance value the team gets compared to how much it has to pay the player. You can think of it like the profit a team gets from the player over the length of his initial contract.

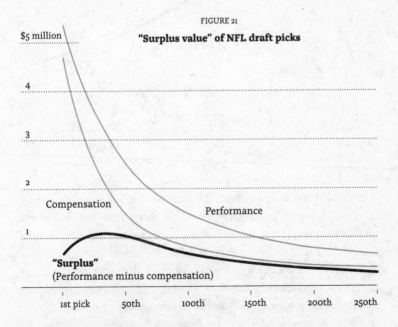

FIGURE 21

"Surplus value" of NFL draft picks

The bottom line on this chart shows the surplus value. The thing to notice is that this curve is sloping upward throughout the first round. What this means is that the early picks are actually worth *less* than the later picks. But remember, the Chart says that early picks are worth a lot more than later picks! Figure 22 shows both curves on the same chart and measured in comparable units, with the vertical axis representing value relative to the first pick, which is given a value of 1.

FIGURE 22

Comparing "The Chart" with player surplus

If the market for NFL players were efficient, these charts would be identical.

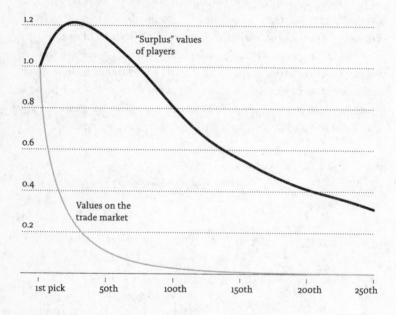

If this market were efficient, then the two curves would be identical. The draft-pick value curve would be an accurate forecast of the surplus that would accrue to the team from using that pick; i.e., the first pick would have the highest surplus, the second pick the second-highest surplus, etc. That is hardly the case. The trade market curve (and the Chart) says you can trade the first pick for five early second-round picks, but we are finding that *each* of those second-round picks yields more surplus to the team than the first-round pick they are together traded for! In all my years of studying market efficiency, this is the most blatant violation I have ever seen.

We made another interesting discovery about the market for picks. Sometimes teams will trade a pick in this year's draft for a pick next year. What is the exchange rate for such trades? Even a casual look at the data reveals that a simple rule of thumb is used for such trades: a pick in a given round this year fetches a pick one round earlier the following year. Give up a third-round pick this year and you can get a second-round pick next year. (Detailed analyses confirm that trades closely follow this rule.) This rule of thumb does not sound unreasonable on the surface, but we found that it implies that teams are discounting the future at 136% per year! Talk about being present-biased! You can borrow at better rates from a loan shark. Not surprisingly, smart teams have figured this out and are happy to give up a pick this year to get a higher-round pick the following year.[*]

So our research yielded two simple pieces of advice to teams. First, trade down. Trade away high first-round picks for additional picks later in the draft, especially second-round picks. Second, be a draft-pick banker. Lend picks this year for better picks next year.

Before discussing the significance of our findings, especially the advice to trade down, it is important to rule out a few potential explanations that will occur to many readers, especially those who think like economists.

Can teams make so much money from jersey sales bearing the player's name that they can still find it profitable to draft a high-profile player, even if he does not become a star? No. The teams share all sales of team jerseys and other official NFL products equally.

Can drafting a high-profile player sell enough tickets to make it worthwhile, even if he does not become a star? No. First of all, most NFL teams have waiting lists to buy season tickets. But more to the point, no one comes to watch a bad player even if he is famous. To thoroughly investigate this possibility, we redid our analysis using only offensive linemen, the largely anonymous behemoths who try

---

[*] A really smart team will trade a second-round pick this year for a first-round pick next year, and then trade that first-round pick for multiple second-round picks the following year, possibly converting one into a first-round pick in the subsequent year, and so forth.

to protect the quarterback from mountain-size defensive players who want to tackle him. Although only the most dedicated fans would be able to name many of the players on the offensive line for their favorite team, our analysis looks the same, so "star appeal" cannot be the missing factor that explains the anomaly.

Could the chance of getting a real superstar make the gamble worthwhile? No. We did one simple analysis to show this. The primary implication of our analysis is that teams with early picks should trade down, that is, trade their early pick for multiple later picks. To test the validity of this strategy, we evaluated every two-for-one trade that would be possible using the Chart as a guideline. For example, the Chart indicates that the team with the first pick could trade it for picks seven and eight, four and twelve, two and fifty, and so forth. For each of these potential hypothetical trades, we looked to see how the team did by using two measures of player performance: games started and years elected as an all-star. We found that trading down yielded a large increase in games started with no sacrifice in the number of all-star seasons.

How could the decision-makers in the league get this so wrong? Why didn't market forces drive the price of draft picks toward the surplus value they provide to the team? The answer provides a good illustration of the *limits to arbitrage* concept that was so important to understanding financial markets. Suppose a team reads and understands our paper, what could they do? If they are a good team that is usually near the top of the standings, there is not much they can do to take advantage of the market inefficiency, aside from being willing to lend this year's picks for better ones the following year. Since there is no way to sell a high draft pick short, there is no arbitrage opportunity for a smart team, much less for outside investors. The best one can hope to do is to buy a bad team, and at least for a while, improve their drafting strategy by trading down.

———

Before we even had our first draft of this paper, we had some interest from one of the NFL teams, and by now we have now worked informally with three teams (one at a time, of course). The first interaction we had was with Daniel Snyder, the owner of the Washington Redskins. Mr. Snyder had been invited by the entrepreneurship club at the Booth

School of Business to give a talk, and one of the organizers asked me to moderate a discussion for the audience. I agreed, knowing I would have some time to talk to Snyder one-on-one during lunch.

Dan Snyder is a self-made man. He dropped out of college to start a company that chartered jets to sell cheap spring break vacation trips to university students. He later went into the direct mail advertising business and had the good fortune or wisdom to sell the company in 2000, at the peak of the market. He used the money from that sale, plus a lot of debt, to buy the Redskins, his favorite team when he was a kid. (Unsurprisingly, many consider the name of the team to be a slur, but Snyder defends keeping it.) He had only been an owner for a brief period when we met.

I told Mr. Snyder about the project with Cade and he immediately said he was going to send "his guys" to see us right away, even though they were in the midst of the season. He said, "We want to be the best at everything." Apparently when Mr. Snyder wants something he gets it. That Monday I got a call from his chief operating officer, who wanted to talk to Cade and me ASAP. We met Friday of that week with two of his associates and had a mutually beneficial discussion. We gave them the basic lessons of our analysis, and they were able to confirm some institutional details for us.

After the season ended, we had further discussions with Snyder's staff. By then, we were pretty sure they had mastered our two take-aways: trade down and trade picks this year for better picks next year. Cade and I watched the draft on television that year with special interest that turned into deep disappointment. The team did exactly the *opposite* of what we had suggested! They moved up in the draft, and then traded away a high draft pick next year to get a lesser one this year. When we asked our contacts what happened we got a short answer. "Mr. Snyder wanted to win now."

This was a good forecast of Snyder's future decisions. In 2012 the Redskins had the sixth pick in the draft, meaning they had been the sixth worst team in 2011, and they were desperate for a high-quality quarterback. There were two highly rated quarterbacks available that year, Andrew Luck and Robert Griffin III, who is known as RG3 for short. Indianapolis had the first pick and had announced their intention to take Luck. The Redskins wanted RG3. The second pick belonged to the St. Louis Rams, who already had a young quarterback they liked, so the Redskins made a deal with the Rams. They moved up four spots from the sixth pick to the second one, and in addition to giving up that sixth pick they gave the Rams their first- and second-round picks for the following year, 2013, and their first-round pick in 2014. This was an astonishing price to pay to move up just four spots.

How did things work out? In the first year, RG3 did his best to make the trade look smart, and us egghead professors look dumb. He was an effective player who was exciting to watch and the team was winning, making the playoffs, suggesting that the trade might have a chance of working out if RG3 became a superstar. But late in the season he was injured and sat out a game. When he came back to play again, possibly too early, he aggravated the injury and needed surgery. The following year, he did not return to the top form he had showed as a rookie, and the Redskins had a terrible season, so bad that the 2014 first-round pick the Redskins had given the Rams turned out to be the second pick in that draft, so giving up that pick turned out to be very expensive. (Recall that it was a number two pick that the Redskins had originally traded up to get.) The 2014 season was also a disappointing one for RG3. In hindsight, another player named Russell Wilson, who was not picked until the third round, appears to be better and less injury-prone than RG3. During his three years in the NFL, Wilson has led his team to the Super Bowl twice, winning once.

Of course, one should not judge a trade using hindsight, and the Redskins were certainly unlucky that Griffen suffered from injuries. But that is part of the point. When you give up a bunch of top picks to select one player, you are putting all your eggs in his basket, and football players, like eggs, can be fragile.*

Our relationship with the Redskins did not last very long, but we soon found that another team (whose identity shall remain confidential) was interested in talking to us about draft strategy. In our dealings

---

* Postscript: The Redskins had a late-season game in 2014 against the St. Louis Rams, the team that received all those picks Washington relinquished to acquire their dream player. At the beginning of the game, the Rams' coach sent out all the players they had chosen with those bonus picks to serve as team captains for the coin toss that began the game. The Rams won the game 24-0 and RG3 was sitting on the bench due to poor play. We will see whether Mr. Snyder learns to be patient.

with that team we learned that there would often be debates among the team's leadership about draft strategy. Some staff members who were comfortable with analytic thinking bought into our analysis and argued for trading down and lending. Others, such as the owner or one of the coaches, would often fall in love with some player and insist on trading up to get their guy. Furthermore, on the few occasions where the team did trade down in the first round, getting a later first-round pick plus an additional second-round pick, the extra pick would not last long. The extra pick had the feel of "house money" and was usually traded away quickly to grab another "sure thing."

———

The failure of teams to draft optimally is a good example of a situation where a principal agent problem would be more accurately labeled a dumb principal problem. When an economist says of a team trading up, "That is just an agency problem," they mean that the general manager or the coach is worried about his job and needs to win now or get fired. Of course, it is perfectly rational for coaches and general managers to be worried about losing their jobs—they do often get fired. But I think blaming their bad decision-making on traditional agency problems is a mischaracterization. In many of these situations, and not only in sports, the owner is at least as responsible for causing the problem as the employees. It is often the case that general managers trade up because the *owner* wants to win now. This is similar to the example discussed in chapter 20 about the CEO who wanted his employees to take on twenty-three risky projects but was only going to get three because his employees were worried about the CEO firing them if the project did not pan out. It was up to the CEO to solve this problem.

The same applies to coaching decisions. In American football, each play is choreographed and there are dozens of specific, strategic decisions that coaches get to make, unlike in European football (soccer), which because of its more fluid nature only offers a small number of set plays, such as corner kicks. Some of the specific decision-making opportunities in the NFL can and have been analyzed. One specific decision is whether to "go for it" on fourth down. A team has four plays, called downs, in which it tries to gain 10 yards or score. If it does not, the other team gets the ball. If a team has failed to gain 10 yards on its first three plays, it has the option of trying to pick up the remainder of the necessary 10 yards (called "going for it"), attempting a field goal, or punting the ball down the field and giving possession to the other team. David Romer, an economist from Berkeley, studied this problem and found that teams don't go for it enough.

Romer's analysis has been replicated and extended with much more data by a football analytics expert named Brian Burke, and in 2013 the *New York Times* used his model to help create an application that computes the optimal strategy in any fourth-down situation: punt, go for it, or kick a field goal. Fans can follow the "*New York Times* 4th Down Bot" in real time and see what the math says a team should be doing. So what effect has this research plus a free app had on the behavior of football coaches? Essentially none. Since Romer wrote his paper, the frequency of going for it on fourth down has marginally gone down, meaning that teams have gotten dumber! (Similarly, there has been no noticeable change in teams' draft strategy since our paper came out.)

Nate Silver, the ex–sports analytics junkie who became famous for his political forecasts and for the excellent book *The Signal and the Noise*, estimates that bad fourth-down decisions cost a football team an average of half a win per season. The *Times* analysts estimate it to be closer to two-thirds of a win per year. That may not seem like a lot, but the season is only sixteen games. A team can win an extra game every other year just by making the smart decision two or three times a game, one they can even check online if they need help.*

Of course, coaches are Humans. They tend to do things the way they have always been done, because those decisions will not be second-guessed by the boss. As Keynes noted, following the conventional wisdom keeps you from getting fired. A smart owner (who reads eco-

---

* Footnote for NFL fans only: I think Silver's estimate may be conservative. It neglects the fact that if you know you are going to go for it on fourth down, it changes the plays you can call on third down. If a team has a third down and five yards to go they almost always try a pass, but if they know they will go for it on fourth and two yards to go, they can try a running play more often on third down, which of course will also improve their chances when they do decide to pass, since they will be less predictable.

nomics journals or hires someone to do that) would urge his staff to follow the strategy that maximizes the chance of winning, and tell them that it is going against the odds that will get you fired. But there are not very many of those owners. So owning a billion-dollar football team does not mean you are in Gary Becker's 10% club, and it certainly does not mean that you will be able to hire people who are in the club or get them to make optimal decisions.

Where should this leave us regarding the validity of the Becker conjecture—that the 10% of people who can do probabilities will end up in the jobs where such skills matter? At some level we might expect this conjecture to be true. All NFL players are really good at football; all copyeditors are good at spelling and grammar; all option traders can at least find the button on their calculators that can compute the Black–Scholes formula, and so forth. A competitive labor market does do a pretty good job of channeling people into jobs that suit them. But ironically, this logic may become less compelling as we move up the managerial ladder. All economists are at least pretty good at economics, but many who are chosen to be department chair fail miserably at that job. This is the famous Peter Principle: people keep getting promoted until they reach their level of incompetence.

The job of being a football coach, department chair, or CEO is multidimensional. For football coaches, being able to manage and motivate a group of young, rich giants over a long season is probably more important than being able to figure out whether to go for it on fourth down. The same goes for many senior managers and CEOs, many of whom were notoriously poor students. Even the ones that were good students have undoubtedly forgotten most of whatever they learned when they took a class in statistics.

One way to salvage the Becker conjecture is to argue that CEOs, coaches, and other managers who are hired because they have a broad range of skills, which may not include analytical reasoning, could simply hire geeks who would deserve to be members of Becker's 10% to crunch the numbers for them. But my hunch is that as the importance of a decision grows, the tendency to rely on quantitative analyses done by others tends to shrink. When the championship or the future of the company is on the line, managers tend to rely on their gut instincts.

Cade and I have now moved on to a third team that has an owner who aspires to get into Becker's elite club, but the more we learn about how professional teams work, the more we understand how difficult it is to get everyone in the organization to adopt strategies that maximize profits and games won, especially if those strategies violate conventional wisdom. It is clear that a necessary condition is to have clear buy-in from the top, starting with the owner, but then that owner has to convince everyone who works for him that they are really going to be rewarded for taking smart but unconventional chances, even (especially!) when they fail. Few teams have achieved this winning formula, as evidenced by the lack of progress on fourth down and draft day decision-making. Clearly, in order to understand how teams or any other organizations make decisions—and therefore how to improve them—we need to be fully aware that they are owned and managed by Humans.

30

Game Shows

With all the research about financial markets, where the stakes are surely high, plus the football paper, we were clearly making headway against the critique that the behavioral anomalies observed in the lab would not be replicated in the so-called real world. But it was too early to declare victory. Myths are hard to kill. Furthermore, there was one limitation to these findings: for the most part, they pertained to market prices rather than specific individual behavior. Yes, the price of draft picks was off, but it was not possible to pin down the specific behavioral cause. Indeed, the fact that many behavioral phenomena, from overconfidence to the winner's curse, predicted that early picks would be overvalued made it impossible to say which bit of misbehaving was producing the mispricing. And although the behavior of cab drivers and individual investors had plausible explanations based on prospect theory, it was impossible to rule out other explanations consistent with expected utility maximization, perhaps associated with biased beliefs. Economists are really good at inventing rational explanations for behavior, no matter how dumb that behavior appears to be.

The highly stylized questions that Kahneman and Tversky had used to build prospect theory were designed to eliminate all possible ambiguities. When a subject is asked: "Would you rather have $300 for sure or a 50-50 chance at winning $1,000 or losing $400?" the probability of winning is known to be precisely 50% and the problem is so simple that there can be no other confounding factors contributing to a subject's answers. Danny and Amos "solved" the high-stakes problem by making the questions hypothetical, so subjects imagined that they were making non-trivial choices, but no one had the budget to make such choices real. Even the researchers using the strategy of going to a poor country in order to raise the stakes rarely used stakes that were for more than a few months' income; important, but not the kinds of stakes that arise in buying a house, choosing a career, or getting married. The search for a way to replicate Amos-and-Danny-type questions at truly high stakes was still unfulfilled when, in 2005, I happened to find an answer in the Netherlands.

The occasion was the award to me of an honorary degree at Erasmus University in Rotterdam. Aside from the honor, the highlight of the visit was a meeting with three economists: Thierry Post, a tenured finance professor, Martijn van den Assem, a new assistant professor, and Guido Baltussen, a graduate student. They had a project that studied the decisions made on a Dutch television game show. I was intrigued by their project, and was excited about their preliminary findings supporting the existence of a house money effect at very high stakes. (Recall that the house money effect, introduced in chapter 10, says that people are more willing to take chances when they think they are ahead in the game.) In this context, contestants faced decisions involving hundreds of thousands of dollars. Perhaps the myth that behavioral findings wilt in the face of high stakes could be finally put to rest. They asked me if I would like to join the team and work with them on the project and I agreed.[*]

If someone had asked me to design a game in order to test prospect theory and mental accounting, I could not have done better than this one. The show was created by a company called Endemol, and although the original version appeared on Dutch television, the show soon spread around the world. We used data from the Dutch, German, and United States versions of the show. The name of the show in Dutch was *Miljoenenjacht* ("Chasing Millions") but in English the show was called *Deal or No Deal*.

The rules were roughly the same in all versions of the show, but

---

[*] I agreed but with some warnings. I said that a collaboration might be unwise on at least two counts. First, I am notoriously slow. (I didn't mention the lazy part.) Second, I worried about the "Matthew effect," a term coined by sociologist Robert K. Merton, which states that excessive credit for any idea will be attributed to the most well-recognized person who is associated with it. Stephen Stigler, a statistician at the University of Chicago, called his alternative version of this effect Stigler's Law (irony intended): "No scientific discovery is named after its original discoverer." The joke, of course, is that Stigler's Law was just a restatement of Merton's proposition. Thierry and the group decided that we would collaborate, with the proviso that if I did not think I was adding anything, I would withdraw.

I will describe the original Dutch version. A contestant is shown a board (see figure 23) showing twenty-six different amounts of money varying from €0.01 to €5,000,000. Yes, you read that correctly, five million euros, or more than six million U.S. dollars. The average contestant won over €225,000. There are twenty-six briefcases, each containing a card displaying one of those amounts of money. The contestant chooses one of those briefcases without opening it and may, if he wishes, keep that until the end of the show and receive the amount of money it contains.

Having chosen his own briefcase, the contents of which remain secret, the contestant must then open six other briefcases, revealing the amounts of money each contains. As each case is opened, that amount of money is removed from the board of possible payoffs, as shown in the figure. The contestant is then offered a choice. He can have a certain amount of money, referred to as the "bank offer," shown at the top of the board, or he can continue to play by opening more cases. When faced with the choice between the bank offer and continuing to play, the contestant has to say "Deal" or "No deal," at least in the English ver-

FIGURE 23

Deal or No Deal scoreboard

€ 13,000 — Current "bank offer"

€ 0.01	€ 50	€ 10,000	€ 400,000
€ 0.20	€ 100	€ 25,000	€ 500,000
€ 0.50	€ 500	€ 50,000	€ 1,000,000
€ 1	€ 1,000	€ 75,000	€ 2,500,000
€ 5	€ 2,500	€ 100,000	€ 5,000,000
€ 10	€ 5,000	€ 200,000	
€ 20	€ 7,500	€ 300,000	

Amounts still left in unopened briefcases   *Amounts no longer available*

sion of the show. If the contestant chooses to continue ("No deal"), he will have to open additional cases on each round. There are a maximum of nine rounds, and the number of cases to be opened on the remaining rounds are five, four, three, two, one, one, one, and one.

The size of the bank offer depends on the remaining prize money left on the board and the stage of the game. To keep players playing and make the show more entertaining, the bank offers in the early rounds of the game are a small proportion of the expected value of the remaining prizes, where the "expected value" is the average of all the remaining amounts. When the game begins, before any cases are opened, the expected value is nearly €400,000. In the first round, the offers are about 10% of expected value, but the offers can reach or even exceed the expected value in the later rounds. By round six, the bank offers on average about three-quarters of the expected value and contestants are facing difficult, high-stakes decisions. Although the fact that the bank offer rises as a percentage of expected value as the game progresses gives players an incentive to keep going, they do run the risk that they will be unlucky in their choice of which cases to open. When cases with large monetary prizes are opened, the expected value drops and so does the bank offer.

Our primary goal in the paper was to use these high-stakes decisions to compare standard expected utility theory to prospect theory,* and beyond that, to consider the role of "path dependence." Does the way the game has played out influence the choices people make? Economic theory says that it shouldn't. The only thing that should matter is the choice the contestant is now facing, not the good or bad luck that occurred along the way. The path is an SIF.

One seemingly mundane finding is of significant importance in evaluating the competing theories. Players are only "moderately risk averse"—they are not extremely risk averse. Many players reject cash offers of 70% of expected value, and thus commit themselves to continuing to take chances, even when hundreds of thousands of euros are on the line. This finding is relevant to the literature on the equity premium puzzle. Some economists pointed out that there would not be a puzzle if investors were very highly risk averse. The results

---

* Prospect theory was the clear winner.

from the game show gave no support to this hypothesis. One simple illustration of this fact is that no player in the Dutch show stopped playing before the fourth round of the game although hundreds of thousands of euros were on the line. A player with a level of risk aversion high enough to explain the equity premium puzzle risk would never make it that far into the game.

Of more interest is the role of path dependence. In my paper with Eric Johnson that had been motivated by my colleague's poker-playing proclivities, we found two situations that induce people to be less risk averse than normal, in fact, actively risk-seeking. The first is when they are ahead in the game and "playing with the house money." The other is when they are behind in the game and have a chance to break even. The contestants on *Deal or No Deal* displayed the same tendencies, and for huge stakes.

To see what can happen to someone who considers himself "behind" in the game, consider the plight of poor Frank, a contestant on the Dutch show. The six cases Frank chose to open in the first round were mostly lucky ones, with only one of the cases having a large number, and his expected value was over €380,000. But in the second round he was very unlucky, picking four of the large prizes. His expected value plummeted to around €64,000, and the bank was offering him only €8,000. Frank was very much in the mood of someone who had just lost a lot of money. Frank pressed on, his luck improved, and he reached an interesting decision at stage six. The remaining prizes were €0.50, €10, €20, €10,000 and €500,000, which average out to €102,006. He was offered €75,000, fully 74% of expected value. What would you do?

Notice that his distribution of prizes is highly skewed. If the next case he opens contains the half million prize, he will have lost any chance of a prize more than €10,000. Frank, still determined to win the big money he had been expecting, said, "No deal." Unfortunately, he next picked the half million case, dropping his expected prize money to €2,508. Despondent, Frank persisted to the end. In the last round there were two amounts left: €10 and €10,000. The banker, feeling sorry for Frank, offered him €6,000, 120% of expected value. Frank again said, "No deal." He left the show with 10 euros.

The other extreme is illustrated by Susanne, who appeared on the less lucrative German version of the show, where the average contestant won "only" €20,602, and the largest prize was €250,000. Susanne had a lucky run of picks, and in the last round had only €100,000 and €150,000 as the remaining prizes, two of the three largest amounts. She received a bank offer of €125,000, exactly the expected value, yet she said, "No deal," undoubtedly thinking that she was only risking €25,000 of "house money." Lucky Suzanne walked away with €150,000.

Frank and Susanne's decisions illustrate the more formal findings of the paper, which show strong support for path dependence. Contestants clearly reacted not just to the gambles they were facing, but also to the gains and losses along the way. The same behavior I had first observed with my poker buddies at Cornell, and then tested for tens of dollars with Eric Johnson, still arises when the stakes are raised to hundreds of thousands of euros.

One concern with using the data from television game shows to study behavior is that people might act differently when they are in public than they would in private. Fortunately, Guido, Martijn, and Dennie van Dolder, then a graduate student, ran an experiment to measure the difference between public and private decisions.

The first stage of the experiment aimed to replicate the results of the televised games with students in front of an audience. They would simulate the television show as closely as possible, with a live master of ceremonies, a crowded auditorium, and cheering fans. The one thing that could not be replicated, of course, was the size of the payoffs. Payoffs were reduced by a factor of either 1,000 (large stakes), or 10,000 (small stakes). The biggest payoffs were €500 and €5,000 in the small- and large-stakes versions respectively. One interesting finding from these experiments is that the choices made were not very different from those in the televised version. As expected, at lower stakes, students were a bit less risk averse overall, but not dramatically so. Also, the pattern of path dependence reemerged, with both big winners and big losers becoming more risk-seeking.

The study went on to compare these experiments with others that had students make private decisions on a computer in the laboratory. The way these experiments were designed, a student in the lab would face exactly the same set of choices and real stakes that occurred in games played in front of a live audience. Time for a thought experiment: in which situation will the students undertake more risk, when choosing by themselves or in front of the crowd?

The results were a surprise to me. I thought that choosing in front of the crowd would induce students to take more risks, but in fact the opposite happened. The students were more risk averse in front of the crowd. Otherwise, the results were quite similar, which is comforting, since my career as a student of game shows was just getting started.

———

Another domain that attracted the "what if you raise the stakes?" complaint was so-called "other-regarding" behavior, such as the Ultimatum Game and Dictator Game. Here again, researchers had been able to raise the stakes to a few months' income, but some still wondered what would happen if "real money" was at stake. Sometime after our *Deal or No Deal* paper appeared, Martijn got in touch with me about a project he was doing with Dennie van Dolder. Endemol had come up with another game show that begged to be analyzed from a behavioral perspective. The show is called, of all things, *Golden Balls*.

The finale of each episode is what captured our attention. The show starts with four contestants, but in preliminary rounds two of them are eliminated, with the two survivors left to play one final game for stakes that can be quite high. At this final stage they play a version of the most famous game in all of game theory: the Prisoner's Dilemma. Recall the basic setup: Two players have to decide whether to cooperate or defect. The selfish rational strategy in a game that will only be played once is for both players to defect, but if they can somehow both cooperate, they do much better. Contrary to the standard theory, in low-stakes experiments of the Prisoner's Dilemma, about 40–50% of people cooperate. What would happen if we raise the stakes? Data from *Golden Balls* allowed us to find an answer.

On the show, the two finalists have accumulated a pot of money and have to make a decision that determines how this prize will be divided; they can choose to "split" or "steal." If both players choose to split, they each get half the pot. If one player says "split" and the other says "steal," the one who says "steal" gets everything and the other gets nothing. And if both players choose to steal, they both get nothing. The stakes are high enough to make even the most stubborn of economists concede that they are substantial. The average jackpot is over $20,000, and one team played for about $175,000.

The show ran for three years in Britain, and the producers were kind enough to give us recordings of nearly all the shows. We ended up with a sample of 287 pairs of players to study. Our first question of interest was whether cooperation rates would fall at these substantial stakes. The answer, shown in figure 24, is both yes and no.

FIGURE 24

How often players cooperated

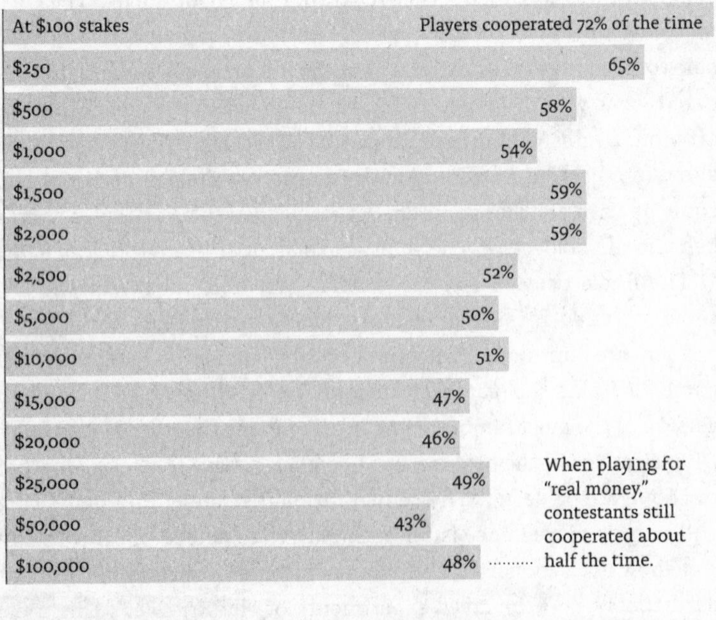

At $100 stakes	Players cooperated 72% of the time
$250	65%
$500	58%
$1,000	54%
$1,500	59%
$2,000	59%
$2,500	52%
$5,000	50%
$10,000	51%
$15,000	47%
$20,000	46%
$25,000	49%
$50,000	43%
$100,000	48%

When playing for "real money," contestants still cooperated about half the time.

The figure shows the percentage of players who cooperate for various categories of stakes, from small to large. As many had predicted, cooperation rates fall as the stakes rise. But a celebration by defenders of traditional economics models would be premature. The cooperation rates do fall, but they fall to about the same level observed in laboratory experiments played hypothetically or for small amounts of money, namely 40–50%. In other words, there is no evidence to suggest that the high cooperation rates in these low-stakes conditions are unrepresentative of what would happen if the stakes went up.

Cooperation rates fall as the stakes rise only because when the stakes were unusually low *by the standards of this show*, cooperation rates were exceptionally high. My coauthors and I have a conjecture for why this happens that we call the "big peanuts" hypothesis. The idea is that a certain amount of money can seem small or large depending on the context. Recall from the List that people were willing to drive across town to save $10 on a small purchase but not a big one. Ten dollars in the context of buying a new television seems like "peanuts," or not enough to worry about. We think the same thing happens on this show. Remember that the average prize pool in this game is about $20,000, so if a pair of contestants find themselves in a final where the pot is just $500, it feels like they are playing for peanuts. If they are playing for peanuts, why not be nice, especially on national television? Of course, $500 would be considered an extraordinarily large prize to be divided in the context of a laboratory experiment.

There is evidence for the same "big peanuts" phenomenon in our *Deal or No Deal* data. Remember unlucky Frank who was, in the last round, offered the choice between a sure €6,000 versus a 50-50 chance of getting either €10,000 or €10, and he chose to gamble. We suspect that after beginning the game with an expected payoff of nearly €400,000 and having been offered as much as €75,000 in past rounds, Frank thought he was down to playing for peanuts and decided to go for it.

We investigated one other aspect of the behavior displayed on *Golden Balls*: could we predict who would split and who would steal? We analyzed a host of demographic variables, but the only significant finding is that young men are distinctly less likely to split. Never trust a man under thirty.

We also analyzed the speeches each player makes before the big decision. Not surprisingly, the speeches all have the same flavor: "I am not the sort of person who would steal, and I hope you are not one of those evil types either." This is an example of what game theorists call "cheap talk." In the absence of a penalty for lying, everyone promises to be nice. However, there turns out to be one reliable signal in all this noise. If someone makes an explicit promise to split, she is 30 percentage points more likely to do so. (An example of such a statement: "I promise you I am going to split it, 120%.") This reflects a general tendency. People are more willing to lie by omission than commission. If I am selling you a used car, I do not feel obligated to mention that the car is burning a lot of oil, but if you ask me explicitly: "Does this car burn a lot of oil?" you are likely to wangle an admission from me that yes, there has been a small problem along those lines. To get at the truth, it helps to ask specific questions.

We had students coding everything that happened on each episode, and I only watched a dozen or so to get a feel for how the game was played. So, it was only after a particular episode went viral on the Internet that I realized *Golden Balls* may well have had one of the best moments ever recorded in a television game show—admittedly not a category with a lot of competition. The players in this game were Nick and Ibrahim, and the star of the game was Nick. It seems that Nick has made a nice sideline career as a game show contestant, appearing on over thirty different shows. He put all his creativity to use on this one.

Before describing his strategy, I need to make a technical point. The game played on *Golden Balls* differs from the standard Prisoner's Dilemma in one way: if you split and the other player steals, you are no worse off than if you had stolen as well. You get zero either way, whereas in the traditional example, if one prisoner stays silent and the other confesses, the silent one gets a severe punishment.* Nick exploited this small difference in devising his plan.

As soon as the discussion period started, Nick jumped in and made a surprising pitch: "Ibrahim, I want you to trust me. I promise you that I am going to steal, but then I will share my winnings with you." Both Ibrahim and the host had a lot of difficulty understanding the logic behind this offer. As Ibrahim pointed out, there would be a much easier way to arrange an even split. Both players could choose the "split" ball. But Nick said no, he was going to steal. The host, who had never heard anything like this, stepped in to clarify that any such

---

* In the game theory literature this is called a "weak" Prisoner's Dilemma (Rapoport, 1988).

promise was not authorized or guaranteed by the show, and the only way to assure that both players got half was for them both to split. Apparently, the discussion went on for much longer than the usual time allotted, and most of it was edited out of the televised version, which had a strict time limit. You might consider what you would do in Ibrahim's shoes.

Poor Ibrahim was clearly under great stress, and could not fathom what Nick was up to. At one point he asked Nick, in total exasperation, "Where do you keep your brains?" Nick smiled and pointed to his head. When the host finally ended the banter and demanded that the two players choose which ball to play, Ibrahim, who had appeared to be highly skeptical of Nick's pitch, suddenly switched from the ball he had originally selected to the other one, giving every indication that he had decided to play along and choose the "split" ball, perhaps feeling that he had no choice. Or perhaps it was one final feint.

Then came the reveal. Ibrahim had indeed selected the "split" ball, but what about Nick? Nick opened his ball, which also read "split."

The National Public Radio show *Radiolab* devoted an episode to this particular show. The hosts asked Ibrahim what he had been planning to do, and he said he was planning to steal right up until the last minute. The hosts reminded him that he had given an impassioned speech about his father telling him that a man is only as good as his word. "What about that?" the hosts asked, somewhat aghast at this revelation. "Oh, that," Ibrahim said. "Actually, I never met my father. I just thought it would be an effective story."

People are interesting.

VIII.

HELPING OUT:

2004–PRESENT

By the mid-1990s, behavioral economists had two primary goals. The first was empirical: finding and documenting anomalies, both in individual and firm behavior and in market prices. The second was developing theory. Economists were not going to take the field seriously until it had formal mathematical models that could incorporate the additional findings from psychology. With talented new behavioral economists entering the field, and even some well-established theorists such as Jean Tirole (the winner of the 2014 Nobel Prize) dabbling with behavioral models, there was continual progress on both fronts. But there was a third goal lurking in the background: could we use behavioral economics to make the world a better place? And could we do so without confirming the deeply held suspicions of our biggest critics: that we were closet socialists, if not communists, who wanted to replace markets with bureaucrats? The time was right to take this on.

31

Save More Tomorrow

Given the attention the behavioral economics community had collectively devoted to the problems of self-control, a natural place to start was ways to help people save for retirement. Designing better retirement savings programs is a task for which standard economic theory is ill-equipped. First of all, the standard theory starts with the assumption that people are saving the exact right amount (not to mention investing intelligently). If people are already doing something perfectly, how can you help? Furthermore, even if an economist did want to help out on such a project, she would only have one policy tool to play with, namely the after-tax financial return on savings. The standard theories of saving such as those offered by Milton Friedman or Franco Modigliani implicitly make the very strong prediction that no other policy variable can matter, since the other factors that determine a household's saving—such as age, income, life expectancy, and so forth—are not controlled by the government. The government cannot change how old you are, but it can change the after-tax return to your saving, for example, by creating tax-free retirement savings plans. And yet, there is a basic problem with the use of this policy tool—economic theory does not tell us how responsive savers will be to such a change. In fact, we cannot even be sure that making saving tax-free will increase or decrease the total amount of money people put aside for retirement.

At first blush, it would seem that increasing the returns to saving by creating tax-free accounts should increase saving, since the rewards for saving have gone up. But upon further reflection, one can see that the higher rates of return mean that it takes less saving to achieve a given retirement savings goal. Someone who is trying to accumulate a specific nest egg can achieve that goal with less saving if rates of return go up.* So economic theory offers only one policy tool, the after-tax rate of return, but we don't know whether to raise or lower it to induce more saving. This is not much help. Of course, empirical tests could tell us what effect changing tax rates will have, but until recently, it was difficult to provide definitive results. As Stanford economist Douglas Bernheim put it in his very thorough review of this literature published in 2002: "As an economist, one cannot review the voluminous literature on taxation and saving without being somewhat humbled by the enormous difficulty of learning anything useful about even the most basic empirical questions."

One of the problems in determining the effect of a change in the tax law is that to qualify for the low tax rate investors have to satisfy other rules, such as putting the money in a special account, possibly with penalties for withdrawals before retirement. The special account may facilitate saving in two ways. First, the penalty for withdrawal acts as an inducement to leave the money invested. Second, a mental account that is designated as "retirement saving" is less tempting to dip into than a simple savings account. In fact, following the introduction of tax-sheltered retirement savings plans in the U.S., there was a heated debate in the economics literature about whether such plans were increasing saving or just shifting money from taxable accounts to tax-free accounts. Only very recently has there been what I consider to be a definitive test, which we will get to later in this chapter.

Behavioral economics offers more potential in this and many other policy domains because more stuff matters, namely, all those SIFs. I first dipped my toe into these waters in 1994 with a short paper entitled "Psychology and Savings Policies." In it I made three policy proposals that drew on behavioral insights. The first two were aimed at the then-popular savings vehicle called the Individual Retirement

---

*Economic theory does predict that the total nest egg people accumulate will go up if saving is made tax-free; it just does not say whether saving *contributions* will go up or down, and as a society we care about both. Here is an analogy. Suppose you trade your old car for a new one that is twice as fuel-efficient. If you are an Econ you will drive more miles since the cost of driving has gone down, but it is unlikely that you will buy more fuel.

Account or IRA. (They became less important when income limits for eligibility were tightened and employer-based retirement savings plans, such as 401(k)s, became more common.) At the time I was writing, individuals could contribute up to $2,000 a year ($4,000 for a married couple) into these tax-sheltered accounts. Since contributions were tax deductible, an individual with a marginal tax rate of 30% who contributed the maximum of $2,000 would reduce his tax bill by $600.

One problem with the IRA design is that a taxpayer must have already made the contribution before filing the tax return. This design is problematic in that for many taxpayers, it is only *after* they have filed their tax return and settled up with the government that they have the cash to invest in an IRA. American taxpayers are more likely to be flush with money after they file their tax return, because 90% of them get a refund that averages about $3,000 per household, and it takes a while for the refund to arrive.

So my first suggestion was to allow taxpayers to use their income tax refund to make a contribution that counts on the return currently being filed (for the previous year's income). Under my proposal, the taxpayer would only have to create an IRA account before filing their taxes, and then could just ask the IRS to send some portion of the refund to that account and repeat this in following years using the same account.

The second proposal was designed to reinforce the first. I suggested that the government adjust the formula used to determine how much money is withheld from workers' paychecks by the Treasury Department as a prepayment of taxes. This formula could be tweaked so that taxpayers would get somewhat larger refunds at the end of the year unless they actively reduced their withholding rates, which anyone can do. The evidence suggests that when people get a windfall—and this seems to be the way people think about their tax refund, despite it being expected—they tend to save a larger proportion from it than they do from regular income, especially if the windfall is sizable. So, my thinking was that if we gave people bigger refunds, we would generate more savings, whether or not we figured out a way to make it easier to funnel those refunds into IRA saving. These two proposals would ideally have been combined.

I suspected that increasing the withholding rates would likely have another beneficial side effect: better tax compliance. My sense was that many taxpayers consider a refund as a gain and an underpayment as a loss, and when faced with a loss, they might get "creative" in filing their tax return. Recall that people tend to be risk-seeking in the domain of losses when they have a chance to break even. A recent study of 4 million tax returns in Sweden has confirmed my hunch. The authors find that taxpayers sharply increase their claimed deductions for "other expenses for earning employment income" if they would otherwise have to write a check to the government. Claims for small amounts in this category studied by the authors (less than 20,000 Swedish kroner or about $2,600) are known to be mostly bogus. When taxpayers are audited (which is rare) such claims are rejected over 90% of the time.

My third proposal involved a simple change to the way in which people sign up for defined contribution savings plans offered by their employers, such as the 401(k) plans offered in the United States. Quite basically, I asked: why not change the default? Under the usual rules, in order to sign up for the plan the employee had to fill out a bunch of forms, choose a saving rate, and decide how to invest the money. Why not make joining the plan the default and tell people that if they do not opt out, they will be enrolled in the plan at some default saving rate and in some default investment product?

Economics makes a clear prediction about this last proposal: it will have no effect. The designation of a particular option as the default is a SIF. The benefits of joining a 401(k) plan can add up to large amounts of money, tens if not hundreds of thousands of dollars, especially if, as is common, the employer matches some portion of the contributions. No Econ would let the minor inconvenience of filling out a couple forms prevent her from cashing in on so much money. To do so would be like buying a winning lottery ticket and not bothering to turn it in because it would require a five-minute stop at the convenience store. But for Humans, for whom filling out forms can be daunting and choosing investment strategies can be frightening, making enrollment in the plan the default option could have a big effect.

I later learned that I was not the first to think of changing the default option for retirement savings plans. A few firms had tried it, most notably McDonald's, the fast food giant. But the name that was commonly used for this plan at that time was unfortunate. In the industry, it was called "negative election." It is hard to get people very excited about a plan that is called negative election.

A few years after publishing this paper, I was asked to give a talk to the retirement plan clients of Fidelity, the American mutual fund giant. Fidelity, of course, had a pecuniary interest in this topic. Firms across the United States had quickly been switching over from the old-style pension plans, in which the employer made all the decisions, to the new defined contribution plans. In response, Fidelity and many other large financial service companies had started new lines of business to administer the plans for employers, and their mutual funds were also offered as potential investment vehicles for the employees. Increasing the account balances would be good for the employees and for Fidelity.

If I could think of something that might put more money into retirement savings accounts, I would have the representatives of several hundred large employers in the audience, and they might be willing to try it. Of course, I would advocate changing the default to automatic enrollment, but it would be good to also come up with something new.

After some brainstorming with Shlomo Benartzi, by that time a regular collaborator, the approach I took was to make a list of the most important behavioral reasons why someone might fail to save enough for retirement, and then design a program that could overcome each of these obstacles. This is an approach I now often use when trying to dream up a behavioral intervention for some problem. For my list, I came up with three factors.

The first obstacle is inertia. Surveys reveal that most people in retirement savings plans think they should be saving more, and plan to take action, uh, soon. But then they procrastinate, and never get around to changing their saving rate. In fact, most plan participants rarely make any changes to their saving options unless they change jobs and are confronted with a new set of forms they have to fill out. Overcoming inertia is the problem that automatic enrollment magically solves. The same concept should be included in a plan to increase saving rates. If we could somehow get people started on a plan to increase their saving rates and let that kick in automatically, inertia could work for us instead of against us.

The second obstacle is loss aversion. We know that people hate losing and, in particular, hate to see their paychecks go down. Based on the findings from our fairness study, we also know that in this domain, loss aversion is measured in nominal dollars, that is, without adjusting for inflation. So, if we could figure out a way that employees would not feel any cuts to their paychecks, there would be less resistance to saving more.

The third behavioral insight was related to self-control. A key finding from the research on this topic is that we have more self-control when it comes to the future than the present. Even the kids in Walter Mischel's marshmallow experiments would have no trouble if *today* they were given the choice between one marshmallow at 2 p.m. tomorrow or three marshmallows at 2:15 p.m. tomorrow. Yet, we know that if we give them that same choice tomorrow at 2 p.m., few would be able to wait until 2:15. They are present-biased.

The proposal I eventually presented at the Fidelity conference was called "Save More Tomorrow." The idea was to offer people the option of deciding *now* to increase their saving rates *later*, specifically, when they get their next raise. Then, keep them enrolled in the program until they opt out or hit some cap. By tying the increases in saving rates to pay increases, loss aversion would be averted. By asking them to make a decision that would take effect sometime in the future, present bias would be mitigated. And by leaving the plan in place unless the person opts out, inertia would work for us. Everything I knew about behavioral economics suggested that such a plan would work. Naively, I was also confident that one of the hundreds of companies that were represented at that conference would soon be getting in touch about how to try out this great new idea. And I was happy to give it away and offer free consulting to anyone who was willing to try it, as long as they let Benartzi and me evaluate what happened.

Boy, was I wrong. Not one company got in touch. And automatic enrollment was not doing much better, even with its improved name.

One thing that was slowing down the adoption of automatic enrollment was that companies were not sure it was legal. Here a lawyer and pensions expert, Mark Iwry, intervened to help. Iwry, then a Treasury Department official in charge of national pension policy, led the Department of the Treasury and the IRS to issue a series of rulings and pronouncements that defined, approved, and promoted the use of what they referred to as automatic enrollment in 401(k) and other retirement savings plans. So Mark Iwry really paved the way for firms to try out this new idea, not only giving it a better name but also giving it a legal stamp of approval. (He did this quite independently, though we later got to know each other and have worked together on other initiatives.)

Yet it remained hard to encourage take-up of the idea without proof that it actually worked. This problem was solved by a colleague at Chicago, Brigitte Madrian, who now teaches at the Kennedy School of Government at Harvard. Brigitte wandered into my office one day to show me some interesting results she had obtained that were so strong she could not quite believe them, even though she had crunched the numbers herself. A company that had tried automatic enrollment asked Brigitte if she would analyze the data. She worked with an employee of the company, Dennis Shea, to see whether automatic enrollment was effective. The results were stunning, at least to Brigitte, who had received traditional training as an economist. She knew that the default option was an SIF and therefore should not matter. But she could see that it did.*

The company had adopted automatic enrollment in June 1999, about a year after the concept had received its official blessing from the government. Brigitte compared the behavior of employees who were newly eligible for the plan in 1998, the year before the change, with those hired in the year after the change. Even the most clueless employees eventually figure out that joining the retirement plan is a good idea, especially in a plan like this with an employer match, so automatic enrollment mostly affects the speed with which people join. Before automatic enrollment, only 49% of employees joined the plan during their first year of eligibility; after automatic enrollment, that number jumped to 86%! Only 14% opted out. That is a pretty impressive change in behavior produced by a supposedly irrelevant factor.

Madrian and Shea aptly called the resulting paper "The Power of Suggestion," and their analyses reveal that the power of default options

---

* Brigitte did not remain a skeptic for long. She soon partnered with David Laibson and a rotating group of coauthors to replicate and extend her original findings. She and David are now prominent experts in the field of retirement saving design.

can have a downside. Any company that adopts automatic enrollment has to choose a default saving rate and a default investment portfolio. Their company had adopted a 3% saving rate as the default, and the money went into a money market fund, an option with little risk but also a very low rate of return, meaning that savings would be slow to accumulate. The government influenced both of these choices. The company had no choice about the selection of the money market account as the default investment because, at that time, it was the only option approved for such use by the U.S. Department of Labor. Since then, the Department of Labor has approved a host of what are called "qualified default investment alternatives," and most plans now choose a fund that mixes stocks and bonds and gradually reduces the percentage in stocks as the worker approaches retirement.

The choice of the 3% default investment level was also influenced by the government, but not intentionally. In official rulings such as the ones Mark Iwry initiated, there are usually specific facts included, and the June 1998 ruling included language along these lines:* "Suppose a firm automatically enrolls employees into a retirement savings plan at a three percent savings rate . . ." Ever since then, the vast majority of firms that use automatic enrollment start people off at that rate. Call it an unintentional default.

Both of these default choices—the money market investment option and the 3% saving rate—were not intended by the employer to be either suggestions or advice. Instead, these options were picked to minimize the chance that the company would be sued. But employees seemed to treat the default options as suggestions. Most ended up saving 3% and investing in a money market fund.

By comparing the choices of people who joined before automatic enrollment with those who came after, Madrian and Shea were able to show that some employees would have selected a higher saving rate if left to their own devices. In particular, many employees had heretofore picked a 6% savings rate—the rate at which the employer

---

* Iwry and his team landed on 3% merely because a low level would be less likely to arouse opposition and at the very least would establish the guiding principle. By 2000, his team tried to recalibrate to a higher level through various other rulings, but the initial anchor stuck.

stopped matching contributions. After automatic enrollment came in, there were fewer people choosing 6% and more choosing 3%. This is the downside of automatic enrollment. And it is a good reason why any firm that adopts automatic enrollment should deploy the Save More Tomorrow plan as well.

Brigitte's paper raised awareness about the effectiveness of automatic enrollment, but there were still no takers for Save More Tomorrow. Then, out of the blue, I got a call from Shlomo Benartzi. A financial services consultant, Brian Tarbox, had heard one of us talking about Save More Tomorrow and had implemented it. We had talked to Brian about the implementation plan, but that had been a couple years earlier and I had forgotten all about it. Brian had gotten back in touch with Shlomo and told him that he now had data and was willing to share it with us. Pop the Champagne corks! We finally had a case study to analyze.

The firm that Tarbox had worked with had started out with a problem. In the case of retirement plans, if its lower-paid employees do not join the plan, a firm can be out of compliance with Department of Labor rules that limit the proportion of benefits that can be given to its highest-paid employees. When that happens, the maximum amount any individual can contribute is reduced. Tarbox's client was desperate to coax their lower-paid employees into saving more, so desperate that they had hired him to meet with each employee for a one-on-one financial planning session. Brian had a laptop loaded with software that could compute how much the employee should be saving, and I think the company hoped he would talk some sense into them. But they needed more than just talking. They needed a plan.

The employees at this firm were currently not saving much, and had not accumulated much in the way of retirement wealth. When Brian would run his program to calculate the employee's optimal saving rate (the one an Econ would choose), the program would often suggest the maximum allowed at this firm, 15%. If Brian suggested to someone who was now saving 5% that they should increase to 15%, the employee would laugh. Most were struggling to make ends meet. A big increase in saving, meaning a big cut in take-home pay, was not in the cards.

Benartzi and Tarbox worked out a more moderate strategy. Rather than report the recommended saving level from the program, Brian would suggest that employees raise their saving rate by five percentage points. If they were unwilling to take this advice, they were offered a version of Save More Tomorrow.

It was good for Tarbox (and the employees) that we had given him this backup plan. Nearly three-quarters of the employees turned down his advice to increase their saving rate by five percentage points. To these highly reluctant savers, Brian suggested that they agree to raise their saving rate by three percentage points the next time they got a raise, and continue to do so for each subsequent raise for up to four annual raises, after which the increases would stop. To his surprise, 78% of employees who were offered this plan took him up on it. Some of those were people who were not currently participating in the plan but thought that this would be a good opportunity to do so—in a few months.

After three and a half years and four annual raises, the Save More Tomorrow employees had nearly quadrupled their savings rate, from a meager 3.5% to 13.6%. Meanwhile, those who had accepted Brian's advice to increase their savings rate by 5% had their saving rates jump by that amount in the first year, but they got stuck there as inertia set in. Brian later told us that after the fact he realized that he should have offered everyone the Save More Tomorrow option initially (see figure 25).

FIGURE 25

Did they Save More Tomorrow?

SAVINGS RATES OF PARTICIPANTS WHO ...	INITIALLY	AFTER FIRST PAY RAISE	SECOND PAY RAISE	THIRD PAY RAISE	FOURTH PAY RAISE
Declined offer of financial advice	6.6	6.5	6.8	6.6	6.2
Took the consultant's recommended savings rate	4.4	9.1	8.9	8.7	8.8
Joined the "Save More Tomorrow" plan	**3.5**	**6.5**	**9.4**	**11.6**	**13.6**
Declined the "Save More Tomorrow" plan	6.1	6.3	6.2	6.1	5.9

Armed with these results, we tried to get other firms to try the idea. Shlomo and I offered to help any way we could, as long as firms would agree to give us the data to analyze. This yielded a few more implementations to study. A key lesson we learned, which confirmed a strongly held suspicion, was that participation rates depended strongly on the ease with which employees could learn about the program and sign up. Brian's setup for this was ideal. He showed each employee how dire his savings situation was, offered him an easy plan for starting down a better path, and then, crucially, helped him fill out and return the necessary forms. Unfortunately, this kind of hands-on implementation is expensive. Some companies have tried group educational seminars, which can be helpful, but unless these are accompanied by a chance to sign up on the spot, their effectiveness is limited. And simply making the option available in some hard-to-find location on the plan administrator's website is not going to attract the lazy procrastinators (a.k.a., most of us) for whom the program was designed. One practical solution to this problem is to make a program like Save More Tomorrow the default (of course with the option to opt out). Certainly, any firms that are still using a 3% initial default saving rate owe it to their employees to ramp them up to a saving ceiling that provides some chance of a decent retirement income. I would say saving 10% of income would be a bare minimum for those without other sources of wealth, and 15% would be better.

Both automatic enrollment and Save More Tomorrow are now finally spreading. Many firms have adopted a simpler version of Save More Tomorrow, called automatic escalation, which delinks saving increases from pay increases. It turns out that many payroll departments are not capable (or willing) to do the computer programming to combine the two. (Fortunately, this does not appear to be a vital feature of the program.) According to a survey conducted by Aon Hewitt that focuses on the largest employers, by 2011, 56% of employers were using automatic enrollment and 51% were offering automatic escalation or Save More Tomorrow. These high participation numbers are in part the result of a law passed in 2006 called the Pension Protection Act, which gave firms a small incentive to adopt these features.

In a recent paper published in *Science*, Shlomo and I estimate that by 2011 about 4.1 million people in the U.S. were using some kind of automatic escalation plan, and by 2013 they were collectively saving an additional $7.6 billion per year as a result. The United Kingdom has recently launched a national personal saving plan that utilizes automatic enrollment, and so far the opt-out rate for those employees who were subject to automatic enrollment has been about 12%. There is talk of adding automatic escalation later on. Similar programs also exist in Australia and New Zealand.

———

One question we were often asked and were unable to answer was whether this sort of automatic saving really increases a household's net worth. Perhaps, some argued, once enrolled, participants reduce their savings elsewhere or take on more debt. There are no American data sets that have adequate information about household wealth to allow this question to be answered. But a team of American and Danish economists led by Harvard's Raj Chetty, a rising star in economics, have used Danish data to provide a definitive answer to this question, as well as to the more general one discussed earlier about whether the tax-free savings aspect of retirement plans is effective in increasing savings. They were able to do so because the Danes keep meticulous records on household wealth as well as income.

There are two principal conclusions from the Danish study. The first is that the bulk of the saving generated by automatic saving plans is "new." When someone moves to a company with a more generous retirement saving plan and automatically starts saving more via that plan, there is neither a discernible decrease in savings in other categories nor an increase in debt. In a world of Econs this result would be surprising because Econs treat money as fungible and are already saving just the right amount, so if an employee is forced or nudged into saving more in one place, she would just save less or borrow more somewhere else. The second conclusion compares the relative contributions of two factors that are combined in these plans: their automatic features and the tax break gained by saving in a tax-free account. In allocating the source of the new saving that comes from these programs, the authors attribute only 1% of the increase to the tax breaks. The other 99% comes from the automatic features. They conclude: "In sum, the findings of our study call into question whether tax subsidies are the most effective policy to increase retirement savings. Automatic enrollment or default policies that nudge individuals to save more could have larger impacts on national saving at lower fiscal cost."

In 2004, several years after Brian Tarbox ran that first experiment, Shlomo and I wrote a paper about the findings. The first time I presented the research at the University of Chicago, it was at a conference in honor of my thesis advisor, Sherwin Rosen, who had recently died prematurely at age sixty-two. The discussant of our paper was Casey Mulligan, one of the several remaining hard-core Chicago School economists in the university's economics department.

The findings of our paper fly in the face of much of what Mulligan believes. We were able to get people to save more simply by using supposedly irrelevant plan design features. An Econ would not enroll in Save More Tomorrow because he would already be saving the right amount, and if he did enroll, it would not affect his saving rate, because he would make adjustments elsewhere to get himself back to saving the optimal amount that he had previously chosen. Mulligan grudgingly admitted that we did seem to be able to perform this black magic, but he worried that we were up to some kind of mischief. He thought we might be tricking them into saving too much. Of course, I was thinking to myself that if people are as clever as rational choice adherents like Mulligan typically assume, they would not be so easily tricked, but I left this unsaid. Instead, I conceded it was possible that we could induce people to save more than the optimal amount an Econ would choose, though this seemed unlikely given the low rates of personal saving in the United States. Still, as a precaution, we built in a maximum saving rate after which the automatic saving increases would cease.

Furthermore, if a household is going to miss its ideal saving target, it seems better to overshoot the desired retirement nest egg than to save too little. I am not taking a position on how people should allocate their consumption over their lifetimes, and surely there are many misers who have lived appropriately miserable lives. Instead, I am concerned with the difficulty of forecasting the rate of return on savings, and the ease of making adjustments later in life. Someone turning sixty who finds herself flush with surplus savings has numerous remedies, from taking an early retirement, to going on lavish vacations, to spoiling the grandchildren. But someone who learns at sixty that she has not saved enough has very little time to make up lost ground, and may find that retirement must be postponed indefinitely.

Casey Mulligan ended his discussion with a question. "Yeah," he said, "it seems like you can get people to save more. But, isn't this 'paternalism'?"

At the University of Chicago, you can call someone a Marxist, an anarchist, or even a Green Bay Packers fan (the archrival of the Chicago Bears, the local NFL team), but calling a colleague a paternalist is the cruelest cut of all. I was genuinely puzzled by this accusation. Normally we think that paternalism involves coercion, as when people are required to contribute to Social Security or forbidden to buy alcohol or drugs. But Save More Tomorrow is a voluntary program. I said as much and went on to say that if this is paternalism, then it must be some different variety of paternalism. Struggling for the right words, I blurted out: "Maybe we should call it, I don't know, libertarian paternalism."

I made a mental note to discuss this new phrase with Cass Sunstein the next time I saw him.

Going Public

W hen I next saw Cass, I told him about my new term, "libertarian paternalism." The phrase was not beautiful, but he had to admit it was more constructive than his term, "anti-anti-paternalism," and he was intrigued.

The notion of paternalism was very much on the minds of behavioral economists at the time. Colin Camerer, George Loewenstein, and Matthew Rabin had collaborated with Ted O'Donoghue and law professor Sam Issacaroff on a paper with a similar idea and an equally forbidding title: "Asymmetric Paternalism." They defined their concept this way: "A regulation is asymmetrically paternalistic if it creates large benefits for those who make errors, while imposing little or no harm on those who are fully rational." Rabin and O'Donoghue had earlier coined the phrase "cautious paternalism" but then raised their ambitions to "optimal paternalism." We were all trying to dig into the question that had been the elephant in the room for decades: if people make systematic mistakes, how should that affect government policy, if at all?

Peter Diamond happened to be serving as president-elect of the American Economic Association in 2002 and was in charge of organizing the annual meeting, to be held in January of 2003. Peter was an early fan of and contributor to behavioral economics, and he took the opportunity to organize a few sessions at the meeting on behavioral topics and invited a session on paternalism. Cass and I wrote a short paper that introduced the idea of libertarian paternalism. With the five published pages we were allotted, Cass was barely getting warmed up, so he took that piece and developed it into a proper law review article, over forty pages. We called it "Libertarian Paternalism Is Not an Oxymoron."

When I printed a draft of the law review version of the paper it looked quite long to me. One day I asked Cass whether he thought there might be a book in it. It would be an understatement to say that Cass loved the idea. There is nothing Cass relishes more than writing a book.

The premise of the article, and later the book, is that in our increasingly complicated world people cannot be expected to have the expertise to make anything close to optimal decisions in all the domains in which they are forced to choose. But we all enjoy having the right to choose for ourselves, even if we sometimes make mistakes. Are there ways to make it easier for people to make what they will deem to be good decisions, both before and after the fact, without explicitly forcing anyone to do anything? In other words, what can we achieve by limiting ourselves to libertarian paternalism?

We knew that the phrase "libertarian paternalism" would raise some hackles. It is not just at the University of Chicago that people dislike the term "paternalism"; many object to the government, or anyone else for that matter, telling them what to do, and that is what the term normally means. The phrase "libertarian paternalism" *is* a mouthful, and it does sound like an oxymoron. But it is not; at least not the way we define the terms.

By paternalism, we mean trying to help people achieve their own goals. If someone asks how to get to the nearest subway station and you give her accurate directions, you are acting as a paternalist in our usage. We use the word "libertarian" as an adjective to mean trying to help in this way but without restricting choices.*

Although we like the term "libertarian paternalism" and can defend its logic, it is safe to say it would never have worked as a book title. That problem was solved when an editor who was considering our book proposal suggested that the word "nudge" seemed to capture what we were trying to do. That publisher ultimately declined the book, but we immediately seized on his idea for a title, a gift for which we are grateful.

Overall, I think it would be fair to say that the level of enthusiasm

---

* While we thought the term was perfectly logical, not everyone agreed. One law professor wrote a comment on our paper titled "Libertarian Paternalism Is an Oxymoron" (Mitchell, 2005). I wanted to post a reply online that would have no text; it would only consist of the three-word title "No It's Not." Cass convinced me that this would not be helpful.

in the publishing community for our book varied between tepid and ice-cold. We ended up with a prestigious but sleepy university press whose skill set, we later learned, did not include marketing. If the book was going to reach any kind of broad audience, it was going to have to come from word of mouth. (The paperback rights were later sold to trade publishers in the U.S. and the U.K., after which the book finally began to appear in bookstores.)

———

It was never our intention to claim that nudging can solve every problem. Some bans and mandates are inevitable. No society can exist without any rules and regulations. We require children to go to school (true paternalism in every sense of the word) and forbid one person from assaulting another. There are rules stipulating on which side of the road one should drive. Countries differ on which side they designate as the correct one, but when a Brit visits America, he is not permitted to drive on the left side of the road. Even ardent libertarians agree that you should not be allowed to shoot your neighbor just because you don't like him. So our goal here was limited. We wanted to see how far one could take the policy of helping without ordering anyone to do anything.

Our premise was simple. Because people are Humans, not Econs (terms we coined for *Nudge*), they make predictable errors. If we can anticipate those errors, we can devise policies that will reduce the error rate. For example, the act of driving, especially for a long distance, can make the driver sleepy, increasing the risk of wandering across the center line and causing an accident. In response, some localities have made the center divider both a painted line and a bumpy strip that makes the car rattle when it is hit, nudging a dozing driver to wake up (and maybe take a break from driving over a cup of coffee). Better yet are bumps that reflect light, making it also easier to navigate in the dark.

The bumpy lane markers example also illustrates a point that critics of our book seem incapable of getting: we have no interest in telling people what to do. We want to help them achieve their *own* goals. Readers who manage to reach the fifth page of *Nudge* find that we define our objective as trying to "influence choices in a way that will make choosers better off, *as judged by themselves.*" The italics are in the original but perhaps we should have also used bold and a large font, given the number of times we have been accused of thinking that we know what is best for everyone. Yes, it is true that we think that most people would like to have a comfortable retirement, but we want to leave that choice up to them. We just want to reduce what people would themselves call errors.

Reducing errors is also a source of *Nudge*'s most famous example, from Schiphol International Airport in Amsterdam. Some obvious genius came up with an idea to get men to pay more attention to where they aim when using the airport urinals. An etched image of a housefly appears near the drain of the urinal. Airport management has reported that installing these flies reduced "spillage," a wonderful euphemism, by some 80%. I don't know of any careful empirical analysis of the effectiveness of these flies, but they (and variations on the theme) have been spotted in other airports around the world. A soccer goal equipped with a ball is particularly popular during the World Cup.

For me, that fly in the urinal has become the perfect exemplar of a nudge. A nudge is some small feature in the environment that attracts our attention and influences behavior. Nudges are effective for Humans, but not for Econs, since Econs are already doing the right thing. Nudges are supposedly irrelevant factors that influence our choices in ways that make us better off. The fly further made clear to me that while Cass and I were capable of recognizing good nudges when we came across them, we were still missing an organizing principle for how to devise effective nudges.

We had a breakthrough in finding our missing organizing principle when I reread Don Norman's classic book *The Design of Everyday Things*. The book has one of the best covers I have ever seen. It is an image of a teapot that has both the handle and the spout on the same side. Think about it. After rereading Norman's book, I realized we could apply many of his principles to the problems we were studying. I had recently bought my first iPhone, a device so easy to use that it didn't need an instruction manual. What if we could design policies that facilitated the creation of choice environments that were just as "user-centered"? At some point we adopted the term "choice architecture" to describe what we were trying to do. In curious ways, simply having that phrase to organize our thoughts helped us create a check-list of principles for good choice architecture, with many of the ideas borrowed from the human design literature. Designing good public policies has a lot in common with designing any consumer product.

Now that we had our new set of tools, one big choice we had to make was which policy issues to try to address with them. Some topics that we had already written about were easy, but others required us to dig into the literature and see whether we could come up with anything useful or interesting. Some of these investigations led to dead ends. We drafted a chapter on Hurricane Katrina but cut it because we only found one remotely interesting idea, and it was not ours. John Tierney, a columnist for the *New York Times*, had a suggestion to encourage people to leave for higher ground before a storm strikes. Tierney's idea was to offer those who opt to stay a permanent ink marker and suggest they use it to write their Social Security number on their body, to aid in the identification of victims after the storm. We had nothing nearly as good as that.

In other cases, the research caused us to change our views on some subject. A good example of this is organ donations. When we made our list of topics, this was one of the first on the list because we knew of a paper that Eric Johnson had written with Daniel Goldstein on the powerful effect of default options in this domain. Most countries adopt some version of an opt-in policy, whereby donors have to take some positive step such as filling in a form in order to have their name added to the donor registry list. However, some countries in Europe, such as Spain, have adopted an opt-out strategy that is called "presumed consent." You are presumed to give your permission to have your organs harvested unless you explicitly take the option to opt out and put your name on a list of "non-donors."

The findings of Johnson and Goldstein's paper showed how powerful default options can be. In countries where the default is to be a donor, almost no one opts out, but in countries with an opt-in policy, often less than half of the population opts in! Here, we thought, was a simple policy prescription: switch to presumed consent. But then we dug deeper. It turns out that most countries with presumed consent do not implement the policy strictly. Instead, medical staff members continue to ask family members whether they have any objection to having the deceased relative's organs donated. This question often comes at a time of severe emotional stress, since many organ donors die suddenly in some kind of accident. What is worse is that family members in countries with this regime may have no idea what the donor's wishes were, since most people simply do nothing. That someone failed to fill out a form opting out of being a donor is not a strong indication of his actual beliefs.

We came to the conclusion that presumed consent was not, in fact, the best policy. Instead we liked a variant that had recently been adopted by the state of Illinois and is also used in other U.S. states. When people renew their driver's license, they are asked whether they wish to be an organ donor. Simply asking people and immediately recording their choices makes it easy to sign up.* In Alaska and Montana, this approach has achieved donation rates exceeding 80%. In the organ donation literature this policy was dubbed "mandated choice" and we adopted that term in the book.

This choice of terminology was unfortunate, as I learned later. Some time after the book was published, I wrote a column in the *New York Times* about organ donations and advocated the Illinois policy, which I continued to call "mandated choice." A few weeks later, someone on the editorial board of *USA Today* called me to talk about the policy because their newspaper was going to endorse it. A couple days later, I got an urgent phone call from the editorial writer. It turns out she had called the state official in charge of this policy, who has the title secretary of state, and he firmly denied that any such policy existed. I was mystified. I had recently renewed my driver's license and was duly asked whether I wanted to be an organ donor. (I said yes.) A few more phone calls solved the mystery. The secretary of state, Jesse White, objected to the word "mandated." He said that no one was required to do anything, and technically he was right. When asked to be a donor, if someone refuses to answer or

---

* Most states wisely combine this policy with a "first person consent" law that stipulates that if the donor should die, his or her wishes should be followed, sparing family members any obligation to make difficult choices in traumatic times.

remains mute, the official at the Department of Motor Vehicles just takes that as a no.

It turns out that Jesse White is a smart politician, and being a smart politician he realized that voters do not like mandates.* In the wake of this lesson on the importance of nomenclature, I have been calling my favored policy "prompted choice," a term both more accurate and less politically charged. When dealing with Humans, words matter.

---

* He might have shared this bit of wisdom with President Obama, whose health care law has a very unpopular feature that is called a "mandate." Because the law forbids insurance companies from discriminating against people with preexisting conditions, it needed to have some provision to prevent people from waiting until they get sick or have an accident to buy insurance, and mandating coverage was chosen as the solution to this problem. But there were other ways to achieve this goal. For example, I would favor a combination of automatic enrollment (with opt-out) plus a provision that anyone who opts out of insurance cannot buy a policy for a specified period of time, such as three years.

33

Nudging in the U.K.

In July of 2008 I spent a few days in London while on my way to Ireland to attend Cass's wedding to Samantha Power. Although *Nudge* had been out for several months in the U.S., only a few copies had made it to London. I was never able to determine the shipping method the publisher used, but I strongly suspected that a fleet of tall sailing ships had come in with the low bid, just beating out the university's rowing team.

One of the enterprising people who had managed to snag a copy of the book was Richard Reeves. Richard is a rare species: a professional intellectual without a permanent post as a professor or pundit. At that time, he was about to become the director of a think tank called Demos, where he invited me to give a talk about *Nudge*.[*] Before Richard and I actually met, I got a call from him on my cell phone. He wanted to know if I would be interested in meeting some of the people who were working in the leadership of the Conservative Party, otherwise known as the Tories. The inquiry had come from his friend Rohan Silva, who also had read *Nudge* and was taken by it.

I was deeply skeptical that anything could come of such a meeting. As best I can recall, there has never been an occasion during my lifetime in which I have been described as conservative. Radical, troublemaker, rabble-rouser, nuisance, and other terms unsuitable for the printed page were all commonly used adjectives, but never conservative.

Still, I was flattered. "Sure," I said. "Give Rohan my number, I'd be happy to talk to him." Rohan called almost immediately and asked whether I might be willing to stop by that afternoon and meet some of his colleagues at the Houses of Parliament. My skepticism about

---

[*] Richard has now moved to the United States and has a post at the Brookings Institution in Washington, DC.

talking to a group of Conservatives was compounded by the fact that I was wandering around London on a rare warm, sunny day, and was dressed in my usual attire of jeans and a T-shirt. At that time, I knew almost nothing about British politics, and my mental image of a group of Conservative Members of Parliament was one of old men in suits, possibly wearing white wigs and robes. I told Rohan that I did not think I was appropriately dressed for a meeting at the Houses of Parliament, but he told me not to worry, they were a casual group. And by the sound of his voice on the phone, he seemed to be quite young. So, I said sure, why not?

My fears about being underdressed were as ill-founded as my stereotypes of the people I was about to meet. Rohan Silva, then twenty-seven and of Sri Lankan descent, always seems to have last shaved three days ago. The only time I remember him actually clean-shaven was at his wedding, years later. His somewhat senior partner among the small team, Steve Hilton, was not yet forty and was dressed in what I later came to know as his favored attire of a T-shirt and Los Angeles Lakers basketball shorts. We met in the office of a senior Conservative Member of Parliament, Oliver Letwin, one of the small group of Tory MPs who surrounded the leadership team of David Cameron and George Osborne, both in their forties. I did not see anyone wearing a wig, and I think Minister Letwin was the only one wearing a suit.

I gave a brief, off-the-cuff talk, and the team seemed to think that the approach to public policy we advocated in *Nudge* was one that the party could support as part of a rebranding that Cameron and Osborne were undertaking. Their stated goal was to make the party more progressive and pro-environment. After the meeting, Rohan and I continued the conversation and I learned that he had travelled to Iowa to support Obama in the 2008 Democratic Party presidential primary campaign. My image of the Conservative Party was rapidly changing.

Rohan somehow managed to buy ten copies of *Nudge*, possibly cornering the U.K. market until the next ship arrived, and piled them up on his desk, nudging passers-by to take a look. One day David Cameron—the future prime minister—saw the pile and asked whether this was the book he had heard some people talking about. Rohan suggested that he take a look. Apparently Cameron liked what he read, because he later put the book on a list of books recommended for summer reading for Tory MPs, though I strongly suspect that Rohan wrote the first draft of that list. Among the many jobs Rohan held was that of "designated reader."

My next trip to London was in the spring of 2009, when I was doing some publicity events with our new U.K. publisher for the paperback edition of the book. Given our earlier experiences, I was shocked to see billboards in tube stations asking in large print, "HAVE YOU BEEN NUDGED TODAY?" At one event, I was told that I would be seated at dinner next to someone called Sir Gus O'Donnell. Again showing my ignorance, I asked who he was, and was told that he was the Cabinet Secretary, the top civil servant in the U.K. I later learned that people would often refer to him as GOD, a play on his initials but also a nod to his power. He basically ran the country. And amazingly, he was already a fan of behavioral economics.

Lord O'Donnell, as he is now called, has a remarkable background. He earned a PhD in economics at Oxford, taught for a while, and then went to work for the government, where he held numerous jobs including, most remarkably, press secretary to the Prime Minister. I have never met an economist who would have lasted a single day as a press secretary to anyone, much less a head of state. After serving in several other capacities, he ended up as the chief civil servant in the country. There is no equivalent to the job of Cabinet Secretary in the United States, and I must say that after my experiences in dealing with Gus and his successor, Jeremy Heywood, I think we would do well to create such a position. When the general election took place in May 2010 and no party won a majority, the government went about its business as usual, with O'Donnell steering the ship while the politicians tried to sort out which parties would form a coalition government.

It turned out that the Conservatives agreed to form a coalition with the Liberal Democrats, and David Cameron would become the next Prime Minister with Nick Clegg, the leader of the Lib Dems, named as Deputy Prime Minister. And whom did Clegg pick as his chief policy advisor? Richard Reeves. Meanwhile, Rohan and Steve Hilton became senior policy advisors to the Prime Minister, if the word "senior" is appropriate for someone who has not yet turned thirty. They had big plans, and the plans included a role for behavioral science, plans that Gus O'Donnell would play an important role in implementing. In only a few days as a visitor in London, I seemed to have stumbled onto the people who could actually take the ideas espoused in *Nudge* seriously, and see if they could be made to work.

———

Soon after the coalition agreement between David Cameron and Nick Clegg was sorted out, Rohan was in touch. The new government was serious about using behavioral economics, and behavioral science more generally, to make government more effective and efficient. He wanted to know if I would be willing to help. Of course I said yes. We had written *Nudge* in the faint hope that a few people with some influence might read it and get some useful policy ideas. Since then, Cass had gone to work for his longtime colleague and friend at the University of Chicago Law School who had become president of the United States, and now the Brits were interested as well.

By some stroke of luck, genius, and timing, David Halpern was selected to run this as yet unnamed operation. David not only is a first-rate social scientist who taught at Cambridge University, but also served as the chief analyst in Prime Minister Tony Blair's strategy unit. He also coauthored previous U.K. reports on how behavioral approaches might be used by government, including one while working for Blair. This meant two things: he possessed vast knowledge and experience about how government works, and had the kind of nonpartisan credentials that would be crucial in establishing the team as a source of impartial information. Halpern is also charming and modest. If you cannot get along with David Halpern, then there is something wrong with you.

During this visit, the team made a quick trip to Paris, where a psychologist, Olivier Oullier, was trying to encourage the Sarkozy government to get interested in behavioral science. On the train ride over, Steve Hilton and I got into a heated debate about what the new team should be called. Steve wanted to use the term "behavior

change," which I thought had awful connotations. David Halpern
and I were lobbying for Behavioural Insights Team, the name finally
chosen. The argument consumed most of the trip to Paris. At some
point Rohan took Steve aside and told him to give in, arguing, pro-
phetically, that "no matter what we name it, everyone will call it the
'nudge unit.'"

———————

By the time of my next trip to London, the initial team had been
established and was set up in temporary facilities in an obscure corner of the Admiralty Arch, located a short walk away from 10 Downing Street and Parliament. It was winter, and London had been hit
with what locals considered a massive snowstorm. Accumulation was
about an inch. And it was not much warmer inside than outside the
drafty building that served as the team's first home.

The official mission of the Behavioural Insights Team (BIT) was
left broad: to achieve significant impact in at least two major areas
of policy; to spread understanding of behavioral approaches across
government; and to achieve at least a tenfold return on the cost of
the unit. The basic idea was to use the findings of behavioral science
to improve the workings of government. There was no manual for
this task, so we had to figure it out on the fly. On this and subsequent
visits, I would often go to meetings with some high-level government
official, the minister of some department or that minister's deputy,
joined by David and another team member. We would typically begin
these meetings by asking what problems the department faced and
then brainstorm about what might be done to help. It was vital to the
success of the project that we let the departments select the agenda,
rather than lecture them on the glories of behavioral science.

The first meeting I attended went so well that I could easily have
gotten the impression that this business of employing behavioral
insights to improve public policy would be easy. Nick Down, of Her
Majesty's Revenue and Customs (HMRC), the British tax collection
authority, had heard about BIT and had reached out. His job was to
collect tax revenues from people who owed the government money.
For most British taxpayers, there is little risk of falling into this situ-

ation. Employers withhold taxes from employees' paychecks through what is called a "pay as you earn" system. For those who earn all their income through wages and salary there is no need to file a tax return and no bill to pay. However, people who are self-employed or have other sources of income besides their regular job have to file a return and can be confronted with a sizable bill.

For taxpayers who have to file a return, payments are required on January 31 and July 31. If the second payment is not received on time, the taxpayer is sent a reminder notice, followed by letters, phone calls, and eventually legal action. As with any creditor, the HMRC views the use of a collection agency or legal action as a last resort, since it is expensive and antagonizes the taxpayer, who is, of course, also a voter. If that first notice could be written more effectively, it could save HMRC a lot of money. That was Nick Down's goal.

He was already off to a good start. He had read the work of psychologist Robert Cialdini, author of the classic book *Influence*. Many people have called Danny Kahneman the most important living psychologist and I would hardly disagree, but I think it would be fair to say that Cialdini is the most practical psychologist alive. Beyond Cialdini's book, Nick Down had also received some advice from a consulting firm that is affiliated with Cialdini to help him think about how he might get people to pay their taxes promptly.

Nick's team had already run a pilot experiment with a letter that used a standard recommendation from the Cialdini bible: if you want people to comply with some norm or rule, it is a good strategy to inform them (if true) that most other people comply.* In *Nudge*, we had reported on a successful use of this idea in Minnesota. In that study, overdue taxpayers were sent a variety of letters in an effort to get them to pay, with messages varying from telling them what their money would be spent on to threatening legal action, but the most effective message was simply telling people that more than 90% of Minnesota taxpayers paid their taxes on time. This latter fact was also true in Britain, and the pilot experiment used a letter with simi-

---

* One can think of this strategy as appealing to people who are "conditional cooperators" as discussed in chapter 15.

lar language. The results seemed supportive, but the pilot had not been done in a scientifically rigorous manner; it lacked a control group and several things were varied at once. Nick was keen to do more but did not have the training or staff to conduct a proper experiment, and did not have the budget to rely on outside consultants.

It was our good fortune to run into Nick Down at such an early stage of BIT's development. He was already sold on the idea that behavioral science could help him do his job better, he was willing to run experiments, and the experiments were cheap. All we had to do was fiddle with the wording of a letter that would be sent to taxpayers anyway. We didn't even have to worry about the cost of postage. Best of all, fine-tuning the letters could potentially save millions of pounds. BIT had a scheduled two-year run, after which it would be up for review. The tax experiment had the potential to provide an early win that would quiet skeptics who thought that applying behavioral science to government policy was a frivolous activity that was doomed to fail.

Our initial meeting eventually led to three rounds of experimentation at increasing levels of sophistication. Michael Hallsworth from BIT and a team of academics conducted the most recent experiment. The sample included nearly 120,000 taxpayers who owed amounts of money that varied from £351 to £50,000. (Taxpayers who owed more were handled differently.) Everyone received a reminder letter explaining how their bill could be paid, and aside from the control condition, each letter contained a one-sentence nudge that was some variation on Cialdini's basic theme that most people pay on time. Some examples:

- *The great majority of people in the U.K. pay their taxes on time.*
- *The great majority of people in your local area pay their taxes on time.*
- *You are currently in the very small minority of people who have not paid their taxes on time.*

If you are wondering, the phrase "the great majority" was used in place of the more precise "90% of all taxpayers" because some of the letters were customized for specific localities, and BIT was unable to confirm that the 90% number was true for every locality used. There is an important general point here. Ethical nudges must be both transparent and true. That is a rule the BIT has followed scrupulously.*

All the manipulations helped, but the most effective message combined two sentiments: most people pay and you are one of the few that hasn't. This letter increased the number of taxpayers who made their payments within twenty-three days† by over five percentage points. Since it does not cost anything extra to add a sentence to such letters, this is a highly cost-effective strategy. It is difficult to calculate exactly how much money was saved, since most people do pay their taxes eventually, but the experiment sped up the influx of £9 million in revenues to the government over the first twenty-three days. In fact, there is a good chance that the lessons learned from this experiment will save the U.K. government enough money to pay for the entire costs of the BIT for many years.

———

The meeting with Nick Down was atypical. More often, the minister or some agency head needed to be sold on both the value of behavioral science and the need to experiment. In many of our meetings, I found myself repeating two things so often they became known as team mantras.

1. *If you want to encourage someone to do something, make it easy.* This

---

* Of course, there is some ambiguity about what is meant by the word "transparent." If a salad bar is placed in a prominent location in the cafeteria (as it is at the Chicago Booth School of Business, I can proudly report), I do not think that it is necessary to post a sign saying that the goal of its prominent location is to nudge you to choose the salad over the burgers. The same goes for the language in the letter. It is not necessary to point out the key sentence and say that we have inserted it to increase the chance that you send us a check promptly. That is what the entire letter is trying to do, after all. So by my definition, transparency means that nothing is hidden, and that eventually the results of all studies will be released to the general public. (This topic is explored at length in a recent article by Cass Sunstein [2014], entitled "The Ethics of Nudging.")

† You might ask what is magic about twenty-three days? It turns out that in the administrative system, if the bill has not been paid by then, another letter goes out, because the HMRC computers are set up to monitor payment on that date. Running experiments in government requires a good deal of accepting the limitations of what is already being measured.

is a lesson I learned from Danny Kahneman, based on the work of Kurt Lewin, a prominent psychologist of the first half of the twentieth century. Lewin described the first step in getting people to change their behavior as "unfreezing." One way to unfreeze people is to remove barriers that are preventing them from changing, however subtle those barriers might be.

2. *We can't do evidence-based policy without evidence.* Although much of the publicity about the BIT has rightly stressed its use of behavioral insights to design changes in how government operates, an equally important innovation was the insistence that all interventions be tested using, wherever possible, the gold-standard methodology of randomized control trials (RCTs)—a method often used in medical research. In an RCT, people are assigned at random to receive different treatments (such as the wording of the letters in the tax study), including a control group that receives no treatment (in this case, the original wording). Although this approach is ideal, it is not always feasible.* Sometimes researchers have to make compromises in order to be able to run any sort of trial. The next example illustrates the importance of both mantras, as well as the practical difficulties associated with running experiments in large organizations, both government and private.

At one point I participated in a meeting in which BIT team members met with representatives of the Department of Energy and Climate Change. It was fitting that this meeting was during that week when everyone was struggling to stay warm, because the topic was how to get more people to insulate their attics, locally known as lofts. In a world of Econs, everyone would have already insulated their attic; the savings in energy costs can repay the costs of the insulation in as

---

* For example, to my knowledge there has never been a randomized control trial test of Save More Tomorrow. The reason is that we could never get a company to agree to pick some employees at random to be offered the plan and not offer it to others. The closest we came was when we were able to get one company to run different tests at two of its plants, with the other twenty-six plants serving as controls. These trials were not perfect, but we still learned things, for example about the value of educational sessions, but interpretations had to be cautious since the employees selected themselves into the educational sessions. When it comes to running experiments in both government and business, you cannot afford to be a purist.

little as one year. Nevertheless, about a third of the homes in Britain still did not have sufficient insulation in their attics, and the department had launched an initiative to encourage the laggards to stop procrastinating. The initiative offered subsidies to both owners and landlords to better insulate their homes and install other energy-saving products. Not many people were taking the department up on their deal. The Behavioural Insights Team promised to think about what might be done.

The proposed intervention embraced the "make it easy" mantra. When homeowners were interviewed and asked why they had not added insulation, even though it would save them money, many replied that it was too much trouble because they had so much clutter in their attics. The BIT proposed that the private firms that installed the insulation should package the insulation upgrade with an attic cleanup service. If a homeowner bought this package, two guys would empty the attic and then help the owners sort through which stuff to give or throw away and which to put back in the attic. Meanwhile, another crew got busy putting in the insulation. Two versions of this deal were offered, one at the installer's cost (£190) and another at retail price (£271). This was on top of the cost of the insulation itself, which was £179.

An experiment was conducted to test this idea, and the results suggest that it might be a winner. I say "might" because the data are so sparse that caution is necessary. In the interest of saving money, the only way the deal was made known to people was by mailing flyers to homes in three distinct but similar neighborhoods, picked because they were thought to have homes that were likely to be eligible for the deal. All the homeowners in a given neighborhood received the same letter,* offering the discounted cleanup, the retail cleanup, or simply the standard green deal (this latter group was the control group). Nearly 24,000 fliers were distributed to each of the three neighborhoods.

Unfortunately, the primary finding from this experiment is that

---

* This design is not pure random assignment because with only three neighborhoods, it is reasonable to worry that there could be subtle differences in the neighborhoods that might confound the results.

very few people were willing to insulate their attics. Whether this was because they did not open their mail, did not find the deals attractive, or rather enjoyed a cold breeze wafting down from their ceilings, take-up was tiny. In total, only twenty-eight attics had insulation installed. However, there is at least a strong hint in the data that the attic cleanup offer was a good idea. Although the sample sizes were all roughly equal, only three families accepted the straight insulation deal, whereas sixteen did with the cheap cleanup condition and nine did with the more expensive version. So nearly everyone who agreed to insulate their attics did it when they were offered some help in getting ready. However, the numbers are small enough that the experiment would need to be replicated to make one confident that the effect was real. For now, I think of this example as something between a scientific finding and a nifty anecdote.

Much as members of the team would love to run a replication, the generally low take-up rates discouraged the department from repeating the experiment. So why include this example out of the many in the BIT portfolio? I have two reasons. First, I have never come across a better example of the Lewin principle of removing barriers. In this case, the removal is quite literal. Whether or not this specific implementation will ever be adopted on a large scale, remembering this example may provide someone with an inspiration for a powerful nudge in another situation.

Second, the example illustrates potential pitfalls of randomized controlled trials in field settings. Such experiments are expensive, and lots of stuff can go wrong. When a lab experiment gets fouled up, which happens all too often in labs run by Humans, a relatively small amount of money paid to subjects has been lost, but the experimenter can usually try again. Furthermore, smart experimenters run a cheap pilot first to detect any bugs in the setup. All of this is hard in large-scale field experiments, and to make matters worse, it is often not possible for the experimenters to be present, on site, at every step along the way. Of course, scientists skilled at running RCTs can reduce the risks of errors and screw-ups, but these risks will never disappear.

Frustrations aside, we must continue to run trials, and continue to test ideas, because there is no other way to learn what works. Indeed, the most important legacy of the Behavioural Insights Team may be to help nudge governments to test ideas before they are implemented. In 2013 the U.K. government established a What Works Network to encourage the testing of ways to improve government effectiveness in every domain, from health to crime to education. Every government, indeed every large organization, should have similar teams conducting tests of new ideas. But we need to be realistic about the outcomes of these tests. Not every idea will work; any scientist can attest to this fact of life.

It is also crucial to understand that many improvements may superficially appear to be quite small: a 1 or 2% change in some outcome. That should not be a reason to scoff, especially if the intervention is essentially costless. Indeed, there is a danger of falling into a trap similar to the "big peanuts" fallacy exhibited by the game show contestants. A 2% increase in the effectiveness of some program may not sound like a big deal, but when the stakes are in billions of dollars, small percentage changes add up. As one United States senator famously remarked, "A billion here, a billion there, pretty soon you're talking about real money."

Tempering expectations about the magnitude of the sizes of effects that will be obtained is important because the success of automatic enrollment and Save More Tomorrow can create the false impression that it is easy to design small changes that will have big impacts. It is not. These savings interventions combined three important ingredients that greatly increase the chance that a program will achieve its stated goal. First, the program designers have a good reason to believe that a portion of the population will benefit by making some change in their behavior. In this case, with many people saving little or nothing for retirement, that was an easy call. Second, the target population must agree that a change is desirable. Here, surveys indicated that a majority of employees thought they should be saving more. Third, it is possible to make the change with one nearly costless action (or in the case of automatic enrollment, no action at all). I call such policies "one-click" interventions. Simply by ticking a box, someone who signs up for Save More Tomorrow sets himself on a course that will increase his saving rate over time, *with no need to do anything else.*

Alas, for many problems, even when the first two conditions are met, there will not be any one-click solution. For example, it is a good bet that someone who weighs 100 pounds more than their recommended body weight would benefit from shedding some pounds, and most people in that situation would agree with that assessment. But short of surgery, there is no easy answer. I have not been able to devise an Eat Less Tomorrow program that works for me or anyone else, and we know that most diet plans fail over the long run. There is no one-click diet. Nevertheless, although we cannot solve every problem with a one-click solution, there surely are some cases where such policies can be devised, and those interested in implementing new behavioral policy changes would be well advised to search for such ideas. They are the low-hanging fruit in the public policy world.

To give one concrete example: if the goal is decreasing teenage pregnancy, the most effective strategy is the use of long-term reversible contraceptives such as an intrauterine device (IUD). Trials with a sample of sexually active young women have found a failure rate of less than 1%, much lower than with other forms of contraception. Once the device is implanted, no further action is needed. Those looking for behavioral interventions that have a high probability of working should seek out other environments in which a one-time action can accomplish the job. If no one-time solution yet exists, invent one!

In some cases, successful interventions are simply reminders to people who might otherwise forget to do something. Many examples of this type have been made possible by the technology of mobile texting, which shows that nudges need not be creative, elaborate, or hidden in any way; simple, straightforward reminders in the form of a text can be extremely effective. One example comes from the domain of health. In a study in Ghana, the nonprofit Innovations for Poverty Action ran a randomized control trial testing whether text message reminders to take malaria medication helped people follow through with the medical regimen. Not only did they find these texts to be effective, but they also found that the most effective messages were brief; it was the reminder, not any additional information, which mattered.

Similarly, a study in the realm of education highlights the efficacy and scalability of simple text reminders. The study measured the effectiveness of READY4K!, a program that sends parents of pre-schoolers regular texts containing tips for good parenting, including ways to help children learn reading and writing skills. The study showed significant increases in parental involvement in literacy activities both at home and at school, in turn increasing learning gains for their children.

Such simple reminders are a good example that nudges can truly be gentle and transparent, and still work.*

The BIT passed its built-in two-year review and was renewed by the Cabinet Office in 2012. Because the team had continued to grow rapidly, it was necessary to find it a new home. The stay in the drafty original quarters was mercifully brief, but the next home, in borrowed space within the Treasury Department, was too small for the growing team's needs. So in 2014, a decision was made to partially privatize the BIT. It is now owned in equal parts by the Cabinet Office, its employees, and its nonprofit partner NESTA, which is providing the team with its current workspace. BIT has a five-year contract with the Cabinet Office, so it can make plans that are independent of the outcome of the general election in May 2015. The team has grown to nearly fifty and now supports a range of public bodies across the U.K., and increasingly helps other national governments too, including an exciting new tax compliance study in Guatemala.

While I was kibitzing the efforts of the U.K. Behavioural Insights Team, Cass was busy in Washington serving as the administrator of the Office of Information and Regulatory Affairs, known as OIRA (pronounced "oh-eye-rah"). Formally a part of the Office of Management and Budget in the White House, OIRA was formed in 1980 with the mission to evaluate the economic impact of new governmental regulations to assure they do more good than harm. Although he did not have a mandate or budget to run randomized control trials, to

---

* Reminders are another example of how in many cases nudges are inherently transparent. There is no reason to add, "By the way, the purpose of this text message was to remind you to take your medicine." Duh!

some extent Cass was able to serve as a one-man Behavioural Insights Team during President Obama's first term.

After four years working for the government, Cass went back to teaching at Harvard Law School, where he had moved just before President Obama was elected. But the U.S. nudging agenda did not end with Cass's departure. In early 2014, Dr. Maya Shankar, a former violin prodigy turned cognitive neuroscientist turned nudger, created a small unit in the White House. Maya, who makes the Energizer bunny look lethargic, has a knack for making things happen. On an American Association for the Advancement of Science fellowship, she served as an advisor in the White House Office of Science and Technology Policy. In this role, Maya made it her mission to create an American version of BIT. Miraculously, she accomplished this in less than a year and without a mandate or any funding from the government.

The team, officially called the White House Social and Behavioral Sciences Team (SBST), began as a small unit of just six behavioral scientists: Maya, two fellows on loan from universities, and three more on leave from not-for-profit think tanks, the North American branch of the Jameel Poverty Action Lab (J-PAL), which specializes in running RCTs, and ideas42, which has behavioral economics as its core strength.

In just the first year, the SBST embedded a dozen behaviorally-informed randomized control trials into federal programs, with policy objectives ranging from increasing uptake of veterans' benefits to helping people pay off their student loans. And the team is growing too. The federal government recently responded to the team's early successes by committing part of its budget to fund additional team members. Thanks to federal support and the continued support of outside partners, the team should have doubled in size by the time this book is published.

Other countries are also joining the movement. A study conducted by the Economic and Social Research Council published in 2014 reports that 136 countries around the world have incorporated behavioral sciences in some aspects of public policy, and 51 "have developed centrally directed policy initiatives that have been influenced by the new behavioural sciences." Clearly word is spreading.

It is worth highlighting that the authors of the report chose the term "behavioral sciences" to describe the techniques being used. The work of the BIT has often been mischaracterized as being based on behavioral economics whereas, in fact, there has been, at least up to now, very little actual economics involved. The tools and insights come primarily from psychology and the other social sciences. The whole point of forming a Behavioural Insights Team is to utilize the findings of other social sciences to augment the usual advice being provided by economists. It is a slur to those other social sciences if people insist on calling any policy-related research some kind of economics.

———

Whenever anyone asks me to sign a copy of *Nudge*, I always add the phrase "nudge for good." Nudges are merely tools, and these tools existed long before Cass and I gave them a name. People can be nudged to save for retirement, to get more exercise, and to pay their taxes on time, but they can also be nudged to take out a second mortgage on their home and use the money on a spending binge. Businesses or governments with bad intentions can use the findings of the behavioral sciences for self-serving purposes, at the expense of the people who have been nudged. Swindlers did not need to read our book to know how to go about their business. Behavioral scientists have a lot of wisdom to offer to help make the world a better place. Let's use their wisdom by carefully selecting nudges based on science, and then subjecting these interventions to rigorous tests.

I am proud to say that my hometown, Chicago, has just launched its own behavioral insights team with the help of ideas42. Encourage your own governments to do likewise. The failure to do so amounts to serious misbehaving.

Conclusion:

What Is Next?

It has now been more than forty years since I first began writing the beginnings of the List on my office blackboard. Much has changed. Behavioral economics is no longer a fringe operation, and writing an economics paper in which people behave like Humans is no longer considered misbehaving, at least by most economists under the age of fifty. After a life as a professional renegade, I am slowly adapting to the idea that behavioral economics is going mainstream. Sigh. This maturation of the field is so advanced that when this book is published in 2015, barring impeachment, I will be in the midst of a year serving as the president of the American Economic Association, and Robert Shiller will be my successor. The lunatics are running the asylum!

But the process of developing an enriched version of economics, with Humans front and center, is far from complete. Here I will say a bit about what I hope will come next, with an emphasis on "hope." I know better than to forecast how a discipline will change over time. The only sensible prediction is to say that what happens will surely surprise us. So, rather than make predictions, I offer a short wish list for the field's progress in years to come. Most of the wishes are aimed at the producers of economic research—my fellow economists—but some are aimed at the consumers of this research, be they managers, bureaucrats, football team owners, or homeowners.

Before looking forward to what economics might become, it seems sensible to look back and take stock. Much to everyone's surprise, the behavioral approach to economics has had its greatest impact in finance. No one would have predicted that in 1980. In fact, it was unthinkable, because economists *knew* that financial markets were the most efficient of all markets, the places where arbitrage was easiest, and thus the domain in which misbehaving was least likely to appear. In hindsight, it is clear that behavioral finance has thrived for two reasons. First, there are tightly specified theories, such as the law of one price. Second, there is fantastic data that can be used to test those theories, including daily data on thousands of stocks going back to 1926. I don't know of any other field of economics that would allow for as clear a refutation of economic theory as the story of Palm and 3Com.*

Of course, not all financial economists have renounced their allegiance to the efficient market hypothesis. But behavioral approaches are taken seriously, and on many issues the debate between the rational and behavioral camps has dominated the literature in financial economics for over two decades.

The linchpin for keeping this debate grounded and (mostly) productive is its focus on data. As Gene Fama often says when he is asked about our competing views: we agree about the facts, we just disagree about the interpretation. The *facts* are that the capital asset pricing model has clearly been rejected as an adequate description of the movements of stock prices. Beta, the only factor that was once thought to matter, does not appear to explain very much. And a pile of other factors that were once supposedly irrelevant are now thought to matter a great deal, although the question of why exactly they matter remains controversial. The field appears to be converging on what I would call "evidence-based economics."

It would be natural to wonder what other kind of economics there could be, but most of economic theory is not derived from empirical observation. Instead, it is deduced from axioms of rational choice, whether or not those axioms bear any relation to what we observe in our lives every day. A theory of the behavior of Econs cannot be empirically based, because Econs do not exist.

The combination of facts that are hard or impossible to square with the efficient market hypothesis, plus the strong voice of behav-

---

* It also didn't hurt that financial markets offer the best opportunities to make money if markets are misbehaving, so a lot of intellectual resources have gone into investigating possible profitable investment strategies.

ioral economists within the field, has made finance the field where claims about the invisible handwave have received the most constructive scrutiny. In a world where one part of a company can sell for more than the entire company, it is clear that no amount of handwaving will suffice. Financial economists have had to take seriously the "limits of arbitrage," which could just as easily be called the limits of handwaving. We now know more about how and when prices can diverge from intrinsic value and what prevents the "smart money" from driving prices back into line. (In some cases, investors who are aspiring to be the "smart money" can make more money by betting on riding the bubble and hoping to get out faster than others, than by betting on a return to sanity.) Finance also illustrates how evidence-based economics can lead to theory development. As Thomas Kuhn said, discovery starts with anomalies. The job of fleshing out the evidence-based version of financial economics is hardly over, but it is very much under way. It is time for similar progress in other branches of economics.

If I were to pick the field of economics I am most anxious to see adopt behaviorally realistic approaches, it would, alas, be the field where behavioral approaches have had the least impact so far: macroeconomics. The big-picture issues of monetary and fiscal policy are vitally important to any country's welfare, and an understanding of Humans is essential to choosing those policies wisely. John Maynard Keynes practiced behavioral macro, but that tradition has long since withered. When George Akerlof and Robert Shiller, two distinguished scholars who are keeping the behavioral Keynesian tradition alive, tried for several years to organize an annual behavioral macroeconomics meeting at the National Bureau of Economic Research, it was hard to find enough good macroeconomics papers to complete a program. (In contrast, the behavioral finance meeting that Shiller and I coordinate, which is held twice a year, attracts dozens of solid submissions for each meeting, and the process of picking the six to include is difficult.) Akerlof and Shiller eventually abandoned the enterprise.

One reason we are not witness to a thriving group of behavioral economists doing work on macroeconomics may be that the field lacks the two key ingredients that contributed to the success of

behavioral finance: the theories do not make easily falsifiable predictions, and the data are relatively scarce. Together, this means that
"smoking gun" empirical evidence of the sort that exists in finance
continues to elude us.

Perhaps more importantly, this also means that economists do not
agree on even the most basic advice about what do to in a financial
crisis like the one we experienced in 2007–08. Those on the left take
the Keynesian view that governments should have taken advantage
of the combination of high unemployment rates and low (or negative)
interest rates to undertake infrastructure investments. Those on the
right worry that such investments will not be well spent and fear that
increasing the national debt will create budgetary crises or inflation
down the road. These economists believe that tax cuts will stimulate
growth, while the Keynesians think that public spending will stimulate growth. Both sides blame the other for the slow recovery: it is
due to either too much or too little austerity. Since we are unlikely to
get governments to agree to let recession-fighting policies be picked
at random, in order to run randomized control trials, we may never
settle this debate.*

Yet the lack of consensus on what constitutes the core "rational"
macroeconomic model does not imply that behavioral economics
principles cannot be profitably applied to big-picture policy issues.
Behavioral perspectives can add nuance to macroeconomic issues
even in the absence of a clear null hypothesis to disprove or build on.
We should not need smoking guns to get busy collecting evidence.

One important macroeconomic policy begging for a behavioral
analysis is how to fashion a tax cut aimed at stimulating the economy.
Behavioral analysis would help, regardless of whether the motive for
the tax cut is Keynesian—to increase demand for goods—or supply
side—aimed at getting "job creators" to create even more jobs. There
are critical behavioral details in the way a tax cut is administered,
details that would be considered SIFs in any rational framework. If
Keynesian thinking motivates the tax cut, then policy-makers will
want the tax cut to stimulate as much spending behavior as possible.

---

* We have benefited by some "natural" experiments, such as the fall of the Berlin
Wall, that have allowed us to compare market vs. planned economies.

And one supposedly irrelevant detail these policy-makers should consider is whether the cut should come in a lump sum or be spread out over the course of the year. Without evidence-based models of consumer behavior, it is impossible to answer that question. (When the goal is to stimulate spending, my advice would be to spread it out.* Lump sums are more likely to be saved or used to pay down debts.)

The same questions apply to a supply-side tax cut. Suppose we are contemplating offering a tax holiday to firms that bring money home to the U.S. instead of keeping it stashed in foreign subsidiaries to avoid taxation. To design and evaluate this policy we need an evidence-based model that will tell us what firms will do with the repatriated money. Will they invest it, return it to shareholders, or hoard it, as many U.S. firms have been doing since the financial crisis? This makes it hard to predict what firms would do if they found themselves with a greater share of that cash held domestically. More generally, until we better understand how real firms behave, meaning those run by Humans, we cannot do a good job of evaluating the impact of key public policy measures. I will have a bit more to say about that later.

Another big-picture question that begs for more thorough behavioral analysis is the best way to encourage people to start new businesses (especially those who might be successful). Economists on the right tend to stress reducing marginal tax rates on high-income earners as the key to driving growth. Those on the left tend to push for targeted subsidies for industries they want to encourage (such as clean energy) or increased availability of loans from the Small Business Administration, a government agency whose mission is to encourage the creation and success of new enterprises. And both economists and politicians of all stripes tend to favor exemptions from many government regulations for small firms, for whom compliance can be costly. All of these policies are worth consideration, but we rarely hear much from economists about mitigating the *downside* risk to entrepreneurs if a new business fails, which happens at least half if not more of the

---

* Even the label given to a tax cut may be relevant. Epley et al. (2006) find that people report a greater propensity to spend from a tax cut that is called a "bonus" rather than a "rebate."

time.* We know that losses loom larger than gains to Humans, so this might be an important consideration. Here is one such suggestion along those lines, offered during an impromptu television interview (so pardon the grammar):

> What we need to do in this country is make it a softer cushion for failure. Because what [those on the right] say is the job creators need more tax cuts and they need a bigger payoff on the risk that they take. . . . But what about the risk of, you're afraid to leave your job and be an entrepreneur because that's where your health insurance is? . . . Why aren't we able to sell this idea that you don't have to amplify the payoff of risk to gain success in this country, you need to soften the damage of risk?

This idea did not come from an economist, not even a behavioral economist. It came from comedian Jon Stewart, the host of *The Daily Show*, during an interview with Austan Goolsbee, my University of Chicago colleague who served for a while as the chairman of President Obama's Council of Economic Advisors. Economists should not need the host of a comedy news show to point out that finding ways to mitigate the costs of failures might be more effective at stimulating new business startups than cutting the tax rate on people earning above $250,000 a year, especially when 97% of small business owners in the U.S. earn less than that amount.

———

Behavioral macroeconomics is on the top of my wish list, but virtually every field of economics could benefit from giving greater scrutiny to the role of Humans. Along with finance, development economics is probably the field where behavioral economists are having

———

* Of course, not everyone should be encouraged to become an entrepreneur. Many start with unrealistic expectations about the chance of success: the vast majority believe their chance of success to be far above average, and a third or so believe their success is a sure thing (Cooper, Woo, and Dunkelberg, 1988)! Perhaps the Small Business Administration should offer training on base rates to budding new business owners, to help curb any overconfidence.

the greatest impact, in part because that field has been revitalized by an influx of economists who are testing ideas in poor countries using randomized control trials. Some poor African country is not going to turn into Switzerland overnight, but we can learn how to make things better, one experiment at a time.

We need more evidence-based economics, which can be either theoretical or empirical. Prospect theory is, of course, the seminal evidence-based theory in behavioral economics. Kahneman and Tversky began by collecting data on what people do (starting from their own experiences) and then constructed a theory whose goal was to capture as much of that behavior as possible in a parsimonious way. This is in contrast to expected utility theory, which, as a normative theory of choice, was derived from rationality axioms. Prospect theory has now been repeatedly and rigorously tested with data taken from a wide variety of settings, from the behavior of game show contestants to golf professionals to investors in the stock market. The next generation of behavioral economic theorists, such as Nicholas Barberis, David Laibson, and Matthew Rabin (to name just three), also start with facts and then move to theory.

To produce new theories we need new facts, and the good news is that I am now seeing a lot of creative evidence collection being published in top economics journals. The growing popularity of randomized control trials, starting with the field of development economics, nicely illustrates this trend, and shows how experimentation can increase economists' tool kit, which often has had a single tool: monetary incentives. As we have seen throughout this book, treating all money as the same, and also as the primary driver of human motivation, is not a good description of reality.

A good example of a domain where field experiments run by economists are having an impact is education. Economists do not have a theory for how to maximize what children learn in school (aside from the obviously false one that all for-profit schools are already using the best methods). One overly simplistic idea is that we can improve student performance just by giving financial incentives to parents, teachers, or kids. Unfortunately, there is little evidence that such incentives are effective, but nuances matter. For example, one intriguing finding by Roland Fryer suggests that rewarding students for *inputs* (such as doing their homework) rather than *outputs* (such as their grades) is effective. I find this result intuitively appealing because the students most in need do not know how to become better students. It makes sense to reward them for doing things that educators believe are effective.

Another interesting result comes directly from the behavioral economics playbook. The team of Fryer, John List, Steven Levitt, and Sally Sadoff has found that the framing of a bonus to teachers makes a big difference. Teachers who are given a bonus at the beginning of the school year that must be returned if they fail to meet some target improve the performance of their students significantly more than teachers who are offered an end-of-year bonus contingent on meeting the same goals.*

A third positive result even further from the traditional tool kit of financial incentives comes from a recent randomized control trial conducted in the U.K., using the increasingly popular and low-cost method of text reminders. This intervention involved sending texts to half the parents in some school in advance of a major math test to let them know that their child had a test coming up in five days, then in three days, then in one day. The researchers call this approach "pre-informing." The other half of parents did not receive the texts. The pre-informing texts increased student performance on the math test by the equivalent of one additional month of schooling, and students in the bottom quartile benefited most. These children gained the equivalent of two additional months of schooling, relative to the control group. Afterward, both parents and students said they wanted to stick with the program, showing that they appreciated being nudged. This program also belies the frequent claim, unsupported by any evidence, that nudges must be secret to be effective.

Public schools, like remote villages in poor countries, are challenging environments for experimenters. That we are learning important lessons about how to teach our children and keep them motivated should embolden others outside of education and development eco-

---

* One caveat to this finding is that the bonus clawback is not popular with teachers, one reason we almost never see "negative" bonuses in the workplace. Taking money back may be viewed as "unfair."

nomics to try collecting data too. Field experiments are perhaps the most powerful tool we have to put the evidence in evidence-based economics.

———

My wish list for non-economists has a similar flavor. Considering that schools are one of the oldest of society's institutions, it is telling that we have not figured out how to teach our children well. We need to run experiments to figure out how to improve, and have only just started doing so. What should that tell us about creations much newer than schools, such as modern corporations? Is there any reason to think we know the best way to run them? It is time for everyone—from economists to bureaucrats to teachers to corporate leaders—to recognize that that they live in a world of Humans and to adopt the same data-driven approach to their jobs and lives that good scientists use.

My participation in the making of behavioral economics has taught me some basic lessons that, with due caution, can be adopted across circumstances. Here are three of them.

Observe. Behavioral economics started with simple observations. People eat too many nuts if the bowl is left out. People have mental accounts—they don't treat all cash the same. People make mistakes— lots of them. To paraphrase an earlier quote, "There are Humans. Look around." The first step to overturning conventional wisdom, when conventional wisdom is wrong, is to look at the world around you. See the world as it is, not as others wish it to be.

Collect data. Stories are powerful and memorable. That is why I have told so many in this book. But an individual anecdote can only serve as an illustration. To really convince yourself, much less others, we need to change the way we do things: we need data, and lots of it. As Mark Twain once said, "It ain't what you don't know that gets you into trouble. It's what you know for sure that just ain't so." People become overconfident because they never bother to document their past track record of wrong predictions, and then they make things worse by falling victim to the dreaded confirmation bias—they only look for evidence that confirms their preconceived hypotheses. The only protection against overconfidence is to systematically collect data, especially data that can prove you wrong. As my Chicago colleague Linda Ginzel always tells her students: "If you don't write it down, it doesn't exist."

In addition, most organizations have an urgent need to *learn how to learn*, and then commit to this learning in order to accumulate knowledge over time. At the very least this means trying new things and keeping track of what happens. Even better would be to run actual experiments. If no one in your organization knows how to go about running a proper experiment, hire a local behavioral scientist. They are cheaper than lawyers or consultants.

Speak up. Many organizational errors could have been easily prevented if someone had been willing to tell the boss that something was going wrong.

One vivid example of this comes from the high-stakes world of commercial aviation, as chronicled by Atul Gawande, a champion of reducing Human error, in his recent book *The Checklist Manifesto*. Over 500 people lost their lives in a 1977 runway crash because the second officer of a KLM flight was too timid to question the authority of the captain, his "boss." After mishearing instructions about another plane still on the same runway, the captain continued to speed the plane forward for takeoff. The second officer tried to warn him but the captain dismissed his warning, and the second officer remained quiet from then on—until the two planes collided. Gawande aptly diagnoses the cause to be an organizational failure: "[The airline was] not prepared for this moment. They had not taken the steps to make themselves a team. As a result, the second officer never believed he had the permission, let alone the duty, to halt the captain and clear up the confusion. Instead the captain was allowed to plow ahead and kill them all."

Another example comes from the mountain climbing disaster on Mount Everest so vividly documented by Jon Krakauer in his book *Into Thin Air*. During the several weeks spent acclimating and slowly reaching high base camp, the expedition leaders for two major climbing companies, Rob Hall and Scott Fisher, repeatedly stressed to their customers the importance of turning around if they had not reached the summit by the designated hour of 1 p.m. Yet both of these experienced guides lost their lives after violating their own rule. Tragically, none of their subordinates tried to intervene to remind these men about their own rules. As both of these examples illustrate, sometimes, even when you are talking to the boss, you need to warn of the threat of an impending disaster.

The making of behavioral economics has included a lot of speaking up to the high priests of economics about the unrealism of hyperrational models. I can't say that I recommend anyone take as risky a career path as I did. I was in unusual circumstances. I was lucky to run into Kahneman and Tversky at just the right moment in time. And as my thesis advisor so bluntly put it, my prospects as an economist were not all that bright: "We didn't expect much of him" says it all. When your opportunity costs are low, it pays to take risks and speak up, especially if the course you pursue is as much fun as the one I have taken.

But we cannot expect people to take risks, by speaking up or in other ways, if by so doing they will get fired. Good leaders must create environments in which employees feel that making evidence-based decisions will always be rewarded, no matter what outcome occurs. The ideal organizational environment encourages everyone to observe, collect data, and speak up. The bosses who create such environments are risking only one thing: a few bruises to their egos. That is a small price to pay for increasing the flow of new ideas and decreasing the risks of disasters.

Although I have at times been critical of economists in this book, I am entirely optimistic about the future of economics. One sign that I find particularly encouraging is that economists who do not identify themselves as "behavioral" wrote some of the best behavioral economics papers published in recent years. These economists simply do solid empirical work and let the chips fall where they may. I already mentioned two such papers earlier in the book: Justine Hastings and Jesse Shapiro's paper on the mental accounting of gasoline, and the paper by Raj Chetty and his team analyzing Danish data on pension saving. Recall that the Chetty team finds that the economic incentive for saving via tax breaks has virtually no effect on behavior. Instead, 99% of the work is done by the choice architecture of the plans, such as the default saving rate—in other words, SIFs. This paper is just one of many in which Chetty and his team of collaborators have found behavioral insights can improve our understanding of public policy.

When all economists are equally open-minded and are willing to incorporate important variables in their work, even if the rational model says those variables are supposedly irrelevant, the field of behavioral economics will disappear. All economics will be as behavioral as it needs to be. And those who have been stubbornly clinging to an imaginary world that consists only of Econs will be waving a white flag, rather than an invisible hand.

NOTES

xi "The foundation of political economy": Pareto ([1906] 2013), ch. 2, p. 21.

Preface

xiv *Choices, Values, and Frames*: Kahneman and Tversky (2000).
xv article about my work for the *New York Times Magazine*: Lowenstein (2000).
xv *When Genius Failed*: Lowenstein (2001).

Chapter 1: Supposedly Irrelevant Factors

7 human "passions": Smith ([1776] 1981, [1759] 1981).
9 behavior of peasant farmers: For evidence on Human farmers making decisions like these, see Duflo, Kremer, and Robinson (2011), Suri (2011), and Cole and Fernando (2012). On the one hand, farmers do seem responsive to information if communicated to them, and they understand how beneficial fertilizer will be on their land. On the other, they also increase their purchase and usage of fertilizer in response to simple behavioral nudges that would have no impact on an Econ.

Chapter 2: The Endowment Effect

12 "Let a six-year-old girl": Schelling (1958).
15 "The Value of Saving a Life": Thaler and Rosen (1976).
19 think about this decision correctly: At Super Bowl XXXV, Alan Krueger (2001) asked fans who had been able to buy tickets for $400 or less (the face value of the tickets) about their willingness to buy and sell at the market price of approximately $3,000. An overwhelming majority (86%) would have been unwilling to buy (if they hadn't managed to secure tickets) yet would also be unwilling to sell at this price.

Chapter 3: The List

21 "hindsight bias": Fischhoff (1975).
22 "Judgment Under Uncertainty: Heuristics and Biases": Tversky and Kahneman (1974).

24 twice as many gun deaths by suicide: DeSilver (2013), reporting on 2010 data from the Centers for Disease Control and Prevention.

Chapter 4: Value Theory

25 "Prospect Theory": Kahneman and Tversky (1979).
27 the theory of human capital formation: See Becker (1962, 1964).
27 Bernoulli in 1738: See Bernoulli ([1738] 1954) for an English translation.
29 *The Theory of Games and Economic Behavior*: von Neumann and Morgenstern (1947).
30 Baumol had proposed an alternative: Baumol (1962).

Chapter 5: California Dreamin'

35 "Consumer Choice: A Theory of Economists' Behavior": Published as Thaler (1980).
38 *Thinking, Fast and Slow*: Kahneman (2011).
40 "slow hunch": Johnson (2010).
40 private value for a token: See Smith (1976).

Chapter 6: The Gauntlet

44 whether *real* managers actually behaved this way: See Mongin (1997) and Frischmann and Hogendorn (2015) for a review of this debate on marginal analysis.
45 "This paper raises grave doubts": Lester (1946).
45 "He would simply rely on his sense or his 'feel' of the situation": Machlup (1946).
46 billiard players: Friedman (1953), p. 21.
48 "preference reversals": Lichtenstein and Slovic (1973).
49 Raising the stakes made things worse: Grether and Plott (1979).
51 "Suppose there were people doing silly things": Markets can actually exacerbate welfare losses resulting from the presence of consumer biases. Firms may not have an incentive to debias consumers since under some circumstances, firm profits are increasing in the degree of naiveté: credit card late payment fees (Heidhues and Kszegi, 2010); gym memberships (DellaVigna and Malmendier, 2006); printer cartridges and hotel room shrouded fees (Gabaix and Laibson, 2006).
51 Adam Smith's invisible hand: For a thoughtful take on how to think about the concept of the invisible hand, see Ullmann-Margalit (1997).
52 transform people into rational agents: The study of how profit-maximizing firms interact with Human consumers is the subject of the exciting field of behavioral industrial organization. For a textbook treatment see Spiegler (2011). The examples discussed in chapter 13 are also relevant.
52 failing to act in accordance with the rational agent model is not fatal: For

a thorough analysis of these kinds of arguments see Russell and Thaler (1985), Haltiwanger and Waldman (1985), and Akerlof and Yellen (1985).
53 "An Economic Theory of Self-Control": Thaler and Shefrin (1981).

Section II: Mental Accounting

55 "mental accounting": My paper was Thaler (1980), and they suggested the term "mental accounting" in Kahneman and Tversky (1984).

Chapter 7: Bargains and Rip-Offs

62 Macy's: Barbaro (2007).
62 surprisingly candid press release: Tuttle (2012).
63 JC Penney claimed the end price consumers paid was effectively the same: Chernev (2012).
63 Johnson was ousted and coupons returned: Clifford and Rampell (2013).
63 [Walmart's] "savings catcher" app: https://savingscatcher.walmart.com.

Chapter 8: Sunk Costs

65 "Knee-Deep in the Big Muddy": Staw (1976).
66 If I want to go to the gym and will feel bad about wasting my membership fee: DellaVigna and Malmendier (2006).
67 "payment depreciation": Gourville and Soman (1998).
67 sunk costs matter . . . but may be forgotten eventually: Arkes and Blumer (1985).
68 survey . . . with one of his newsletters: Shafir and Thaler (2006). See also Thaler (1999a) for a discussion of the study.
72 "kill their darlings": A nice piece on this phrase is Wickman (2013).

Chapter 9: Buckets and Budgets

75 most MBA students had . . . budgets: Heath and Soll (1996).
75 the most rigorous demonstration of the effects of mental budgeting to date: Hastings and Shapiro (2013).
78 *House of Debt*: Mian and Sufi (2014).

Chapter 10: At the Poker Table

80 a study showing that the odds on long shots: The study cited by Kahneman and Tversky (1979) is McGlothin (1956).
82 started work on a real paper: Thaler and Johnson (1990).
84 Mutual fund portfolio managers take more risks in the last quarter of the year: Chevalier and Ellison (1997).

Chapter 11: Willpower? No Problem

87   "invisible hand": Smith ([1776] 1981, p. 456): vol. 1, book 4, ch. 2, par. 9.

87   The same can be said of much of behavioral economics: See Ashraf, Camerer, and Loewenstein (2005) for a full discussion of this point. My discussion here draws heavily on their work and also that of George Loewenstein (1992), who has long had a interest in this topic, and is not too lazy to read very long books.

88   "The pleasure which we are to enjoy ten years hence": Smith ([1759] 1981, p. 190): part 4, ch. 2, par. 8; cited in Ashraf, Camerer, and Loewenstein (2005).

88   preference for present consumption over future consumption: "The change, again, must be less rapid the further we are from the moment, and more rapid as we come nearer to it. An event which is to happen a year hence affects us on the average about as much one day as another; but an event of importance, which is to take place three days hence, will probably affect us on each of the intervening days more acutely than the last" (Jevons [1871], 1957, ch. 2).

88   "Our telescopic faculty is defective": Pigou (1920), cited by Loewenstein (1992), which gives a nice historical overview of ideas about time preference.

89   "This is illustrated by the story of the farmer": Fisher (1930, p. 82): par. 9.

89   "those working men who, before prohibition": Ibid., p. 83: par. 9.

90   annual rate of about 10%: To be precise, the exact discount rate is 11.11...%. If next year's consumption is valued as 10% less than today's, then the discount rate is usually defined as the value x that satisfies $1/(1+x)=.9$, which is .11.... That is, saying that the value of consumption next year is 90% of its value today is equivalent to saying that the value of consumption today is 111.11...% of its value next year. For discount rates close to zero, the difference between these two numbers (here 10% and 11.11...%) is small.

91   *present-biased*: The generalized hyperbolic discounting function introduced by Loewenstein and Prelec (1992) took a kind of faulty telescope as a starting assumption, namely that the interval between two future dates seems a fraction as long as an equivalently-sized interval that starts today.

93   adding mathematical rigor to economics.: On Pareto's important role in divorcing economics from psychology see Bruni and Sugden (2007).

94   *The General Theory of Employment, Interest and Money:* Keynes (1936).

95   *permanent income hypothesis*: Friedman (1957).

95   a discount rate of 33% per year: Friedman (1963) clarifies the analysis of this case.

95   Modigliani, writing with his student: Modigliani and Brumberg (1954).

96   Robert Barro: Barro (1974).

98   *behavioral life-cycle hypothesis*: Thaler and Shefrin (1988).

98   when investors in retirement plans earn high returns: Choi, Laibson, Madrian, and Metrick (2009).

Chapter 12: The Planner and the Doer

99 the only economics paper on self-control I found: Strotz (1955–56).

101 Mischel himself had done considerable research: Mischel (1968), p. 146, and Mischel (1969), p. 1014. For an update on the longitudinal research, see Mischel et al. (2011) and Mischel's (2014) recent book for the general public.

102 a large literature studying delay of gratification: Ainslie (1975) worked out a version of hyperbolic discounting that Loewenstein and Prelec (1992) would later build on.

103 "The idea of self-control is paradoxical": McIntosh (1969), p. 122.

103 the two-system view: The two-system model is not a Kahneman creation. Many other psychologists had written about such models. See for example Sloman (1996) and Stanovich and West (2000).

104 Hersh Shefrin . . . to join the effort: Thaler and Shefrin (1981).

105 a famous paper on the topic: Jensen and Meckling (1976).

109 Recent research in neuro-economics: See Banich (2009) for a review of some of the relevant psychology and neuroscience.

110 PhD dissertation: Laibson (1997).

110 Two other behavioral economic theorists . . . elaborated: O'Donoghue and Rabin (1999).

110 references to the key papers: An influential survey article on time preference is Frederick, Loewenstein, and O'Donoghue (2002).

111 "hot-cold empathy gaps": Loewenstein (2005).

Chapter 13: Misbehaving in the Real World

118 decoupled the purchase decision: Prelec and Loewenstein (1998).

121 excess inventory: Another factor driving the pile-up of inventory was that President Nixon had imposed price controls around 1971–72. The next year, when the fixes were lifted, manufacturers raised prices more steeply than consumers were used to, to make up for the past fixes. This created highly negative transaction utility for consumers, such that fewer were willing to buy and inventory piled up.

121 One innovation was the rebate: Technically, the first rebate was offered by Ford in 1914, but once it disappeared it didn't come back until the 1970s as Chrysler's "Car Clearance Carnival" campaign response to the inventory pile-up (Jewett, 1996).

121 discounted auto loans: GM reluctantly offered loans after Chrysler and Ford first did so. "It is understood that GM had been resisting following Ford and Chrysler for fear of triggering an industrywide battle on incentives. In the past, many consumers who didn't buy cars before such programs expired have simply held off on purchases until the next round of incentives" (Nag, 1985).

121 A reporter had crunched the numbers: Buss (1986).

Chapter 14: What Seems Fair?

128   experimental philosophy: Actual philosophers do this now. See Knobe and Nichols (2013), or for a shorter introduction, Knobe et al. (2012).

130   "repugnant": Roth (2007).

131   wages and salaries appear to be sticky: Daly, Hobijn, and Lucking (2012); Kaur (2014).

133   the cheapest place in the country to buy plywood: Lohrn (1992).

133   "FIRST CHICAGO LOSES TOUCH WITH HUMANS": Miller (1995).

135   "tin ear": McKay, Deogun, and Lublin (1999).

135   The *Guardian* was the first . . . to break the story: Halliday (2012).

135   The *Daily Mail* quoted one customer . . . "is totally parasitic.": "Apple accused of exploiting Whitney Houston's death after cost of albums soar on iTunes," *Daily Mail*, February 14, 2012.

135   Whitney Houston albums sold in the U.S.: Nielsen SoundScan (2012).

137   multiples charged during a blizzard in New York City: Brown (2014).

139   "It is incredibly important for any business": Kokonas (2014).

Chapter 15: Fairness Games

141   three German economists: Güth, Schmittberger, and Schwarze (1982). I wrote a survey article on this and other papers studying Ultimatum Games (Thaler, 1988b).

141   Dictator Game: Kahneman, Knetch, and Thaler (1986).

142   some remote tribes: The Machiguenga people in the Peruvian Amazon rarely turn down any offer of free money, and the offers they make tend to be low (Henrich, 2000). See also Henrich et al. (2002). For a popular treatment, see Watters (2013).

143   results did not differ much from lower-stakes games: Hoffman, McCabe, and Smith (1996).

143   virtually no difference in the behavior of Proposers: Cameron (1999). Slonim and Roth (1998) find similar results in Slovakia, though Andersen et al. (2011) find lower rejection rates with a different experimental design in northeast India.

145   "The *purely* economic man": Sen (1977), p. 336.

145   "Economists Free Ride: Does Anyone Else?": Marwell and Ames (1981). See also Frank, Gilovich, and Regan (1993), who argue that training in economics causes students to behave self-interestedly.

145   tested this interpretation with a brilliant twist: Andreoni (1988).

146   *conditional cooperators*: Fehr and Gächter (2000, 2002); Fischbacher, Gächter, and Fehr (2001); Fehr and Fischbacher, (2003); Kocher et al. (2008).

146   an article about cooperation: Dawes and Thaler (1988).

Chapter 16: Mugs

148 *Laboratory Experimentation in Economics*: Roth (1987).
148 a paper written by Jack Knetsch: Knetsch and Sinden (1984).
149 joined forces with him: Kahneman, Knetsch, and Thaler (1991).
154 "status quo bias": Samuelson and Zeckhauser (1988).

Chapter 17: The Debate Begins

159 a conference at the University of Chicago: The proceedings of the conference were published, first as an issue of the *Journal of Business* (Hogarth and Reder, 1986), and then as a book, *Rational Choice* (Hogarth and Reder, 1987).
161 "Let me dismiss a point of view": Arrow (1986), p. S385.
161 When prices change, the consumer chooses: He notes that even this theory still involves some maximization. In fact, since this time economists have developed habit-based theories that are considered to be "rational." See Becker and Murphy (1988) and Becker (1992).
162 "We have the curious situation": Arrow (1986), p. S391.
162 "Obviously I am accepting the insight": Ibid., p. S397. See also Simon (1957), chs. 14–15, and Conlisk (1996).
162 "Well, some people just can't tell a joke": Stigler (1977), p. 441.
163 "the advantages of the division of labor are reaffirmed": Ibid., p. 442.
163 "I will end my remarks with the following two false statements": Thaler (1986), p. S283.
164 "Don't laugh. We proved it rigorously!": Modigliani and Miller (1958). See also Miller (1988).
164 behavioral finance paper: Shefrin and Statman (1984).
165 *did* pay dividends: Baker and Wurgler (2004) provide evidence that firms cater to investor's desire for dividends, offering them more at times when the market puts a premium on dividend-paying firms.
166 In Lintner's model: Lintner (1956).
166 "I assume it to be a behavioral model": Miller (1986), p. S467.
166 "The purpose of this paper": Ibid., p. S466.
167 "Behind each holding": Ibid., p. S467.
168 "I tend to view": Shiller (1986), p. S501.

Chapter 18: Anomalies

169 *The Structure of Scientific Revolutions*: Kuhn (1962).
174 the first two columns: Thaler (1987a, 1987b).
174 A burst of papers: Rozeff and Kinney (1976).
174 Another anomaly came from bettors at the racetrack: Thaler (1992).

8192

Chapter 19: Forming a Team

176 game theory in the 1940s: The catalyst was arguably von Neumann and Morgenstern (1947), the first edition of which was published in 1944.

176 the field of behavioral game theory: Camerer (2003).

180 Stanley Schachter: Schachter et al. (1985a, 1985b), Hood et al. (1985).

180 generating new psychology of our own: An exception is the research associated with Sendhil Mullainathan and Eldar Shafir's (2013) book *Scarcity*, one of those rare collaborations between an economist and a psychologist.

182 paper by Fehr that captured our attention: Fehr, Kirchsteiger, and Riedl (1993).

182 employment contracts could be viewed partially as a gift exchange: Akerlof (1982).

182 Rabin's model: Rabin (1993).

Chapter 20: Narrow Framing on the Upper East Side

186 bold forecasts and timid choices: Kahneman and Lovallo (1993).

186 described . . . in *Thinking, Fast and Slow*: Kahneman (2011), ch. 22.

189 benefits are demonstrably large: Mullainathan (2013), Baicker, Mullainathan, and Schwartzstein (2013).

191 *equity premium puzzle*: Mehra and Prescott (1985).

192 six years to get the paper published: Rajnish Mehra told me this.

192 none of the explanations had proven to be completely satisfactory: Mehra (2007).

194 words with one syllable: Samuelson (1979), p. 306.

194 "Risk and Uncertainty: A Fallacy of Large Numbers": Samuelson (1963).

195 "myopic loss aversion": Benartzi and Thaler (1995).

195 The only way you can ever take 100 attractive bets: Barberis, Huang and Santos (2001) formalize this intuition in a dynamic model.

195 experiment using recently hired non-faculty employees: Benartzi and Thaler (1999).

197 *Quarterly Journal of Economics* dedicated to Amos's memory: Thaler et al. (1997).

198 A paper by . . . Maya Shaton: Shaton (2014).

198 Benartzi and I used: Benartzi and Thaler (1995).

199 the actual decision-making of cab drivers: Camerer et al. (1997).

200 The higher the wage, the less drivers worked: This result has been debated in the literature, with contrary findings by Farber (2005, 2008, 2014) and Andersen et al. (2014), and supportive results from Fehr and Goette (2007), Crawford and Meng (2011), Dupas and Robinson (2014), and, with the best data so far (on Singaporean cab drivers), Agarwal et al. (2014).

Chapter 21: The Beauty Contest

205 "I believe there is no other proposition in economics": Jensen (1978), p. 95.

207 Michael Jensen's PhD thesis: Published as Jensen (1969).

209 his thoughts on financial markets: Keynes (1936), ch. 12.

209 "the element of real knowledge . . . seriously declined": Ibid., ch. 12, p. 153.

209 "Day-to-day fluctuations . . . market": Ibid., p. 154.

210 "Worldly wisdom teaches . . . unconventionally": Ibid., p. 158.

210 "Professional investment may be likened": Ibid.

212 *A Beautiful Mind*: Nasar (1998).

212 commonly referred to as the "beauty contest": Camerer (1997).

212 first studied experimentally by . . . Rosemarie Nagel: Nagel (1995).

212 zero was the Nash equilibrium: Researchers have explored various alternatives to Nash equilibrium. See, for example, Geanakoplos, Pearce, and Stachetti (1989), McKelvey and Palfrey (1995), Camerer, Ho, and Chong (2004), Eyster and Rabin (2005), Hoffmann et al. (2012), and Tirole (2014).

215 "In the long run, we are all dead": Keynes (1923), ch. 2, p. 80.

Chapter 22: Does the Stock Market Overreact?

217 Groucho Marx theorem: This idea was formalized by Milgrom and Stokey (1982).

217 why shares would turn over at a rate of about 5% per month: Based on data from New York Stock Exchange (2014).

218 given a decile score . . . on a test of "sense of humor": Kahneman and Tversky (1973).

219 *Security Analysis . . . The Intelligent Investor*: Graham and Dodd ([1934] 2008), Graham ([1949] 1973).

220 Buying the entire original thirty-stock portfolio: Graham ([1949] 1973), ch. 7, p. 164.

220 "overenthusiasm or artificial stimulants": Graham and Dodd ([1934] 2008), p. 270.

221 "In conclusion, the behavior of security prices": Basu (1977), p. 680.

221 "Given its longevity": Banz (1981), p. 17.

221 *The New Contrarian Investment Strategy*: Dreman (1982).

224 My paper with Werner: De Bondt and Thaler (1985).

Chapter 23: The Reaction to Overreaction

225 This subtlety was first articulated by Eugene Fama: Fama (1970).

226 capital asset pricing model (CAPM): Sharpe (1964) and Lintner (1965a, 1965b). For a textbook treatment, see Cochrane (2005). The reason that these methods don't use the variance of price as a measure of a stock's risk is that in a wide portfolio of stocks, these movements would be a wash on average. Instead, the idea is to measure risk based on how sensitive the stock price is to market movements (e.g., an index like the S&P 500), so that you have a measure of how much riskier (or less risky) owning this stock would make your portfolio.

228 the small firm effect: Banz (1981).

228 "The CAPM Is Wanted, Dead or Alive": Fama and French (1996).

228 Fama–French Three Factor Model: Fama and French (1993).

228 "Contrarian Investment, Extrapolation, and Risk": Lakonishok, Shleifer, and Vishny (1994).

228 Fama concedes . . . risk or overreaction: See Fama's Nobel lecture, published as Fama (2014).

229 a new five-factor model: Fama and French (2014). A related model is Asness, Frazzini, and Pedersen (2014).

Chapter 24: The Price Is Not Right

230 Shiller . . . published a paper: Shiller (1981).

232 one of those papers . . . presented at the Chicago conference: Kleidon (1986).

232 U.S. stock market dropped 4.4%: Cutler, Poterba, and Summers (1989).

233 "Stock Prices and Social Dynamics": Shiller (1984).

233 book with George Akerlof: Akerlof and Shiller (2009).

234 Bob later borrowed that phrase: Shiller (2000).

236 a thriving and mainstream component of financial economics research: You can find a list of all the programs from these workshops on Bob's website: http://www.econ.yale.edu/~shiller/behfin/.

Chapter 25: The Battle of Closed-End Funds

240 "THERE ARE IDIOTS. Look around": Quoted in Fox (2009), p. 199.

240 more rigorous, thorough, and polite version of the "idiots" paper: De Long et al. (1990).

241 "an expensive monument": Graham ([1949] 1973), p. 242.

242 That is exactly what we found: Lee, Shleifer, and Thaler (1991).

242 thesis on closed-end funds: Thompson (1978).

242 *A Random Walk Down Wall Street*: Malkiel (1973).

243 "But they can't": Chen, Kan, and Miller (1993), p. 795.

243 the last set of stones: The five papers are: Lee, Shleifer, and Thaler (1991), Chen, Kan, and Miller (1993a), Chopra et al. (1993a), Chen, Kan, and Miller (1993b), and Chopra et al. (1993b).

Chapter 26: Fruit Flies, Icebergs, and Negative Stock Prices

249 LTCM had collapsed: Lowenstein (2000).

249 in a paper they published on this topic: Shleifer and Vishny (1997).

250 an academic paper about the . . . episode: Lamont and Thaler (2003).

251 "we might define an efficient market": Black (1986), p. 553.

252 "liar loans": See Mian and Sufi (2014).

Chapter 27: Law Schooling

258 The published version of the paper: Jolls, Sunstein, and Thaler (1998).

259 "Posner evidently writes": Solow (2009).

262 "The Problem of Social Cost": Coase (1960).

262 "This is, of course, a very unrealistic assumption": Ibid., p. 15.

265 *More Guns, Less Crime*: Lott (1998).

268 In not a single case did the parties even attempt to negotiate: Farnsworth (1999).

269 *Oxford Handbook of Behavioral Economics and the Law*: Zamir and Teichman (2014).

269 "The battle . . . has been won": Korobkin (2011).

Chapter 28: The Offices

275 If there is a number, people will use it: Hsee et al. (2009).

Chapter 29: Football

277 "Division of labor strongly attenuates": Stewart (1997).

278 football paper: Massey and Thaler (2013).

280 *The winner's curse*: For a review, see my "Anomalies" column on the subject (Thaler, 1988a).

280 *The false consensus effect*: Ross, Greene, and House (1977).

284 If a team is paying a high draft pick a lot of money: Camerer and Weber (1999).

292 teams don't go for it: Romer (2006).

292 *New York Times* used his model: For an example of Brian Burke's work, see http://www.advancedfootballanalytics.com/.

292 "*New York Times* 4th Down Bot": The bot's recommendations can be found at http://nyt4thdownbot.com/. For a comparison between coaches and the *NYT* Bot's performances, see Burk and Quealy (2014).

292 *The Signal and the Noise*: Silver (2012).

293 Peter Principle: Peter and Hull (1969).

Chapter 30: Game Shows

296 They asked me if I would like to join the team: Post et al. (2008).

299 my paper with Eric Johnson: Thaler and Johnson (1990).

300 an experiment to measure the difference between public and private decisions: Baltussen, van den Assem, and van Dolder (2015).

301 more risk averse in front of the crowd: This lines up with findings that investors take more risks online than in front of others. Barber and Odean (2002) find that investors trade more and more speculatively after switching from phone-based to online trading.

301 "other-regarding" behavior, such as the Ultimatum Game and Dictator Game: Rabin (1993); Tesler (1995); Levitt and List (2007).

301 low-stakes experiments of the Prisoner's Dilemma: See Sally (1995) for a meta-study of papers published over 35 years. Holfstadter (1983) and Rapoport (1988) are some representative examples.

302 a sample of 287 pairs of players to study: Van den Assem, van Dolder, and Thaler (2012).

305 "an effective story": WNYC (2014).

Section VIII: Helping Out

307 well-established theorists: See, for example, Ellison and Fudenberg (1993), Ellison (1997), Fudenberg and Levine (2006), and Bénabou and Tirole (2003).

Chapter 31: Save More Tomorrow

309 standard theories of saving: Friedman (1957); Modigliani and Brumberg (1954).

310 "As an economist, . . . empirical questions": Bernheim (2002).

310 a heated debate in the economics literature: Poterba, Venti, and Wise (1996) argued that IRAs did increase savings. They pointed out that those who started such plans tended to keep contributing each year, and their balances steadily rose, with no apparent offset in other forms of saving. Engen, Gale, and Scholz (1996) focused on a different question: whether an increase in the maximum contribution would increase saving. They concluded that it would not. I think both were right. IRAs did increase saving because they induced some people who were not doing any retirement saving to put something aside each year. But an increase in the maximum contribution would only affect the affluent, who were already saving more than the maximum, and would merely shift money from taxable to non-taxable accounts. My reading of the Chetty et al. (2014) paper discussed at the end of this chapter supports this view.

310 "Psychology and Savings Policies": Thaler (1994).

311 The evidence suggests that when people get a windfall: Landsberger (1966); Epley, Mak, and Idson (2006); Shapiro and Slemrod (2003).

312 When taxpayers are audited: Engstrm, Nordblom, Ohlsson, and Persson (2015).

313 inertia could work for us instead of against us: Choi et al. (2003); Choi, Laibson, and Madrian (2004).

315 "The Power of Suggestion": Madrian and Shea (2001).

316 "Suppose a firm automatically enrolls employees": Internal Revenue Service (1998).

319 survey conducted by Aon Hewitt: Hess and Xu (2011).

319 recent paper published in *Science*: Benartzi and Thaler (2013).

319 a national personal saving plan: U.K. Department for Work and Pensions (2014).

320 Australia and New Zealand: Summers (2013) provides a brief and friendly description of Australian retirement saving plans. John and Levine (2009) describe the New Zealand model, among others.

320 a team of American and Danish economists: Chetty et al. (2014).

321 Shlomo and I wrote a paper: Benartzi and Thaler (2004).

Chapter 32: Going Public

323 "Asymmetric Paternalism": Camerer et al. (2003).

323 "A regulation is asymmetrically paternalistic": Ibid., p. 1212.

323 "cautious paternalism"; "optimal paternalism": O'Donoghue and Rabin (1999, 2003).

323 Cass and I wrote a short paper: Thaler and Sunstein (2003).

323 "Libertarian Paternalism is Not an Oxymoron": Sunstein and Thaler (2003).

325 paperback rights were later sold to trade publishers: Thaler and Sunstein (2008).

326 *The Design of Everyday Things*: Norman (1988).

327 John Tierney . . . had a suggestion: Tierney (2005).

327 paper . . . on the powerful effect of default options in this domain: Johnson and Goldstein (2004).

328 In Alaska and Montana: Donate Life America (2014).

328 "mandated choice": This was first called "mandated choice" in a report on organ donation by the Institute of Medicine (Childress et al., 2006).

328 which I continued to call "mandated choice": Thaler (2009).

Chapter 33: Nudging in the U.K.

335 the classic book *Influence*: Cialdini (2006).

335 a consulting firm: Cialdini's consulting firm is called Influence at Work.

336 the most recent experiment: Hallsworth et al. (2014).

338 One way to unfreeze people: See Lewin (1947).

340 something between a scientific finding and a nifty anecdote: Behavioural Insights Team (2013), p. 3.

341 "A billion here, a billion there": For those who are curious, this is Senator Evvert Dirksen of Illinois.

342 it was the reminder . . . which mattered: Raifman et al. (2014).

343 READY4K!: York and Loeb (2014).

344 "have developed . . . behavioural sciences": Whitehead et al. (2014).

Conclusion: What Is Next?

349 Akerlof and Shiller eventually abandoned the enterprise: See Akerlof (2007) for one perspective on the questions to be answered.

352 Jon Stewart: Stewart (2012).

353 testing ideas in poor countries using randomized control trials: Two recent books that describe what we have learned from many such experiments are Banerjee and Duflo (2011) and Karlan and Appel (2011). Mullainathan and Shafir (2013) and Haushofer and Fehr (2014) argue that for behavioral and psychological reasons, being in poverty can lead to worse decision-making, which makes it hard to escape poverty. See also World Bank (2015).

353 repeatedly and rigorously tested: See Post et al. (2008) and van den Assem, van Dolder, and Thaler (2012) on game shows, Pope and Schweitzer (2011) on golf, Barberis and Thaler (2003) and Kliger, van den Assem, and Zwinkels (2014) for reviews of behavioral finance, and Camerer (2000) and DellaVigna (2009) for surveys of empirical applications of behavioral economics more generally.

353 intriguing finding by Roland Fryer: Fryer (2010).

354 The team of Fryer, John List, Steven Levitt, and Sally Sadoff: Fryer et al. (2013).

354 a recent randomized control trial: Kraft and Rogers (2014).

355 Field experiments are perhaps the most powerful tool we have: Gneezy and List (2013).

356 "If you don't write it down, it doesn't exist": Ginzel (2014).

356 his recent book *The Checklist Manifesto*: Gawande (2010), pp. 176–77.

356 *Into Thin Air*: Krakauer (1997).

357 99% of the work is done by the choice architecture: Another example is Alexandre Mas who (sometimes collaborating with Alan Krueger) has shown that after labor disputes that go badly for workers, the quality of work declines. See Mas (2004) on the value of construction equipment after a dispute, Mas and Krueger (2004) on defects in tires after a strike, and Mas (2006) on police work after arbitration. One other example of mainstream economists doing research with a behavioral economics bent would be Edward Glaeser (2013) on speculation in real estate.

358 improve our understanding of public policy: See Chetty's (2015) Ely lecture delivered at the American Economic Association Meeting that I organized in January 2015. In this case you can literally see it by going to the AEA website: https://www.aeaweb.org/webcasts/2015/Ely.php.

BIBLIOGRAPHY

Agarwal, Sumit, Mi Diao, Jessica Pan, and Tien Foo Sing. 2014. "Labor Supply Decisions of Singaporean Cab Drivers." Available at: http://ssrn.com/abstract=2338476.

Akerlof, George A. 1982. "Labor Contracts as Partial Gift Exchange." *Quarterly Journal of Economics* 97, no. 4: 543–69.

———. 2007. "The Missing Motivation in Macroeconomics." *American Economic Review* 97, no. 1: 3–36.

———, and Robert J. Shiller. 2009. *Animal Spirits: How Human Psychology Drives the Economy, and Why It Matters for Global Capitalism.* Princeton: Princeton University Press.

———, and Janet L. Yellen. 1985. "A Near-Rational Model of the Business Cycle, With Wage and Price Inertia." *Quarterly Journal of Economics* 100, supplement: 823–38.

Andersen, Steffen, Alec Brandon, Uri Gneezy, and John A. List. 2014. "Toward an Understanding of Reference-Dependent Labor Supply: Theory and Evidence from a Field Experiment." Working Paper 20695, National Bureau of Economic Research.

Andersen, Steffen, Seda Ertaç, Uri Gneezy, Moshe Hoffman, and John A. List. 2011. "Stakes Matter in Ultimatum Games." *American Economic Review* 101, no. 7: 3427–39.

Andreoni, James. 1988. "Why Free Ride?: Strategies and Learning in Public Goods Experiments." *Journal of Public Economics* 37, no. 3: 291–304.

Arkes, Hal R., and Catherine Blumer. 1985. "The Psychology of Sunk Cost." *Organizational Behavior and Human Decision Processes* 35, no. 1: 124–40.

Arrow, Kenneth J. 1986. "Rationality of Self and Others in an Economic System." *Journal of Business* 59, no. 4, part 2: S385–99.

Ashraf, Nava, Colin F. Camerer, and George Loewenstein. 2005. "Adam Smith, Behavioral Economist." *Journal of Economic Perspectives* 19, no. 3: 131–45.

Asness, Clifford S., Andrea Frazzini, and Lasse Heje Pedersen. 2014. "Quality Minus Junk." Available at: http://ssrn.com/abstract=2312432.

Baicker, Katherine, Sendhil Mullainathan, and Joshua Schwartzstein. 2013. "Behavioral Hazard in Health Insurance." Working paper.

Baker, Malcolm, and Jeffrey Wurgler. 2004. "A Catering Theory of Dividends." *Journal of Finance* 59, no. 3: 1125–65.

Baltussen, Guido, Martijn J. van den Assem, and Dennie van Dolder. 2015 (forthcoming). "Risky Choice in the Limelight." *Review of Economics and Statistics*. Available at: http://ssrn.com/abstract=2526341.

Banerjee, Abhijit Vinayak, and Esther Duflo. 2011. *Poor Economics: A Radical Rethinking of the Way to Fight Global Poverty*. New York: PublicAffairs.

Banich, Marie T. 2009. "Executive Function: The Search for an Integrated Account." *Current Directions in Psychological Science* 18, no. 2: 89–94.

Banz, Rolf W. 1981. "The Relationship between Return and Market Value of Common Stocks." *Journal of Financial Economics* 9, no. 1: 3–18.

Barbaro, Michael. 2007. "Given Fewer Coupons, Shoppers Snub Macy's." *New York Times*, September 29. Available at: http://www.nytimes.com/2007/09/29/business/29coupons.html.

Barber, Brad M., and Terrance Odean. 2002. "Online Investors: Do the Slow Die First?" *Review of Financial Studies* 15, no. 2: 455–88.

Barberis, Nicholas C., and Richard H. Thaler. 2003. "A Survey of Behavioral Finance." In Nicholas Barberis, Richard H. Thaler, George M. Constantinides, M. Harris, and René Stulz, eds., *Handbook of the Economics of Finance*, vol. 1B, 1053–128. Amsterdam: Elsevier.

Barberis, Nicholas, Ming Huang, and Tano Santos. 2001. "Prospect Theory and Asset Prices." *Quarterly Journal of Economics* 116, no. 1: 1–53.

Barner, Martin, Francesco Feri, and Charles R. Plott. 2005. "On the Microstructure of Price Determination and Information Aggregation with Sequential and Asymmetric Information Arrival in an Experimental Asset Market." *Annals of Finance* 1, no. 1: 73–107.

Barro, Robert J. 1974. "Are Government Bonds Net Wealth?" *Journal of Political Economy* 82, no. 6: 1095–117.

Basu, Sanjoy. 1977. "Investment Performance of Common Stocks in Relation to Their Price-Earnings Ratios: A Test of the Efficient Market Hypothesis." *Journal of Finance* 32, no. 3: 663–82.

Baumol, William J. 1962. "On the Theory of Expansion of the Firm." *American Economic Review* 52, no. 5: 1078–87.

Becker, Gary S. 1962. "Investment in Human Capital: A Theoretical Analysis." *Journal of Political Economy* 70, no. 5: 9–49.

——. 1964. *Human Capital: A Theoretical Analysis with Special Reference to Education*. New York and London: National Bureau for Economic Research and Columbia University Press.

——. 1992. "Habits, Addictions, and Traditions." *Kyklos* 45, no. 3: 327–45.

——, and Kevin M. Murphy. 1988. "A Theory of Rational Addiction." *Journal of Political Economy* 96, no. 4: 675–700.

Behavioural Insights Team. 2013. "Removing the Hassle Factor Associated with Loft Insulation: Results of a Behavioural Trial." UK Department of Energy & Climate Change, September. Available at: https://www.gov.uk/government/publications/loft-clearance-results-of-a-behavioural-trial.

Bénabou, Roland, and Jean Tirole. 2003. "Intrinsic and Extrinsic Motivation." *Review of Economic Studies* 70, no. 3: 489–520.

Benartzi, Shlomo, and Richard H. Thaler. 1995. "Myopic Loss Aversion and the Equity Premium Puzzle." *Quarterly Journal of Economics* 110, no. 1: 73–92.

———. 1999. "Risk Aversion or Myopia? Choices in Repeated Gambles and Retirement Investments." *Management Science* 45, no. 3: 364–81.

———. 2013. "Behavioral Economics and the Retirement Savings Crisis." *Science* 339, no. 6124: 1152–3.

Bernheim, B. Douglas. 2002. "Taxation and Saving." In Martin Feldstein and Alan J. Auerbach, eds., *Handbook of Public Economics*, vol. 3, 1173–249. Amsterdam: Elsevier.

Bernoulli, Daniel. (1738) 1954. "Exposition of a New Theory on the Measurement of Risk." Translated from Latin by Louise Sommer. *Econometrica* 22, no. 1: 23–36.

Brown, Gary S. 2014. "Letter from State of New York Office of the Attorney General to Josh Mohrer, General Manager, Uber NYC." July 8. Available at: http://ag.ny.gov/pdfs/Uber_Letter_Agreement.pdf.

Burke, Brian, and Kevin Quealy. 2013. "How Coaches and the NYT 4th Down Bot Compare." *New York Times*, November 28. Available at: http://www.nytimes.com/newsgraphics/2013/11/28/fourth-downs/post.html.

Buss, Dale. 1986. "Rebate or Loan: Car Buyers Need to Do the Math." *Wall Street Journal*, October 1.

Camerer, Colin F. 1989. "Bubbles and Fads in Asset Prices." *Journal of Economic Surveys* 3, no. 1: 3–41.

———. 1997. "Progress in Behavioral Game Theory." *Journal of Economic Perspectives* 11, no. 4: 167–88.

———. 2000. "Prospect Theory in the Wild: Evidence from the Field." In Daniel Kahneman and Amos Tversky, eds., *Choices, Values, and Frames*. Cambridge, UK: Cambridge University Press.

———. 2003. *Behavioral Game Theory: Experiments in Strategic Interaction*. Princeton: Princeton University Press.

———, Teck-Hua Ho, and Juin-Kuan Chong. 2004. "A Cognitive Hierarchy Model of Games." *Quarterly Journal of Economics* 119, no. 3: 861–98.

———, Samuel Issacharoff, George Loewenstein, Ted O'Donoghue, and Matthew Rabin. 2003. "Regulation for Conservatives: Behavioral Economics and the Case for 'Asymmetric Paternalism.'" *University of Pennsylvania Law Review* 151, no. 3: 1211–54.

———, and Roberto A. Weber. 1999. "The Econometrics and Behavioral Economics of Escalation of Commitment: A Re-examination of Staw and Hoang's NBA Data." *Journal of Economic Behavior and Organization* 39, no. 1: 59–82.

Cameron, Lisa Ann. 1999. "Raising the Stakes in the Ultimatum Game: Experimental Evidence from Indonesia." *Economic Inquiry* 37, no. 1: 47–59.

Carlson, Nicolas. 2014. "What Happened When Marissa Mayer Tried to Be Steve Jobs." *New York Times Magazine*, December 17. Available at: http://www.nytimes.com/2014/12/21/magazine/what-happened-when-marissa-mayer-tried-to-be-steve-jobs.html.

Case, Karl E., and Robert J. Shiller. 2003. "Is There a Bubble in the Housing Market?" *Brookings Papers on Economic Activity*, no. 2: 299–362.

Case, Karl E., Robert J. Shiller, and Anne Thompson. 2012. "What Have They been Thinking? Home Buyer Behavior in Hot and Cold Markets." Working Paper 18400, National Bureau of Economic Research.

Chang, Tom Y., Samuel M. Hartzmark, David H. Solomon, and Eugene F. Soltes. 2014. "Being Surprised by the Unsurprising: Earnings Seasonality and Stock Returns." Working paper.

Chen, Nai-Fu, Raymond Kan, and Merton H. Miller. 1993a. "Are the Discounts on Closed-End Funds a Sentiment Index?" *Journal of Finance* 48, no. 2: 795–800.

———. 1993b. "Yes, Discounts on Closed-End Funds Are a Sentiment Index: A Rejoinder." *Journal of Finance* 48, no. 2: 809–10.

Chernev, Alexander. 2012. "Why Everyday Low Pricing Might Not Fit J.C. Penney." *Bloomberg Businessweek*, May 17. Available at: http://www.businessweek .com/articles/2012-05-17/why-everyday-low-pricing-might-not-be-right -for-j-dot-c-dot-penney.

Chetty, Raj. 2015 (forthcoming). "Behavioral Economics and Public Policy: A Pragmatic Perspective." *American Economic Review* 105, no. 5. Video of lecture available at: https://www.aeaweb.org/webcasts/2015/Ely.php.

———, John N. Friedman, Søren Leth-Petersen, Torben Heien Nielsen, and Tore Olsen. 2014. "Active vs. Passive Decisions and Crowd-Out in Retirement Savings Accounts: Evidence from Denmark." *Quarterly Journal of Economics* 129, no. 3: 1141–219.

Chevalier, Judith, and Glenn Ellison. 1997. "Risk Taking by Mutual Funds as a Response to Incentives." *Journal of Political Economy* 105, no. 6: 1167–200.

Childress, James F., Catharyn T. Liverman, et al. 2006. *Organ Donation: Opportunities for Action.* Washington, DC: National Academies Press.

Choi, James J., David Laibson, and Brigitte C. Madrian. 2004. "Plan Design and 401(k) Savings Outcomes." *National Tax Journal* 57, no. 2: 275–98.

———, and Andrew Metrick. 2003. "Optimal Defaults." *American Economic Review* 93, no. 2: 180–5.

———. 2009. "Reinforcement Learning and Savings Behavior." *Journal of Finance* 64, no. 6: 2515–34.

Chopra, Navin, Charles Lee, Andrei Shleifer, and Richard H. Thaler. 1993a. "Yes, Discounts on Closed-End Funds Are a Sentiment Index." *Journal of Finance* 48, no. 2: 801–8.

———. 1993b. "Summing Up." *Journal of Finance* 48, no. 2: 811–2.

Choudhry, Niteesh K., Jerry Avorn, Robert J. Glynn, Elliott M. Antman, Sebastian Schneeweiss, Michele Toscano, Lonny Reisman, Joaquim Fernandes, Claire Spettell, Joy L. Lee, Raisa Levin, Troyen Brennan, and William H. Shrank. 2011. "Full Coverage for Preventive Medications aft Myocardial Infarction." *New England Journal of Medicine* 365, no. 22: 2088–97.

Cialdini, Robert B. 2006. *Influence: The Psychology of Persuasion.* Revised edition. New York: Harper Business.

Clifford, Stephanie, and Catherine Rampell. 2013. "Sometimes, We Want Prices to Fool Us." *New York Times*, April 13. Available at: http://www.nytimes .com/2013/04/14/business/for-penney-a-tough-lesson-in-shopper-psych ology.html.

Coase, Ronald H. 1960. "The Problem of Social Costs." *Journal of Law and Economics* 3: 1–44.

Cochrane, John H. 2005. *Asset Pricing*. Princeton: Princeton University Press.

Cole, Shawn, and A. Nilesh Fernando. 2012. "The Value of Advice: Evidence from Mobile Phone-Based Agricultural Extension." Finance Working Paper 13-047, Harvard Business School.

Conlisk, John. 1996. "Why Bounded Rationality?" *Journal of Economic Literature* 34, no. 2: 669–700.

Cooper, Arnold C., Carolyn Y. Woo, and William C. Dunkelberg. 1988. "Entrepreneurs' Perceived Chances for Success." *Journal of Business Venturing* 3, no. 2: 97–108.

Crawford, Vincent P., and Juanjuan Meng. 2011. "New York City Cab Drivers' Labor Supply Revisited: Reference-Dependent Preferences with Rational Expectations Targets for Hours and Income." *American Economic Review* 101, no. 5: 1912–32.

Cutler, David M., James M. Poterba, and Lawrence H. Summers. 1989. "What Moves Stock Prices?" *Journal of Portfolio Management* 15, no. 3: 4–12.

Daly, Mary, Bart Hobijn, and Brian Lucking. 2012. "Why Has Wage Growth Stayed Strong?" *Federal Reserve Board of San Francisco: Economic Letter* 10: 1–5.

Dawes, Robyn M., and Richard H. Thaler. 1988. "Anomalies: Cooperation." *Journal of Economic Perspectives* 2, no. 3: 187–97.

De Bondt, Werner F. M., and Richard H. Thaler. 1985. "Does the Stock Market Overreact?" *Journal of Finance* 40, no. 3: 793–805.

De Long, J. Bradford, Andrei Shleifer, Lawrence H. Summers, and Robert J. Waldmann. 1990. "Noise Trader Risk in Financial Markets." *Journal of Political Economy* 98, no. 4: 703–38.

DellaVigna, Stefano. 2009. "Psychology and Economics: Evidence from the Field." *Journal of Economic Literature* 47, no. 2: 315–72.

———, John A. List, and Ulrike Malmendier. 2012. "Testing for Altruism and Social Pressure in Charitable Giving." *Quarterly Journal of Economics* 127, no. 1: 1–56.

DellaVigna, Stefano, and Ulrike Malmendier. 2006. "Paying Not to Go to the Gym." *American Economic Review* 96, no. 3: 694–719.

DeSilver, Drew. 2013. "Suicides Account for Most Gun Deaths." Fact Tank, Pew Research Center, May 24. Available at: http://www.pewresearch.org/fact-tank/2013/05/24/suicides-account-for-most-gun-deaths/.

Donate Life America. 2014. "National Donor Designation Report Card." Available at: http://donatelife.net/wp-content/uploads/2014/06/Report-Card-2014-44222-Final.pdf.

Donohue III, John J., Abhay Aneja, and Alexandria Zhang. 2014. "The Impact of Right to Carry Laws and the NRC Report: The Latest Lessons for the Empirical Evaluation of Law and Policy." Working Paper 430, Stanford Law and Economics Olin.

Dreman, David N. 1982. *The New Contrarian Investment Strategy*. New York: Random House.

Duflo, Esther, Michael Kremer, and Jonathan Robinson. 2011. "Nudging Farmers to Use Fertilizer: Theory and Experimental Evidence from Kenya." *American Economic Review* 101, no. 6: 2350–90.

Dupas, Pascaline, and Jonathan Robinson. 2014. "The Daily Grind: Cash Needs, Labor Supply and Self-Control." Working Paper 511, Stanford Center for International Development.

Ellickson, Paul B., Sanjog Misra, and Harikesh S. Nair. 2012. "Repositioning Dynamics and Pricing Strategy." *Journal of Marketing Research* 49, no. 6: 750–72.

Ellison, Glenn. 1997. "Learning from Personal Experience: One Rational Guy and the Justification of Myopia." *Games and Economic Behavior* 19, no. 2: 180–210.

———, and Drew Fudenberg. 1993. "Rules of Thumb for Social Learning." *Journal of Political Economy* 101, no. 4: 612–43.

Engen, Eric M., William G. Gale, and John Karl Scholz. 1996. "The Illusory Effects of Saving Incentives on Saving." *Journal of Economic Perspectives* 10, no. 4: 113–38.

Engström, Per, Katarina Nordblom, Henry Ohlsson, and Annika Persson. 2015 (forthcoming). "Tax Compliance and Loss Aversion." *American Economic Journal: Economic Policy*.

Epley, Nicholas, Dennis Mak, and Lorraine Chen Idson. 2006. "Bonus or Rebate?: The Impact of Income Framing on Spending and Saving." *Journal of Behavioral Decision Making* 19, no. 3: 213–27.

Eyster, Erik, and Matthew Rabin. 2005. "Cursed Equilibrium." *Econometrica* 73, no. 5: 1623–72.

Fama, Eugene F. 1970. "Efficient Capital Markets: A Review of Theory and Empirical Work." *Journal of Finance* 25, no. 2: 383–417.

———. 2014. "Two Pillars of Asset Pricing." *American Economic Review* 104, no. 6: 1467–85.

———, and Kenneth R. French. 1993. "Common Risk Factors in the Returns on Stocks and Bonds." *Journal of Financial Economics* 33, no. 1: 3–56.

———. 1996. "The CAPM Is Wanted, Dead or Alive." *Journal of Finance* 51, no. 5: 1947–58.

———. 2014. "A Five-Factor Asset Pricing Model." Working paper, Fama–Miller Center for Research in Finance. Available at: http://ssrn.com/abstract= 2287202.

Farber, Henry S. 2005. "Is Tomorrow Another Day? The Labor Supply of New York City Cabdrivers." *Journal of Political Economy* 113, no. 1: 46.

———. 2008. "Reference-Dependent Preferences and Labor Supply: The Case of New York City Taxi Drivers." *American Economic Review* 98, no. 3: 1069–82.

———. 2014. "Why You Can't Find a Taxi in the Rain and Other Labor Supply Lessons from Cab Drivers." Working Paper 20604, National Bureau of Economic Research.

Farnsworth, Ward. 1999. "Do Parties to Nuisance Cases Bargain after Judgment? A Glimpse Inside the Cathedral." *University of Chicago Law Review* 66, no. 2: 373–436.

Fehr, Ernst, and Urs Fischbacher. 2003. "The Nature of Human Altruism." *Nature* 425, no. 6960: 785–91.

Fehr, Ernst, and Simon Gächter. 2000. "Cooperation and Punishment in Public Goods Experiments." *American Economic Review* 66, no. 2: 980–94.

———. 2002. "Altruistic Punishment in Humans." *Nature* 415, no. 6868: 137–40.

Fehr, Ernst, and Lorenz Goette. 2007. "Do Workers Work More If Wages re High? Evidence from a Randomized Field Experiment." *American Economic Review* 97, no. 1: 298–317.

Fehr, Ernst, George Kirchsteiger, and Arno Riedl. 1993. "Does Fairness Prevent Market Clearing? An Experimental Investigation." *Quarterly Journal of Economics* 108, no. 2: 437–59.

Fehr, Ernst, and Klaus M. Schmidt. 1999. "A Theory of Fairness, Competition, and Cooperation." *Quarterly Journal of Economics* 114, no. 3: 817–68.

Fischbacher, Urs, Simon Gächter, and Ernst Fehr. 2001. "Are People Conditionally Cooperative? Evidence from a Public Goods Experiment." *Economics Letters* 71, no. 3: 397–404.

Fischhoff, Baruch. 1975. "Hindsight $\neq$ Foresight: The Effect of Outcome Knowledge on Judgment Under Uncertainty." *Journal of Experimental Psychology: Human Perception and Performance* 1, no. 3: 288.

Fisher, Irving. 1930. *The Theory of Interest: As Determined by Impatience to Spend Income and Opportunity to Invest It.* New York: MacMillan.

Fox, Justin. 2009. *The Myth of the Rational Market: A History of Risk, Reward, and Delusion on Wall Street.* New York: HarperCollins.

Frank, Robert H., Thomas Gilovich, and Dennis T. Regan. 1993. "Does Studying Economics Inhibit Cooperation?" *Journal of Economic Perspectives* 7, no. 2: 159–71.

Frederick, Shane, George Loewenstein, and Ted O'Donoghue. 2002. "Time Discounting and Time Preference: A Critical Review." *Journal of Economic Literature* 40, no. 2: 351–401.

Friedman, Milton. 1953. "The Methodology of Positive Economics." In *Essays in Positive Economics* (ch. 1), 3–43. Chicago: University of Chicago Press.

———. 1957. "The Permanent Income Hypothesis." In *A Theory of the Consumption Function* (ch. 2), 20–37. Princeton: Princeton University Press.

———. 1963. "Windfalls, the 'Horizon,' and Related Concepts in the Permanent-Income Hypothesis." In *Measurement in Economics: Studies in Mathematical Economics and Econometrics in Memory of Yehuda Grunfeld* (ch. 1), 3–28. Stanford, CA: Stanford University Press.

Frischmann, Brett M., and Christiaan Hogendorn. 2015. "Retrospectives: The Marginal Cost Controversy." *Journal of Economic Perspectives* 29, no. 1: 193–206.

Fryer, Jr., Roland G. 2010. "Financial Incentives and Student Achievement: Evidence from Randomized Trials." Working Paper 15898, National Bureau of Economic Research.

———, Steven D. Levitt, John List, and Sally Sadoff. 2012. "Enhancing the Efficacy of Teacher Incentives through Loss Aversion: A Field Experiment." Working Paper 18237, National Bureau of Economic Research.

Fudenberg, Drew, and David K. Levine. 2006. "A Dual-Self Model of Impulse Control." *American Economic Review* 96, no. 5: 1449–76.

Gabaix, Xavier, and David Laibson. 2006. "Shrouded Attributes, Consumer Myopia, and Information Suppression in Competitive Markets." *Quarterly Journal of Economics* 121, no. 2: 505–40.

Gawande, Atul. 2010. *The Checklist Manifesto: How to Get Things Right.* New York: Metropolitan Books.

Geanakoplos, John, David Pearce, and Ennio Stacchetti. 1989. "Psychological Games and Sequential Rationality." *Games and Economic Behavior* 1, no. 1: 60–79.

Ginzel, Linda E. 2015. "The Green Pen—Linda Ginzel: In the Classroom." *Chicago Booth Magazine,* Winter.

Glaeser, Edward L. 2013. "A Nation of Gamblers: Real Estate Speculation and American History." Working Paper 18825, National Bureau of Economic Research.

Gneezy, Uri, and John A. List. 2013. *The Why Axis: Hidden Motives and the Undiscovered Economics of Everyday Life.* New York: Random House.

Gourville, John T., and Dilip Soman. 1998. "Payment Depreciation: The Behavioral Effects of Temporally Separating Payments from Consumption." *Journal of Consumer Research* 25, no. 2: 160–74.

Graham, Benjamin. (1949) 1973. *The Intelligent Investor: A Book of Practical Counsel.* Fourth revised edition. New York: Harper and Row.

———, and David L. Dodd. (1934) 2008. *Security Analysis.* Sixth edition. New York: McGraw Hill.

Grether, David M., and Charles R. Plott. 1979. "Economic Theory of Choice and the Preference Reversal Phenomenon." *American Economic Review* 69, no. 4: 623–38.

Grynbaum, Michael M. 2011. "Where Do All the Cabs Go in the Late Afternoon?" *New York Times,* January 11. Available at: http://www.nytimes.com/2011/01/12/nyregion/12taxi.html.

Güth, Werner, Rolf Schmittberger, and Bernd Schwarze. 1982. "An Experimental Analysis of Ultimatum Bargaining." *Journal of Economic Behavior and Organization* 3, no. 4: 367–88.

Halliday, Josh. 2012. "Whitney Houston Album Price Hike Sparks Controversy." *Guardian,* February 13. Available at: http://www.theguardian.com/music/2012/feb/13/whitney-houston-album-price.

Hallsworth, Michael, John A. List, Robert D. Metcalfe, and Ivo Vlaev. 2014. "The Behavioralist as Tax Collector: Using Natural Field Experiments to Enhance Tax Compliance." Working Paper 20007, National Bureau of Economic Research.

Haltiwanger, John, and Michael Waldman. 1985. "Rational Expectations and the Limits of Rationality: An Analysis of Heterogeneity." *American Economic Review* 75, no. 3: 326–40.

Hastings, Justine S., and Jesse M. Shapiro. 2013. "Fungibility and Consumer Choice: Evidence from Commodity Price Shocks." *Quarterly Journal of Economics* 128, no. 4: 1449–98.

Haushofer, Johannes, and Ernst Fehr. 2014. "On the Psychology of Poverty." *Science* 344, no. 6186 (May 23): 862–7.

Heath, Chip, and Jack B. Soll. 1996. "Mental Budgeting and Consumer Decisions." *Journal of Consumer Research* 23, no. 1: 40–52.

Heidhues, Paul, and Botond Kszegi. 2010. "Exploiting Naïveté about Self-Control in the Credit Market." *American Economic Review* 100, no. 5: 2279–303.

Henrich, Joseph. 2000. "Does Culture Matter in Economic Behavior? Ultimatum Game Bargaining among the Machiguenga of the Peruvian Amazon." *American Economic Review* 90, no. 4: 973–9.

———, Wulf Albers, Robert Boyd, Gerd Gigerenzer, Kevin A McCabe, Axel Ockenfels, and H. Peyton Young. 2002. "What Is the Role of Culture in Bounded Rationality?" In Gerd Gigerenzer and Reinhard Selten, eds., *Bounded Rationality: The Adaptive Toolbox* (ch. 19), 343–59. Cambridge, MA: MIT Press.

Hess, Pamela, and Yan Xu. 2011. "2011 Trends & Experience in Defined Contribution Plans." Aon Hewitt. Available at: http://www.aon.com/attachments/thought-leadership/2011_Trends_Experience_Executive_Summary_v5.pdf.

Hoffman, Moshe, Sigrid Suetens, Martin A. Nowak, and Uri Gneezy. 2012. "An Experimental Test of Nash Equilibrium versus Evolutionary Stability." In *Proc. Fourth World Congress of the Game Theory Society* (Istanbul, Turkey), session 145, paper 1.

Hofstadter, Douglas R. 1983. "Computer Tournaments of the Prisoners-Dilemma Suggest How Cooperation Evolves." *Scientific American* 248, no. 5: 16.

Hogarth, Robin M., and Melvin W. Reder, eds. 1986. "The Behavioral Foundations of Economic Theory: Proceedings of a Conference October 13–15, 1985." *Journal of Business* 59, no. 4, part 2 (October): S181–505.

———, eds. 1987. *Rational Choice: The Contrast Between Economics and Psychology.* Chicago: University of Chicago Press.

Hood, Donald C., Paul Andreassen, and Stanley Schachter. 1985. "II. Random and Non-Random Walks on the New York Stock Exchange." *Journal of Economic Behavior and Organization* 6, no. 4: 331–8.

Hsee, Christopher K., Yang Yang, Yangjie Gu, and Jie Chen. 2009. "Specification Seeking: How Product Specifications Influence Consumer Preference." *Journal of Consumer Research* 35, no. 6: 952–66.

Internal Revenue Service. 1998. "Revenue Ruling 98–30." *Internal Revenue Bulletin* 25 (June 22): 8–9. Available at: http://www.irs.gov/pub/irs-irbs/irb98-25.pdf.

Jackson, Eric. 2014. "The Case For Apple, Facebook, Microsoft Or Google Buying Yahoo Now." *Forbes.com*, July 21. Available at: http://www.forbes.com/sites/ericjackson/2014/07/21/the-case-for-apple-facebook-microsoft-or-google-buying-yahoo-now.

Jensen, Michael C. 1969. "Risk, The Pricing of Capital Assets, and the Evaluation of Investment Portfolios." *Journal of Business* 42, no. 2: 167–247.

———. 1978. "Some Anomalous Evidence Regarding Market Efficiency." *Journal of Financial Economics* 6, no. 2: 95–101.

Jevons, William Stanley. (1871) 1957. *The Theory of Political Economy.* Fifth edition. New York: Augustus M. Kelley.

Jewett, Dale. 1996. "1975 Cars Brought Sticker Shock, Then Rebates." *Automotive News*, June 26. Available at: http://www.autonews.com/article/19960626/ANA/606260830/1975-car-prices-brought-sticker-shock-then-rebates.

John, David C., and Ruth Levine. 2009. "National Retirement Savings Systems in Australia, Chile, New Zealand and the United Kingdom: Lessons for the

United States." The Retirement Security Project, Brookings Institution. Available at: http://www.brookings.edu/research/papers/2010/01/07-retirement-savings-john.

Johnson, Eric J., and Daniel G. Goldstein. 2004. "Defaults and Donation Decisions." *Transplantation* 78, no. 12: 1713–6.

Johnson, Steven. 2010. *Where Good Ideas Come From: The Natural History of Innovation.* New York: Riverhead.

Jolls, Christine, Cass R. Sunstein, and Richard Thaler. 1998. "A Behavioral Approach to Law and Economics." *Stanford Law Review* 50, no. 5: 1471–550.

Kahneman, Daniel. 2011. *Thinking, Fast and Slow.* New York: Macmillan.

——, Jack L. Knetsch, and Richard H. Thaler. 1986. "Fairness and the Assumptions of Economics." *Journal of Business* 59, no. 4, part 2: S285–300.

——. 1991. "Anomalies: The Endowment Effect, Loss Aversion, and Status Quo Bias." *Journal of Economic Perspectives* 5, no. 1: 193–206.

Kahneman, Daniel, and Dan Lovallo. 1993. "Timid Choices and Bold Forecasts: A Cognitive Perspective on Risk Taking." *Management Science* 39, no. 1: 17–31.

Kahneman, Daniel, and Amos Tversky. 1973. "On The Psychology of Prediction." *Psychological Review* 80, no. 4: 237.

——. 1979. "Prospect Theory: An Analysis of Decision under Risk." *Econometrica* 47, no. 2: 263–91.

——. 2000. *Choices, Values, and Frames.* Cambridge, UK: Cambridge University Press.

Karlan, Dean, and Jacob Appel. 2011. *More Than Good Intentions: Improving the Ways the World's Poor Borrow, Save, Farm, Learn, and Stay Healthy.* New York: Penguin.

Kaur, Supreet. 2014. "Nominal Wage Rigidity In Village Labor Markets." Working Paper 20770, National Bureau of Economic Research.

Keynes, John Maynard. 1923. *A Tract on Monetary Reform.* London: Macmillan.

——. 1936. *The General Theory of Employment, Interest and Money.* London: Macmillan.

Kleidon, Allan W. 1986. "Anomalies in Financial Economics: Blueprint for Change?" *Journal of Business* 59, no. 4, part 2: S469–99.

Kliger, Doron, Martijn J. van den Assem, and Remco C. J. Zwinkels. 2014. "Empirical Behavioral Finance." *Journal of Economic Behavior and Organization* 107, part B: 421–7.

Knetsch, Jack L., and John A. Sinden. 1984. "Willingness to Pay and Compensation Demanded: Experimental Evidence of an Unexpected Disparity in Measures of Value." *Quarterly Journal of Economics* 99, no. 3: 507–21.

Knobe, Joshua, Wesley Buckwalter, Shaun Nichols, Philip Robbins, Hagop Sarkissian, and Tamler Sommers. 2012. "Experimental Philosophy." *Annual Review of Psychology* 63: 81–99.

Knobe, Joshua, and Shaun Nichols. 2013. *Experimental Philosophy.* Oxford and New York: Oxford University Press.

Kocher, Martin G., Todd Cherry, Stephan Kroll, Robert J. Netzer, and Matthias Sutter. 2008. "Conditional Cooperation on Three Continents." *Economics Letters* 101, no. 3: 175–8.

Kokonas, Nick. 2014. "Tickets for Restaurants." Alinea restaurant blog, June 4.

Available at: http://website.alinearestaurant.com/site/2014/06/tickets-for-restaurants/.

Korobkin, Russell. 2011. "What Comes after Victory for Behavioral Law and Economics." *University of Illinois Law Review* 2011, no. 5: 1653–74.

Kraft, Matthew, and Todd Rogers. 2014. "The Underutilized Potential of Teacher-to-Parent Communication: Evidence from a Field Experiment." Working Paper RWP14-049, Harvard Kennedy School of Government.

Krakauer, Jon. 1997. *Into Thin Air: A Personal Account of the Mount Everest Disaster.* New York: Random House.

Krueger, Alan B. 2001. "Supply and Demand: An Economist Goes to the Super Bowl." *Milken Institute Review*, Second Quarter: 22–9.

———, and Alexandre Mas. 2004. "Strikes, Scabs, and Tread Separations: Labor Strife and the Production of Defective Bridgestone/Firestone Tires." *Journal of Political Economy* 112, no. 2: 253–89.

Kuhn, Thomas S. 1962. *The Structure of Scientific Revolutions.* Chicago: University of Chicago Press.

Laibson, David. 1997. "Golden Eggs and Hyperbolic Discounting." *Quarterly Journal of Economics* 112, no. 2: 443–78.

Lakonishok, Josef, Andrei Shleifer, and Robert W. Vishny. 1994. "Contrarian Investment, Extrapolation, and Risk." *Journal of Finance* 49, no. 5: 1541–78.

Lamont, Owen A., and Richard H. Thaler. 2003. "Can the Market Add and Subtract? Mispricing in Tech Stock Carve-Outs." *Journal of Political Economy* 111, no. 2: 227–68.

Landsberger, Michael. 1966. "Windfall Income and Consumption: Comment." *American Economic Review* 56, no. 3: 534–40.

Lee, Charles, Andrei Shleifer, and Richard H. Thaler. 1991. "Investor Sentiment and the Closed-End Fund Puzzle." *Journal of Finance* 46, no. 1: 75–109.

Lester, Richard A. 1946. "Shortcomings of Marginal Analysis for Wage-Employment Problems." *American Economic Review*, 36, no. 1: 63–82.

Levitt, Steven, and John List. 2007. "What Do Laboratory Experiments Measuring Social Preferences Reveal About the Real World?" *Journal of Economic Perspectives* 21, no. 2: 153–74.

Lewin, Kurt. 1947. "Frontiers in Group Dynamics: II. Channels of Group Life; Social Planning and Action Research." *Human Relations* 1, no. 2: 143–53.

Lichtenstein, Sarah, and Paul Slovic. 1973. "Response-Induced Reversals of Preference in Gambling: An Extended Replication in Las Vegas." *Journal of Experimental Psychology* 101, no. 1: 16.

Lintner, John. 1956. "Distribution of Incomes of Corporations Among Dividends, Retained Earnings, and Taxes." *American Economic Review* 46, no. 2: 97–113.

———. 1965a. "The Valuation of Risk Assets and the Selection of Risky Investments in Stock Portfolios and Capital Budgets." *Review of Economics and Statistics* 47, no. 1: 13–37.

———. 1965b. "Security Prices, Risk, and Maximal Gains from Diversification." *Journal of Finance* 20, no. 4: 587–615.

List, John A. 2011. "The Market for Charitable Giving." *Journal of Economic Perspectives* 25, no. 2: 157–80.

Loewenstein, George. 1992. "The Fall and Rise of Psychological Explanations in the Economics of Intertemporal Choice." In George Loewenstein and Jon Elster, eds., *Choice Over Time*,. 3–34. New York: Russell Sage Foundation.

———, and Drazen Prelec. 1992. "Anomalies in Intertemporal Choice: Evidence and an Interpretation." *Quarterly Journal of Economics* 107, no. 2: 573–597.

Lohr, Steve. 1992. "Lessons From a Hurricane: It Pays Not to Gouge." *New York Times*, September 22. Available at: http://www.nytimes.com/1992/09/22/business/lessons-from-a-hurricane-it-pays-not-to-gouge.html.

Lott, John R. 1998. *More Guns, Less Crime: Understanding Crime and Gun Control Laws*. Chicago: University of Chicago Press.

Lowenstein, Roger. 2000. *When Genius Failed: The Rise and Fall of Long-Term Capital Management*. New York: Random House.

———. 2001. "Exuberance Is Rational." *New York Times Magazine*, February 11. Available at: http://partners.nytimes.com/library/magazine/home/20010211 mag-econ.html.

Machlup, Fritz. 1946. "Marginal Analysis and Empirical Research." *American Economic Review* 36, no. 4: 519–54.

MacIntosh, Donald. 1969. *The Foundations of Human Society*. Chicago: University of Chicago Press.

Madrian, Brigitte C., and Dennis F. Shea. 2001. "The Power of Suggestion: Inertia in 401(k) Participation and Savings Behavior." *Quarterly Journal of Economics* 116, no. 4: 1149–87.

Malkiel, Burton Gordon. 1973. *A Random Walk Down Wall Street*. New York: Norton.

Marwell, Gerald, and Ruth E. Ames. 1981. "Economists Free Ride, Does Anyone Else? Experiments on the Provision of Public Goods." *Journal of Public Economics* 15, no. 3: 295–310.

Mas, Alexandre. 2006. "Pay, Reference Points, and Police Performance." *Quarterly Journal of Economics* 121, no. 23: 783–821.

———. 2008. "Labour Unrest and the Quality of Production: Evidence from the Construction Equipment Resale Market." *Review of Economic Studies* 75, no. 1: 229–58.

Massey, Cade, and Richard H. Thaler. 2013. "The Loser's Curse: Decision Making and Market Efficiency in the National Football League Draft." *Management Science* 59, no. 7: 1479–95.

McGlothlin, William H. 1956. "Stability of Choices among Uncertain Alternatives." *American Journal of Psychology* 69, no. 4: 604–15.

McKay, Betsy, Nikhil Deogun, and Joann Lublin. 1999. "Clumsy Handling of Many Problems Cost Ivester Coca-Cola Board's Favor." *Wall Street Journal*, December 17. Available at: http://online.wsj.com/article/SB945394494360188276.html.

McKelvey, Richard D., and Thomas R. Palfrey. 1995. "Quantal Response Equilibria for Normal Form Games." *Games and Economic Behavior* 10, no. 1: 6–38.

Mehra, Rajnish. 2007. "The Equity Premium Puzzle: A Review." *Foundations and Trends in Finance* 2, no. 1: 1–81.

———, and Edward C. Prescott. 1985. "The Equity Premium: A Puzzle." *Journal of Monetary Economics* 15, no. 2: 145–61.

Mian, Atif, and Amir Sufi. 2014. *House of Debt: How They (and You) Caused the Great Recession, and How We Can Prevent It from Happening Again.* Chicago: University of Chicago Press.

Miller, Mark. 1995. "First Chicago Loses Touch with Humans." *Chicago Sun-Times*, May 2, 25. Accessed via ProQuest, http://search.proquest.com/docview/258111761.

Miller, Merton H. 1986. "Behavioral Rationality in Finance: The Case of Dividends." *Journal of Business* 59, no. 4, part 2: S451–68.

———. 1988. "The Modigliani–Miller Propositions after Thirty Years." *Journal of Economic Perspectives* 2, no. 4: 99–120.

Mischel, Walter. 1968. *Personality and Assessment.* Hoboken, NJ: John Wiley.

———. 1969. "Continuity and Change in Personality." *American Psychologist* 24, no. 11: 1012.

———. 2014. *The Marshmallow Test: Mastering Self-Control.* New York: Little, Brown.

———, Ozlem Ayduk, Marc G. Berman, B. J. Casey, Ian H. Gotlib, John Jonides, Ethan Kross, Theresa Teslovich, Nicole L Wilson, Vivian Zayas, et al. 2010. "'Willpower' over the Life Span: Decomposing Self-Regulation." *Social Cognitive and Affective Neuroscience* 6, no. 2: 252–6.

Mitchell, Gregory. 2005. "Libertarian Paternalism Is an Oxymoron." *Northwestern University Law Review* 99, no. 3: 1245–77.

Modigliani, Franco, and Richard Brumberg. 1954. "Utility Analysis and the Consumption Function: An Interpretation of Cross-Section Data." In Kenneth K. Kurihara, ed., *Post-Keynesian Economics*, 383–436. New Brunswick, NJ: Rutgers University Press.

Modigliani, Franco, and Merton Miller. 1958. "The Cost of Capital, Corporation Finance and the Theory of Investment." *American Economic Review* 48, no. 3: 261–97.

Mongin, Philippe. 1997. "The Marginalist Controversy." In John Bryan Davis, D. Wade Hands, and Uskali Mäki, eds., *Handbook of Economic Methodology*, 558–62. London: Edward Elgar.

Mullainathan, Sendhil. 2013. "When a Co-Pay Gets in the Way of Health." *New York Times*, August 10. Available at: http://www.nytimes.com/2013/08/11/business/when-a-co-pay-gets-in-the-way-of-health.html.

———, and Eldar Shafir. 2013. *Scarcity: Why Having Too Little Means So Much.* London: Macmillan.

Nag, Amal. 1996. "GM Is Offering Low-Cost Loans on Some Cars." *Wall Street Journal*, March 21.

Nagel, Rosemarie Chariklia. 1995. "Unraveling in Guessing Games: An Experimental Study." *American Economic Review* 85, no. 5: 1313–26.

Nasar, Sylvia. 1998. *A Beautiful Mind.* New York: Simon and Schuster.

New York Stock Exchange. 2014. "NYSE Group Volume in All Stocks Traded." *NYSE Facts and Figures.* Available at: http://www.nyxdata.com/nysedata/asp/factbook/viewer_edition.asp?mode=table&key=3133&category=3.

Norman, Donald A. 1998. *The Design of Everyday Things.* New York: Basic Books.

O'Donoghue, Ted, and Matthew Rabin. 1999. "Procrastination in Preparing for Retirement." In Henry Aaron, ed., *Behavioral Dimensions of Retirement Eco-*

nomics, 125–56. Washington, DC: Brooking Institution, and New York: Russell Sage Foundation.

———. 2003. "Studying Optimal Paternalism, Illustrated by a Model of Sin Taxes." *American Economic Review* 93, no. 2: 186–91.

Pareto, Vilfredo. (1906) 2013. *Manual of Political Economy: A Variorum Translation and Critical Edition.* Reprint edited by Aldo Montesano et al. Oxford: Oxford University Press.

Peter, Laurence J., and Raymond Hull. 1969. *The Peter Principle: Why Things Always Go Wrong.* New York: William Morrow.

Pigou, Arthur Cecil. 1920. *The Economics of Welfare.* London: Macmillan.

Pope, Devin G., and Maurice E. Schweitzer. 2011. "Is Tiger Woods Loss Averse? Persistent Bias in the Face of Experience, Competition, and High Stakes." *American Economic Review* 101, no. 1: 129–57.

Post, Thierry, Martijn J. van den Assem, Guido Baltussen, and Richard H. Thaler. 2008. "Deal or No Deal? Decision Making under Risk in a Large-Payoff Game Show." *American Economic Review* 98, no. 1: 38–71.

Poterba, James M., Steven F. Venti, and David A. Wise. 1996. "How Retirement Saving Programs Increase Saving." *Journal of Economic Perspectives* 10, no. 4: 91–112.

Prelec, Drazen, and George Loewenstein. 1998. "The Red and the Black: Mental Accounting of Savings and Debt." *Marketing Science* 17, no. 1: 4–28.

Rabin, Matthew. 1993. "Incorporating Fairness into Game Theory and Economics." *American Economic Review* 83, no. 5: 1281–302.

Raifman, Julia R. G., Heather E. Lanthorn, Slawa Rokicki, and Günther Fink. 2014. "The Impact of Text Message Reminders on Adherence to Anti-malarial Treatment in Northern Ghana: A Randomized Trial." *PLOS ONE* 9, no. 10: e109032.

Rapoport, Anatol. 1988. "Experiments with N-Person Social Traps I: Prisoner's Dilemma, Weak Prisoner's Dilemma, Volunteer's Dilemma, and Largest Number." *Journal of Conflict Resolution* 32, no. 3: 457–72.

Romer, David. 2006. "Do Firms Maximize? Evidence from Professional Football." *Journal of Political Economy* 114, no. 2: 340–65.

Ross, Lee, David Greene, and Pamela House. 1977. "The 'False Consensus Effect': An Egocentric Bias in Social Perception and Attribution Processes." *Journal of Experimental Social Psychology* 13, no. 3: 279–301.

Roth, Alvin E. 2007. "Repugnance as a Constraint on Markets." *Journal of Economic Perspectives* 21, no. 3: 37–58.

———, ed. 1987. *Laboratory Experimentation in Economics: Six Points of View.* Cambridge, UK: Cambridge University Press.

Rozeff, Michael S., and William Kinney. 1976. "Capital Market Seasonality: The Case of Stock Returns." *Journal of Financial Economics* 3, no. 4: 379–402.

Russell, Thomas, and Richard H. Thaler. 1985. "The Relevance of Quasi Rationality in Competitive Markets." *American Economic Review* 75, no. 5: 1071–82.

Sally, David. 1995. "Conversation and Cooperation in Social Dilemmas: A Meta-Analysis of Experiments from 1958 to 1992." *Rationality and Society* 7, no. 1: 58–92.

Samuelson, Paul A. 1937. "A Note on Measurement Utility." *Review of Economic Studies* 4, no. 2: 155–61.

———. 1954. "The Pure Theory of Public Expenditure." *Review of Economics and Statistics* 36, no. 4: 387–9.

———. 1963. "Risk and Uncertainty: A Fallacy of Large Numbers." *Scientia* 98, no. 612: 108.

———. 1979. "Why We Should Not Make Mean Log of Wealth Big Though Years to Act Are Long." *Journal of Banking and Finance* 3, no. 4: 305–7.

Samuelson, William, and Richard J. Zeckhauser. 1988. "Status Quo Bias in Decision Making." *Journal of Risk and Uncertainty* 1, no. 1: 7–59.

Schachter, Stanley, William Gerin, Donald C. Hood, and Paul Anderassen. 1985a. "I. Was the South Sea Bubble a Random Walk?" *Journal of Economic Behavior and Organization* 6, no. 4: 323–9.

Schachter, Stanley, Donald C. Hood, William Gerin, Paul Andreassen, and Michael Rennert. 1985b. "III. Some Causes and Consequences of Dependence and Independence in the Stock Market." *Journal of Economic Behavior and Organization* 6, no. 4: 339–57.

Schelling, Thomas C. 1968. "The Life You Save May Be Your Own." In Samuel B. Chase Jr., ed., *Problems in Public Expenditure Analysis*, vol. 127, 127–176. Washington, DC: Brookings Institution.

———. 1984. "Self-Command in Practice, in Policy, and in a Theory of Rational Choice." *American Economic Review: Papers and Proceedings* 74, no. 2: 1–11.

Sen, Amartya K. 1977. "Rational Fools: A Critique of the Behavioral Foundations of Economic Theory." *Philosophy and Public Affairs* 6, no. 4: 317–44.

Shafir, Eldar, and Richard H. Thaler. 2006. "Invest Now, Drink Later, Spend Never: On the Mental Accounting of Delayed Consumption." *Journal of Economic Psychology* 27, no. 5: 694–712.

Shapiro, Matthew D., and Joel Slemrod. 2003. "Did the 2001 Tax Rebate Stimulate Spending? Evidence from Taxpayer Surveys." In James Poterba, ed., *Tax Policy and the Economy* (ch. 3), vol. 17, 83–109. Cambridge, MA: National Bureau of Economic Research and MIT Press.

Sharpe, William F. 1964. "Capital Asset Prices: A Theory of Market Equilibrium Under Conditions of Risk." *Journal of Finance* 19, no. 3: 425–42.

Shaton, Maya. 2014. "The Display of Information and Household Investment Behavior." Working paper, University of Chicago Booth School of Business.

Shefrin, Hersh M., and Meir Statman. 1984. "Explaining Investor Preference for Cash Dividends." *Journal of Financial Economics* 13, no. 2: 253–82.

Shefrin, Hersh M., and Richard H. Thaler. 1988. "The Behavioral Life-Cycle Hypothesis." *Economic Inquiry* 26, no. 4: 609–43.

Shiller, Robert J. 1981. "Do Stock Prices Move Too Much to Be Justified by Subsequent Changes in Dividends?" *American Economic Review* 71, no. 3: 421–36.

———. 1984. "Stock Prices and Social Dynamics." *Brookings Papers on Economic Activity* 2: 457–510.

———. 1986. "Comments on Miller and on Kleidon." *Journal of Business* 59, no. 4, part 2: S501–5.

———. 2000. *Irrational Exuberance*. Princeton: Princeton University Press.

Shleifer, Andrei, and Robert W. Vishny. 1997. "The Limits of Arbitrage." *Journal of Finance* 52, no. 1: 35–55.

Silver, Nate. 2012. *The Signal and the Noise: Why So Many Predictions Fail—But Some Don't*. New York: Penguin.

Simon, Herbert A. 1957. *Models of Man, Social and Rational: Mathematical Essays on Rational Human Behavior in a Social Setting*. Oxford: Wiley.

Sloman, Steven A. 1996. "The Empirical Case for Two Systems of Reasoning." *Psychological Bulletin* 119, no. 1: 3.

Slonim, Robert L., and Alvin E. Roth. 1998. "Learning in High Stakes Ultimatum Games: An Experiment in the Slovak Republic." *Econometrica* 66, no. 3: 569–96.

Smith, Adam. (1759) 1981. *The Theory of Moral Sentiments*. Reprint edited by D. D. Raphael and A. L. Macfie. Indianapolis: LibertyClassics.

———. (1776) 1981. *An Inquiry into the Nature and Causes of the Wealth of Nations*. Reprint edited by R. H. Campbell and A. S. Skinner. Indianapolis: LibertyClassics.

Smith, Vernon L. 1976. "Experimental Economics: Induced Value Theory." *American Economic Review* 66, no. 2: 274–9.

———, Gerry L. Suchanek, and Arlington W. Williams. 1988. "Bubbles, Crashes, and Endogenous Expectations in Experimental Spot Asset Markets." *Econometrica* 56, no. 5: 1119–51.

Solow, Robert M. 2009. "How to Understand the Disaster." *New York Review of Books*, May 14. Available at: http://www.nybooks.com/articles/archives/2009/may/14/how-to-understand-the-disaster/.

Spiegler, Ran. 2011. *Bounded Rationality and Industrial Organization*. Oxford and New York: Oxford University Press.

Stanovich, Keith E., and Richard F. West. 2000. "Individual Differences in Reasoning: Implications for the Rationality Debate." *Behavioral and Brain Sciences* 23, no. 5: 701–17.

Staw, Barry M. 1976. "Knee-Deep in the Big Muddy: A Study of Escalating Commitment to a Chosen Course of Action." *Organizational Behavior and Human Performance* 16, no. 1: 27–44.

Stewart, Jon. 2012. "Interview with Goolsbee, Austan." *Daily Show*, Comedy Central, September 6.

Stewart, Sharla A. 2005. "Can Behavioral Economics Save Us from Ourselves?" *University of Chicago Magazine* 97, no. 3. Available at: http://magazine.uchicago.edu/0502/features/economics.shtml.

Stigler, George J. 1977. "The Conference Handbook." *Journal of Political Economy* 85, no. 2: 441–3.

Strotz, Robert Henry. 1955–56. "Myopia and Inconsistency in Dynamic Utility Maximization." *Review of Economic Studies* 23, no. 3: 165–80.

Sullivan, Gail. 2014. "Uber Backtracks after Jacking Up Prices during Sydney Hostage Crisis." *Washington Post*, December 15. Available at: http://www.washingtonpost.com/news/morning-mix/wp/2014/12/15/uber-backtracks-after-jacking-up-prices-during-syndey-hostage-crisis.

Summers, Nick. 2013. "In Australia, Retirement Saving Done Right." *Bloomberg BusinessWeek*, May 30. Available at: http://www.businessweek.com/articles/2013-05-30/in-australia-retirement-saving-done-right.

Sunstein, Cass R. 2014. "The Ethics of Nudging." Available at: http://ssrn.com/abstract=2526341.

———, and Richard H. Thaler. 2003. "Libertarian Paternalism Is Not an Oxymoron." *University of Chicago Law Review* 70, no. 4: 1159–202.

Telser, L. G. 1995. "The Ultimatum Game and the Law of Demand." *Economic Journal* 105, no. 433: 1519–23.

Thaler, Richard H. 1980. "Toward a Positive Theory of Consumer Choice." *Journal of Economic Behavior and Organization* 1, no. 1: 39–60.

———. 1986. "The Psychology and Economics Conference Handbook: Comments on Simon, on Einhorn and Hogarth, and on Tversky and Kahneman." *Journal of Business* 59, no. 4, part 2: S279–84.

———. 1987a. "Anomalies: The January Effect." *Journal of Economic Perspectives* 1, no. 1: 197–201.

———. 1987b. "Anomalies: Seasonal Movements in Security Prices II: Weekend, Holiday, Turn of the Month, and Intraday Effects." *Journal of Economic Perspectives* 1, no. 2: 169–77.

———. 1988a. "Anomalies: The Winner's Curse." *Journal of Economic Perspectives* 2, no. 1: 191–202.

———. 1988b. "Anomalies: The Ultimatum Game." *Journal of Economic Perspectives* 2, no. 4: 195–206.

———. 1992. *The Winner's Curse: Paradoxes and Anomalies of Economic Life.* New York: Free Press.

———. 1994. "Psychology and Savings Policies." *American Economic Review* 84, no. 2: 186–92.

———. 1999a. "Mental Accounting Matters." *Journal of Behavioral Decision Making* 12: 183–206.

———. 1999b. "The End of Behavioral Finance." *Financial Analysts Journal* 55, no. 6: 12–17.

———. 2009. "Opting in vs. Opting Out." *New York Times*, September 26. Available at: http://www.nytimes.com/2009/09/27/business/economy/27view.html.

———, and Shlomo Benartzi. 2004. "Save More Tomorrow™: Using Behavioral Economics to Increase Employee Saving." *Journal of Political Economy* 112, no. S1: S164–87.

———, and Eric J. Johnson. 1990. "Gambling with the House Money and Trying to Break Even: The Effects of Prior Outcomes on Risky Choice." *Management Science* 36, no. 6: 643–60.

———, and Sherwin Rosen. 1976. "The Value of Saving a Life: Evidence from the Labor Market." In Nestor E. Terleckyj, ed., *Household Production and Consumption*, 265–302. New York: National Bureau for Economic Research.

———, and Hersh M. Shefrin. 1981. "An Economic Theory of Self-Control." *Journal of Political Economy* 89, no. 2: 392–406.

———, and Cass R. Sunstein. 2003. "Libertarian Paternalism." *American Economic Review: Papers and Proceedings* 93, no. 2: 175–9.

———. 2008. *Nudge: Improving Decisions about Health, Wealth, and Happiness.* New Haven, CT: Yale University Press.

———, Amos Tversky, Daniel Kahneman, and Alan Schwartz. 1997. "The Effect of Myopia and Loss Aversion on Risk Taking: An Experimental Test." *Quarterly Journal of Economics* 112, no. 2: 647–61.

———, and William T. Ziemba. 1988. "Anomalies: Parimutuel Betting Markets: Race-tracks and Lotteries." *Journal of Economic Perspectives* 2, no. 2: 161–74.

Thompson, Rex. 1978. "The Information Content of Discounts and Premiums on Closed-End Fund Shares." *Journal of Financial Economics* 6, no. 2–3: 151–86.

Tierney, John. 2005. "Magic Marker Strategy." *New York Times*, September 6. Available at: http://www.nytimes.com/2005/09/06/opinion/06tierney.html.

Tirole, Jean. 2014. "Cognitive Games and Cognitive Traps." Working Paper, Toulouse School of Economics.

Tuttle, Brad. 2012. "In Major Shakeup, J.C. Penney Promises No More 'Fake Prices.'" *Time*, January 26. Available at: http://business.time.com/2012/01/26/in-major-shakeup-j-c-penney-promises-no-more-fake-prices/.

Tversky, Amos, and Daniel Kahneman. 1974. "Judgment under Uncertainty: Heuristics and Biases." *Science* 185, no. 4157: 1124–31.

Ullmann-Margalit, Edna. 1997. "The Invisible Hand and the Cunning of Reason." *Social Research* 64, no. 2: 181–98.

UK Department for Works and Pensions. 2014. "Automatic Enrolment Opt Out Rates: Findings from Qualitative Research with Employers Staging in 2014." Ad Hoc Research Report 9, DWP. Available at: https://www.gov.uk/government/uploads/system/uploads/attachment_data/file/369572/research-report-9-opt-out.pdf.

van den Assem, Martijn J., Dennie van Dolder, and Richard H. Thaler. 2012. "Split or Steal? Cooperative Behavior When the Stakes Are Large." *Management Science* 58, no. 1: 2–20.

von Neumann, John, and Oskar Morgenstern. 1947. *Theory of Games and Economic Behavior.* Second edition. Princeton: Princeton University Press.

Wald, David S., Jonathan P. Bestwick, Lewis Raiman, Rebecca Brendell, and Nicholas J. Wald. 2014. "Randomised Trial of Text Messaging on Adherence to Cardiovascular Preventive Treatment (INTERACT Trial)." *PLOS ONE* 9, no. 12: e114268.

Wason, Peter C. 1968. "Reasoning About a Rule." *Quarterly Journal of Experimental Psychology* 20, no. 3: 273–81.

Watters, Ethan. 2013. "We Aren't the World." *Pacific Standard*, February 5. Available at: http://www.psmag.com/magazines/magazine-feature-story-magazines/joe-henrich-weird-ultimatum-game-shaking-up-psychology-economics-53135/.

Whitehead, Mark, Rhys Jones, Rachel Howell, Rachel Lilley, and Jessica Pykett. 2014. "Nudging All Over the World: Assessing the Global Impact of the Behavioural Sciences on Public Policy." *Economic and Social Research Council*, September. Available at: https://changingbehaviours.files.wordpress.com/2014/09/nudgedesignfinal.pdf.

Wickman, Forrest. 2013. "Who Really Said You Should 'Kill Your Darlings'?" *Slate*, October 18. Available at: http://www.slate.com/blogs/browbeat/2013/10/18/_kill_your_darlings_writing_advice_what_writer_really_said_to_murder_your.html.

WNYC. 2014. "The Golden Rule." *Radiolab* 12, no. 6 (February 25). Available at: http://www.radiolab.org/story/golden-rule/.

World Bank. 2015. *World Development Report 2015: Mind, Society, and Behavior.* Washington, DC: World Bank.

York, Benjamin N., and Susanna Loeb. 2014. "One Step at a Time: The Effects of an Early Literacy Text Messaging Program for Parents of Preschoolers." Working Paper 20659, National Bureau of Economic Research.

Zamir, Eyal, and Doron Teichman. 2014. *The Oxford Handbook of Behavioral Economics and the Law.* Oxford and New York: Oxford University Press.

Zielinski, Sarah. 2014. "A Parrot Passes the Marshmallow Test." *Slate*, September 9. Available at: http://www.slate.com/blogs/wild_things/2014/09/09/marshmallow_test_of_self_control_an_african_grey_parrot_performs_as_well.html.

LIST OF FIGURES

Unless otherwise noted, all figures created by Kevin Quealy

ACKNOWLEDGMENTS

A lazy man does not manage to write a book without a lot of help. Thanks go to John Brockman, who tricked me into writing this book, as only he can. My publishers, W. W. Norton and Penguin UK, were patient and highly supportive, even when I ended up writing a book that was not the one they were expecting. Brendan Curry at Norton provided a level of editorial support that is increasingly rare. He read every word of this manuscript at least twice; most authors are lucky to get such treatment even once. Alexis Kirschbaum at Penguin helped encourage me to take the book in this direction, and has been great at seeing the big picture. Both of them have also been a lot of fun to work with. Allegra Huston applied the final spit and polish with aplomb.

Many friends read early drafts of the book, and given their level of talent and the generosity of the time they gave me, this really should be a much better book. Caroline Daniel of the *Financial Times* read the entire manuscript and gave me handwritten comments that were almost legible. My writer's dream team of Stephen Dubner, Malcolm Gladwell, and Michael Lewis also read and commented on various drafts. Michael took a chunk of the book on a hiking trip and sent me a three-word email saying "It's not boring!" That kept me going for a while. All three gave me the kind of advice that only true masters of their craft can provide.

Cass Sunstein was a constant source of encouragement and sound advice, though he cannot understand why I didn't finish this book at least three years ago. Danny Kahneman offered his sage wisdom at every stage, including during the copyediting. Not surprisingly, Danny is amazed that I finished the book at all. Maya Bar-Hillel, Drew Dickson, Raife Giovinazzo, Dean Karlan, Cade Massey, Manny

Roman, Rohan Silva, and Martijn van den Assem all read and gave detailed comments on an early draft that greatly improved the book. And what can I say about the amazing Jesse Shapiro, who has now read and edited every word of my last two books. If Jesse ever writes a book, buy it. It will be fantastic. Other friends who offered opinions about various sections include Nick Barberis, Shlomo Benartzi, Alain Cohn, Owen Lamont, Andrei Shleifer, and Rob Vishny. As usual, I talked for many hours with Sendhil Mullainathan about this book, and he made it smarter, as he always does. Craig Fox, one of our many summer campers, came up with the title last summer at a conference. This long list does not include all the friends who had to listen to me talking about this project for the past few years. Thanks, you guys!

Kevin Quealy created all the figures in the book, doing so with creativity and patience. In my post-book life I look forward to watching some football with him and talking about fourth down strategy.

The University of Chicago Booth School of Business provided financial support for this project via the Center for Decision Research and the Initiative on Global Markets. They also pay me to go to work at a place where I can look forward each day to learning something from someone smarter than me. Oh, and they also provide me with a great office. If you read this far, you deserve to know that I lucked into the seventh draft pick.

To produce the book three people did yeoman's work. Two Russell Sage summer camp graduates compiled and checked the references: Paolina Medina spent part of her summer getting us started on that task, which was then taken over by Seth Blumberg, who went into a work frenzy in the final stages in which he checked everything at least twice and even helped out on some of the figures. If the facts in this book are mostly right, give them the credit, and expect to start reading their great behavioral economics papers soon. Paolina, Seth, and I all reported to the great Linnea Meyer Gandhi, who managed the entire book production process as only a Chicago Booth–trained consultant can. I simply cannot imagine how I would have ever finished this thing without her. (Neither can she.) Especially in the final stages, with lots of people working on various parts of the book simultaneously, Linnea kept us (and especially me) organized.

I expect Linnea to be running a company soon. If she hires you, be prepared to work hard. No one would ever call Linnea lazy.

Finally, against all odds France Leclerc continues to put up with me when she would rather be traveling the world looking for those images that only she can capture. She makes my world more beautiful and interesting.

INDEX

Page numbers in *italics* refer to illustrations.
Page numbers beginning with 359 refer to endnotes.

Schachter, Stanley, 180
Schelling, Thomas, 12–13, 14, 37*n*,
    100, 104*n*, 178
  in Behavioral Economics
    Roundtable, 181
Schiphol International Airport, 326
Scholes, Myron, 208
Schwartz, Alan, 197
Science, 22, 319
scientific revolutions, 167–68, 169–70
secret sales, 119–20
Security Analysis (Graham and Dodd),
    219–20
Seeger, Pete, 65
self-control, 54, 85–86, 99–111, 115
  as about conflict, 103
  retirement savings and, 314
  and savings for retirement, 309
  two selves in, 103–5
  willpower and, 87–99, 363
self-interest, bounded, 258
selfishness, 145–46
Sen, Amartya, 145
sense of humor, 218, *219*, 223
Shafir, Eldar, 58*n*, 67–68, 69, 71, 179,
    257, 366
Shankar, Maya, 344
Shapiro, Jesse, 75–76, 357
Sharpe, William, 208, 226, 229
Shaton, Maya, 198
Shea, Dennis, 315–17
Shefrin, Hersh, 98, 104, 164–66, 167,
    223–24
Shiller, Robert, 5*n*, 176, 242
  in behavioral economics debate,
    159, 167–68
  in Behavioral Economics
    Roundtable, 181
  behavioral finance workshop
    organized by, 236
  and behavioral macroeconomics,
    349
  housing prices studied by, 235, 252
  as president of AEA, 347
  on variability of stock prices, 230–
    33, *231*

Shleifer, Andrei, 175, 178
  closed-end fund paper of, 240–43,
    244
  on limits of arbitrage, 249
Signal and the Noise, The (Silver), 292
Silva, Rohan, 330–33, 334
Silver, Nate, 47, 292
Simon, Herbert, 23, 29
  in behavioral economics debate,
    159, 162
Sinden, John, 148–49
skiing, 115–20, 138
Slovic, Paul, 21, 36, 48
slow hunch, 39–40
Small Business Administration, 351,
    352*n*
Smith, Adam, 7, 51–52, 58, 87–88, 89,
    103
Smith, Cliff, 206
Smith, Roger, 123
Smith, Vernon, 40, 41, 148, 149
  "learning" critique of
    experimental economics, 153
snow shovels, 20, 64–65, 127–29, 133,
    136, 137
Snyder, Daniel, 288–89, 290*n*
Social Security, 322
Society for Judgment and Decision
    Making, 180*n*
Society of Actuaries, 14
Soll, Jack, 75
Solow, Robert, 259
Soman, Dilip, 66–67
Sony, 135–36
sophisticated agents, 110–11
sporting events, tickets for, 18–19,
    57–58
spreadsheets, 214*n*
Stanford Law Review, 258–59
Stanford University, 35–41, 125, 126,
    185
statistical lives, 13
Statman, Meir, 104, 164–66, 167
status quo, 131
  bias, 154
  and Weber–Fechner law, 32